Introduction to Sociology

FIRST EDITION

Introduction to Sociology

EDITED BY Sebahattin Ziyanak

The University of Texas Permian Basin

cognella®

SAN DIEGO

Bassim Hamadeh, CEO and Publisher
John Remington, Executive Editor
Gem Rabanera, Project Editor
Christian Berk, Production Editor
Emely Villavicencio, Senior Graphic Designer
Trey Soto, Licensing Coordinator
Natalie Piccotti, Director of Marketing
Kassie Graves, Vice President of Editorial
Jamie Giganti, Director of Academic Publishing

3970 Sorrento Valley Blvd., Ste. 500, San Diego, CA 92121

CONTENTS

Editor's Introduction

The academic field of sociology is the study of everyday human interactions. Interactions from around the world construct our global social world and the study is more germane than ever before. Readers will find the examples include our world in change, real world issues and debates, and a diverse array of topics to critically examine the social world and global impacts of social life.

I am a classroom professor and have been fortunate to teach Introduction to Sociology. My teaching experiences are always exciting, fascinating, inspiring, and ever-changing. My students are from diverse educational backgrounds and disciplines. For the past four years, there are more than 20 countries represented among about 500 students in my global classroom. Over the years, student feedback, insight, and class discussions have helped me to decide which topics to cover in this textbook. Essentially, the topics are those selected by your peers. Along the way, this book has evolved from my lectures, teaching experiences, and assessment of students. Having spent 20 years in the field of sociology, I feel grateful to contribute my knowledge, observations, and analyses to introduce sociology from sociological angles and aspects that will help guide students to better understand the social world. We view this examination through what we call the sociological lens.

I found the readings fascinating. The articles on the global social world are carefully selected to provide specific examples and a sociological imagination so that readers will have various perspectives from which to apply and understand sociological concepts and perspectives as well as sociology itself.

One of the unique aspects of this textbook is to show how sociological perspectives, theories, and concepts are detailed at a national or international level and presented in every chapter so that readers and students can make connections between sociology and their everyday lives.

The textbook is divided into 13 chapters.

Chapter 1: An Introduction to Sociology. This is a general introduction to sociology and describes three basic types of sociological traditions.

Chapter 2: Social Research. Introduces the reader to research methods step by step. It also explains concepts, variables, and the causal process with empirical evidences to demonstrate a particular social condition or some aspect of social function.

Chapter 3: Culture. Presents culture and the explosion of cultural studies in sociology. It seeks to explain how social structure, symbols, meanings, and cultural practices affect people's rational action.

Chapter 4: Socialization. Introduces socialization, along with the symbolic interactionist tradition, George Herbert Mead's distinct perspective on self and society, and Charles Horton Cooley's insights to understand how identities are developed through a social process.

Chapter 5: Deviance and Crime. Compiles the perceptions of deviance, the fluidity of deviance, and how deviance is constructed and by whom. This chapter also explores the distinctions between deviance and crime. To present social control, deviance, and crime, various approaches are discussed about how people perceive and engage in deviant behaviors.

Chapter 6: Social Stratification. Focuses on the relevant view of inequality and poverty. This chapter includes a more detailed account of the accelerating gap between the 99 percent and the one percent. Finally, it addresses dynamic and underlying aspects of inequality and how inequality erodes social mobility, public services, and equal opportunity.

Chapter 7: Race and Ethnicity. Covers the analysis of race as a social construct. This chapter provides an insight into group dynamics, racial conflict, race-based social movements, whiteness, racial domination, cultural nationalism, prejudice, segregation, and forms of discrimination.

Chapter 8: Gender and Sexuality. This chapter turns our attention to the contemporary constructions of gender and sex. This chapter also seeks to explain sexual orientation, gender socialization, gender norms, distribution of power, feminization of poverty, and sexism.

Chapter 9: Marriage and Families. Emphasizes that marriage is still an indispensable association in many societies, but not all societies. In addition, family, marriage forms, rationale of marriage, divorce, remarriage, how marriage and family function around the world, and theoretical perspectives on marriage and family are illustrated.

Chapter 10: Education. Provides an understanding of education and modernity in the context of sociological perspectives. This chapter focuses on the goal of education, the function of education pertaining to the ability of people to change their status, cultural deprivation, multiculturalism, educational programs with different educational philosophical and disciplinary approaches.

Chapter 11: Politics and Globalization. This chapter explores the aspects detailing the rise of transnational corporations. We explore the political climate from a historical context as well as examine contemporary views. Major scopes of economic and political power within the world system are presented.

Chapter 12: Population and Urbanization. This chapter focuses on the transition to urban society and suburbanization.

Chapter 13: Social Change and Social Movements. This chapter analyzes the information society and the foremost characteristics of collective action and social movements.

Lastly, this book studies the social world. It illustrates how sociological theories will be helpful to understand how we each are a part of the social world. My hope is that as you read this book, you will delve into the captivating world of sociology in general as well as the newly emerging area of global sociology.

An Introduction to Sociology

Sociology is the macro- and micro-level analysis of the social structures and social order linked to group interactions, organizations, cultures, social interactions, and societies in the world. As you explore the social world, you are influenced by social events around the world. Sociological study is vital to look beyond an inadequate understanding of individuals, society, and social structures. Chapter 1 provides a fundamental outline for the textbook by offering sociological perspectives for studying social behavior and understanding human groups. Buechler (2014) examines three basic types of sociology—scientific sociology, humanistic sociology, critical sociology—employed to explain social issues, social interactions, patterns, and how and why things work in your daily life. This chapter provides a more systematic sociological approach in order to gain a broader understanding of society.

The Legacy of the Discipline

Steven M. Buechler

For more than two centuries, sociology has developed a rich legacy of theoretical approaches that help make sense out of the world. This chapter describes three basic types of sociology (Habermas 1969). Scientific sociology applies the scientific method of the natural sciences to the social world. Humanistic sociology emphasizes how consciousness and reflexivity distinguish people from other topics of scientific study. Critical sociology examines and challenges relations of domination while promoting more egalitarian relations. Good (and bad) sociology has been done within each of these traditions.

Scientific Sociology

Auguste Comte (the "father" of sociology) was among the first to argue that sociology should model itself on the natural sciences. From Comte to the present, the premise of scientific sociology is that there is a single, universal, scientific approach to knowledge that applies to both the natural and the social worlds. This approach involves systematic testing of hypotheses through experimental methods to discover the most general laws that govern the world around us. Whether one is a physicist, botanist, economist, or sociologist, the differences in subject matter are less important than the similarities in how all these subjects are handled by the scientific method.

Durkheim's Sociology

The best classical spokesperson for scientific sociology was the French sociologist Emile Durkheim (1858–1917). He was a strong advocate for sociology and the idea of emergentism. For Durkheim, society was more than the sum of its parts; it was a reality sui generis, or unto itself. Society consists of social facts, which must be explained by other social facts. Durkheim relentlessly argued for the superiority of sociological explanations over individual, biological, or physiological ones. His argument was strengthened when he advocated a scientific sociology, linking this new discipline to established sciences.

Durkheim's early work on the division of labor (1893) contrasted traditional and modern societies. In traditional societies, people are very similar to one another. In these small-scale societies, everybody does everything. What unites people is a common set of cultural beliefs known as the collective conscience. As societies become larger and more differentiated, the bond of common beliefs weakens and conflict over scarce resources intensifies. Some societies disintegrate, but others survive because they find a new method of integration. In modern societies, the division of labor provides the social glue that holds things together. In these societies, people are different from one another and do different things. These differences create interdependency among people. Social evolution involves a transition from worlds united by common beliefs to ones united by functional differences. This social evolution is best understood through the same scientific method used to understand biological evolution.

In subsequent work on suicide (1897), Durkheim strengthened the case for a scientific sociology. He chose suicide because the decision to end one's life seems intensely personal. Durkheim, however, sought sociological explanations of this seemingly individual act. He de-emphasized individual suicides and focused on variations in suicide rates between different groups of people. Group suicide rates are social facts that need to be explained by other social facts rather than individual predispositions. The most important social fact in the explanation of suicide rates is the degree of social integration. Whenever people become less integrated into a group, suicide rates are likely to increase. People become "unplugged" in two ways. *Egoism* means the bonds linking people to the group are broken. *Anomie* means the norms guiding people's lives are weakened or irrelevant. Egoistic and anomic suicides are thus extreme expressions of much broader social problems that occur whenever individuals are disconnected and set adrift from their normal social anchors. Social facts like suicide rates are thus best explained by other social facts like changing degrees of social integration.

Durkheim's sociology of religion (1912) also illustrates his scientific sociology. He argued that some form of religion is virtually universal in human societies but that specific beliefs are highly variable. He claimed that the single common thread in all religions is a distinction between the sacred and the profane. That which is sacred is seen as external, powerful, constraining, and eternal in relation to the individual. Durkheim concluded that there is one reality that has the qualities that religion attributes to the sacred realm. That reality is society itself. When people worship their respective gods, they are recognizing a genuinely higher power. What they are not recognizing is that power is society itself.

Whether addressing evolution, suicide, or religion, Durkheim advocated a scientific sociology that analyzed society as an emergent reality of social facts that could be explained through the scientific method.

Functionalist Analysis

Many of Durkheims concerns were revived in Talcott Parsons's functionalist theory in the mid-twentieth century. Parsons sought a general theory applicable to all times and places; this quest for generality is another hallmark of scientific sociology. Parsons's early focus was the structure of social action (1937). He saw people as selecting means to pursue goals. Such choices are shaped by situational conditions and cultural values. Parsons stressed that people make choices; at the same time, their choices are guided by common values that predispose them to conform. Having analyzed these "unit acts," Parsons then became interested in how these unit acts were linked together.

The new problem was *interaction*; the new answer was the social system (1951). A social system is an ongoing, patterned relationship between social actors. Systems provide actors with status-roles; these are positions in the system along with guidelines for how to act. Roles are reciprocal and complementary. In Parsons's language, imagine two actors: Ego and Alter. Ego's role obligates her to do certain things that are identical to Alter's role expectations. In reverse order, Alter's role obligations match Ego's role expectations. Integrated social interaction occurs whenever people meet their role obligations because they are simultaneously meeting the role expectations of others.

Consider this example. If teachers are knowledgeable in their subject and fair in their grading, they are meeting not only their role obligations as teachers but also the expectations of students, because "teacher's obligations = student's expectations." By a similar logic, if students study hard and participate in class, they meet not only their role obligations but also the expectations of teachers, because "student's obligations = teacher's expectations." Integrated social systems thus arise whenever people learn their roles and are motivated to play them. Learning occurs through socialization that links the personality system (people) to the social system; motivation is provided by the cultural system and its core values. Parsons thus proposed a highly general and abstract model of how social order was possible.

If a social system is to survive over time, it must fulfill certain functions. Adaptation means systems must get resources from outside the system and distribute them throughout the system. Goal attainment means that systems must set priorities and allocate resources to them. Integration means that systems must maintain cohesion and connections among various parts of the system. Latency means that systems must motivate people to meet their obligations and smooth over tensions that might arise. Healthy societies develop social institutions that meet these functions on a regular basis.

Consider another example. The United States is a social system with various institutions that meet functional needs. The economy accomplishes adaptation by producing and distributing resources. The political system achieves goal attainment by setting priorities and allocating resources. The need for integration is met both by informal community norms and formal legal procedures. Finally, the latency function of providing motivation to people is met by family, religion, and education. Parsons thus continued the quest for a scientific sociology through a theory of systems and functions that could he applied to any ongoing social system.

By the 1950s, Parsons's functionalism dominated sociology. It then attracted much criticism. Robert Merton (1968) thought sociology should develop more modest, middle-range theories. C. Wright Mills (1959) accused Parsons of a hopelessly abstract "grand theory" that obscured more than it revealed. Many claimed that functionalism exaggerated social integration and ignored social conflict. These criticisms redirected sociology toward conflict while maintaining the quest for a scientific sociology.

Conflict Theory

Lewis Coser (1956) used functionalist logic to provide a novel understanding of conflict. He argued that conflict was a constant element in social life. On the other hand, conflict can have beneficial consequences. It can be a source of creativity, innovation, and healthy social change. Moreover, conflict actually causes much of the integration in society. When conflict occurs within groups, it can be a healthy release that resolves tensions and solidifies the group. When conflict occurs between groups, it increases integration within each group as they conduct the conflict. When conflict occurs in society, it clarifies group boundaries and identities by forcing people to commit to a side. In all these ways, conflict creates order that might not otherwise be there.

When societies have cross-cutting conflicts, opponents on one issue are allies on another issue. This reduces the violence and intensity of conflict and promotes smoother resolution of conflict. As a final example, imagine two groups who share a common enemy. Because "the enemy of my enemy is my friend," new alliances often emerge between previously unconnected groups. Although not all conflict is beneficial, much conflict has functional consequences. Conflict and order are intimately connected. We cannot explain order without acknowledging how conflict helps create it.

Other conflict theorists focused on how modern society is dominated by large bureaucratic organizations that rest on a hierarchical and unequal distribution of authority (Dahrendorf 1959). In any such organization, there are a small number of positions at the top that have authority and a larger number of positions below them that do not. This structure creates conflicting interests. Those with authority will seek to maintain the organization and their position within it. Those without authority will seek to change both the organization and their positions within it. Such conflicts are built into the very structure of authority; they are endemic to bureaucracy. Under the right conditions, such latent conflicts become overt Battles between political parties, labor and management, students and administration, or soldiers and officers. Because bureaucratic authority is so widespread in modern society, this form of conflict will also be common.

The social conflicts of the 1960s moved conflict theory to the center of academic sociology. Randall Collins (1975) revived the call for a scientific sociology of conflict. His logic went like this: Coercion is always a potential resource in social life. Some people are better at threatening or using coercion than others. When coercion is directed at people, they resist in whatever ways they can.

People compete for scarce and valued resources like wealth, status, and power. On the basis of these plausible principles, Collins concluded that conflict is the central social process in modern life. At the same time, he recognized that the form of conflict varies tremendously. It can involve subtle battles for strategic advantage, competition for educational credentials, claims to moral high ground, or overt, violent, and even deadly struggles.

Collins sought to synthesize sociology around conflict by linking macro-level institutions with micro-level interaction. On the macro level, social stratification and complex organizations are the outcome of past conflicts and the seeds of future ones. But macro-institutions don't exist on their own; they always have micro-level foundations in everyday interaction. This "micro-conflict" is evident in conversational strategies people use to manipulate others so they can achieve their goals. Conflict sociology would thus link micro and macro levels through a scientific approach.

Rational Choice

A final example of scientific sociology is rational choice, or exchange theory. It borrows from economic theory and behavioristic psychology. The challenge is to take premises from other disciplines and make them sociological. This means recognizing that people seek symbolic as well as material rewards, that social norms limit self-interested behavior, and that people are not always or fully rational in their behavior. With such adjustments, rational choice theorists argue that scientific explanations of human behavior become possible.

George Homans (1974) followed the psychological behaviorism of B. F. Skinner to identify a small number of general laws to explain a wide range of behavior. These laws are straightforward: rewarded actions will be repeated; the more valuable the result, the more likely the action that leads to it; frequent rewards have declining value; and the like. Homans argued that when sufficiently tested, refined, and combined, these laws could scientifically explain human behavior. Many sociologists criticized this work. With its strong focus on individual behavior, it seemed to deny the emergent level of social reality and to reduce macro-level sociology to micro-level psychology.

Peter Blau's (1964) version of exchange theory recognized emergentism and the need to explain exchange on both micro and macro levels. Blau argued that all social exchange rests on a social norm of reciprocity: In order to get something, we must give something. It is even in our self-interest to give something, because that is how we get something back. When exchanges are satisfactory to both parties, they foster trust. It is the trust established through small exchanges that makes people willing to risk larger exchanges; by this logic, the sequence from casual dating to serious commitment to formal marriage is a spiral of increasing trust born of successful exchanges.

Micro-level exchange includes situations where coworkers exchange favors, knowledge, or status, as long as it serves their interests. In contrast, macro-level exchange is long-term, indirect, and involves multiple parties. A nice example is the Social Security system, in which younger workers support older retirees, with the expectation that they will get the same deal when they retire. When exchanges succeed, order results. When they don't, conflict occurs. For most of the twentieth century, the Social Security system "succeeded" and was widely supported through what Blau called "legitimating values." More recently, "oppositional values" about its long-term viability have sown the seeds of generational conflict as younger workers question whether they will receive future benefits commensurate with their current costs. In this way, rational choice principles can explain both order and conflict.

The connections between exchange and power are most interesting. Consider the principle of lesser interest: In any relationship, the side with less interest in maintaining the relationship has more power. This principle applies to everything from romantic involvements to labor negotiations to international alliances. More generally, power arises whenever one side is dependent on the other for a needed resource. In its emphasis on power and micro-macro linkages, Blau's rational choice theory resembles Collins's conflict theory.

Scientific sociology analyzes a wide variety of topics. What links them is not the subject matter but the approach. The common thread is the quest for a genuinely scientific sociology modeled on the natural sciences. This thread distinguishes scientific from both humanistic and critical sociology.

Humanistic Sociology

When scientific sociologists do social science, they emphasize the word *science,* linking it to other sciences. When humanistic sociologists do social science, they emphasize the word *social,* separating it from other sciences. For humanistic sociology, people have unique traits like reflexivity and self-consciousness that require a different approach. As a result, humanistic sociology is less interested in general theories with universal applicability and more interested in how people create meanings that shape their actions. These distinctive human traits must be at the center of any worthwhile sociology. As a result, the best humanistic sociology can be more like a good novel exploring people's motivation than an analytical research report documenting human behavior.

Weber's Sociology

The classical theorist Max Weber (1864–1920) was a complex thinker whose work crossed the categories of scientific, humanistic, and critical sociology. Nonetheless, one dimension of his work nicely typifies humanistic sociology: his emphasis on the role of subjective meanings in human actions. Indeed, Weber argued sociology must begin with an interpretive understanding of social action in order to arrive at causal explanations. Without subjective meaning, we have mere behavior that hardly merits sociological study.

Because people attach different meanings to actions, Weber distinguished different types of social action. Purposive-rational action pursues goals efficiently; think of economic behavior. Value-rational action embodies commitment to a transcendent value; think of religious worship. Affectual action expresses an emotional state; think of maternal love. Traditional action repeats social customs; think of sheer habits. In each case, the action means something to the actor, and that meaning must be part of any worthwhile sociological explanation.

Sociological analysis thereby needs a unique method Weber called *Verstehen*. This requires researchers to empathetically understand the meanings motivating someone's action. Consider Weber's study *The Protestant Ethic and the Spirit of Capitalism* (1904). He wanted to understand why Protestants were so prominent among early entrepreneurs. His explanation required understanding how the Calvinist belief in predestination created anxiety among true believers. They responded by throwing themselves into productive activity. Their religious beliefs made this activity into a moral imperative. Capitalism thus arose less from material greed than from a spiritual incentive to demonstrate one's worth and salvation through productive activity. The rise of capitalism was, in part, an unintended consequence of religious motivations. But it could not be explained without first grasping the subjective meaning of these actions to the people doing them.

Weber's sociology ranged far and wide but was always rooted in this principle. Consider his analysis of authority. Power is the ability to achieve one's will against resistance; although effective, it is often unstable. Hence, power holders try to convert power into authority by seeking legitimacy. This can be done in several ways: by appealing to traditional customs, to charismatic leaders, or to rational-legal rules. What is crucial is that leaders cannot create legitimacy. It can only be granted by followers, when they attach a subjective meaning to the power being exercised over them. If they see it as legitimate, they will obey, and social order will be stable. If they don't, they might disobey and undermine social order. Even when analyzing macro-level issues in political sociology, social action involves subjective meanings.

Weber saw rationalization as the master trend of Western society. Rationalization meant that in all human activity, the emphasis was on maximizing efficiency, calculability, predictability, and control. George Ritzer's (2000) analysis of how the cultural experience of eating has been reduced to the industrial production of fast food is one example of rationalization. Although it brings the efficiency of abstract technique, rationalization sacrifices the sensuality of direct experience. This is why Weber took a dim view of this trend. He was especially troubled by the rise of giant bureaucracies, seeing them as "iron cages" from which we could not escape. Rationalization threatened human qualities like spontaneity, creativity, sensuality, and myth-making. Weber's humanistic approach is evident in his distress over modern trends that threatened the very qualities that make us human.

Symbolic Interactionism

Among contemporary approaches, symbolic interactionism is the best example of humanistic sociology. George Herbert Mead (1934) is the founder of this approach, which reveals how people literally become human through socialization. Only when we are immersed in social relations with others do we develop the seemingly individual traits of mind and self that allow us to become fully human.

In rare cases of children reared in extreme isolation, they fail to develop a mind and a self because they are deprived of the social interactions that create our humanity.

Although behaviorism speaks of stimulus and response as if they are transparently obvious and similar for all social actors, Mead argues that stimuli and responses involve symbolic interpretation. They are not objectively meaningful; they become intersubjectively meaningful when people relate to them in certain kinds of ways. It is interaction that creates, sustains, and transforms the meanings that are crucial to human action and that distinguish it from the instinctive responses of other organisms.

It is this meaningful interaction that triggers the development of minds and selves. To have a mind is to engage in thinking and reflection. This process is like having a conversation with oneself. Mead's point is that we must have conversations with others before we can have conversations with ourselves. It is the others in our environment who provide the conversational and interactional tools that we need to engage in thinking. Infants begin with random babbling and untutored impulses. Through interaction with others, we gradually move from babbling to meaningful speech and from impulses to purposive action. Having learned through others, we can then internalize these lessons, talk to ourselves, and have a mind.

We are born with a brain but must develop a mind. In a parallel way, we are born with a body but must develop a self. Just as social interaction is necessary to develop a mind, it is also necessary to develop a self. Having a self means the ability to take oneself as an object. We only develop a self through interaction with others. What such interaction provides is the opportunity to "take the role of the other," or imaginatively adopt someone else's viewpoint. Their viewpoint helps us learn to see ourselves as objects. Children start by imitating particular people; they end up with a more generalized notion of how others see them. Once again, society comes first because it provides the others whose roles we need to take in order to develop a self. The social world is thus the mechanism by which we become human.

The development of mind and self is a generic process making us human. It is the foundation for the more specific process of acquiring an individual identity. Identity refers to the symbolic meanings attached to our self-object. Like our generic self, our individual identity is a product of what others reflect back to us about who we are. When we detect consistent messages from other people about who we are, that gradually becomes internalized as our identity. If the messages are largely positive, we develop an equally positive identity; if they are negative, our self-image is likely to suffer. In this way, our perceptions of the perceptions of others become a self-fulfilling prophecy producing our identity.

By emphasizing symbolic meanings, this approach focuses on the distinctive processes and properties that make us human. Therefore, it is central to humanistic sociology.

Phenomenological Sociology

A similar emphasis is evident in phenomenological sociology, which studies the life-world of immediate experience. This lifeworld involves a "here and now" that rests on many taken-for-granted assumptions.

We assume that our "here and now" is part of a larger, objective world that is shared with others. Phenomenological sociologists are less interested in whether these beliefs are true than in how we sustain them.

One way we do this is by routinely assuming that our perspective is the same as others' (Schutz 1932). In other words, we assume the world we experience is the same one they experience. We also rely on culturally learned techniques to sustain belief in an orderly world. These techniques are learned through socialization, but then they become second nature. We forget that we had to learn them and instead believe that they reflect the natural order of things. For American drivers, nothing could be more "natural" than driving on the right side of the road, which is why they find it so difficult to drive in England, whose native drivers find it equally "natural" to drive on the left side of the road. Unless we have such unsettling experiences, however, we don't question the socially learned, deeply rooted, taken-for-granted beliefs that motivate our actions and shape our understandings of the world. Every time our beliefs "work" and interaction proceeds smoothly, we convince ourselves that our world is objectively real. In so doing, we deny our own role in creating whatever order exists around us.

Ethnomethodology refers to methods people use in everyday life to make sense of their world (Garfinkel 1967). Through such methods, people create their social worlds. Thus, when we interpret words or actions, we begin with what people say or do but we "fill in" a great deal of other information as well. It is only by adding what we know about people's biographies, the context of the situation, or our history with them that we fully know what their words or actions mean. Whatever order we experience is less "out there" than a projection of our methods of making sense of the world.

Another way we assign meaning is by using mental categories to make sense. When we experience a situation—especially if it contains novel or unexpected elements—we search our categories to find one that best fits the moment. Once we do, our understanding of "what is going on" is as much a function of the category we bring to it as the raw experience. Again, the order we presume to be "out there" is inseparable from our own efforts to find it. We don't just live in society; we *accomplish* it through such methods.

These techniques sustain our belief in an orderly, objective, shared world. Despite our best efforts, however, such beliefs can unravel quite easily You can unravel them by entering a familiar situation and doing things that contradict the expectations of others. But you'd best be prepared for unpleasant consequences. People might become angry, question your sanity, or quickly withdraw because they find things too disorienting. So here's the point. If "social order" can be disrupted this easily, doesn't this show that it is not objectively real but rather a collaboration sustained by people's beliefs and actions?

Phenomenological sociology is thus about the social construction of reality (Berger and Luckmann 1966). It reveals that the world we assume to be real is relative and arbitrary. It "feels" real because of the sense-making techniques we employ. A final example is a relevance structure. This is a purpose, goal, or intention that focuses attention and motivates action. It is through relevance structures that individuals come to experience the world as a meaningful, orderly place, and to act accordingly. Once they act, the outcomes of their actions take on a life of their own and seem to exist independently of the people who created them. We thereby trick ourselves into thinking that we live in an objective, orderly, and shared social world.

Like scientific sociology, humanistic sociology addresses many topics. The thread that connects them is the premise that people create, interpret, and act on meanings. For humanistic sociology, this fundamental fact must be at the center of sociological analysis. Because these qualities distinguish humans from other objects of scientific study, a *social* science must be quite different from natural science.

Critical Sociology

Critical sociology shares some concepts, approaches, and techniques with both scientific and humanistic sociology. What distinguishes it is a value commitment to create and use knowledge to promote emancipation. To paraphrase Marx, the point is not merely to understand the world; the point is to change it. Critical sociology analyzes social forces that limit human potential, narrow people's freedom, and sustain social domination. Critically understanding such forces can help move society in more egalitarian directions. Good critical sociologists know that the application of knowledge is fraught with dangers and unintended consequences. But they nonetheless remain committed to doing sociology to promote emancipation.

Marx's Sociology

Karl Marx (1818–1883) argued that the human capacity for labor is our distinguishing trait. Through productive activity, we not only survive; we also develop our humanity. Under capitalism, however, people become alienated from this potential. Under capitalism, the process of labor is controlled by others and the products of labor are owned by capitalists. Capitalism reduces workers to commodities who must sell themselves in a labor market. Capitalism alienates workers and deforms human potential. Rather than living to work (as the expression of creative activity), people must work (under alienated conditions) to live. Because labor makes us human, its alienation is a fundamental assault on our human nature.

Marx was also a materialist who believed that the most important feature of any society is how it meets people's material needs. The material base of society is the foundation for everything else. It contains forces of production, such as technology, resources, and labor. It also contains relations of production, consisting of a small, powerful group of owners who benefit from the labor of a much larger group of producers. This material base is an engine of change as new technologies and skills are developed. It is also a source of conflict as producers resist exploitation by owners. Arising from the material base, there is a superstructure consisting of politics, kinship, and culture as well as ideas, beliefs, and worldviews. This superstructure is largely controlled by the same powerful class that controls material production. They shape politics, culture, and ideas to reinforce their power over the masses. Marx was highly critical of how these relations allowed the few to benefit at the expense of the many.

Under capitalism, the relations of production involve capitalists who own the means of production and live off profits and workers who sell their labor-power and live off wages. Marx endorsed the labor theory of value: that workers create all economic value. Capitalists create no value, although they organize the productive process. Because capitalists have economic control, political power, and legal rights, they own the products created by labor. When they sell them, they divide the proceeds between their profits and workers' wages. This arrangement is exploitative because workers create all value but only get a portion back as wages. Moreover, competition between capitalists drives each to maximize exploitation of their workers. Marx recognized that capitalism revolutionizes technology and creates unprecedented wealth. The problem is that this wealth is created by one class but owned by another. Once again, the human capacity for productive labor is turned against the vast majority who actually do the labor. This exploitation was the main target of Marx's critique.

As capitalism developed, Marx expected that workers would resist exploitation and become class-conscious agents of social change. He thought that as workers were brought together in large factories, they would realize their shared exploitation, identify with each other, recognize their common enemy, and challenge capitalist power. Over time, Marx thus expected increasing solidarity within classes and polarization between them. As the battle lines became clearer, he expected workers to overthrow capitalism and create a more equitable society.

Worker resistance creates instability, but capitalism experiences increasingly severe economic crises for several reasons. Overproduction occurs because the value of the goods workers produce is greater than the value of the wages they receive; hence there is a shortage of purchasing power that can become an overproduction crisis. There is also a tendency for the rate of profit to fall because capitalism replaces human labor with technology. If labor is the source of all value, and if labor shrinks while technology expands, then profits become harder to realize. Many capitalist practices are responses to these crisis tendencies. By seeking new markets, cutting labor costs, destroying surplus goods, and offering consumer credit, capitalism has sought to maintain profitable production. But the structural tendency toward crisis remains. When combined with worker resistance, the potential exists for a revolutionary transformation to a more equal society.

Marx's sociology could assume both scientific and humanistic forms. What ultimately places it in the critical sociology camp is its overriding commitment to promoting progressive social change on the basis of sociological knowledge.

Critical Theory

By the early twentieth century, it was evident that history was not following Marx's script for socialist revolution. In this context, a group of German, Jewish intellectuals founded the Frankfurt School for Social Research in 1923 (Jay 1973). Along with other neo-Marxists, their collective work came to be known as critical theory. This school is a major contribution to critical sociology. These thinkers were sympathetic to Marx's analysis, but they had serious doubts that the working class would become the revolutionary agent of history. The challenge before the Frankfurt School was to critically build on Marx's work. The central question was how a society based on class exploitation could nonetheless remain stable over time.

The Frankfurt School argued that Marx focused too narrowly on labor and the material base of society. Although economic exploitation is important, modern capitalism controls people in many different ways. Whereas Marx focused on one dimension, the Frankfurters focused on multiple dimensions of domination. They accepted his analysis of economic exploitation, but were most interested in other methods of social control. This led the Frankfurters to focus on the superstructure of society. In many respects, they saw this superstructure of politics, culture, symbols, and ideas as just as important as the material base in sustaining an unjust and unequal society.

Antonio Gramsci (1971) was not a member of the Frankfurt School, but his work exemplifies critical theory. He was interested in hegemony, or cultural domination. Hegemony is like a subtle kind of thought control. When this occurs, people embrace beliefs that contradict their own interests. With hegemony, domination becomes almost invisible, because people don't realize how they are being manipulated by their beliefs. Marx expected workers to develop class consciousness around their real interests. Hegemony is a kind of false consciousness that obscures real interests. Such distorted beliefs often rest on a false unity; people identify with their rulers, their nation, their culture, their race, or their religion—but not with their real interests or allies. The concept of hegemony allowed critical theory to explain the persistence of capitalism because material control over resources was reinforced by symbolic control over ideas; both benefited elites at the expense of ordinary people.

Nazi Germany confirmed the worst fears of the Frankfurt School, as Hitler rose to power in a nightmarish example of hegemonic control. However, although the Nazi movement was specific to Germany, the broader phenomenon of fascism occurred in Italy, Spain, and elsewhere. The most chilling message of the Frankfurt School was that an authoritarian, militaristic fascism could emerge in any modern, capitalist nation.

The contributions of the Frankfurt School continued throughout the twentieth century and will receive more extensive treatment. Their work continued Marx's critical spirit even while subjecting his ideas to critical scrutiny.

World System Theory

Whereas critical theorists expanded Marx's analysis "up" into the superstructure, world system theorists expanded it "out" across national boundaries. Marx recognized the expansionary tendency of capitalism, but world system theorists make it the centerpiece of their analysis. Thus, Immanuel Wallerstein (1974, 1980, 1989) details how capitalism has been a global, world system for several centuries. This world system is politically divided but economically integrated.

This integration is not harmonious. It is rooted in the same exploitation that Marx identified. The extraction of profits from the labor of workers is simply a global rather than a national phenomenon. This means that capitalism's relations of production have become international. The working class includes everyone on the globe who sells his or her labor for a wage. The capitalist class includes everyone who owns means of production and purchases labor to derive a profit. This poses new challenges to class formation, because cheaper labor in poorer nations is used to undermine living standards for workers everywhere else. Before workers can defend their interests in a world system, there must be communication, consciousness, and solidarity *across* national boundaries. It is only by improving the position of the worst off that the position of all workers can be defended.

The current composition of the world system reflects the imperialism and colonialism that helped create it. The core of the world system consists of former colonial and neocolonial powers. They retain the economic power, political clout, and military might to ensure that the world system provides substantial profits to them. The periphery of the world system consists of former colonies. Their natural resources and cheap labor continue to generate profits that flow from the periphery to the core. Standing between these two extremes is the semi-periphery. It is a diverse group that includes former socialist nations and more advantaged former colonies. Core nations exploit both peripheral and semi-peripheral nations. Semi-peripheral nations exploit peripheral nations while being exploited by core nations. And peripheral nations experience a double exploitation by both core and semi-peripheral nations.

Inequalities between nation-states make the class relations of the world system very complex. Nation-states are good examples of "status groups" (Weber 1921) that provide their members with cultural identity and group affiliation. In the world system, national status identity can undermine global class identity. When workers follow nationalistic, patriotic, or militaristic appeals, it weakens class solidarity across national boundaries and strengthens global capitalist interests. But this is not simply "false consciousness." In core countries, workers derive real material benefits from their national identity; they might be exploited as workers but benefit as consumers with comfortable standards of living. The world system creates real contradictions among classes and nations. These political divisions within an economically integrated world system help maintain the power of the dominant class.

The world system has a dynamic history. Different nations have changed positions over time, and the leadership of the core and the system as a whole has changed hands. As we shall see in a later exploration of globalization, these dynamics have important global and domestic ramifications.

World system theory is a prime example of critical sociology. It explains why the demise of formal colonialism has not ended global inequality. It illuminates how ongoing postcolonial struggles continue to challenge the core's domination over the labor, resources, and cultures of the world's peoples. It studies global capitalism to identify the changes that could create a more equitable system for producing and distributing the world's resources.

Feminist Sociology

Another example of critical sociology and its commitment to progressive social change is feminist sociology. It analyzes gender in much the same way that Marxism analyzes class. Most importantly, feminist sociology focuses on how gender is socially constructed to create inequality.

The emergence of feminist sociology is itself revealing. Sociology prides itself on seeing beyond appearances, but sociology historically ignored gender. In part, this was because sociology was a male-dominated discipline. Because gender rarely works to the disadvantage of men, this helps explain why it remained off sociology's radar screen. There have always been women who provided incisive understandings of how gender shapes the world (Freedman 2002), but their work was rarely accepted as "real" sociology. It was the feminist movement that provided leverage for feminist sociology. As feminism challenged male domination in the late 1960s, a feminist perspective gradually entered sociology.

This perspective took multiple forms. Liberal or equal-rights feminism criticized segregation and discrimination that limited opportunity for women and advocated for their integration into mainstream institutions. Social or cultural feminism emphasized distinctively female temperaments and aptitudes and argued for their preservation as core social values in place of male competition, aggression, and violence. Socialist feminists and feminists of color analyzed how multiple inequalities rooted in class and race as well as gender intersected and reinforced each other. Through such feminist insights, gender eventually took its place on sociology's agenda.

Feminism entered sociology relatively recently, but its insights have always been profoundly sociological. The slogan "the personal is political" means that seemingly individual issues are shaped by gender power differences. The "personal" is "political" when female self-esteem is tied to male-defined body images reinforced by relentless advertising and marketing. This recalls Mills's (1959) distinction between personal troubles and public issues. If the sociological perspective involves seeing public issues in place of psychological troubles, then feminists have always been solid sociologists. This also suggests that good sociology is as likely to be done by people challenging domination as by credentialed professionals.

Another link between feminism and sociology concerns levels of analysis. Whereas sociologists have struggled to integrate their understandings of macro and micro levels of social order, feminists have always understood gender as a multilevel phenomenon. In so doing, they have enriched sociology's understanding of both levels of analysis.

On the macro level of social structure, including gender has meant broadening conventional notions of material production. Although such activities are often male-dominated, they are sustained by equally basic forms of *social* production and reproduction. The latter are often female-dominated, and sexist biases have frequently ignored or trivialized the social significance of domestic labor, household production, and child rearing in sustaining social life.

Through the gender division of labor, gendered assumptions are embedded in major social institutions. Whether the focus is economics, politics, media, culture, education, medicine, religion, or sports, each institution incorporates and perpetuates basic assumptions about gender differences and inequality. The daily operation of these institutions makes these appearances seem utterly natural. As critical sociology, feminism looks beyond these seemingly natural appearances to examine the social mechanisms that sustain them.

Macro-level gendered patterns are intertwined with micro-level gendered practices. Gender is part of social structure; it is also a fundamental social identity. Sociologists have long studied socialization, but feminism reinvigorated the topic by revealing how socialization is always gendered. As such, it constructs differences between women and men that in turn foster gender inequality.

Gender-laden notions about women and men circulate in the culture but also get embedded in individual minds. As people come to see themselves through a gendered lens, they learn commonsense understandings about the world and their place in it that differ sharply by gender. When they act on those understandings, they perpetuate a world so familiar that it seems like the only possible social order. When micro-level common sense dovetails with macro-level social reproduction, gender becomes a pervasive type of inequality and domination.

Feminist sociology grew out of political struggles for social change. Sociology has been greatly enriched by its understanding of gender, and feminist sociology has retained a commitment to both analyzing and changing gender dynamics.

Postmodern Insights

Postmodern analysis provides a final example of critical sociology. This work spans many disciplines, and some of it challenges critical sociology's project of emancipation. Nonetheless, there are important strands of postmodernist thinking that exemplify critical sociology.

Postmodernism implies we are in a transition from the modern era that has always been sociology's subject matter to something else. Although economics and politics retain many modern features, culture best illustrates postmodernist claims. Here's an example: Modernism assumes we can distinguish between reality and representations of reality. In a postmodern era, such distinctions break down.

Consider how much of our daily experience is mediated through television and other symbolic media. We often take these images as faithful representations of an underlying reality. Yet, if you have ever been at a televised event and later seen it rebroadcast, you know that media representations are partial and selective at best. Given how many such images we see, how selective they inevitably are, and how we nonetheless take them as "real," it could be said that the images are more "real" to us than the "reality" they supposedly represent. It could even be said that media create our reality rather than reflecting a preexisting reality. A postmodern world is like a house of mirrors in which we mistake images for the "real" thing when they are all merely reflections of other reflections.

Consider another example. Every spring I attend a "Festival of Nations," where people from dozens of cultural groups prepare ethnic food, dress in native costumes, and perform traditional music and dances. This event seems to authentically represent existing cultures around the world. In actual fact, many of these cultures exist mainly in the memories of the people staging the festival. For better and for worse, many of these traditional practices have been superseded by social change, cultural diffusion, colonial domination, and globalizing forces. Hence, we have the peculiar situation of witnessing a copy of something for which there is no longer an original. In such a "hyperreal" world of endless "simulations" (Baudrillard 1983), modernist distinctions between reality and representations no longer hold up.

Some postmodern thinking thus recalls sociology's debunking tendency. It questions not only the surface appearance, but also whether there even is an underlying reality. Some other postmodernist thinking resembles the critique of domination that is central to critical sociology. And still other postmodernist thinking challenges critical sociology itself.

Good examples of the "critique of domination" version of postmodernism can be found in Foucault's (1965, 1975, 1979) historical case studies of the rise of modern psychiatry, medicine, and corrections. Although each discipline claimed to be more humane than its predecessors, Foucault detects new forms of domination in each case. This domination derived from new discourses about madness, disease, or deviance. While couched in the language of scientific objectivity, these discourses created new power relations between privileged experts with specialized knowledge and dependent clients, patients, or prisoners at their mercy. The rise of expertise through scientific discourses created a new elite with the power to define reason and madness, health and sickness, and conformity and deviance. Behind the benevolent facade, new forms of power are embedded in many contemporary social institutions.

The most radical, postmodern challenge is to the Enlightenment premise that reason and knowledge can lead to freedom and equality. Foucault (1980) speaks of "power/knowledge" to suggest that every quest for knowledge is really a grab for power, and that knowledge inevitably leads to domination rather than freedom. For other postmodernists, the Enlightenment dream of reason leading to emancipation is merely another "grand narrative" (Lyotard 1979) that cannot possibly be true because "Truth" itself is no longer possible in a postmodern era. Such arguments challenge the foundations of critical sociology (and every other modern system of knowledge). Although I do not find them ultimately persuasive, they provide critical sociologists with a critical lens on their own work even as they seek to analyze and change a problematic world.

This dual commitment to analyzing and changing domination is the hallmark of critical sociology. It is the common thread running through Marx's work, critical theory, world system theory, feminist sociology, and some versions of postmodernist thought. It is also the thread that sets critical sociology apart from scientific and humanistic sociology.

Conclusion

Sociological theories are complex, and any attempt to categorize them is somewhat arbitrary. My purpose here has been to highlight critical sociology as one of several orientations within the discipline.

We can now see how all sociological approaches are *critical* in the first sense of the term. They all have a debunking quality that does not take the world at face value. They look beyond surface appearances. They assume the world is something other than what it claims to be. They look for unintended consequences and latent functions.

Both scientific and humanistic sociology are critical in this sense. The functional analysis that typifies scientific sociology specializes in finding latent consequences of social action. It recognizes that while people are doing one thing, their actions create other outcomes as well. It reveals precisely how the world is not always (or only) what it appears to be. Humanistic sociology is also critical in this sense. It gave rise to the idea of debunking in the first place (Berger 1963). Humanistic sociology is especially good at seeing how society consists of multiple, symbolic meaning systems. Any system that claims to be the central one is ripe for a debunking analysis.

Among my categories, only critical sociology is also critical in the second sense. Scientific and humanistic approaches embrace value neutrality and scientific detachment that limit their critique. Critical sociology is rooted in particular values that motivate sociological work from the start. It advocates freedom, equality, and emancipation. It is the only approach that fully embodies sociology's double critique.

Critical sociology is also best qualified to address the flawed legacy of Enlightenment thought more generally. The critique of domination has traditionally focused on inequalities of class and injustices of capitalism, and those topics loom large in what follows. But this critique has also been extended to inequalities of race, ethnicity, and gender as well as injustices of colonialism and globalization. These issues also receive more detailed analysis in subsequent chapters.

References

Baudrillard, Jean. 1983. *Simulations*. New York: Semiotext(e).

Berger, Peter. 1963. *Invitation to Sociology*. New York: Doubleday.

Berger, Peter, and Thomas Luckmann. 1966. *The Social Construction of Reality*. Garden City, NY: Anchor.

Blau, Peter. 1964. *Exchange and Power in Social Life*. New York: Wiley.

Collins, Randall. 1975. *Conflict Sociology*. New York: Academic Press.

Coser, Lewis. 1956. *The Functions of Social Conflict*. New York: Free Press.

Dahrendorf, Ralf. 1959. *Class and Class Conflict in Industrial Society*. Stanford, CA: Stanford University Press.

Durkheim, Emile. 1893/1964. *The Division of Labor in Society*. New York: Free Press.

———. 1897/1951. *Suicide*. New York: Free Press.

———. 1912/1965. *The Elementary Forms of the Religious Life*. New York: Free Press.

Foucault, Michel. 1965. *Madness and Civilization.* New York: Vintage.

———. 1975. *The Birth of the Clinic.* New York: Vintage.

———. 1979. *Discipline and Punish.* New York: Vintage.

———. 1980. *Power/Knowledge.* New York: Pantheon.

Freedman, Estelle. 2002. *No Turning Back.* New York: Ballantine Books.

Garfinkel, Harold. 1967. *Studies in Ethnomethodology.* Englewood Cliffs, NJ: Prentice Hall.

Gramsci, Antonio. 1971. *Selections from the Prison Notebooks.* New York: International Publishers.

Habermas, Jürgen. 1969. *Knowledge and Human Interests.* Boston: Beacon.

Homans, George. 1974. *Social Behavior: Its Elementary Forms.* New York: Harcourt, Brace Jovanovich.

Jay, Martin. 1973. *The Dialectical Imagination.* Boston: Little, Brown.

Lyotard, Jean-François. 1979. *The Postmodern Condition.* Minneapolis: University of Minnesota Press.

Mead, George Herbert. 1934/1962. *Mind, Self and Society.* Chicago: University of Chicago Press.

Merton, Robert. 1968. *Social Theory and Social Structure.* New York: Free Press.

Mills, C. Wright. 1959. *The Sociological Imagination.* New York: Oxford University Press.

Parsons, Talcott. 1937. *The Structure of Social Action.* New York: McGraw-Hill.

———. 1951. *The Social System.* Glencoe, IL: Free Press.

Ritzer, George. 2000. *The McDonaldization of Society.* Thousand Oaks, CA: Pine Forge Press.

Schutz, Alfred. 1932/1967. *The Phenomenology of the Social World.* Evanston, IL: Northwestern University Press.

Wallerstein, Immanuel. 1974. *The Modern World-System.* New York: Academic Press.

———. 1980. *The Modern World-System II.* New York: Academic Press.

———. 1989. *The Modern World-System III.* New York: Academic Press.

Weber, Max. 1904/1958. *The Protestant Ethic and the Spirit of Capitalism.* New York: Charles Scribner's Sons.

———. 1921/1968. *Economy and Society.* 3 volumes. Totowa, NJ: Bedminster Press.

CHAPTER 2

Social Research

The topics discussed in this book are taken from your daily life. Sociologists pose questions about social phenomena and engage in social research to provide relevant answers to those questions. You will learn how sociologists study and collect data on social issues. Sociologists need a guide to start their journey in gathering, ordering, and interpreting their findings and facts. Chapter 2 introduces the key subjects in social research including samples, variables, concepts, theories, validity, legality, trust, research ethics, and bias. You will identify scientific methods and compare their strengths and weaknesses. Alexander and Thompson (2008) explain why some methods are chosen rather than others and what qualitative (in the form of words) and quantitative (in the form of numbers or statistics) methods are employed to do so. In other words, qualitative methods yield detailed descriptions and verbal reports while quantitative methods yield numerical data. This chapter stresses how to select a proper research method to study sociological explanations for human actions. Similarly, you will learn how tools are used from both methods of sociological research to engage in data analysis.

Sociological Methods

Jeffrey C. Alexander and Kenneth Thompson

....

Once, it was thought that sociological research could be undertaken and understood only by an elite. In the nineteenth century the elite was composed of "armchair scholars," who attempted to explain the whole course of social development on the basis of information that they could find in the library. Auguste Comte, the reputed founder of sociology, even stopped reading after some years and practiced what he called "mental hygiene," which meant avoiding being "contaminated" by other people's writings. Needless to say, this is not a procedure that we recommend to sociology students who have exams to pass! After all, Comte had been a brilliant student and had read extremely widely before writing his major works. Karl Marx, another scholar whose work left a lasting mark on sociology, spent most of his time in the British Library in London, where he not only read books but also studied the statistics being gathered by government factory inspectors and local health officers. Herbert Spencer, also based in London, whose social evolutionary sociology had a major impact in America, was reputed to have done most of his reading in the Athenaeum, a gentlemen's club.

In the twentieth century, sociological research became a professional occupation and was directed by a new elite of trained scholars and researchers, based in universities and research centers. Exhaustive graduate training leading to a Ph.D. became the minimum entry requirement to this elite. The research model was that of the expensively funded natural sciences.

One of the distinguishing features of the postmodern culture of the twenty-first century is that sociological thinking and research have spread through all levels of society. In a sense, then, sociology has been diversified and democratized, because all sorts of people undertake research and almost everyone is exposed to it. This is particularly true of the various kinds of sociological knowledge and research disseminated by the mass media. Society itself has become a kind of **text** into which diverse meanings are woven [...].

How do you react to this kind of media research? Would you be inclined to regard it as scientifically sound and its findings valid, or do you find yourself asking critical questions about the methods the producers used? Bear in mind that, nowadays, television producers often have some knowledge of sociological research methods and findings, perhaps as a result of taking a sociology course or reading sociology books. They may even claim to be carrying out sociological studies, as in the case of renowned director Michael Apted, who, not content with merely making an entertaining documentary, claims in his television series *Married in America* to provide the basis of "a sociological study about what the institution of marriage means in America today" [...]. We will examine that claim in the next section, when we discuss basic research issues concerning **samples** and **interviews.** But, first, we need to consider this example of a mass-media documentary as part of a wider postmodern phenomenon of **infotainment.**

The mass media are constantly engaged in the systematic gathering and dissemination of information. Postmodern culture does not lack information; indeed, it may suffer from information overload. The mass media are part of our everyday lives, and we depend on them for much of our understanding of what goes on in the world. Compared with earlier generations, we are fortunate in having the mass media to bring the world into our living rooms. The problem is, we may tend to assume that what they bring is a fair reflection of that world, and that they observe the same rigorous standards as those of social science research. This is not to suggest that the mass media should be regarded suspiciously as inclined to be biased or sloppy. Rather, it is a matter of raising questions about the differences between mass media procedures and reports, on the one hand, and those of social science, on the other. You can probably think of some of these differences for yourself, but here are some suggestions.

Because they are competing for attention with other media outlets, the mass media must give the "customers" what they want, or at least what can be afforded, bearing in mind that the media must make a profit or at least balance their budget. So, unlike academic research, media coverage of a topic is partly determined by the criterion of what will attract or entertain consumers.

The information must be readily available and be presented in such a way that the consumers of the media can understand it. This places heavy demands on the information-gathering capacities of the media as well as on those who interpret and present the information (usually journalists). Frequently, journalists will call in experts, sociological researchers among them, to help them—but in the end it is the journalist who has to take the responsibility. Unlike professional social scientists, journalists do not have to qualify in research methods! They may present the results of social science research, but they are less likely to discuss and evaluate the methods used.

Limitations of time (deadlines) and space (column inches or program length) add to the pressures affecting what information is collected and how it is presented. The book-length research monograph does not have an equivalent in the mass media. In addition, the values and priorities of the media may not be the same as those they are reporting on, sometimes leading to unconscious bias even when fairness is intended. Journalism often depends on finding an "angle" that shapes the story. The angle may draw on various implicit theories or hypotheses, but not necessarily in a rigorous or testing way that would meet the standards expected in social science research. The angle is often more like a hunch or a slant.

The criteria for verifying whether media research results are valid are not spelled out or formally agreed upon. This contrasts with sociological research, in which such issues are constantly debated and there is a shared knowledge about the kinds of criteria that should be used in evaluating research methods—even in cases where specific disagreements have occurred.

These are just a few of the points that come to mind when considering the differences between media reports and sociology research reports. But there are also positive similarities. Both the journalist and the sociologist are interested in accurately describing and plausibly explaining some social phenomenon that they judge to be significant. And both professions are committed to certain values and standards, such as accuracy and fairness in the pursuit of truth. They may even use the same or similar sets of data, such as government statistics, surveys of attitudes and opinions based on questionnaires or in-depth interviews, and observations of people's behavior.

The key differences are in the natures of the two institutions—the media and the scientific community. The latter has been developing as an institution over several centuries and sociology has accepted its rules, while insisting on the distinctive character of its human subject matter. The mass media, by contrast, are a relatively new institution. Although small-circulation and short-lived newspapers began to appear in the seventeenth century, mass-circulation newspapers date from the nineteenth century. The electronic mass media—film, television, and radio—developed in the postmodern period, which started around the mid-twentieth century. They were not around during the time of the classical sociologists—namely, Emile Durkheim and Max Weber. Even the sociologists of the immediate post–World War II era tended to regard just a few newspapers, such as the *New York Times* and the *Washington Post*, as the only serious mass media of information. The way in which television has developed since then has not reassured sociologists about the seriousness of the medium as a reliable means of gathering data and presenting findings, for some of the reasons that we mentioned above. And yet, television is tremendously active and influential in providing the general public with versions of sociological knowledge that cannot be ignored [...].

The postmodern dilemma about knowledge is that there is so much of it, and in such a variety of forms, that it is difficult to sift through and evaluate. This is why an understanding of the basics of social scientific research and analysis is vital. The task is complicated by the fact that sociologists themselves are engaged in lively debates about the validity of different types of research and analysis. Feminists have objected that some well-established methods of research and analysis are undertaken from a masculine position that neglects women's perspective and experience. Similar arguments have been made by gays and lesbians, and other groups, such as nonwhites and nonwesterners. The question of "relativism" then becomes unavoidable. Is all knowledge, including "scientific knowledge," only relatively valid, its validity restricted by the fact that it derives from a limited perspective? And if this is so, are all perspectives or standpoints equally valid? Before trying to answer these questions, we will look at some of the basic terms used in various types of sociological research and analysis.

Some Key Research Terms

What does it mean to select a sample of a population? In support of Michael Apted's claim to be undertaking sociological research, a commentator on *Married in America* states that Apted and his producers "selected the couples demographically as well as telegenically." In other words, he tried to cover a representative sample of the American population. A sample is a small number of individuals drawn from a larger population. A **representative sample** (also called a *stratified sample*) is one that aims to provide an accurate representation of the different sections that make up the population, distinguished by attributes such as race, religion, income, location, education, and sexual preference. (This contrasts with a **random sample,** which is selected purely statistically—as when, say, every tenth person in the population is chosen for a sample.) In fact, Apted's sample might more accurately be termed a *purposive sample*, on the grounds that he selected people on the basis that they were likely to be relevant to the subject he was studying. The drawback of such a sample is that it reflects the prior judgments of the researcher-producer, which may be open to question, especially as another criterion of selection was that the participants should be "telegenic." Presumably, boringly "average" people were not selected because they were not sufficiently interesting or attractive. Another intention was to do follow-up interviews with the couples after a certain period of time, and this resembles the kind of sample referred to as a *panel sample,* whereby the same group of people is studied at intervals in order to record any changes. Sometimes, for convenience, a researcher may use a **snowball sample,** which involves asking the first few interviewees for the names of other people who might fit the criteria of the study. This is probably the most problematic type of sample, because it depends so much on the recommendations of a small number of people, who, in turn, are likely to recommend people like themselves.

Modern **survey** techniques rely on random sampling, making it possible for social scientists to use relatively small samples to arrive at generalizations about an entire population. For example, election polls using a sample of 1,500 to 2,000 respondents may be used to predict the distribution of votes in a presidential election. Such surveys are used not just for election polling but for many other sociological and governmental data-gathering purposes as well. For example, the U.S. Census Bureau's Current Population Survey (CPS) uses sample surveys to provide monthly estimates of marriages, divorces, births, deaths, poverty, employment and unemployment, and many other social indicators.

Opinion polls are another form of sociological survey that is widely used by governmental and other agencies. One of the best known of these is the General Social Survey (GSS) conducted by the National Opinion Research Center (NORC). Using a nationwide random sample of at least 1,500

United States Census 2000

U.S. Department of Commerce • Bureau of the Census

This is the official form for all the people at this address. It is quick and easy, and your answers are protected by law. Complete the Census and help your community get what it needs — today and in the future!

Start Here

Please use a black or blue pen.

1. How many people were living or staying in this house, apartment, or mobile home on April 1, 2000?

Number of people

INCLUDE in this number:
- foster children, roomers, or housemates
- people staying here on April 1, 2000 who have no other permanent place to stay
- people living here most of the time while working, even if they have another place to live

DO NOT INCLUDE in this number:
- college students living away while attending college
- people in a correctional facility, nursing home, or mental hospital on April 1, 2000
- Armed Forces personnel living somewhere else
- people who live or stay at another place most of the time

2. Is this house, apartment, or mobile home — Mark ☒ ONE box.
- ☐ Owned by you or someone in this household with a mortgage or loan?
- ☐ Owned by you or someone in this household free and clear (without a mortgage or loan)?
- ☐ Rented for cash rent?
- ☐ Occupied without payment of cash rent?

3. Please answer the following questions for each person living in this house, apartment, or mobile home. Start with the name of one of the people living here who owns, is buying, or rents this house, apartment, or mobile home. If there is no such person, start with any adult living or staying here. We will refer to this person as Person 1.

What is this person's name? Print name below.

Last Name

First Name   MI

4. What is Person 1's telephone number? We may call this person if we don't understand an answer.

Area Code + Number

5. What is Person 1's sex? Mark ☒ ONE box.
- ☐ Male   ☐ Female

6. What is Person 1's age and what is Person 1's date of birth?

Age on April 1, 2000

Print numbers in boxes.
Month   Day   Year of birth

➔ **NOTE: Please answer BOTH Questions 7 and 8.**

7. Is Person 1 Spanish/Hispanic/Latino? Mark ☒ the "No" box if **not** Spanish/Hispanic/Latino.
- ☐ No, not Spanish/Hispanic/Latino   ☐ Yes, Puerto Rican
- ☐ Yes, Mexican, Mexican Am., Chicano   ☐ Yes, Cuban
- ☐ Yes, other Spanish/Hispanic/Latino — Print group. ↗

8. What is Person 1's race? Mark ☒ one or more races to indicate what this person considers himself/herself to be.
- ☐ White
- ☐ Black, African Am., or Negro
- ☐ American Indian or Alaska Native — Print name of enrolled or principal tribe. ↗

- ☐ Asian Indian   ☐ Japanese   ☐ Native Hawaiian
- ☐ Chinese   ☐ Korean   ☐ Quamanian or Chamorro
- ☐ Filipino   ☐ Vietnamese   ☐ Samoan
- ☐ Other Asian — Print race. ↗   ☐ Other Pacific Islander — Print race. ↗

- ☐ Some other race — Print race. ↗

➔ **If more people live here, continue with Person 2.**

OMB No. 0607-0856: Approval Expires 12/31/2000

Form **D-61A**

The U.S. Census, taken every ten years, gathers crucial data that sociologists use to analyze American society. (U.S. Census Bureau)

respondents, the GSS is able to generalize about the whole American adult population's opinions on a wide range of selected issues.

Concepts and Theories

In some respects, media documentaries and sociological research are similar in their resemblance to detective work. Sometimes there are brilliant insights; at other times it seems to be more a matter of sifting through evidence to find clues and then meeting with failure or success in finding a solution. The aim in all three contexts is to get at the truth or the facts about something that is a puzzle. What constitutes the puzzle for sociologists is different from that which presents itself to the television producer or the detective. The detective has to solve a crime, whereas the sociologist has to solve a puzzle about society. The detective's object of study—a crime—is defined by the law and how the police and the legal system interpret the law in each case. The sociologist's puzzle is defined by his or her application of sociological concepts and theories. The television producer may seem to be investigating the same puzzle as the sociologist, such as what factors are affecting people's decisions about marriage? The difference is that the television producer—in this case, Michael Apted—need not be explicit about concepts and theories (although these may be implicit in the way he chooses to angle the program). The sociologist is not permitted such license.

Concepts and theories are important for the sociological researcher because they make it possible to pose relevant questions about social phenomena in ways that indicate clearly what would constitute an adequate answer. A **concept** is a mental construct that represents some aspect of the world in simplified form. It may also be a category or classification, such as social class, race, or gender. People can then be classified in these terms—for example, as upper-class, middle-class, or lower-class; black or white; male or female.

A **variable** is a concept whose value changes from case to case. This changing value is demonstrated by an indicator. According to Weberian theory (deriving from the sociologist Max Weber), for example, income is the key indicator for deciding the variable of class. A researcher would be interested in discovering whether two variables seem to change their values in tandem, as this might mean there is a relation between them—a **correlation.** However, a correlation does not mean that one variable is the cause of the other's change. During summer, there appears to be both a rise in ice cream sales and a rise in sports participation. This is a correlation. It would be erroneous, obviously, to assume any causal relation. Ice cream eating does not cause sports participation, or (usually!) vice versa. It may be the operation of a third variable—hot weather—that explains the correlation, in the sense of specifying a cause. In developing causal explanations, it is customary to distinguish between an independent variable and a dependent variable. An **independent variable** is a factor that causes change in another variable—namely, the **dependent variable.**

Concepts and variables, and the causal processes they lay out, are linked together to make up a theory. A **social theory** is an organizing framework of concepts, based on empirical evidence, that explains why society, or some aspect of society, works as it does. Facts do not speak for themselves. We need a theory to guide us in gathering, ordering, and interpreting facts. An **explanatory theory** contains one or more hypotheses about cause and effect, proposing that a specified independent variable is the cause of an effect on a dependent variable. (A *hypothesis* is a conjecture that relates two or more concepts.) A famous example in sociology is Durkheim's theory of social integration, according to which he posited that for every society there is an optimum level of social integration. From this he made deductions about the probable occurrence of various social problems, such as suicide, when social integration is weakened. In particular, he deduced that a decrease in social integration (independent variable) would cause an increase in the suicide rate (dependent variable) (Durkheim 1897). Using this theory, Durkheim went on to test more specific hypotheses. Protestants would have higher rates of suicide than Catholics, he hypothesized, because Protestantism is more individualist and produces less forceful social integration. (Jews ranked even higher than Catholics on social integration and had lower suicide rates.) Durkheim tested his theory of suicide by making statistical samples of suicides and then testing them, in turn, by seeing if there were correlations with other variables. His results seemed to validate the theory, as regions or countries with higher numbers of Protestants than Catholics did have higher rates of suicide.

Durkheim's study, *Suicide*, provides one of the earliest examples in sociology of the use of *secondary data*—information collected for another purpose often, as in this case, by governments. Its chief advantage is that it can provide the sociologist with extensive statistical or other information that is not readily available or would be costly and time-consuming to gather. The disadvantage is that it is usually collected for some other purpose than that envisaged by the sociologist, and so it may have to be adapted or reinterpreted. In the case of suicide statistics, Durkheim had to bring together data from different government sources and different dates. He was also conscious that societies differed in their attitudes to suicide and that this might have affected the figures. Despite these problems, he decided that the figures were sufficiently reliable to make it worth advancing conclusions (e.g., "Thus, everywhere, without exception, Protestants show far more suicides than the followers of other confessions") on the basis of data such as those shown in Table 2.1.

Because Durkheim believed that sociological explanation (like exploration in the natural sciences) should be based on externally observable factors, he rejected explanations in terms of individuals' internal motives and purposes. He sought to formulate his explanations solely in terms of externally observable rates of covariation of variables. So, variations in the recorded rates of suicide corresponded to variations in the rate of social integration between religious denominations: Protestant doctrines and practices encouraged individual responsibility, whereas Catholicism offered absolution for sins through the ministration of the priest. Jews, in Durkheim's day, were supported by the close-knit bonds of the ghetto and, hypothetically as a result of this high level of social integration, had the lowest rates of suicide.

Sociologists following the example of Max Weber and his **interpretive sociology** have taken a different approach to explanation, insisting that sociological explanations should try to interpret the motives and meanings that lie behind the actions of individuals. In the context of explaining suicide, J. Jacobs (1970) examined suicide notes in order to find the reasoning used by would-be suicides in

Table 2.1 Suicides in Different Countries per Million Persons of Each Faith

		Protestants	Catholics	Jews
Austria	(1852–59)	79.5	51.3	20.7
Prussia	(1849–55)	159.9	49.6	46.4
Prussia	(1869–72)	187	69	96
Prussia	(1890)	240	100	180
Baden	(1852–62)	139	117	87
Baden	(1870–74)	171	136.7	124
Baden	(1878–88)	242	170	210
Bavaria	(1844–56)	135.4	49.1	105.9
Bavaria	(1884–91)	224	94	193
Württemberg	(1846–60)	113.5	77.9	65.6
Württemberg	(1873–76)	190	120	60
Württemberg	(1881–90)	170	119	142

Source: Adapted from Durkheim (1951 [1897]), p. 154.

overcoming the moral prohibitions against suicide found in each of the three religions. Like Weber, Jacobs believed it is possible to reconstruct typical processes of reasoning that make it possible to put forward general explanations (as opposed to those specific to an individual). After studying the reasoning in a sample of suicide notes, Jacobs pointed to differences among the religious groups in their moral evaluation of suicide.

Comparing the beliefs taught by Christianity to Judaism, he argued on the basis of his evidence about motives that Christianity promises rewards in the hereafter whereas Judaism does not, and that Christians represent their deaths as "going to heaven" whereas Jews do not. Jacobs suggested that what encourages potential Christian suicides is their ability to convince themselves of ending an intolerable life on earth and obtaining a better one in the beyond. On these grounds, Jews will have a lower suicide rate than Christians, whether Catholic or Protestant. Protestantism is more rationalistic than Catholicism and stresses the ability of the individual to work out his or her own balance sheet of salvation. Catholicism lays greater stress on the supremacy of dogma. Therefore, Protestants will find it easier to construct a justification of their suicide than will Catholics, who are more constrained by the dogmatic prohibition of suicide.

Jacobs thus arrived at an explanation of the same observed differences in religious suicide rates that Durkheim found. However, it is a very different form of explanation. Jacobs constructed schemes of motives for suicide that could be shown to typify the different religious groups and, in this sense, arrived at causes for suicide that were intelligible for being "understandable." In contrast, Durkheim's explanation was deliberately free of any terms that would ascribe purposes or motives to the individual.

Both explanations could be considered correct, since they both predict the effect of the religious factor in the same way. So, the choice between the explanations depends on what the researcher considers to be an "adequate" explanation. Those who, like Durkheim, believe sociology should follow the model of explanation favored by the natural sciences do not emphasize the distinctive nature of human action—the role played by cultural meanings and emotional motives. Others, like Jacobs, following Weber's lead, would insist on explanations that link remote causes (such as social integration) and effects (suicide rates), whereby the necessary link is provided by an understandable scheme of motives. They would argue that Durkheim's explanation can be made "intelligible" only by the addition of certain assumptions about how individuals react to different levels of social integration. In other words, if one added a subsidiary theory containing hypotheses such as "a subject's experience of low social integration produces subjective feelings of purposelessness," these individual suicides could be explained. However, Durkheim did not think that sociology could use concepts relating to individual purposes or inner feelings. In this respect, he was attempting to follow the *hypothetical-deductive model* of natural science.

Science aims to establish certain laws based on predictable and reliable theories about causal relationships between dependent and independent variables. And, indeed, Durkheim believed that his theory of social integration would provide such laws in sociology. But critics have objected on two counts. The first is that sociological theories are far below the level of precision achieved in natural science. Durkheim's theory of social integration is said to suffer from this lack of precision. It is difficult, for example, to be precise about what is meant by *social integration*—the bonds between individuals that constitute social integration are not objective and visible but rather vague and indistinct. The other, more radical criticism is the one we have been discussing: The natural science form of explanation is said to be inappropriate for sociological explanations of human actions. Two reasons are given for this. Human actors (unlike the "objects" of physics) follow rules in deciding on and carrying out their actions, rather than responding mechanically to scientific laws. Order and regularity in social life stem from the sharing of common beliefs, values, and purposes among individuals in society. Behavior becomes understandable only when we find out *why* certain actions are being performed. If we see a roomful of students frantically writing in bluebooks, we may explain their behavior by finding out that they are taking a sociology exam. Their actions are intelligible to us, and thus explained, when we come to know the purpose behind what they are doing. Conversely, a researcher who does not share, or cannot readily imagine, a culture in common with those she is studying may be unable to understand the purpose of actions she observes. Australian aborigines' ritual of killing and eating a totemic animal puzzled anthropologists until they were able to learn the aborigines' own reasons why their ritual was performed. (Interestingly, Durkheim used the same kind of anthropological data in his last great book, *The Elementary Forms of Religious Life* [1912], suggesting that he was more flexible about models of sociological explanation than was evident either in *Suicide* [1897] or in his earlier book, *The Rules of Sociological Method* [1895]—both of which insisted, as we have seen, on examining social facts as "things," from the outside.) What is true of exotic tribal people is true in a less dramatic way of street gangs; they, too, have their own cultures, and these need to be understood by the academic researcher before he or she can comprehend and explain their actions.

Thus far, we have contrasted two forms of sociological explanation as extremes. In actual research, however, since a sociologist may well use aspects of both forms, the opposition between ways of explaining social patterns is not always so stark. Still, the two poles of the hypothetical-deductive model—sometimes referred to as a *covering-law explanation*, on the one hand, and as the *interpretive approach* or *explanation-by-understanding method*, on the other—are real and have consequences for the choice of methods adopted by the researcher. Explanation by understanding requires evidence of meaning—the purposes and motives of individuals and groups—and so usually requires methods such as participant observation (joining in with those being studied) or documentary research (written documents, such as files, government reports, and personal diaries; and visual documents, such as photographs or films). Covering-law explanations ideally prefer to use quantified concepts of observable behavior (such as divorce rates) in which the element of motive or purpose is lost, owing to the emphasis placed on the need for precise models and hypotheses. Quantification is one way of looking for precision. Careful qualitative research can also be "precise," but it is harder to put qualitative hypotheses in a form that can be rigorously replicated—namely, in the form of tests that the covering-law model of explanation requires. The use of interviewers to administer questionnaire surveys of attitudes and opinions, perhaps supplemented by observation of actual behavior, is one way in which researchers have tried to bridge the gap between quantification and qualitative understanding of motives and meanings.

In short, opinions differ among sociologists as to what is an adequate explanation. The covering-law model requires theories with precisely stated hypotheses and explanations that take the form of validly deducing a conclusion. A good or well-grounded theory is one that has withstood determined attempts to falsify one or more of its hypotheses. And, indeed, application of the covering-law model in sociology is often held back by the weakness of sociological theories (imprecise hypotheses) that are difficult to test. Alternatively, the explanation-by-understanding model is a scheme of explanation in which the purposive nature of human action is recognized, with the result that culture and meaning become necessary parts of the sociological theory in question. This purposive nature of action requires a scheme of explanation that makes human action intelligible. Each of the two forms of explanation has its preferred research methods.

As noted earlier, sociologists often use a combination of approaches and methods. Most researchers are reconciled to the fact that sociological theories cannot be as precise and quantifiable as natural science theories and thus tend to be rather tentative and "sensitizing"—composed of hypotheses suggesting what connections may exist between variables and where to look for possible relations of cause and effect. At some point, then, such theories are likely to depend on assumptions about the typical motives and meanings of those involved in the action being described or explained. This is one unavoidable reason for the relativism of sociological theory. To understand *motive*, we must be thoroughly enmeshed in our own time, or at least believe ourselves to be.

Methodology and Methods

There is a wide range of research methods available to sociologists. Why some methods are chosen rather than others, and what the different methods are intended to do, is the subject of methodology (literally: the study of methods). The methodological reasons for choosing a particular research method (or combination of methods) may reflect a preference for either the natural science model of explanation or the interpretive approach. If it is the former, then there will be a desire to employ methods that produce **quantitative** data (i.e., in the form of numbers or statistics). If the preference is for the interpretive approach, then the inclination will be to use methods that produce **qualitative** data (i.e., in the form of words).

In principle, methods are simply technical tools for getting a job done. But, in practice, methodological reasons may lie behind the choice of a particular method or set of methods for a research project:

> In a sense, methods are a-theoretical and a-methodological (meaning, independent from methodology). Interviews, for instance, like observation, experiments, content analysis, etc., can be used in any methodology type, and serve any chosen research purpose. The same methods can be used in the context of different methodologies, and the same methodology can employ different methods. ...
>
> Nevertheless, although methods are in general a-methodological, their content structure and process are dictated by an underlying methodology. Although interviews, for instance, can be used in a qualitative and a quantitative methodology, the former employs an unstructured, open or in-depth interview, while the latter normally opts for a standardized interview. In a similar vein, participant observation is used in qualitative studies while structured observation is employed in quantitative studies. (Sarantakos 1993: 33)

Quantitative data in the form of statistics are useful because they allow researchers to consider trends over time. Statistics have also become the common currency for making public comparisons between groups. For example, we could compare church attendance rates for various income groups. If there seemed to be a correlation, such as "the lower the income, the higher the church attendance," we might hypothesize that the two variables are linked in some way. But remember, the fact that there is a correlation between two variables does not necessarily mean that one has caused the other. There may be another variable that intervenes (an intervening variable). For example, it could be a difference in ethnic origin that has led to the correlation between church attendance and income, with poor Mexican-American Catholics ranking higher on church attendance but lower on income, compared with white Anglo-Saxon Protestants. (In fact, the links between income and church attendance vary considerably, because there are, indeed, many intervening variables, including not only ethnicity but such other cultural factors as differences between religious denominations.) Sociologists who prefer a qualitative methodology are likely to want to emphasize the importance of getting at the motives and meanings that lie behind people's actions. In our example of the correlation between church attendance and income or ethnicity, they would concentrate on posing probing questions about what church attendance means to people from a particular income or ethnic group.

The availability of computers has made it possible to manipulate large bodies of statistical data very quickly, making it relatively easy for sociologists to obtain findings from social surveys with large samples. In addition, computers can be used for reanalysis of data, so that sociologists years from now can reuse data that had been collected earlier. They also enable sociologists to make large-scale comparisons between groups; consider, for instance, the cross-national comparisons that yield statistics on health, education, poverty, and so on that are compiled by the United Nations and its agencies.

Despite these advantages, quantitative methods have some drawbacks as well. In the case of *descriptive statistics* (numbers that communicate characteristics of a population, such as income, marital status, race, or ethnic background), the disadvantage may be that they do not go into sufficient detail and so gloss over significant differences. For example, the U.S. Bureau of Justice uses "racial" categories, such as "whites, blacks, American Indians, and Asians," in tables of statistics on "Violent Victimization and Race." But there are various ethnic groups included within the very broad category "Asians" (e.g., Chinese, Indian, and Japanese), and the possibility that these ethnicities are associated with very different cultures may be highly significant with respect to violence and crime. Another sort of problem emerges when quantitative sociologists wish to use *secondary statistics* (statistics first collected earlier for another purpose). The fact that someone else collected them for a different purpose may mean that they are not suitable for reuse without adaptation, and the process of adaptation may distort the findings.

The **census** is a specific form of social survey, using questions designed to gather information that will provide a description of a whole population [...]. There are other types of survey research, too, as we will see in subsequent chapters dealing with topics that have attracted academic researchers using surveys. However, the two main types are the interviewer-administered questionnaire and the self-administered questionnaire. Whichever type is used, the basic characteristics of the survey method are as follows:

1. The survey method requires that a sample of respondents reply to a number of fixed questions under comparable conditions.

2. The survey must be administered by an interviewer who completes a form for each respondent by asking him or her the survey questions; alternatively, a form on which the questions are printed is sent to each respondent for self-completion.

3. The respondents in the survey represent a defined population. If all the members of a population are interviewed or fill in a self-completion form, then a *census* (i.e., a 100 percent sample survey) has been taken. If only a fraction of the population is covered, then a *sample survey* has been conducted.

4. A sample survey should be representative of its population. If it is, then we can generalize results from the sample to the population.

5. By using the same questions for a sample of respondents, we can make comparisons of individuals within the sample.

The advantages of the social survey method are that it allows information from large samples to be collected quickly and relatively cheaply, and it allows comparisons among individuals because answers to questions are comparable. The main disadvantage, compared with participant observation, is that it may be superficial in measuring sensitive or difficult aspects of behavior. A researcher can minimize this oversimplification of replies by testing questions on a small part of the sample beforehand, using a less structured and more conversational method of interview in which replies are probed more deeply than is possible in the full-scale survey in the main sample. Well-conducted surveys often utilize a number of *"pilot" interviews* before the main questionnaire is finalized.

All surveys are structured to some extent, even though the more open and conversational forms of interviewing are sometimes referred to as "unstructured." In the category of highly structured methods of asking questions, the two main ones—the *self-administered questionnaire* and the *interview schedule*—have many points in common. Note, however, that the interviewer-administered questionnaire allows for more control over the interview situation than does the self-administered questionnaire, which is either sent by mail or administered to a group such as workers in an office or factory.

The interviewer (or a *coder* working after the event) should be able to organize the responses to any question into a set of mutually exclusive and exhaustive categories, such as "Yes," "No," and "Don't know." A less simple categorization of responses—named after its inventor, Rensis Likert—involves coding into one of five or seven categories. Typical Likert categories are as follows:

Strongly agree
Agree
Neither agree nor disagree
Disagree
Strongly disagree

(with a particular statement).

This is a fivefold Likert categorization. (Sevenfold categorizations, by contrast, list three categories on either side of the neutral category of "Neither agree nor disagree.") The language used for these categories either invites agreement with a given statement or asks for responses to a question that the interviewer then has to code into a specific category. An example using a fivefold Likert scale can be found in this statement from a study of Americans' views of the police as a public service: "How would you rate the overall quality of police services in your neighbourhood? Remember, we mean the two or three blocks around your home. Are they outstanding, good, adequate, inadequate, or very poor?" (paraphrasing Zeller and Carmines 1980).

Questionnaire Surveys

A popular quantitative method (or research instrument) is the questionnaire survey, which is often composed of closed questions that allow only a limited number of possible responses. Often these responses are written on the questionnaire itself, where a space or box is allocated for a tick or cross. Another kind of closed question elicits attitudes of people by providing them with a set of scales ranging from "strongly agree" to "strongly disagree" or some other set. For example, a survey of people's attitudes toward their neighborhood might ask a closed question such as "Which answer best sums up your feelings about the number of shops in your neighborhood?"

Too few
About right
Too many
Don't know

Alternatively, questions may be more open-ended, and these are capable of producing data that are more qualitative. Here the respondents are provided with spaces in which they can construct their own answers. For example: "How do you feel about the shopping facilities in your neighborhood?" Although open-ended questions are more difficult to code—and thus to quantify and analyze statistically—than closed questions, they offer more scope for individuals' expression of real opinions and attitudes. The criticism of closed questions is that they impose a limited set of options, and that these are the products of the mind of the researcher rather than of the respondent. The meanings of the possible responses may vary among respondents, and so what appears to be a block of like-minded people may in reality be no such thing.

Open-ended questions are aimed at avoiding these problems by allowing respondents to speak for themselves. However, the problem with such questions is that they make it difficult to compare answers, because these can be so varied in their expression. The researcher is left with a great deal of work to do in trying to categorize the answers. Sometimes this may be done through content analysis, whereby a computer program picks out certain words or phrases that are taken to represent a certain attitude or position on an issue. (This method can also be used in research on documents, such as newspaper articles.)

Written questionnaires are the easiest to administer to a large sample (especially if they can be mailed out), and they usually feature closed questions. The completed questionnaires can then be fed directly into the computer, which quickly produces quantitative data. Face-to-face interviews are more time-consuming, but they offer the advantage of raising the response rate (securing an adequate response rate to written questionnaires is more difficult). The interview schedule (design of questions) may be structured or semistructured. A *structured interview* is one consisting of questions that allow the interviewer little scope for varying the way the questions are presented or followed up. A *semistructured interview* allows the interviewer more scope in these respects. The semistructured interview schedule initially provides a brief guide as to what should be asked (perhaps also including some closed questions of a factual sort, such as those concerning biographical facts—name, age, education, occupation, etc.) and then lists broad subject headings for further questioning. An in-depth interview is one in which the interviewer can encourage the interviewee to talk at length in answer to "prompt questions."

Observation

Observation of behavior is a sociological research method that can take various forms. Experiments are a favored form for quantitative research because they are the epitome of research methods in the natural sciences, allowing the researcher to control the situation—holding some variables constant in order to study the effects of change in one variable. However, experiments are difficult to set up in sociological research and so are less frequently used than other methods, although they have been attempted in research on social psychological factors, such as group behavior and social interaction in a small-scale, laboratory-like setting. Observation of real-life groups may be more feasible, but these situations are harder to control than experimental situations.

Researchers may be nonparticipant observers, perhaps observing from a distance or hidden from view, so as not to disturb the normal functioning of the group. This is necessary in order to avoid the "Hawthorne effect," which occurred when Elton Mayo (1933) and Fritz Jules Roesthlisburger and William J. Dickson (1939) undertook a **field research** experiment at the Hawthorne factory of the General Electric Company in Chicago. The intention was to study the effect of certain variables on group performance, including physical changes in the work situation, such as the lighting. However, productivity seemed to go up in response to *all* changes, not just one or two. Eventually it became clear that the workers were reacting to the fact that they knew they were being observed, and this seemed to increase their group morale.

In participant observation the researcher has a choice regarding the degree to which he or she gets involved in the activities of those being observed, and also whether the subjects of the research are informed that they are being studied. A good example of partial involvement is Ned Polsky's

(1967) study of poolroom hustlers. Using the methods of direct observation, informal talks, and participant observation during the poolroom activities, Polsky was sufficiently involved to be able to further his research objectives, but without becoming engaged in other aspects of the hustlers' lives (especially the illegal ones). In contrast, William Foote Whyte, during his study of an Italian-American street gang in Chicago, *Street Corner Society* (1943), lived in a house with the group and joined in on most of their activities. Both studies are examples of ethnographic fieldwork. *Ethnography*, broadly defined as the study of a way of life, was originally associated with anthropology and the analysis of small-scale societies. It was developed in sociology for the purpose of studying deviant groups, such as gangs—a topic of particular interest to the Chicago School of Sociology during the 1930s. Another early example of an ethnographic study in Chicago is Paul Cressey's *The Taxi-Dance Hall* (1932), which investigated the "taxi-dance" halls where attractive young women were paid by male partners for each dance. Cressey described the taxi-dance hall as a distinct "cultural world," comprising not just lonely immigrant men but also the sons of some of Chicago's most respectable families: "For those who attend the taxi-dance hall, even irregularly, it is a distinct world, with its own ways of acting, talking, and thinking. It has its own vocabulary, its own activities and interests, its own conception of what is significant in life, and—to a certain extent—its own scheme of life" (Cressey 1932: 31).

Polsky, who did his graduate training in the Sociology Department at the University of Chicago, described his ethnographic method as an effort to "present hustlers and hustling on their own terms" rather than from a "social problems" focus. In other words, he deliberately reversed the usual perspective: Instead of spotlighting the problems the hustlers posed for society, he approached the study from the perspective of the hustlers themselves: "In so far as I treat social problems, they are not the problems posed by the hustler but for him; not the difficulties he creates for others, but the difficulties that others create for him as he pursues his career" (Polsky 1971: 32–33). Polsky admitted that "the disadvantage for the scientifically minded reader is that the underlying sociological framework may be obscured." However, he explained that his framework was the same as that of one of his Chicago teachers, Everett Hughes, who had studied more legitimate work occupations with the same ethnographic approach. Although Polsky attempted to adopt the perspective of his subjects, there were sociological questions regarding them that he was seeking to answer: (1) How was the hustler's work situation structured? (2) What was the career pattern of the hustler? (3) How was the hustler's work situation affected by changes in the larger society? [...]

Ethnographic Research

The central characteristic of ethnographic research is that it asserts that all social action has meaning for those involved in it. If we want to understand others' behavior (regardless of our own view of it), then we must examine it from their perspective—we must try to get inside their heads. As Colin Robson (1993: 148) describes it: "[Ethnography] seeks to provide a written description of the implicit rules and traditions of a group. An ethnographer, through involvement with the group, tries to work out these rules. The intention is to provide a rich, or 'thick,' description which interprets the experiences of people in the group from their own perspective."

Ethnographic research is both expensive and time-consuming. It is labor-intensive and can take months or even years to complete. Critics maintain that it produces "soft" data that are less reliable than the "hard" data produced by quantitative methods, since there is no way of checking the data and conclusions through replication. For example, it may well be that researchers like Polsky become overinvolved with the group being studied, such that some of the necessary researcher detachment is lost. However, the advantage is that ethnography and participant observation can produce rich data, especially for understanding the meanings and informal rules that shape a culture and motivate the actions of those who share it.

The Ethnographic Case Study and Participant Observation

A classic example of the ethnographic method is Donald Roy's study of a work group in an American machine shop (1952). Roy was investigating a well-known problem in the sociology of work and organizations—namely, the effect of different systems of payment on workers' productivity. Piecework payment, whereby a worker's pay is bigger the more he or she produces, appears to be rational on the assumption that workers wish to maximize their earnings. However, experience shows that workers in the same job tend to have outputs that are very similar to one another—and that these outputs are generally less than expected by management. Why is this so, given that one would expect to see considerable differences among individual workers in the quantity of work each produced, according to their various skills or the amount of money they need to earn? Roy became an operative in the machine shop in order to find out how and why workers control the outputs of their group. His role as researcher was unknown to both management and workers; to all appearances, he was simply another worker.

Roy's method involved participant observation inasmuch as he fully shared the experience and work of the group he had joined. Every day he kept a diary of the conversations he had with fellow workers. Some jobs had piece-rates that workers thought to be unfair, and the "rule" here was to underproduce so as to force the rate-fixers into re-timing the task. Other jobs had very easy piecework norms, which the workers "protected" by producing a comfortable amount, but not too much. The workers shared the belief that the easy rates would be retimed by management if the fact of their "easyness" became known. Roy noted that new recruits were guided by their fellow workers on how to perform, and that a new worker's failure to pick up on the hints and suggestions of the "old hands" led to harassment and even ostracism. Eventually, nearly all the workers conformed to the group's own rules of factory life.

It was only by fully immersing himself in the group, and sharing its ways of thinking and speaking, that the participant observer, Roy, was able to understand these subtle processes of group control. A survey would not have yielded such knowledge.

A major advantage of the ethnographic method is that it is *naturalistic*. It involves the study of individuals and groups in their natural settings, specifically with regard to how behaviors and meanings depend on interaction with others and how statements taken from their contexts can be distorted and lead to bias. It is thus a good method for investigating covert behaviors and meanings, but it is not limited to these. Any given social group is full of spontaneous activity, which, in turn, reflects a structure and culture that are difficult to capture through a formal method of questioning. Since the actual performance of members in a group is what defines social positions and shared culture, questioning a respondent in isolation can easily miss the group nature of social behavior. And, indeed, since individuals are often inarticulate when asked to reflect on the full meaning of their actions, an observer inferring meanings by understanding the context (through participation in the group's "life") is in a better position to get an account of the group's collective purpose than is a researcher who is limited to "artificial" interviews or the use of a questionnaire.

The most obvious disadvantages of the ethnographic method, as suggested earlier, are that it is laborious and time-consuming. To do the job effectively, the researcher must gain acceptance by the group. If he or she is keeping the research role secret for fear of biasing the results, then two roles have to be performed—the normal group role as well as that of the researcher. A naturalistic method of study requires that a group's activities be followed throughout the whole of their cycle. The observer is observing and recording as things happen in real time. He or she cannot short-circuit natural processes. For example, if Roy had asked individual members of the group "Why do you limit output?" or "How do you get new workers to toe the line on how much they produce?" he would perhaps have been met with suspicion or incomprehension (especially if members were not conscious that they were deliberately limiting production). In short, group rules are informal, not formal; they are embedded in concrete behavior and must be inferred from actual performances rather than from what group members say they do.

Another problem has to do with *representativeness* (or *typicality*). If limitations of resources and time mean that only one group can be studied, how do we know that this particular group is typical of all such groups in a complex society? There is a limit, therefore, on the capacity for *generalization* from an ethnographic study.

Two further problems concern *reliability* and *replication*. The reliability of the observer's analysis depends on his or her personal abilities in techniques of observation and recording data. Selection of significant actions or comments has to be made by the researcher, who, if not careful, may miss or discard potentially significant data. Reliability in science normally means that another observer using the same methods on the same group would obtain the same results. But ethnography does not involve fixed procedures that can be written down and followed exactly by another observer.

Indeed, it is much more elastic and flexible than the above rule of reliability allows. The observer is necessarily unique in terms of his or her own behavior (and how it affects respondents), what he or she selects for recording, and how it is interpreted. The replication of an ethnographic study in order to check the original author's findings is thus very difficult (Roy 1952).

Life Histories and Personal Narratives

Personal narratives, as collected and used by social scientists, are stories that provide accounts of lives and events as told by or from the perspective of the narrator—usually the person(s) being studied. To call a personal narrative a story is not to call it a fiction, although, like any other sociological data, it is "constructed"—put together from a particular perspective. Figuring out what it is constructed *for* is one of the tasks of sociological analysis. In particular, the sociologist may be trying to understand the emotions and intentions of the author of the narrative, as well as taking account of the social context in which the narrative was constructed—for example, the hopes and fears of moving from a European farm to an American inner-city ghetto, as experienced by many Polish immigrants at the beginning of the twentieth century. This was the challenge taken up by the best-known and earliest use of personal narratives in American sociology: *The Polish Peasant in Europe and America*, by W. I. Thomas and Florian Znaniecki (1927).

Personal narratives come in a wide variety of forms, including autobiographies, oral histories, and life history interviews. Various types of personal writing may also have a narrative dimension: biographies, diaries, personal journals, correspondence, even obituaries. These personal writings are forms of data that historians are familiar with, and sociologists have learned a great deal from the research practices of historians about how to analyze such documents. Oral histories and life history interviews, which are similar to the interview forms of research that sociologists customarily undertake, demonstrate the contribution that can be made by recording the words of people who are not accustomed to writing down their experiences. In addition, they can reveal how the lives and perceptions of individuals relate to social networks and institutions over a period of social change.

A good example is provided by the oral histories brought together by Brigid O'Farrell and Joyce Kornbluh in *Rocking the Boat: Union Women's Voices, 1915–1975* (1996). They tell us about the individual lives of women trade-union activists and the organizational forms, social networks, and historical changes that were witnessed throughout six decades of American history. Unlike questionnaire surveys, a study based on oral histories is likely to have a relatively small number of contributors; in this case, volunteer interviewers collected life stories from eighty-seven female trade-union activists. Although it is difficult to draw generalizations from such small numbers, tentative conclusions are possible. For example, *Rocking the Boat* shows how workers' involvement in educational programs figured into the development of social activism in this period. Many of the early women activists, especially those from immigrant and less-educated backgrounds, were taught, encouraged in their activism, and formed solid networks through their participation in the "school for union organizers established in 1914 by the Women's Trade Union League, the Bryn Mawr Summer School for Women Workers, and government-sponsored programs established in the mid-1930s under the New Deal" (O'Farrell and Kornbluh 1996: 7) as well as in schools within their own unions. Another interesting conclusion reached in this study is that the inclusion of "union feminists" in definitions of feminism has the potential to bring about change in contemporary perceptions of feminism. Specifically, the authors argue that referring to women who seek economic justice and occupational advancement as a "group," rather than discussing them individually in terms of upward mobility, creates a more inclusive definition of feminist activism. The suggestion here is that too much of the theorizing about feminism is based solely on the experiences of academic women. Collecting the life stories of those who do not normally publish their ideas can raise important questions about how feminism is conceptualized and what effect it has on sociological theory. Indeed, one of the best tests of sociological research, whatever the method employed, is to see whether it leads to modifications in sociological theory.

Postmodernism, Relativism, and Research Methods

In the nineteenth century, Auguste Comte expressed the belief that sociology would develop research methods enabling it to discover laws of social behavior, following the example of the natural sciences. This view, which has been termed **positivism,** often lies behind the preference for quantitative research methods. In the twentieth century, positivism was countered by sociologists, such as Max Weber, who emphasized the need for "interpretive" analyses using qualitative methods that would facilitate an understanding of the cultural meanings that motivated social actions. Many ethnographic studies follow this approach, as do studies that focus on interpreting the content of documents (including not just written accounts but also visual documents such as television programs and photographs) and oral histories. What these interpretive approaches have in common is an appreciation of the "standpoint" of the actors themselves. The researcher should not elevate herself above those she is studying and impose her own meanings on them. Instead, she should seek to put herself in their place and understand the situation from their standpoint.

Comte's hope that sociology could discover laws of social behavior and promulgate them with authority in a scientific "grand narrative" is no longer on the agenda for most sociologists. Sociologist Zygmunt Bauman (1987) suggests that sociologists should now see themselves more as "interpreters" than as "legislators" (Bauman 1987). He argues that, whereas earlier sociologists believed they were developing a science that would hand down judgments of what is true, based on laws, their successors today should be content with reconstructing and analyzing the varieties of discourse that exist in the many different cultures of postmodernity.

Feminist sociologists contributed to this discussion by arguing that ways of seeing and describing social phenomena are relative to the particular standpoint of the investigator—and, in so doing, they identified with the perspective known as **relativism.** Beginning in the 1960s, many feminist sociologists have argued that positivist methodology and quantitative methods favor a male perspective, and that an interpretive methodology and qualitative methods are better suited to the feminist perspective. Canadian sociologist Dorothy Smith, in particular, suggests that the notion of a feminist "standpoint" is the only valid position from which to undertake research that is respectful of women's experience. For her, research in itself begins with everyday life and routines. She recommends what she calls "institutional ethnography" as the core of a feminist methodology. Such an ethnography uses methods based on in-depth interviewing of selected samples of women, attention to the details of what women say, and forms of analysis dedicated to reproducing these details as "faithfully" as possible (Smith 1988). Feminists also reject Max Weber's idea that sociological research should be "value free." Specifically, they see their research as a means of furthering women's emancipation from a male-dominated (patriarchal) society, not as a scientifically neutral activity.

However, not all female sociologists accept the argument that qualitative methods are more suited to feminist research. Ann Oakley (1988) has argued that quantitative methods, too, can serve the ends of emancipatory research. She points out that historical innovations in quantitative methods, such as the social survey, were made primarily by people, including women, who sought policy-relevant knowledge as ammunition for social reform. For example, activists such as Jane Addams in America and Harriet Martineau in Britain carried out social investigations that served the reformist cause by revealing the extent of poverty and inequality in the nineteenth century (McDonald 1993). Feminist social reformers have also advocated the need for statistics to demonstrate the conditions of women's lives. In 1875 the astronomer Maria Mitchell urged the collection of statistics to describe the inadequate opportunities for women scientists in the United States. And in the campaign against women's exclusion from higher education, statistics were used to disprove the masculinist medical notion that education damaged women's health (Reinharz 1992). Oakley further argues that the tendency of some feminist sociologists to polarize quantitative and qualitative methods, identifying the former as masculine and the latter as feminine, risks playing into the hands of those who use gender differences as a means of discriminating against women. It is a short step from accepting that men and women are bound to think differently, on the one hand, to saying that men are essentially rational and women are emotional, on the other. According to Oakley, this is exactly the kind of discriminatory thinking that feminism aims to dispel.

Oakley is clearly not convinced by the arguments of feminists who believe that qualitative methods are more in tune with women's experience and feminist values than quantitative methods. Sometimes, the way we judge an issue like this depends on the purpose at hand, which may lead us to find one type of study more insightful and useful than another. Many women (but perhaps also men) have found that ethnographic studies help them to see their own experiences in a new light; they also feel ethically comfortable with the procedures used in such studies. Others, engaged in a struggle against inequalities, may find that quantitative methods better suit their purpose.

Research in the Future

In a special symposium titled "Charting Futures for Sociology" and published at the beginning of the new millennium, the official review journal of the American Sociological Association, *Contemporary Sociology*, invited the Australian sociologist R. W. Connell to write the opening article. Connell (2000) began by noting that it was not preordained that sociology should come into existence in the way that it did, and goes on to say that its continued existence cannot be guaranteed unless it draws on new sources of experience and discovers new standpoints. After all, there are many competing sources of knowledge about society, including those of the mass media. The question Connell poses is whether there is a future for sociology if it is confined to being a "reformist science"—helping government and other institutions to carry on their activities more efficiently by providing expertise in carrying out surveys and making field observations in the form of small-scale ethnographies—and, indeed, whether it might have a more challenging future. You may well react to this criticism by asking what's wrong, after all, with being reformist and useful. Fair enough. But it's important to note that Connell is being true to the more ambitious project envisaged by early sociologists. His fear is that sociology will become nothing more than a "salvage ethnography" of marginalized lifestyles, which he disparagingly describes as similar to the old ethnographies of "nuts, sluts, and perverts" and to the science of "losers"—the poor, the chronically sick, the disturbed, the violent, the linguistically challenged, the illiterate (including the computer illiterate), and the unemployed. None of these functions, in Connell's view, matches the comprehensive scope and critical edge of the earlier sociological tradition. To escape such marginalization, he argues, sociological research must be "reconstituted as a democratic science," which entails stepping outside the confines of the Western academic world and entering into partnerships with new participants in research.

Where are these new partnerships to be found? Among those Connell mentions as possible partners are activists in various spheres of society—community activists, social reformers, educators, and mass media professionals. The idea is that, in a knowledge-based society, knowledge is an important tool of power and social control, and so it is crucial to spread access to that tool, especially to those who are disadvantaged. In some cases, it's simply a matter of using research to reveal the facts about inequalities; in others, a community might be given the tools to reveal processes that have been obscured by ideology. Connell has in mind dominant discourses through which society classifies things as binary opposites (e.g., "rational/emotional," "modern/traditional," "normal/deviant") and then relegates the second term in each of those pairs to an inferior position. He calls, instead, for a kind of research that "deconstructs" such binary opposites. For example, in responding to feminist and gay-lesbian movements, some sociologists have engaged with the ways in which issues of sexuality and sexual difference destabilize and de-essentialize such categories as "woman," "heterosexual," and "homosexual." Such stereotyping is not confined to marginal groups. Indeed, Jeffrey Alexander and Philip Smith (1993) have shown how binary thinking pervades public discourse about economic crisis, political scandal, election fraud, and war. Their "deconstructive" analysis of texts, including media texts such as television programs, is a fairly recent development in sociological research. But when allied with a commitment to a radical vision of the future of sociology, as in Connell's case, it can be particularly forceful and productive. Connell proposes this approach as an alternative to what he sees as the dominant tendency at present, whereby sociological information is to be collected and used for commercial purposes and to the advantage of the powerful.

Key Terms

Text   Anything, whether written or nonwritten, that is capable of carrying or conveying meaning. Society itself is a text, made up of multiple texts about social nature, social relationships, social processes, and so on.

Sample   A portion of a population selected to be the subjects of a particular research project. In most cases a sample is expected to be a microcosm of the whole population in some respect, such that the findings are generalizable.

Interview   A method of research whereby subjects are asked questions. Interviews can be formal, involving a set list of questions and topics to address, or informal, resembling a conversation or dialogue.

Infotainment   A genre of mass media prevalent in postmodern society that provides research results, information, and knowledge in the form of an entertaining media product. Mass media documentaries are a good example of infotainment, inasmuch as they strive to be informative about a particular subject but also to entertain.

Representative sample (or *stratified sample*)   A sample that accurately represents the various attributes (e.g., race, religion, income, age, gender) found in the whole population.

Random sample   A sample that is selected purely statistically. For example, a random sample might include every tenth person in a population, or every hundredth person.

Snowball sample   A sample created through a process whereby the researcher asks the first few interviewees for the names of other individuals who might fit the study, then asks those individuals for names, and so on. The problem with snowball samples is that they may be heavily skewed toward particular demographics, because people tend to know and recommend others like themselves.

Survey   A method of research whereby information is gathered from a sample of a population about a specific list of variables and questions.

Opinion poll   A type of sociological survey in which the members of a population sample are asked about their attitudes and beliefs on a wide range of issues. An example is the General Social Survey (GSS), which asks a nationwide random sample of at least 1,500 respondents to address issues such as capital punishment, family statistics, and religiosity.

Concept   A mental construct that represents some part of the world in a simplified form. A concept might also be a category or classification, such as race, gender, or social class.

Variable   A concept whose value changes from case to case. The changing value is noted by an indicator. For example, income might be an indicator of the variable *class*.

Correlation   A term that refers to the relationship between two variables whose values change together. It is important to note, however, that correlation does not imply causation. For example, in wintertime, people tend to wear scarves and car accidents tend to occur more often. Increased scarf wearing and increased car accidents are correlated, but this does not mean that wearing a scarf causes car accidents.

Independent variable   A variable that causes change in another factor. In our wintertime example, weather can be considered an independent variable, since ice, snow, and cold temperatures cause people to wear scarves and can increase car accidents.

Dependent variable   A variable that changes as a result of independent variables. In our wintertime example, scarf wearing and car accidents are the dependent variables.

Social theory   A framework based on empirical evidence that is used to organize concepts, and that explains why society or some aspect of society functions as it does.

Explanatory theory   A theory that has one or more causal hypotheses suggesting that a particular independent variable causes a particular effect on the dependent variable.

Interpretive sociology   A form of sociology that bases its approach to the task of sociological explanation on the assumption that social actions can be fully understood only by interpreting the motives and meanings that guide individuals' actions.

Quantitative   Referring to research that relies on numerical or statistical data for calculating findings. Quantitative research is typically used in cases where one is trying to apply a natural science model of explanation, as opposed to an interpretive model.

Qualitative   Relating to research that is typically used in cases where one is taking an interpretive approach. The data are often textual; examples include interview transcripts and ethnographic field notes.

Census   A type of social survey in which the questions are designed to gather information that is descriptive of an entire population.

Field research   Research that is based on the observation of behavior rather than on the use of existing quantitative data. Field researchers select a location and a field site and then spend time observing. They may be participant observers who engage directly in the activities of their field site, or they may remain at a distance. Field research raises important issues regarding consent and research ethics. Ethnography is an example of field research.

Personal narrative   A type of qualitative data in which an account of life events is given from the perspective of a narrator, usually the individual being studied. The term *narrative* connotes not fiction but, rather, a story that is socially constructed and put together. Personal narratives can come in many forms, including autobiography, oral history, and life history interviews.

Positivism   An approach to research that follows the example of the natural sciences in that it assumes sociology will employ methods that enable it to discover laws of social behavior. Positivists are often inclined toward the use of quantitative data and methods.

Relativism   An approach to research that counters positivism by asserting that a particular social behavior may be understood differently if viewed from different perspectives or in different social contexts. In other words, the interpretation of a behavior may vary depending on the perspective or setting. Relativists tend to prefer an interpretive approach to sociology and to rely on qualitative data.

Exercises

Exercise 1

Write an outline detailing a sociological research project that you would like to undertake in your hometown. Then, explain which methods you would adopt, giving reasons why they are appropriate.

Exercise 2

It has been suggested that, in the postmodern culture in which we live, much of our knowledge is mediated by television. Think of a television documentary or news program that you viewed recently. How much attention did you give to the broadcast? (Recall Ron Lembo's findings about television viewing, which are summarized in the box titled "Conceptualizing and Investigating the Viewing Culture: Research Strategy and Methods.") Do you have a clear recollection of the main conclusions you reached while watching the program? How would you go about verifying those conclusions if you could undertake further research?

Study Questions

1. In what ways can society be regarded as a "text"?

2. What differences are there between the procedures involved in constructing a television documentary and the procedures used in social science research?

3. One notable difference between television documentaries and much social science research has to do with how they are received by their "audiences." Discuss this difference in audience reception in terms of the combination of methods employed in Lembo's research.

4. Why might some groups want to emphasize that all knowledge, including scientific knowledge, is only relatively valid?

5. List the different types of samples that may be used in social science research.

6. What is the difference between an independent variable and a dependent variable?

7. Distinguish between the two forms of sociological explanation of suicide offered, respectively, by Durkheim and Jacobs.

8. Outline the different methods of gathering quantitative versus qualitative data, and list some of their advantages and disadvantages.

9. The postmodern culture has been described as "mediatized"—meaning that much of the knowledge and information that we accumulate has been constructed and transmitted by the mass media. Sometimes the process seems to spiral out of control and people are panicked into believing that a threatening social trend is advancing upon them, when in fact a more critical analysis of statistics would counter this belief. How does Joel Best illustrate this point with regard to school violence?

Further Reading

Alvesson, Mats. 2002. *Postmodernism and Social Research*. Buckingham, U.K./Philadelphia: Open University Press.

Bellah, Robert N., R. Madsen, W. M. Sullivan, A. Swidler, and S. M. Tipton. 1997. *Habits of the Heart*. Berkeley: University of California Press.

Best, Joel. 2001. *Damned Lies and Statistics*. Berkeley/Los Angeles: University of California Press.

Denzin, N., and Y. Lincoln, eds. 2000. *Handbook of Qualitative Research*, 2nd ed. Thousand Oaks, CA: Sage.

Fonow, Margaret, and Judith A. Cook. 1991. *Beyond Methodology: Feminist Scholarship as Lived Research*. Bloomington: Indiana University Press.

Jacobs, J. 1970. "The Use of Religion in Constructing the Moral Justification of Suicide." In *Deviance and Respectability: The Social Construction of Moral Meanings,* edited by J. D. Douglas. New York: Basic Books, 229–250.

Oakley, Ann. 1988. "Gender, Methodology, and People's Ways of Knowing: Some Problems with Feminism and the Paradigm Debate in Social Science." *Sociology* 32, no. 4: 707–731.

Polsky, Ned. 1967. *Hustlers, Beats, and Others*. Chicago: Aldine.

Postman, Neil. 1987. *Amusing Ourselves to Death: Public Discourse in the Age of Show Business*. London: Methuen.

Roy, Donald. 1952. "Quota Restriction and Goldbricking in a Machine Shop." *American Journal of Sociology* 57: 427–442.

Smith, Dorothy. 1988. *The Everyday World as Problematic: A Feminist Sociology*, Milton Keynes, U.K.: Open University Press.

Sudman, S., and N. Bradburn. 2004. *Asking Questions: A Practical Guide to Questionnaire Design*. San Francisco: Jossey-Bass.

Bibliography

Alexander, Jeffrey C., and Philip Smith. 1993. "The Discourse of American Civil Society: A New Proposal for Cultural Studies." *Theory and Society* 22, no. 2: 151–207.

Bauman, Zygmunt. 1987. *Legislators and Interpreters: On Modernity, Post-Modernity, and Intellectuals*. Ithaca, NY: Cornell University Press.

Brough-Williams, Ian. 1996. "War Without End? The Bloody Bosnia Season on Channel Four." In *Bosnia by Television*, edited by Richard Paterson, James Gow, and Alison Preston, 19–33. London: British Film Institute.

Connell, Robert W. 2000. "Sociology and World Market Sociology." *Contemporary Sociology* 29, no. 2: 291–296.

Cressey, Paul G. 1932. *The Taxi-Dance Hall: A Sociological Study in Commercialized Recreation and City Life*. Chicago: University of Chicago Press.

Durkheim, Emile. 1895. *The Rules of Sociological Method*. Glencoe, IL: Free Press. Reprinted in 1938.

———. 1897. *Suicide, a Study in Sociology*. Glencoe, IL: Free Press. Reprinted in 1951.

———. 1915. *The Elementary Forms of the Religious Life*. Glencoe, IL: Free Press. Reprinted in 1965.

Gitlin, Todd. 1983. *Inside Prime Time*. New York: Pantheon.

Mayo, Elton. 1933. *Human Problems of an Industrial Civilization*. New York: Macmillan.

McDonald, Lynn. 1993. *The Early Origins of the Social Sciences*. Montréal: McGill-Queen's University Press.

Oakley, Ann. 1998. "Gender, Methodology, and People's Ways of Knowing: Some Problems with Feminism and the Paradigm Debate in Social Science." *Sociology* 32, no. 4 (1998): 707–731.

O'Farrell, Brigid, and Joyce L. Kornbluh. 1996. *Rocking the Boat: Union Women's Voices, 1915–1975*. New Brunswick, NJ: Rutgers University Press.

Polsky, Ned. 1967. *Hustlers, Beats, and Others*. Chicago: Aldine.

Postman, Neil. 1985. *Amusing Ourselves to Death: Public Discourse in the Age of Show Business*. London: Heinemann.

Reinharz, Shulamit. 1992. *Feminist Methods in Social Research*. New York: Oxford University Press.

Robson, Colin. 1993. *Real World Research: A Resource for Social Scientists and Practitioner-Researchers*. Cambridge, UK: Blackwell.

Roethlisberger, Fritz Jules, and William J. Dickson. 1939. *Management and the Worker*. Cambridge, MA: Harvard University Press.

Roy, Donald. 1952. "Quota Restriction and Goldbricking in a Machine Shop." *American Journal of Sociology* 57, no. 427–442.

Sarantakos, S. 1993. *Social Research*. Melbourne, Australia: Macmillan.

Smith, Dorothy E. 1987. *The Everyday World as Problematic: A Feminist Sociology*. Boston: Northeastern University Press.

Thomas, William Isaac, and Florian Znaniecki. 1927. *The Polish Peasant in Europe and America*. New York: Knopf.

Whyte, William Foote. 1943. *Street Corner Society*. Chicago: University of Chicago Press.

Zeller, Richard A., and Edward G. Carmines, eds. 1980. *Measurement in the Social Sciences: The Link Between Theory and Data*. Cambridge, UK: Cambridge University Press.

CHAPTER 3

Culture

Culture applies to the total aspects of life for individuals. Culture includes shared characteristics such as ideas, values, norms, beliefs, language, and practices. Chapter 3 defines culture and its basic components including material and non-material culture. Further, it explains emerging issues in culture, such as the connection between belief and behaviors, the mainstream culture, subcultures, counter-cultures, and global and consumer culture. Plume (2017) emphasizes cultural patterns of society and elements of culture including values and beliefs. Theoretical perspectives—structural functionalism, conflict approach, and interactionist approach—are applied to understanding these values and beliefs. The chapter raises important questions such as: Is culture learned? How is culture transmitted across generations? Is culture dynamic? How is social change connected to cultural change? How can we promote cultural understanding? Is cultural conflict inevitable?

Culture Is Everything, Everything Is Culture

Mark Plume

"Culture is as natural as life. We shortchange ourselves if we view culture as artifice to be opposed to nature. On the other hand, we must separate cultural information from genetic information. The two are in no sense opposed; indeed, the confusion arises because they are so totally commingled in our experience. In the course of growing up, we learn culture as ways to exercise our genetic capacities." —Paul Bohannan, 1995

The Trobriand Islanders

In traditional Trobriand Island culture, Trobrianders do not see a connection between sexual intercourse and pregnancy. As a consequence, their culture is highly sexualized. Children as young as six years old are encouraged to engage in various sexual activities, and intercourse is encouraged in those as young as eleven. Young people frequently engage in what they call "sex picnics." These picnics include food and then lots of sexual activity, including intercourse. For the Trobriand Islanders, sex includes mild violence, many times heavy scratching and drawing of blood. They particularly enjoy biting the eyelashes of their partners during orgasm. Yet, when they see Westerners kissing on the lips, they are disgusted. They enjoy these robust sexual lifestyles mainly because in their culture, they do not believe that pregnancy is the consequence of sexual intercourse. Magic plays a very important part in the Trobriand island culture, and they believe that magic and spirits are responsible for impregnating women. When they are ready, the spirits, or *baloma*, which dwell on the island of Tuma, will inhabit women, impregnating them. Then, women's magic plays an important part by placing the magic pregnancy jacket on the woman and placing her in a center of a circle of women, therefore ensuring a successful pregnancy (Malinowski, 1929).

Figure 3.1 Branislaw Malinowski with Trobriand Islanders

Yams are also a central feature of the Trobriand island culture; they eat yams multiple times a day prepared in a variety of ways throughout their lives. Yams are so important to the Trobriand Islanders that their yam storage huts are sturdier and more highly adorned than their own homes. An interesting fact about yams is that they contain diosgenin, which was used to make the first birth control pills in the 1960s. So, imagine young Trobriand girls eating yams all day long over their entire lifetimes; the result would be no consistent relationship between intercourse and pregnancy because of the contraceptive effect of the yams! Are the practices of the Trobriand people good or bad, right or wrong? The ways of the Trobriand Islanders are no more or less correct or valuable than the practices of other cultures; they simply represent another way of being.

What Is Culture?

Culture Is Everything. Everything Is Culture*

"Culture emerges from life, like life emerges from matter" (Bohannan, 1995). So where there is human life, there is culture. **Culture** is the total way of life of a people—their learned and shared values, beliefs, customs, and habits, the things they make and use, and the common viewpoints that bind them together. While we don't see culture directly, it shapes the way we act, what we believe, and how we see the world. Remember, we don't see the world the way it is; we see the world the way we are, and culture shapes who we are. Culture is of great interest to sociologists because it affects all aspects of our lives.

Culture influences what we eat, what we wear, the way we think, the way we see the world, and how we judge right from wrong, the sacred from the profane, and beauty from ugliness. Is going to the opera culture? Is watching NASCAR culture? Is eating birthday cake on your birthday culture? Is believing in God culture? Are the contents of your dreams culture? How about getting married, is that culture? Yes, to all.

Every idea, feeling, action, and thing in the world and that humans create is culture. Even elements of the natural world become coopted by human culture. Nothing escapes inclusion in human culture.

Culture is everything. Everything is culture. Now think of something that is not culture. Yep, you read it correctly. Well, if you thought of something like the moon, you would be right—kind of. Culture, as we will learn later, is created by humankind, and the moon is not made by humans. But once humans label some natural feature like the moon, it has been *coopted* by language into culture. That is, once we have a linguistic handle on something, we can manipulate it through language and apply our own particular beliefs, values, and impression on it. Let's take the moon, for example.

Once we label the moon with language, we have brought it into our culture; the next step is to fold it into our **world view**—our collective perspective from which we see and interpret the world. Think about three things you could say about the moon. Those things would probably include the moon influences tides, it is about a quarter million miles away from earth, it's composed of rock, it orbits the earth, we only see its light side, and we have been there (if you believe that). We have been taught in our Western, rational, scientific culture all about the various objective characteristics of the moon. Our *cultural* ideas about the moon are a reflection of our rational, scientific world view. While some

Figure 3.2 What do you see when you look at the moon?

people in the United States still believe that phases of the moon influence things like increased birth rates, aggressive behaviors, and psychiatric illnesses (lunacy ... get it, lunar), there is NO scientific research that supports these ideas.

What if we asked an Inuit person from Greenland to tell us three things about the moon? That person would most likely tell us that Anningan (the moon) chases his sister, Malina (the sun), across the sky. Anningan is so consumed by the chase that he forgets to eat and over the course of a few weeks, he becomes thinner, representing the phases of the moon. Not to worry—he disappears for three days to eat (new moon), then reappears full (gibbous moon), ready to begin the chase again. In order to keep her distance from her mischievous brother, Malina rises and sets at different times than him (Freed, 2012).

Try using that Inuit story to explain the moon to your neighbor. He will probably look at you funny and wonder what you are smoking. Our culture tends to reject animism—the idea that all animals, plants, and inanimate objects have a spiritual essence—and seeks a logical-scientific explanation. But the Inuit people, and the people of hundreds of cultures around the world, believe that objects like the moon are imbued with spirits, which help them explain how the world works. The *cultural* beliefs and practices of the Inuit are a reflection of their animistic world view.

Before we go any further, I want to make clear the distinction between the terms culture and society. *Culture*, as we have discussed, is the underlying shared characteristics (language, beliefs, values, world view, etc.) of a group of people; **society** refers to the people of that group and their patterned interactions with each other—people conducting their daily interactions with each other in their homeland. Let's broaden that out. Culture is not bound by any geography, but a society typically is. You can find pieces of American culture all over the world. For instance, elements of American culture like McDonald's restaurants can be found in over one hundred countries, Coca-Cola can be found all over the world, and Levi's jeans are found in just about every corner of the world. But American society can only be found in the United States. I can find sushi restaurants, which represent Japanese culture, all over my hometown, but I would have to travel to Japan to experience Japanese society.

Language and Culture

> *"If culture was a house, then language was a key to the front door, to all the rooms inside."* —Khaled Housseini

Language—a shared collection of symbols that allow people to communicate with each other—is the largest system of symbols that we use on a regular basis to communicate.

I believe that we can assign the relationship below to our understanding of culture.

Language (communication) = Culture

What do I mean by this? Let's go back in time, let's say fifty thousand years ago. At that time, according to the recent African origin of modern humans theory, also known as the *out of Africa theory*, modern humans had come out of Africa and inhabited much of the world, but not the Americas (Meredith, 2011). Most likely, we traveled in small bands of twenty to thirty individuals. How could this happen without language, some recognized form of communication shared by the members of the collective? It couldn't. We could have never made tools, organized hunts, or worked cooperatively without

It has been estimated that in the past fifty years, twenty-eight of the world's language families have gone extinct. Today, there are 3,176 languages that are endangered; this represents about 46% of all living languages. This means that nearly half of all languages spoken today, as well as the richness of their cultures, could go silent (Weicha, 2013).

language, however primitive. When languages die, cultures die with them. Language is the vehicle upon which culture emerges, is transmitted, and flourishes.

Ethnocentrism and Cultural Relativism

> *"People from different cultures have different definitions for beauty, isn't that sad to judge others with our standards. ... rather than appreciate them?"* —Mizuki Namura

Before we go any further in our discussion of culture, there are two important practices we need to discuss. These are important for several reasons, but perhaps the most important, as you will see, is how one practice leads to the subjugation and death of culture, while the other leads to a richer understanding of other cultures.

> *"No culture can live, if it attempts to be exclusive."* —Mahatma Gandhi

Ethnocentrism is the habit of judging other cultural practices from the perspective of one's own culture and deeming them as primitive, inadequate, or inferior. Ethnocentrism is learned in all cultures because it serves some useful functions. It promotes solidarity of the group, or that "we" feeling. It unites us though our cultural practices, and promotes the idea that our way of life is worth preserving and reproducing. In a crystal-clear example of ethnocentrism, President Obama, in a 2013 speech to the United Nations, declared, "I believe that America is exceptional." With this statement, he was obviously implying that the American way of life/world view and all Americans are superior to others and other ways of life.

However, these beliefs of superiority may hinder cooperation with other cultures. If one's ways are superior to the ways of others, there seems little incentive for promoting or practicing inferior ways. This could lead to attitudes of contempt, ridicule, and downright hostility. The very real global extension of ethnocentrism is **cultural imperialism**—imposing one's cultural values, beliefs, and practices on the members of another culture. The results of this practice fill the pages of history with the records of war and religious, economic, and racial colonialism. For centuries, it was common for the ships of colonial powers to roll up on the shores of a Caribbean paradise, the invaders telling the local people to cover themselves, to speak their language, and to worship their god and their king. As local customs and languages were extinguished, so were the local cultures. These ethnocentric practices resulted in the death of hundreds of cultures around the world, depriving humankind of the variety and richness of ways of thinking, being, and seeing the world. In some ways, this practice continues today with the destruction of the world's rainforests and the ways of life of those who dwell in them. This destruction is in large part driven by the appetites of some far-off developed nation willing to exploit others to satisfy its needs.

In contrast, the perspective of **cultural relativism** views each culture as possessing its own distinct but equally valid sets of beliefs, values, and practices, which can only be understood from the viewpoint of that culture itself. Practicing cultural relativism allows researchers to understand the beliefs, values, and behaviors of other peoples from their viewpoint and not judge them by the cultural standards of the researcher. This gives us an understanding of *why* other cultures believe what they believe and *why* they engage in their particular behaviors. You cannot come to understand or appreciate other cultures if you are comparing or judging them by your standards; you will never see the world the way others do and never know why people of other cultures do what they do and believe what they believe.

Even though this perspective was developed by anthropologists, its principles act as a sort of guide to the ethical conduct of researchers of other disciplines, such as sociology. One of the basic tenets of cultural relativism is the relative worth of a culture and its component parts. That is, one culture is not superior to others (American culture is not superior to the culture of the Tiv people of Nigeria or the Tuva people of Siberia); these cultures merely represent different ways of being. Another important element of cultural relativism is the relative importance of the contents of cultures such as language, customs, rituals, and aesthetics.

Right and wrong and good and bad are only defined within the context of each culture. Remember in the opening story, the Trobriand Islanders view sexual acts between young children as part of the Trobriand childhood experience and as acceptable for their way of life. In contrast, in the United States, most people would be appalled by sexual behavior among six- and seven-year-old children; we see that behavior as deviant in our culture. So, who's right? Both. Acceptable and unacceptable behaviors are defined in the context of culture and are relative; there are no absolutes. Pedophilia is criminally wrong in our culture; does that make it *absolutely* wrong? If so, we should not find any culture in the world practicing pedophilia. However, as a rite of passage to manhood, young Sambia boys must perform fellatio and ingest the semen of the single men of their village; many engage in homosexual relationships with the older men. This is considered wrong among Americans but is an integral part of constructing manhood among the Sambia people.

Read More

- *The Sexual Lives of Savages* by Bronislaw Malinowski (1929). Malinowski relays detailed descriptions of the sexual practices and beliefs of the Trobrianders.
- *The Sambia: Ritual, Sexuality and Change in Papua New Guinea* by Gilbert Herdt (1987). The author explores the lengthy (twelve years) rite of passage to manhood among the Sambia people of Papua New Guinea in striking detail.

The Characteristics of Culture

Culture is created by humans. We are the only species that possesses and uses culture to the degree that we can adapt to worlds other than earth and to the point that we can modify our own essence—our DNA. Some argue that other species possess culture; I do not view rudimentary tool making, communication, social organization, and social learning sufficient to rise to the level of culture. No other species possesses the complex interplay of concept, creation, and self-reflexivity found in human cultures. Moreover, if we understand culture to be, in part, a tool for adaptation to the physical environment, there is no single species, except for humans, that inhabits the entire globe. However, this is my position; you may believe differently.

Culture Is an Adaptive Mechanism

Culture is an adaptive tool used by humans; its complexity allows us to thrive anywhere on earth. Even though we essentially remain a warm-climate animal, adaptive strategies such as the use of fire, hunting technologies, shelter, clothing, and cooperative work has allowed us, as a species, to occupy all climate regions on earth. The cumulative effect of these adaptive strategies, discoveries, inventions, and cooperation is culture. Our ability to develop culture comes in part from our physical features: our large brains, binocular vision, upright posture, and free hands with an opposable thumb and a prehensile grip. This unique combination of human physical features allowed our ancestors to start the culture train rolling by fashioning crude stone tools about two million years ago.

Culture is partly a response to the challenges of adapting to various physical environments and partly creative responses to satisfying our

Figure 3.3 Inuit Children

biological imperatives. That is, humans must eat, drink, eliminate waste, sleep, and reproduce. Even a cursory look at the cultures of the world shows us that people in different cultures satisfy human imperatives/drives in myriad ways.

Take, for instance, the Inuit of Greenland. Elements of their culture such as food, clothing, and language are reflections of their adaptation to a harsh Arctic environment. Like many people around the world, the Inuit eat foods found in their local environment. However, the climate of the Arctic is not suited for agriculture, so they eat a diet high in animal protein such as whale, seal, fish, polar bear, and caribou. The high fat and protein content of their diet helps them stay warm, along with heavy clothing made from the skins of the animals they kill to eat. This makes sense—they are capitalizing on the game found in their environment. This is also true of their language—it reflects their understanding of their physical environment. You have probably heard that the Inuit have hundreds of words for snow and ice. Actually, the number of root words for snow in the Inuit language is roughly equivalent to those in English. However, the Inuit language is structured so the number of distinct words for snow that can be derived from root words is not just a few hundred, but infinite. Additionally, researchers have identified at least ninety-three terms for distinctly different forms of ice (Krupnik et al., 2010; Pullum, 1991).

In contrast, the Polynesian culture is an island culture located over a vast area of the Pacific Ocean, encompassing more than a thousand islands. Their environment is distinctly different from that of the Inuit; they enjoy coconuts, rice, sugar cane, yams, taro, fish, and many other seagoing creatures. Additionally, their clothing reflects the relatively mild year-round climate; traditionally, both men and women would wear simple loin clothes (tapa) or nothing at all. Nowadays, men wear shorts, t-shirts, and flip-flops, and variations on the sarong are worn by both sexes. Their language reflects their connection to the ocean. Naturally, the Hawaiian (which is part of Polynesia) language has about twice as many words to describe ocean waves as English. This makes sense, as most of Polynesia is made of coral islands, and wave motion is important in navigating the coral reefs that encircle the islands—and for surfing!

As all cultures do, they develop over time in response to the physical environment, exploiting the local natural resources in order to feed, clothe, and shelter members of the collective. Language is also a response to the natural environment, developing specifically to identify in detail the features prominent in the environment: snow for the Inuit and waves for Hawaiians. However, the specificity of language is not just because the Inuit are bored and sit around making up snow vocabulary and Polynesians like to name waves. It's about survival: identifying features in the physical environment in precise ways can protect members of the group. Our seal hunter, Yoskolo, knows that he can't go out on the ice floes if Yutu tells him conditions are *qautsaulittuq*—ice that breaks after its strength has been tested by a harpoon—because he may risk falling into the frigid water. And our Hawaiian friend, Keanu, knows it is dangerous to paddle his sup when the waves are *hanupanupa*—surging waves (Krupnik et al., 2010; Pukui and Elbert, 1986).

Culture Is Not Genetic, and People Are Not Born with It; Culture Is Learned

You could drop off a human infant with any family in any culture of the world, and that child would grow up to understand and accept it as her own. We are all born with our own genetic profile that says "human being," but only through learning our culture can we understand and be understood by others. Additionally, we are all born with certain biological drives like hunger and thirst, but as infants, we do not possess the instinctual patterns to satisfy them—we must learn. We are, however, genetically predisposed to learn language, which is the mechanism we use to learn, create, and share culture.

Culture Is Shared and Transmitted

In order for each new generation of individuals to survive, the individuals have to be taught how to navigate their particular culture. Sociologists refer to this process as **socialization**—the lifelong process by which children and adults learn from others—and it is necessary to ensure the development and adjustment of all humans so they can form identities and function properly in society. For humans, it takes some time before one can successfully navigate society. We do not have the biological capacity to fend for ourselves; human infants are fragile creatures. Humans are unlike giraffes, for example, who can stand up and run with the herd within an hour of being born. Moreover, by eighteen months, both male and female giraffe calves leave their moms to form their own giraffe street gangs (sort of). Humans need nurturing, education, financial support, and considerable social experience before we are able to run with our herd. This may take anywhere from eighteen to forty years.

Culture Is Dynamic

It changes from place to place and over time. We have already discussed a number of cultures and how different they look from our own. We know that we will encounter differences in foods, clothing, language, and ways of behaving if we travel from place to place, but all cultures also change over time due to several factors:

- **Discovery**—the process of learning about something that was not known before. When humans discovered and controlled fire, it profoundly influenced the development of human culture. Before fire, our ancestors huddled together in caves, cold and quivering, fearing the sounds of the night, waiting for the great fiery orb in the sky to reappear. Fire extended the time early humans could devote to daily activities, and it protected them from many predators. Once they started gathering around the fire for its warmth and light, they most likely started telling stories of the hunt, which led to more celebratory behaviors like singing and dancing. In fact, Polly Wiessner (2014), an anthropologist who studied hunting-gathering societies in the Kalahari of Africa, which resemble early human groups, found that most daytime conversations were devoted to issues of hunting and gathering or gossip, while conversations around the fire at night were dominated by storytelling and magic. Also, we started cooking our food, which led to increased cranial capacity, and cooked meat proteins afforded us more nutritional value (James, 1989; Weiner et al., 1998). Other notable discoveries that have profoundly impacted human culture include gravity, penicillin, and stem cells.

- **Invention**—the creation of something completely new. Imagine culture as a still mountain lake and you take a stone and throw it into the middle of the lake. What happens? Once the stone breaks the lake's surface, it creates ripples, which move out into wider and wider rings. Invention is the stone that gets thrown into culture, creating a ripple effect of changes within culture. The invention of the plow, for example, precipitated the agricultural revolution. This transformed human society, making large, widespread crop production possible, resulting in greater food surpluses, which created huge human population growth and freed people to engage in a variety of other types of work. Air conditioning changed where we live, what our houses look like, and what we do on a hot summer evening, for example. Air conditioning also managed to influence housing architecture: no need for a porch or "sleeping porch" to cool off on, just turn up the air conditioning. It has also influenced human interaction by drawing families into their isolated, air-conditioned homes and off the front porch where they used to wave at and chat with neighbors. Paper, guns, steam engines, automobiles, the computer, and the Internet are all significant inventions in human history. Can you list ways these inventions changed our language and the way we interact with each other?

- **Innovation**—refers to taking an existing object, idea, or system and modifying or improving it. Apps are good examples of innovation. They claim to enhance your dining, shopping, viewing, or listening experience by improving on previous methods of delivering goods or services. Spotify lets you stream music, gets to know what music you like, and suggests additional or alternate titles you may enjoy, which is a lot easier than going to a music store and searching through titles or dealing with physical media like CDs, cassette tapes, or eight-track tapes. YourMechanic, an app that allows you to schedule auto repairs at your home or office, didn't invent the engine, the oil change, or mechanics, but it did improve on auto-repair service by putting an auto mechanic at your fingertips—the mechanic comes to you. Uber is another good example of an app that enhances the taxi experience by not requiring in-vehicle payment;

Read More

- *Losing our Cool: Uncomfortable Truths about our Air-Conditioned World (and Finding New Ways to get through the Summer)* by Stan Cox (2010). He explores the impact the invention of air conditioning has had on our political, social, and economic lives in the U.S. He also looks at the environmental impact of worldwide air-conditioning use.

there's no need to carry cash or credit cards, and the drivers are regular citizens like you and me. My wife and I use Uber frequently, and it is much more convenient (and cheaper) than taxis. Apps make things like grocery shopping, doctor's visits, learning statistics, or finding a local restaurant with the best beer selection really simple; they are an improvement over a previous way to do these things, or at least more convenient. Other types of innovations throughout history include domestication of livestock, containerized shipping, and jet aircraft. Why are these examples of innovation and not invention or discovery?

- **Diffusion**—the movement of parts of one culture into another. Food is a good example of diffusion of culture; as people move around the world, they take familiar elements of their home culture with them, such as food. My wife and I regularly cook Mexican, Italian, Japanese, and Thai food. We also go out for Vietnamese, Greek, Lebanese, French, and Basque food. All this exotic food from around the world is accessible in central Virginia. What kind of food can you find in your neck of the woods? Other parts of culture become diffused like yoga, which came to the U.S. via Eastern religious and meditational practices. Do you wear *pajamas*, use *shampoo*, or know a *thug*? All these words come from the Hindi language. These and many other words were coopted by the British when they occupied modern-day India and Pakistan, then they just spread through the English-speaking world. A few years ago, my wife and I were scuba diving in Roatan, Honduras, and on the drive from the airport to our hotel, we passed by a Bojangles fast food restaurant! Roatan is not a highly developed island, and it is located forty miles off the coast of mainland Honduras. We were surprised to see Bojangles there, to say the least. Probably the most common symbol of American culture around the world is Coca-Cola, with McDonald's a close second. You can find a McDonald's restaurant in 119 countries (there are 196 countries in the world), and you can buy a Coke in all countries of the world except for Cuba and North Korea, and I bet you can scratch Cuba off that list soon.

- **External Pressure** from outside forces can be applied directly to societies to produce cultural change. This pressure can be exercised through patterns of domination like colonization or conquest. The Islamic State of Iraq and the Levant (ISIL) has invaded parts of Syria and Iraq, leaving in its wake of destruction and barbarism a population that either converted to its interpretation of the Qu'ran and sharia (Islamic law) or were killed. The people of those regions have had to abandon their mainstream interpretation of their religion and adopt a radicalized, fundamental interpretation of Islam, altering the locals' way of life. External pressure can be applied in less militant ways. Widely viewed as a human rights violation against girls and women, female genital mutilation (FGM), sadly, is still practiced in about twenty-eight countries. The practice is a deeply held cultural custom that transcends religion but is in some areas encouraged by religious leaders. Many organizations have used a range of tactics to eliminate FGM. Pressure from the United Nations and a host of other organizations has led to the reduction in the number of cases of FGM and the criminalization of FGM in eighteen

African countries. This has been achieved through education and outreach programs, lobbying governments, and sharing some African nations' abysmal human rights records with the world in an attempt to pressure them to change their laws (Center for Reproductive Rights, 2008; World Health Organization, 2008).

As we have discussed, there are a number of ways culture can change, from new inventions to adopting parts of other cultures to being forced to change from outside pressures. With all the change taking place in society, it takes time for all elements of culture to catch up with those changes. Just like when you acquire some new technology, for example, you need to learn how it works, the various ways you can use it, and, ultimately, how it changes the way you live your life. The same holds true for culture. Rules that guide social behavior take time to adjust and catch up with social changes.

Cultural lag is a term used to describe how cultural values, beliefs, and norms take time to catch up with technological advances, and this lag can create social problems and conflict. With new inventions and innovations come social change. Societies have to develop acceptable ways of behaving relative to the use of new technologies. Is it acceptable to talk on your phone or text while you are checking out at a grocery store? It seems to be a gray area of social behavior, unless you're in line behind that cell phone user—then it's pretty clear-cut. I've noticed that some stores have posted signs asking customers to refrain from cell phone use during checkout, which indicates that social rules have yet to catch up with cell phone use—we still don't quite know how to act. Similarly, rules about mobile phone use in movie theaters *lagged* behind the *technology*. I lived in L.A. when cell phone use took off, and I noticed then that people were free to gab on their phones in theaters. Over a period of time, theater owners asked moviegoers to refrain from phone use during movies, but it was completely voluntary on the part of the customers. Now, nearly all theaters prohibit mobile device use during movies, using clever and amusing short videos to make the rules crystal clear. If you have ever been in a movie theater when someone was talking or texting on his phone, you can understand the conflict this can create. You can see from these examples how rules of social behavior had to catch up to the use of new mobile phone technology.

Laws that regulate Internet usage lagged behind that technology. Widespread availability and access to the Internet dates to about 1990. Many of the first laws were aimed at preventing harassment. The Communications Decency Act of 1995 basically extended to computers a law that prohibited obscene and harassing phone calls. Laws protecting children online didn't appear until 1998. Napster, an Internet site that allowed users to swap/download music for free, burst onto the cyber scene in 1999. The music industry soon realized that Napster was costing them billions of dollars, and they went to court. Napster was essentially shut down in 2001 as a free file-swapping site, as Internet practices and copyright laws were reconciled. Napster was in violation of copyright laws and had to pay out millions of dollars (Cannon, 1996; History, 2015; Kravets, 2007). It takes some time for people to realize how new technologies can affect their lives, both positively and negatively. That time between the introduction of new technology and its regulation, formal or informal, is cultural lag.

Culture Is Symbolic

You may notice that there is considerable variation in the way people behave and interact, but there exist many common characteristics. Some of these common characteristics are **symbols**, which are anything that represents something else. Symbols are really important in culture because they allow us to interpret things and events, then act appropriately. The only way this works is if everyone shares the meaning behind the symbols. Symbols can be material: I wear a wedding band, for example, which symbolizes my marital status.

Symbols can also be non-material like a sound, a facial expression, or a gesture. Here in the U.S., for example, we commonly use the hand gesture for OK (thumb and index finger joined in a circle) to mean everything is, well, OK. However, if you were traveling in Brazil and you wanted to let your bartender know your caipirinha (the national drink of Brazil) is super tasty, and you throw up the OK sign, you have just told him to f**k off—oops. If you raise your hand, palm out, in the direction of another person here in the U. S., you are saying "talk to the hand" or "hold it right there, buddy." Don't use this gesture if you find yourself in Greece. The hand raised and held palm outward from the body means you're throwing shit on your Greek friend—your now-angry Greek friend. It's all about the shared meaning and keeping your hands by your sides when traveling.

These examples of hand gestures illustrate a phenomenon called **culture shock**, the feeling of disorientation, surprise, and even fear one can experience when encountering a new culture. Not knowing the rules of a culture, such as what gestures are appropriate, can disorient visitors to unfamiliar cultures. When I traveled through Egypt, I encountered men who I thought were in heated arguments, waving their arms about while using a very firm and loud tone. I finally realized this style of interaction was common when haggling or conducting certain transactions. I was confused and a bit fearful until I learned it was a common social interaction. Sometimes the social customs of cultures may surprise travelers. Many Americans are surprised when they find that many beaches around the Mediterranean Sea are topless, clothing optional or fully nude. Many travelers from Islamic countries are shocked when they see young women wearing what they perceive as revealing clothing here in the U.S. Most Westerners traveling to Vietnam will be surprised, and maybe sickened, when they learn that cats and dogs are common items on restaurant menus. While lounging poolside at my resort in Belize a few years ago, I saw a *fully clothed* Mennonite couple step into the pool. They proceeded to walk into the pool to about shoulder depth, stop, and stand there and talk for about fifteen minutes. Everyone around the pool was trying to look without appearing to look. You have to admit that in our culture, and many others, you wear a swimsuit in a pool. Even though they were a honeymooning couple, modesty in public is an important element of their culture.

Components of Culture: Material and Non-Material Culture

Culture can broadly be broken into two component parts: material culture and non-material culture.

Material Culture is all the things that we make and use as humans—all our stuff. These are the physical artifacts of our existence. Material culture includes clothing, iPads, food, makeup, sneakers, skyscrapers, and the International Space Station.

Most people in the world do not eat with spoons, knives, and forks; despite this, people manage to feed themselves. Most people in the world do not sleep on what we consider to be a bed, and our social rules about reproduction are considerably different than those of other cultures. For example, the Yanomamo sleep in hammocks, not in beds on or near the ground. Sleeping in an elevated hammock eliminates the risk of having some slithering, crawling creature finding its way into one of your orifices as you sleep. It also allows air to circulate around you, keeping you cool, which makes adaptive sense if you live in the thick jungles and humid rainforests of South America like they do. So, these material artifacts represent human adaptive strategies.

While it seems on the surface that this is just stuff, you should know that stuff has meaning. That is, material objects have a **symbolic nature**—an object can represent or stand for something else (Oxford English Dictionary, 2015). Think about all the stuff you have; all that stuff may symbolize our materialistic culture. Think about what your car symbolizes. Do you drive a hybrid, a big SUV, a highline car, or maybe a POS (piece of shit)? Your hybrid may symbolize your concern for the environment, and that big SUV may be emblematic of the need for lots of room for your outdoor gear, the Bentley Continental GT may symbolize your social status, and that POS may say "Hey, I'm broke." There is meaning in material possessions.

We know this for several reasons, but it is best illustrated using archaeology. Rarely do archaeologists find instruction manuals for ancient cultures or things that say "Hey, this is who we were, what we believed in and valued, and how we behaved." What they do find is stuff, artifacts that humans left behind in the remote past. And what they do with those artifacts is reconstruct ancient cultures. The only way they come to know about ancient people's ways of life, their culture, is from the meaning that their possessions held for them.

Figure 3.4 (a) and (b) Automobiles and smart phones are part of our Material Culture.

For example, the Moche people (100 CE–800 CE), who inhabited the northern coastal area of modern-day Peru, left behind a surprising array of ceramics that depict a wide range of subject matter encompassing many aspects of life. Moche ceramics portray people, animals, gods at war, hunting scenes, caring for the sick, and burying the dead (Weismantel, 2004). These scenes have painted a vivid picture of many parts of Moche life and a fuller understanding of Moche culture for anthropologists. However, over five hundred pots found depict sex acts that include fellatio, masturbating male skeletons, and anal sex. The majority of sex pottery discovered represented heterosexual anal sex, usually showing an infant breastfeeding while the couple has sex. What do these artifacts say about the Moche way of life? While it is controversial, Weismantel has hypothesized that the Moche may have believed that many sex acts were responsible for pregnancy. Therefore, for them, they are simply depicting mainstream sexual habits.

Non-material Culture includes the knowledge, beliefs, values, and norms that help shape society and promote solidarity and stability. Let's start with a look at social **norms**—standards of behavior for a group or society. Norms are the rules and regulations that members of a group or society have agreed upon and are expected to adhere to or suffer some consequence. Norms also elicit conformity so that our social interactions become patterned, social life has regularity to it, and social order is maintained.

Because norms are guidelines for social interaction, they are manifested in a range of *expected behaviors*. When you pass someone on campus and greet them with "How are you doing?" you *expect* a response like "Fine," "OK," or "Good." We *expect* people in the United States to drive on the right-hand side of the road, when you are introduced to someone you are *expected* to shake their hand, and you are *expected* to use the restroom to relieve yourself, not the streets. Norms are a part of every culture, and they range in importance from very serious, such as paying your taxes, to not very important, such as wearing clean clothes.

Formal Norms are social rules that are so important that they have been written down and there is usually a serious consequence for their violation. Laws are formal norms; so are the official rules of Major League Baseball (MLB), your student handbook, and the "no turn on red" sign at your local intersection. So, formal norms are the most clearly stated and strictly enforced type of norms.

There are a great number of laws; in fact, in 2011, all U.S. states and territories created 40,000 new ones (National Conference of State Legislatures, 2013). However, the number of unwritten, mainly unspoken social rules or **informal norms**—rules that govern everyday behaviors that are widely understood and conformed to and carry no serious consequence for violation—seem infinite. These informal norms or *folkways* greatly influence our day-to-day interactions with others. From the minute we get up in the morning until we go to bed at night, our daily routines are guided by a host of informal social rules. Everything from swearing at your roommates for drinking all your beer, to how close you stand to a stranger on the bus, to where you stand in the elevator, to how you behave in the classroom is guided by informal norms.

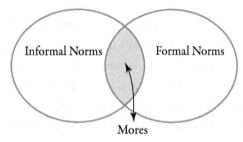

Figure 3.5 This diagram illustrates that Mores represent the subset of all norms, both Informal and Formal that have a strong moral component.

In my sociology classes, we discuss elevator behavior as a good example of a set of informal norms. How did you learn about acceptable elevator behavior? Did your parents sit you down one day and say "It's time we had a talk about elevator behavior"? Probably not, I hope not, that would be really weird! We do learn some things that way, such as when you were told to "Look both ways before crossing the street" or "Don't talk with food in your mouth." We also learn informal norms by imitation and observation, especially observing the consequences of their violation, as part of the process of our socialization into society.

Mores are a subset of both formal and informal norms that are believed to have great moral significance, and typically, their violation produces serious consequences. As we have discussed, every day our behaviors are guided by a slew of formal and informal norms. However, not all norms have a significant moral element to them. If you speed in your car to get to school on time, do you think you are immoral? No. If you accidently trespass on your neighbor's property, does that make you an immoral person? No. So of all the formal and informal norms that guide our lives, only a subset of them have a strong element of morality—mores. Figure 3.5 shows how mores represent only those norms that have moral significance among all possible formal and informal norms.

For example, murder and rape are highly immoral and illegal; we have formal norms or laws that prohibit these acts. Informal rules about cheating on your partner exist, and while it may not be illegal, it is still immoral, and it makes you a creep. These examples illustrate that both formal and informal norms that possess moral significance can be considered mores.

Taboos are acts that are so strongly prohibited in a culture that they elicit feelings of disgust, repugnance, and revulsion. Taboos in the United States include such acts as *incest* (sexual activity with close relatives), *necrophilia* (sexual attraction to or sex acts with a dead person), *pedophilia* (sexual attraction to or sexual contact with pre-pubescent children), *bestiality* (sexual acts with non-human animals), and *cannibalism* (eating the flesh or internal organs of other humans). Notice a common thread? All of these acts are not really productive for any collective of humans or the species in general. Sex with young children, sex with dead people, and sex with barnyard animals are all reproductive dead ends. Incest leads to physical and developmental birth defects, and eating each other just reduces the population and seems quite disgusting. These acts rise to the level of revulsion in the United States, but each of these acts is or has been practiced by some culture somewhere in world.

A Brief Discussion About Norms

Norms are a part of every culture and therefore change from place to place. For example, a friend of mine was working in the Philippines a few years ago and got to be pretty friendly with his Filipino coworker, Fred. One night after work, he was invited to Fred's house for drinks. My friend is a hearty beer drinker and gladly accepted. Fred poured my friend a beer, he finished it, and Fred immediately poured another beer. This went on for several hours, and my friend began to plot his escape, but every time he finished his beer, the glass was immediately filled. My friend, being American, did not want to be rude to his host by not finishing his beer, but he was now quite drunk. What my friend did not know is that while he was trying to be polite by finishing each beer, he was actually indicating, by finishing each beer, that Fred was a terrible host who could not supply enough beer to his guest. In Filipino culture, in order not to insult your host, you leave a small amount of beer in the glass or a tiny morsel of food on the plate, indicating that your host has been so generous you could not finish the abundance he provided. In contrast, Americans think it rude not finish all that is offered. Norms like these are subtle and many times lost on those who were not raised in the culture or who have not been fully immersed in it.

Norms also change over time within a culture. I was certain that I would grow up to have one arm longer than the other. Why, you ask? When I was a child, my mother would quite frequently yank my arm vigorously when I would not come along voluntarily or was acting the fool. When I was young, it was not uncommon for me or my friends to be spanked, struck, or hit with a belt as punishment, sometimes in public. How would an arm yank or a slap on the bottom of a child in public play out these days? A parent using physical punishment in public today could be subjected to the disapproval of other parents or even be reported to Child Protective Services. Norms about the physical punishment of children, especially in public places, has changed considerably just in the last few decades. Research indicates that it is not widely accepted to use corporal punishment on children in public or private unless there are unusual circumstances. FYI, in Sweden, it is against the law to use corporal punishment on children, and in Canada, you cannot use physical punishment on children younger than two or older than twelve. In fact, both the European Union and the United Nations have asked all nations of the world to prohibit corporal punishment by parents (Straus, 2010; Gershoff, 2010). So, if you travel with kids. ...

Norms can either encourage or restrict/prohibit behaviors. Because norms have these qualities, we make a distinction between prescriptive and proscriptive norms. **Prescriptive norms** refer to socially encouraged behaviors such as applauding after a really good Fourth of July fireworks show or wearing somber-colored clothing to a funeral. In contrast, **proscriptive norms** are behaviors that one should not or must not engage in, such as murder, placing your hands in fire, or playing air guitar during my lectures. Our social lives, then, are guided by a number of both types of norms. Can you name several prescriptive and proscriptive norms that have influenced your behavior today?

Regardless of what type of norm you obey, they all encourage conformity, which promotes social stability and social order.

Norms are bound by social context. Expected social behavior may vary depending on the social setting and who is involved. Say you are at the park on a picnic with your love interest, the sun is shining, and people are out and about. You both notice a small child, about two years old, stripping off her clothes down to her diaper, laughing, and running carefree through the grass. How would you react? If you are like most people, it would probably bring a smile to your face, and you might even let out a slight giggle. Then, you turn in horror to see a forty-five-year-old man strip off his clothes down to his tighty-whities, twirling his pants about his head, laughing, and running carefree through the grass ... until he is arrested. You see, a little kid can run nearly naked through the park and she is adorable, but a grown man does the same thing and he's in jail for indecent exposure. The application of norms depends on a number of factors, such as who is involved in the behavior and where the act is taking place. Even our adorable two-year-old could not get away with her strip-down dance if she were to do it in a museum, library, or the DMV. You can get away with a lot of socially unacceptable behaviors in the privacy of your own home that you couldn't get away with on the streets of your hometown.

When I was younger, I had a real issue with authority—I didn't really like obeying rules. Now I'm like the overwhelming majority of people: I have a career, a home, a family, and follow the rules ... for the most part. The big question is, why do the vast majority of people follow the rules? Like with any set of rules for behavior, there are rewards and punishments established to encourage conformity to social norms; sociologists refer to these as **sanctions. Positive sanctions** are rewards for conforming to norms like a work promotion, good grades, or a smile for holding a door open for someone. Positive sanctions are used to promote desirable behaviors like working hard, doing well on exams, and positive responses from others. These rewards are distributed so that people

---

Try This

Norm violation. Try violating some informal norm like not shaking someone's hand when you first meet them, interrupt someone's conversation or offer to trade your jacket for a cup of coffee instead of using money at your local coffee shop. There are hundreds of informal norms that guide our behaviors every day, pick one, violate it and note how people react. Then let them off the hook by telling them you were just engaging in a bit of social research. Discuss with them why they reacted the way they did. Try to get beyond that you had broken a social rule, and explore why they think the rule exists and how does it help make social interactions run smoothly.

Figure 3.6 Police officers, an umpire, and a teacher in a classroom are all authorized to apply formal sanctions.

will continue to engage in acceptable and productive social behaviors. On the other hand, **negative sanctions** are punishments for the violation of social norms. Examples include a speeding ticket, jail time, and dirty looks from other customers when you have fifty items in the 15 or fewer items express checkout lane. Negative sanctions are applied in order to extinguish unacceptable, unproductive, or dangerous behaviors.

Who can impose sanctions? Well, anybody really. You can't pull someone over because he failed to use his turn signal (if you lived in Virginia you wish you could), but you can shush someone for being loud in a movie theater. Sociologists make a distinction between these types of sanctions and who can apply them.

Formal sanctions are rewards or penalties that are applied by an authorized agent. For example, police are authorized to enforce laws and can write traffic tickets, issue warnings, or arrest suspects. The dean of students at your college is authorized to expel students who violate the honor code or honor students who beautify the college campus. Formal sanctions are used to promote compliance with laws or official institutional policies.

When you shake your head in displeasure, wag your finger at someone, or laugh at someone's silly behavior, you are applying **informal sanctions**—approval or disapproval that does not come from an authorized agent but from everyday interactions with others. These can range from mild, such as giving someone a dirty look for talking on his cell phone in an elevator, to severe, such as ending a friendship because your friend drinks too much. We all have the capacity to administer informal sanctions, and we all have. Have you ever flipped someone off after that person cut you off in traffic? If so, you applied an informal sanction.

Table 3.1 Some Weird (to us) Food Rules from Around the World

Country/Region	Food Rule	Why?
Jamaica and Nigeria	Do not feed young children eggs.	They will grow up to be thieves.
China	Do not leave your chopsticks standing up in the remaining rice in your bowl.	In private homes, that practice is restricted to offerings to the ghosts of family ancestors. Doing this in a restaurant would cast a terrible curse on the owner.
Japan	If you want to share a tasty morsel with your meal-mate, do not pass the food from chopstick to chopstick. Rather, place the morsel on a separate plate and pass it to your partner.	Passing food from chopstick to chopstick references the Japanese practice of sifting through the cremated remains of loved ones looking for bones.
Alaska	It is illegal to give beer to a moose.	Have you ever seen a drunk moose?
France	As of 2011, ketchup is banned in all schools in France.	It threatens all things French. Ketchup is also viewed as an American encroachment on French culture.
The Middle East	Be sure to shake your cup after you have enjoyed your coffee with your new Bedouin friends.	If you don't, they will keep refilling it.
Nunavut (Canada) Inuit People	Be sure to fart after you finish your narwhal—the unicorn of the sea.	It shows appreciation for the meal, your host, and the cook.
Portugal	If they are not on the table, do NOT ask for salt and pepper.	To do this is to insult the cook's ability to season the food.
Thailand	Do NOT place the fork in your mouth. The fork is used to push food onto the spoon, which is then placed in the mouth.	You will appear both crude and rude.

Sources: Audiger, 2016; El Gedida, 2007; Graff and Ramadhana, 2011; Gray-Kanatiiosh, 2002; "Japanese Table Manners", 2015; Meyer-Rochow, 2009; Reid, 2012 Willsher, 2011.

The Etiquette App (Android and Apple) helps you with dining, dating, business and cultural etiquette. This could help in a variety of social situations in which you are unsure of the proper behavior. Don't know which fork to use first, unsure about how to greet your new Chinese boss, wondering how many times to kiss a French woman on the cheek or what the proper tip for the pizza delivery person is … just use The Etiquette App and never be embarrassed again (Solaz Dazen srl, 2016).

Norms are not random. Rules for social conduct are generated by social values. That is, norms are based on the shared values of a society. All cultures possess **values**—culturally defined standards that guide people's interpretation about what is good or bad, right or wrong, desirable or undesirable, and just or unjust. If you want to know what a society values, take a look at its social rules. Let me start with a concrete example and move to a more abstract one. What do desert cultures value? Water. Desert cultures around the world have elaborate social rules surrounding consuming, finding, and distributing their limited water supply. The Bushmen of the Kalahari Desert have a complicated system of exchange called *hxaro,* which is guided by a complex set of social rules that determine who, how, when, and where people can, for example, drink water (Wiessner, 1977).

According to University of Michigan researcher Wayne Baker (2014), one of the ten core American values is "*getting*

Figure 3.7 Eating food with chopsticks is more widely practiced than eating with silverware.

Figure 3.8 San People—The Bushmen of the Kalahari.

ahead—individual achievement, status, and success." This idea of getting ahead or being successful is a fairly abstract concept, and one that people may define differently. Even so, most Americans would include possessions like a home, car, and clothing as indicators of status and success. Think about all the rules we have that protect people's stuff. You can't damage, trespass, take, or use other people's stuff. There are thousands of laws that prohibit robbery, theft, vandalism, and trespassing. These laws were established to protect the things that people work so hard for as they strive to get ahead. These laws also reflect our value of private property.

> *"Don't believe anything. Regard things on a scale of probabilities. The things that seem most absurd, put under 'Low Probability,' and the things that seem most plausible, you put under 'High Probability.' Never believe anything. Once you believe anything, you stop thinking about it."* —Robert A. Wilson

In daily conversations, people commonly use the terms values and beliefs interchangeably, not really making a clear distinction. We sociologists, on the other hand, like to point out the distinction between the two terms. While values are culturally defined standards about what is *good* and *desirable*, which serve as broad guidelines, **beliefs** are commonly held ideas about what is *true* or *real*. As Americans, we *value* success and we *believe* that we can be successful if we get an education and work hard. We also value freedom; therefore, we believe that people should be free to live where they want, work at what they want, be free to say what they want, and worship as they like. We also value independence, which leads to the belief that people should achieve things on their own, not rely on others, and achievement or success is an individual's responsibility. In contrast, Japanese culture values dependence; one must consider others before themselves, dependence on others is a natural part of the human condition, and contributing to the collective is emphasized.

You can see that values and beliefs are intertwined but different. One important difference between values and beliefs, and a unique characteristic of beliefs, is that people tend to maintain beliefs even when there is little or no evidence to support them or even if there is considerable evidence that contradicts them. For instance, in light of centuries of empirical evidence, including photographs, videos, and eyewitness reports (astronauts, cosmonauts, and other space men), that the earth is spherical in shape, as of 2015, there is still a Flat Earth Society, which believes the earth is a flat disc (I am not kidding: check out theflatearthsociety. org). Billions of people around the world believe in ghosts, spirits, angels, gods, and extraterrestrial beings without any support for their existence and considerable evidence suggesting they don't exist.

While beliefs can sustain people, sometimes they become the engine that drives immoral, unethical, or barbaric acts. In June 2014, for example, the Islamic State of Iraq and the Levant (ISIL) published a manifesto, which, among other things, indicated that anyone who does not *believe* in its severe interpretation of Islam must convert or die. The extremist beliefs of ISIL's members have led them to burn, shoot, rape, torture, and behead anyone who does not believe what they believe. The group has gone as far as to produce and publish, on the Internet, videos of the gruesome beheadings of innocent people.

The Connection Between Beliefs and Behaviors

The Fore (FOR-ray) people of Papua New Guinea greatly value the affection and respect of family members above nearly all other traits. According to their customs, there is only one powerful way to demonstrate one's love and loyalty to a dead relative: you must eat them. The Fore people are ritual cannibals: they eat the flesh and internal organs of deceased loved ones as a ritual celebration. They *believe* that this practice is the highest tribute of affection and respect you can bestow on your dead relative. Additionally, consuming your dead relatives keeps them near you always (Whitfield et al., 2008).

Unfortunately, one particular *behavior*, eating your dead loved ones' brains, has serious health consequences. Many times, the brains of the deceased contain a prion that causes a disease known as kuru. Kuru, or the "laughing sickness," is a spongiform encephalopathy, which is an incurable, degenerative brain disorder. It creates thousands of tiny holes in your brain so that it resembles a sponge. It is a degenerative disorder that passes through three stages. The first stage includes difficulty walking, talking, and seeing, muscle tremors, shivering, and slurred speech. In the second stage, a patient would experience the following symptoms: inability to walk without support, muscle jerks, outbursts of laughter (the "laughing sickness"), depression, and mental slowing. In the third and final stage, one would be unable to walk or sit up on his own, be incontinent, be unable to speak, and suffer a general cognitive disintegration. All this in a three- to six-month period after consuming the tainted brains.

Despite being informed of the danger associated with eating the brains of the deceased, they continued the *behavior* because the cultural *belief* in honoring the dead was so powerful. Knowing full well that they would die, and so would anyone who consumed brains of the dead, such as their children and spouses, they continued the custom. Fortunately, the ritual has effectively been extinguished. Do you believe in something so strongly you would risk the lives of your children, your parents, or other loved ones?

Dominant Culture, Subcultures, and Countercultures

It is safe to say that a culture like ours is not monolithic—not solid, unbroken, and uniform. Our society is composed of a number of similar and dissimilar groups—everyone is not the same in the way they think or act. However, in the United States, like in other cultures, there is a dominant culture. The **dominant culture** refers to the mainstream culture in a society whose values, beliefs, and practices are shared and accepted by the majority of its members. That is, most people buy into our way of life without much oppositions. While there are groups who protest racial inequality, economic conditions, and gender inequality, they are exercising freedom of speech, and they don't really threaten social order. Production and maintenance of the dominant culture is usually, though not always, achieved by the majority population through control of social institutions such as schools, media, law, the political process, and the economy. In the United States, we might identify economically and politically powerful white males as those who control the dominant culture.

Just as there is considerable diversity of cultures across societies, there can be variation within a single society. Within nearly all cultures, there are groups of people who differ in some practice, custom, or habit from the general mainstream culture. The United States is a complex society composed of many groups; some have developed cultural patterns that are different from the dominant culture. Think about it this way: within the larger American culture, many smaller cultures, or subcultures, exist.

Subcultures are groups in society whose beliefs, behaviors and interests differ from the larger cultural patterns of society. While members of subcultures share a specific identity within that group, they are still part of and participate in the larger culture. There are countless subcultures in the United States that center around a number of social identities. Subcultures include different types of groups that can be formed by religion, age, class, region, sexual preference/identity, disability, race/ethnicity, occupation, or even interest. You can see by this list that whether we realize it or not, most of us have membership in a number of subcultures.

Ethnic and racial subcultures form around the language, food, and customs of their ancestors. Others form around shared experiences. Combat veterans are united by their unique journeys that only those who have known combat can share. Some subcultures are united by common traits, characteristics, or preferences. The corseting community, for example, embraces an aesthetic preference for tightly laced corsets and the physical sensation the members derive from wearing corsets. (There is a shop in Jacksonville, Florida, devoted to corsets and corset fashion appropriately named Subculture). Groups like Alcoholics Anonymous, Online Gamers Anonymous, and Clutterers Anonymous emerge to support those suffering from various addictions. Even though members of subcultures coalesce around their particular lifestyle, they still identify with and participate in the larger society.

Goths, hipsters, furries, and hip-hop are all examples of subcultures. Many times, like in these examples, groups have a particular style of dress, listen to certain music, and have a central focus, trait, or interest, which adds up to what members consider a lifestyle. The Goth lifestyle, the hipster lifestyle, and the vampire lifestyle represent alternate ways of living within the larger culture. Goths wear black, and hipster males have a "uniform": boots, jeans with the cuffs rolled up, plaid shirt, and oh, don't forget the facial hair. Furries like to dress as their favorite furry animal, and rap music is central to the hip-hop culture. While members of subcultures share beliefs or practices that differ from mainstream culture, they still participate in the larger general culture. I see Goths in my classes along with hipsters, athletes, and hackers, earning degrees so they can get jobs, buy homes, and have families like most in American culture.

I have many friends who ride Harleys. They wear a lot of black, take care and pride in their bikes, ride frequently, and share road stories. Many of these "weekend warriors" take on the persona of the "Harley Rider" on the weekends but are back in the classroom or office come Monday morning, participating in the big culture. Moreover, they identify with Harley bike owners no matter where they may ride—Alaska or Arizona, Croatia or Japan, membership in many subcultures is not bound by geography. When I travel to scuba dive, I meet divers from around the world, and we immediately bond over our common interest.

This is by no means a comprehensive list of subcultures. There are also many **deviant subcultures** that are less tolerated or aren't as acceptable as others. These are unusual subcultures that most people can't relate to and may mock or deride. Vampire culture, for example, is a growing subculture in which people may believe that they are vampires. Some have night jobs so they can sleep during the day and avoid daylight, they may sleep in coffins, and they may have their teeth ground down into fangs or have custom prosthetic fangs made. They dress in exotic vampire attire, and some even consume the blood of others, usually close friends who consent to the practice. But not all vampires consume blood; some get their sustenance from the psychic energy of crowds or the power in nature, such as waves or lightning. Yet others are highly spiritual, and some believe they have an immortal soul. Take a look at Table 3.3 if you want to keep your vampire types straight. Finally, there are groups in society who remain marginalized because criminal activity is their central unifying activity. *Criminal deviant subcultures* include groups such as the mafia, street gangs, or drug users.

Table 3.2 Several Examples of Subcultures by Type

Subculture Type	Examples
Religion	Amish, Hasidim, and Fundamentalist Church of Jesus Christ of Latter-Day Saints (FLDS)
Age	Boomers, Gen Xers, Millennials
Class	Lower Class, Middle Class, Upper Class
Region	Southerner, New Englander
Sexual Preference/ Identity	LGBPTTQQIIAA+ (Lesbian, Gay, Bisexual, Pansexual, Transgender, Transsexual, Queer, Questioning, Intersex, Intergender, Asexual, Ally)
Disability	Deaf and Disabled Punk Rockers
Race/Ethnicity	African American, Latino, and German American
Occupation	Operating Room Nurses, College Professors, and Piano Tuners
Interest	Scuba Divers, Cheerleaders, and Hackers

Table 3.3 Know Your Vampires

Vampire Type	What They're Into
Sanguinarians	Consume their own blood or that of others
Psychic (Pranic)	Thrive on the psychic or aural energy of individuals or groups
Living	Highly spiritual vampires who do not drink blood or draw on the energies of others. Organized into clans (Temple of the Vampire, Ordo Strigoi Vii and The Order of the Black Dragon)
Transcendental	Believe that they can obtain immortality by transferring their soul into the body of a younger vampire.

Source: Vampireunderworld.com

In contrast, **countercultures**—groups that engage in lifestyles that include beliefs and practices that are in direct opposition to the prevailing norms of mainstream culture—do not always identify with and participate in the larger society. Typically, countercultures reject some of the values, beliefs, or norms of the larger society, and unlike subcultures that operate relatively smoothly within the larger society, countercultures actively defy mainstream society by developing their own social organization, many times in isolated communities.

Some examples include the counterculture movements of the yippies (members of the Youth International Party, a political party for young progressives) and hippies of the 1960s, which opposed the war in Vietnam, the federal government, and capitalist economic systems in general. They protested the social, political, economic, and sexual inequalities of the time and essentially called for a reordering of society. Radical groups like Earth First! are in opposition to environmental policies and practices they believe don't do enough to conserve or protect natural resources. This counterculture organization advocates "monkey wrenching," or "ecotage," the practice of environmental sabotage. Followers of Earth First! are suspected of "spiking" old growth trees, putting large, hidden spikes in trees so that

Figure 3.9 Hippies of the 1960s and 1970s and Black Panthers both represented counterculture groups.

when loggers cut into them they are injured or killed (Roselle and Mahan, 2009; Earth First!, 2015). These acts of ecotage were meant to protest the unsustainable practice of logging old growth forests and the subsequent damage to the ecosphere and bring about radical social change.

Some counterculture movements have lofty aims and are opposed to the larger society because they believe that they can affect real, positive social change. The hippies wanted to transform the United States into a fair and free society, and Earth First! wants human societies to stop destroying the earth so future generations can enjoy a healthy planet. However, some countercultures are more militant and antisocial. The Black Panther Party (BPP) of the 1960s and '70s was a militant counterculture movement originally formed to monitor police brutality. Then the movement grew, ultimately advocating violent revolution as the only path to black liberation. The party called on all African Americans to arm themselves in preparation for the revolution that would topple the white establishment (Bloom and Martin, 2013).

Another race-based counterculture, the White Supremacy Movement, seeks to expel or enslave all people of color and anyone who practices any religion other than protestant Christianity. Groups like the Ku Klux Klan, Aryan Brotherhood, and the Aryan Nations have popularized this movement. These groups differ slightly on tactics, but they all espouse the same message of eliminating or subjugating all non-white, non-Christians in the United States.

Theoretical Perspectives on Culture

Recall that the functionalist perspective assumes that society is a complex system of interrelated parts that work together cooperatively. Functionalists are highly concerned with social order. There are more than 323 million Americans; if people are pursuing their own self-interests, how does society hang together? The reality is people do cooperate and there is a degree of social integration, because most people are invested in their families, communities, and society. Functionalists believe that cooperation is a result, in part, of compliance and conformity to social rules. Generally, the roadways of my city and of yours run fairly smoothly because drivers cooperate with each other. People want to get to their jobs or home to their families, so they obey traffic laws, avoiding accidents and all the hassle those bring. Everyone's behavior on the road is constrained by the same rules, which leads to cooperation and creating a sort of social order of the roadways; the same is true for the larger society.

[...] The conflict perspective argues social order is maintained by the elite classes through coercion and power. Conflict theorists don't view social order as emerging from cooperation; rather, they believe the powerful classes use ideologies to maintain their positions of dominance. The dominant classes manipulate social institutions and other elements of culture, ideas, values, and beliefs to ensure their economic supremacy. The elements of culture like values, beliefs, and norms are designed to reinforce the economic relations in society. Culture is essentially constructed by the elite classes as a mechanism of social control.

The interactionist approach emphasizes the interactions of individuals in everyday life and how they shape social life. This stands in contrast to both the functionalist and conflict approaches, which focus on how large scale social structures pattern our daily lives. The interactionist approach sees humans as continually adjusting their behavior in response to the actions of others, interpretation of the situation, and meaning found in symbols. Thus, people are seen as active, creative participants who construct their social world, not simply conform to it. For interactionists, culture is constructed through human interaction and negotiation.

For instance, imagine you find yourself at a house party, music is playing, people are dancing, and there are kegs of beer. It's Friday night, and you don't have any sociology homework, so you decide to have a few beers. You have a few beers, meet and talk with some interesting people, and dance a bit. After a few hours and many beers, you are feeling pretty buzzed, your speech is slightly slurred, your balance is a little uneven, and you're drunk. Then the music stops, the lights come on, and everyone goes silent. You are then informed that all the beer served at the party was non-alcoholic! Huh? You are now stone-cold sober. From all the symbols and given the social environment, you interpreted the situation as a party, and when you are at a party and drink beer all night long, you get drunk.

The Bottom Line

Culture is everything, everything is culture. This is my phrase, which emphasizes that human culture is ubiquitous. Culture is what has allowed us as a species to adapt, survive, and flourish. However, the birth and development of culture was impossible without language. The development of complex languages allowed humans to organize, work cooperatively, and survive. Language is so intimately intertwined with culture that it links users in common modes of thought and perception. It also makes us uniquely human because language can relate present to past and future.

Culture has been an effective adaptive mechanism for humans, the only single species that can inhabit all geographical regions of the planet. Culture is learned, shared, and transmitted across generations, and it is dynamic. Culture changes as new discoveries and inventions are introduced and

Table 3.4 Theoretical Perspectives and Elements of Culture

Theoretical Perspective

Element of Culture	Structural Functionalism	Conflict Approach	Interactionist Approach
Norms	Social rules are necessary for conformity and compliance, which promote solidarity and stability, maintaining social order.	Norms reinforce the economic power of the dominant group. Conformity and compliance to social rules maintain the dominant group's consent to rule.	During daily interactions, people interpret the actions of others and the social context in order to know what social rules apply.
Values and Beliefs	Common values and beliefs are central to maintaining consensus, leading to stable social order. Generally, Americans share the belief that hard work will get you ahead. So, the overwhelming majority of people get jobs, work hard, pay taxes and buy stuff, helping maintain our way of life.	The powerful classes use ideologies—systems of ideas, values, and beliefs that guide the way people think and act—to maintain their positions of dominance. Members of society who do not buy into the dominant ideology are marginalized and portrayed as radical or deviant. Those who practice non-standard religions, for example, are seen as weird and pushed to the margins of society.	During daily interactions, individuals use symbols to reflect and reinforce social values and beliefs. Some political candidates use American flag lapel pins as symbols to reflect their patriotism, which people will notice during interactions.

when improvements or innovations are made to existing technology. Social change comes in several forms. Language is always altered when new technologies emerge in society, because we need to label those new things the associated beliefs and behaviors. Sometimes change in behaviors lag behind the technologies, and rules about how to use the technologies have to catch up. Culture is symbolic: signs and symbols can be used as a sort of shorthand because members of the culture share their meaning.

However, languages can be extinguished through the ethnocentric practice of cultural imperialism. Human history is filled with examples of the conquest and destruction of cultures, but this has been tempered in the past century as many researchers and governments have taken a more relativistic approach to understanding other cultures. Not only has this practice preserved many cultures, it has raised awareness of cultures that are endangered by identifiable external forces.

Culture is composed of two distinct components: material culture and non-material culture. Material culture is all those things we make and use. Food, cell phones, computers, underwear, and cigars are all representatives of material culture. But these are not just things; these things have meaning. Meaning attached to material objects allows us to interpret the value, status, or worth of those objects. Non-material culture is composed of values, beliefs, and norms. Values are important shared standards of right and wrong, good and bad, desirable and undesirable, and just and unjust. These cultural standards drive beliefs about what is true and real, potentially binding us together. In turn, we act according to our beliefs. Our behaviors are constrained and regulated through the application of social norms. These rules of social conduct can encourage social cooperation and promote social stability and social order.

Within the larger culture, there exist many little cultures. And despite their distinctive values and practices, subcultures are still subsumed under the larger cultural system. Subcultures in the United States include such groups as the Hmong, Eastern Orthodox, competitive cheerleaders, and vampires. Most of us are members of a number of subcultural groups at any given time and over the course of our lives. Countercultures, on the other hand, do not operate smoothly within the mainstream culture. These groups seek to destroy or dismantle the larger culture and social structure. Many of these groups are at odds with government policies or practices, oppose cultural practices and lifestyles, or feel that members of their group are being systematically mistreated.

Finally, in this chapter, we examined the way that the three major sociological perspectives viewed culture. Functionalists argue adherence to values and beliefs promotes solidarity and consensus, contributing to stable social order. Again, conformity and compliance with social norms promotes stable social order, with all people doing what they are supposed to be doing. In contrast, the conflict approach maintains that the elements of culture are created by the elite classes to maintain their position of dominance. The elements of culture, including social institutions, are simply tools of the dominant class used to secure consent to their rule. Unlike either functionalism or conflict theories, the interactionist approach sees culture as constructed by the interaction of individuals in everyday life. For interactionists, social order is derived from interactions among individuals rather than being imposed by larger social structures. This focus shifts their interpretation away from stable values and beliefs and toward more malleable, continually readjusting social processes.

Figure Credits

Figure 3.1: "Branislaw Malinowski with Trobriand Islanders," https://commons.wikimedia.org/wiki/File: Bronis%C5%82aw_Malinowski_among_Trobriand_tribe.jpg. Copyright in the Public Domain.
Figure 3.2: Copyright © Saperaud~commonswiki (CC BY-SA 3.0) at https://commons.wikimedia.org/wiki/ File:Moon_merged_small.jpg.
Figure 3.3: Captain George E. Mack, "Inuit Children," https://commons.wikimedia.org/wiki/File:Enfants_ Inuits_1925.jpg. Copyright in the Public Domain.

Figure 3.4a: Copyright © Philipp Rath (CC BY-SA 3.0) at https://commons.wikimedia.org/wiki/File:Bmw_525d.jpg.

Figure 3.4b: Copyright © Janitors (CC by 2.0) at https://commons.wikimedia.org/wiki/File:Size_comparison_of_iPhone_5C_5S_4S.jpg.

Figure 3.6a: Copyright © Elliot Moore (CC BY-SA 2.0) at https://commons.wikimedia.org/wiki/File:G20_police_lines.jpg.

Figure 3.6b: Copyright © Paul L Dineen (CC by 2.0) at https://commons.wikimedia.org/wiki/File:Safe_(4779502220).png.

Figure 3.6c: Cruise Reviewer, "Jpg_port_pollenca," https://commons.wikimedia.org/wiki/File:Jpg_port_pollenca.jpg. Copyright in the Public Domain.

Figure 3.7: Copyright © Opponent (CC by 2.0) at https://commons.wikimedia.org/wiki/File:Okonomi-yaki_by_chou_i_ci_at_Sumiyoshi_Taisha,_Osaka.jpg.

Figure 3.8: Copyright © Mopane Game Safaris (CC BY-SA 4.0) at https://commons.wikimedia.org/wiki/File:Bosquimanos-Grassland_Bushmen_Lodge,_Botswana_09.jpg.

Figure 3.9a: Copyright © Mombas (CC by 2.5) at https://commons.wikimedia.org/wiki/File:1981_People_Pix.jpg.

Figure 3.9b: http://www.loc.gov/pictures/item/2005677025/. Copyright © 1967 by New YorkWorld-Telegram.

Bibliography

Audiger, Stephan. "Thai Food Etiquette: Do's and Don'ts." *Phuket*. Hotels.com, 2016. Web. 26 July 2016.

Baker, Wayne. *United America*. Canton: Read The Spirit Books, 2014. Print.

Bloom, Joshua, and Waldo E. Martin Jr. *Black Against Empire: The History and Politics of the Black Panther Party*. Berkeley: University of California Press, 2013. Print.

Bohannan, Paul. *How Culture Works*. New York: The Free Press, 1995. Print.

Bump, Philip. "The New Congress is 80 Percent White, 80 Percent Male and 92 Percent Christian." *Washington Post*. Washington Post, 5 Jan. 2015. Web. 9 Aug. 2015.

Cannon, Robert. "The Legislative History of Senator Exon's Communications Decency Act: Regulating Barbarians on the Information Superhighway." *Cybertelecom*. Cybertelecom, Nov. 1996. Web. 9 Aug. 2015.

Center for Reproductive Rights. "Female Genital Mutilation (FGM): Legal Prohibitions Worldwide."*Center for Reproductive Rights*. Center for Reproductive Rights, 11 Dec. 2008. Web. 5 Aug. 2015.

Cox, Stan. *Losing Our Cool: Uncomfortable Truths about our Air-Conditioned World (and Finding New Ways to Get Through the Summer)*. New York: The New Press, 2010. Print.

Dennis, Steven, and Jay Hunter. "Wealth of Congress Jumps $150 Million." *Hill Blotter*. Hill Blotter, 22 Oct. 2014. Web. 9 Aug. 2015.

"Earth First! Journal: Media from the Frontlines of Ecological Resistance." *Earth First! Journal | Media from the Frontlines of Ecological Resistance*. Earth First!, 2015. Web. 9 Aug. 2015. <http://earthfirstjournal.org/>.

El Gedida, El Manshia. "The Bedouin Hospitality." *Bedawi*. Bedawi, 2007. Web. 26 July 2016.

Freed, Andrea B. "School of Education at Johns Hopkins University-Multicultural Science Education: Myths, Legends, and Moon Phases." *Johns Hopkins School of Education*. Johns Hopkins University, 2012. Web. 5 Aug. 2015.

Gershoff, Elizabeth T. "More Harm ˝an Good: A Summary of Scientific Research on the Intended and Unintended Effects of Corporal Punishment on Children." *Law and Contemporary Problems* 73.31 (2010): 31–56. Web. 5 Aug. 2015.

Graff, Kristen and Rio Ramadhana. *Chinese Dining Etiquette*. Austin: Magnolia, 2011. Print.

Gray-Kanatiiosh, Barbara A. *Inuit*. New York: Abdo Publishers, 2002. Print.

Herdt, Gilbert. *The Sambia: Ritual and Gender in New Guinea*. New York: Holt, Rinehart and Winston, 1987. Print.

History. "The Death Spiral of Napster Begins." *This Day in History*. History, 6 Mar. 2015. Web. 9 Aug. 2015.

James, Steven R. "Hominid use of fire in the Lower and Middle Pleistocene." *Current Anthropology* 30 (1989): 1–26. Web. 5 Aug. 2015.

"Japanese Table Manners." *Japan-guide*. Japan-guide, 18 Feb. 2015. Web. 26 July 2016.

Kravets, David. "Napster Trial Ends Seven Years Later, Defining Online Sharing Along the Way." *Wired*. Wired, 31 Aug. 2007. Web. 9 Aug. 2015.

Krupnik, Igor, Claudio Aporta, Shari Gearheard, Gita J. Laidler, and Lene Kielsen Holm, eds. *SIKU: Knowing Our Ice: Documenting Inuit Sea Ice Knowledge and Use*. New York: Springer, 2010. Print.

Malinowski, Bronislaw. *The Sexual Lives of Savages in North-Western Melanesia*. 1929. New York: Kessinger Publishing, 2005. Print.

Mellins, Maria. *Vampire Culture*. New York: Bloomsbury, 2013. Print.

Meredith, Martin. *Born in Africa: The Quest for the Origins of Human Life*. New York: Public Affairs, 2011. Print.

Meyer-Rochow, Victor Benno. "Food taboos: their origins and purposes." *Journal of Ethnobiology and Ethno-medicine* 5.18 (2009): 1–10. Web. 26 July 2016.

National Conference of State Legislatures. "New Laws for a New Year: 2014." *NCSL: National Conference of State Legislatures*. National Conference of State Legislatures, 2013. Web. 5 Aug. 2015.

Oxford English Dictionary "Symbol." *Oxford Dictionaries*. Oxford University Press, 2015. Web. 7 Dec. 2015.

Pukui, Mary Kawena, and Samule H. Elbert. *Hawaiian Dictionary: Hawaiian-English, English-Hawaiian*. Hawaii: University of Hawaii Press, 1986. Print.

Pullum, Geoffrey K. *The Great Eskimo Vocabulary Hoax and Other Irreverent Essays on the Study of Language*. Chicago: University of Chicago Press, 1991. Print.

Reid, Robert. "Fine tune your table manners." *Lonely Planet*. Lonely Planet, May 2012. Web. 26 July 2016.

Roselle, Mike, and Josh Mahan. *Tree Spiker: From Earth First! To Lowbagging: My Struggles in Radical Environmental Action*. New York: St. Martin's Press, 2009. Print.

Solaz Dazen srl. *Good Manners: Improve your etiquette.* Computer software. Apple App Store. Vers. 2.0 Solaz Dazen srl, 22 Jan. 2016. Web. 3 Aug. 2016.

Strauss, Murray A. "Criminogenic Effect of Corporal Punishment by Parents." *Transnational Criminology Manual: Vol. I.* Eds. M. Herzog-Evans, and Isabelle Dréan-Rivette. Amsterdam: Wolf Legal Publishing, 2010. 373–390. Web. Aug. 5 2015.

Tucker, Jim B. *Return to Life: Extraordinary Cases of Children Who Remember Past Lives.* New York: St. Martin's Press, 2013. Print.

Weicha, Karin. "New Estimates on the Rate of Global Language Loss." *The Rosetta Blog.* The Rosetta Project, 28 Mar. 2013. Web. 5 Aug. 2015.

Weiner, Steve, Qinqi Xu, Paul Goldberg, Jinyi Liu, and Ofer Bar-Yosef. "Evidence for the Use of Fire at Zhoukoudian, China." *Science* 281.5374 (1998): 251–253. Web. 5 Aug. 2015.

Weismantel, Mary. "Moche Sex Pots: Reproduction and Temporality in Ancient South America." *American Anthropologist* 106.3 (2004): 495–505. Web. Aug. 5 2015.

Whitfield, Jerome T., Wandagi H. Pako, John Collinge, and Michael P. Alpers. "Mortuary Rites of the South Fore and Kuru." *Philosophical Transactions of the Royal Society* 363 (2008): 3721–3724. Web. Aug. 9 2015.

Wiessner, Pauline Wilson. *Hxaro: A Regional System of Reciprocity for Reducing Risk Among The!Kung San.* Ann Arbor: University of Michigan, 1977. Print.

Wiessner, Polly W. "Embers of Society: Firelight talk among the Ju/'hoansi Bushmen." *Proceedings of the National Academy of Sciences* 111.39 (2014): 14013–14014. Web. 5 Aug. 2015.

Wilsher, Kim. "France bans ketchup in cafeterias." *Los Angeles Times.* Los Angeles Times, 6 Oct. 2011. Web. 26 July 2016.

World Health Organization. "Eliminating Female genital mutilation: An interagency statement: OHCHR, UNAIDS, UNDP, UNECA, UNESCO, UNFPA, UNHCR, UNICEF, UNIFEM, and WHO." Geneva: World Health Organization, 2008. Web. 5 Aug. 2015.

CHAPTER 4

Socialization

Chapter 4 describes how individuals emerge through socialization, develop self-awareness, and establish identity. It also discusses the significance of socialization in childhood and adulthood, the concept of the individual as performer, and what makes each individual unique. Buechler (2014) focuses on patterns of interaction as well as key aspects of social relationships and how you maintain and construct your sense of self and identity in the context of symbolic interaction. Symbolic interactionism is a main notion in the sociological study of how you establish a sense of self. The personality yields oneself as a thing and over time develops a sense of who one is. The chapter raises important questions such as: Who are you? Why do you differ from others? Why don't you exit from your social ties? What distinguishes human actions from animal behavior? Why do you use significant symbols and simple gestures? What are the processes of thinking, involving consciousness and meaning?

How We Become Who We Are

Steven M. Buechler

....

[...]

This chapter traces the biography of the individual. Here, the individual arrives late in a different sense. We become individual only through socialization. We begin this process utterly dependent on others. Only after extensive social support do we develop self-awareness, become individuals, and acquire identity. In both historical and biographical terms, individuals only emerge through social connections with others. We are always social before we are individual (Lemert 2008).

When we ponder what makes one person different from another, there are at least two types of answers. A psychological answer seeks unique traits to explain personal differences. A sociological answer examines the relationships people have with others. Here individuality arises not from something internal, but rather from our external ties to others. A classic version of this idea sees the individual existing at the center of a "web of group affiliations" (Simmel 1908).

A modern variant is the sociograph. You can construct your own. Draw a small circle in the center of a piece of paper to symbolize you. Now draw spokes radiating out to other circles that represent the people in your life. Your relationships with those people differ in many ways: the length of time you have known them, the closeness or intensity of your bonds with them, and the like. Imagine drawing spokes in differing colors, thicknesses, or lengths to capture such nuances.

If you took this exercise seriously, the resulting sociograph would be different from those constructed by others. Sociographs illustrate how no two people occupy the same location in a web of group affiliations. Put differently, we all have unique locations in social networks.

A sociological perspective thus explains the uniqueness of individuals not by focusing inward on personal traits but rather by focusing outward on social networks. We differ from others because we occupy different locations in different networks. Even individuality is not "personal" as much as it is "social."

Take the exercise a step further. Imagine moving to some other circle in your sociograph and constructing that person's sociograph. Their web would include you and some people you know in common, but it would also include people who aren't in your web. Now imagine constructing a sociograph for everyone in your sociograph. As the number of spokes multiply exponentially, the circles representing individuals become less prominent than the ties linking them together. Indeed, the circles representing people come to look like fleeting interruptions in a flow of social forces and connections between them.

This imaginary exercise dramatizes how individuals don't exist apart from social ties with other individuals and groups. Moreover, individuality itself (even with its connotation of uniqueness) is best seen as a product of our distinctive ties with others rather than a purely personal set of traits.

In what follows, we explore how individual selves emerge through social processes. The exploration begins with C. H. Cooley's looking-glass self and proceeds to the synthesis of George Herbert Mead. We then examine symbolic interactionism and identity theory. The chapter closes with observations about how human beings are reflexive actors who bring self-awareness to every situation they encounter.

Cooley's Contributions

Charles Horton Cooley made two vital contributions to understanding how selves emerge through a social process. His work anticipates that of George Herbert Mead, who inspired the symbolic interactionist tradition, which remains sociology's best guide to unraveling questions about self and society.

The first of Cooley's (1998) contributions concerns the role of primary groups in social life. Primary groups involve intimate, face-to-face interaction with others. Within primary groups, we know others and are known to them as whole people, because our involvement is ongoing, all-inclusive, and central to our sense of self.

People also belong to secondary groups, but their connections to such groups are less personal, less intimate, more formal, and often shorter lived than with primary groups. In the sociograph you imagined a moment ago, your primary group consists of the people with whom you have the strongest (and often longest) bonds. They are probably the people closest to you in the sociograph. Farther away from you and your primary group, there are probably other nodes and networks that represent your secondary groups.

The vast majority of people begin their lives within a primary group of family members and perhaps others who are regarded as "family." For better or worse, whether "functional" or "dysfunctional," such familial primary groups are the first and most important social group through which most of us are socialized and develop a sense of self and individuality.

As our self develops, we venture out and join other groups. On the first day of school, we become members of a secondary group of other students. What might start as a frightening social encounter with strangers often develops into another primary group. As we come to know, interact, and play with the same circle of kids, we might form increasingly intimate bonds that become primary relationships.

In adolescence, such peer groups often become more primary and intimate than our family groups. When young people feel as if their friends understand them in ways their parents no longer do (and when parents feel the same way), it is a good indication of multiple primary ties (and tension between them). A more intense emotional tie might then arise, as a romantic partner displaces both the peer group and the family. And somewhat later, we might marry one of those partners and begin a family that will become our next primary group.

Throughout the life cycle, our web of group affiliations consists of shifting combinations of primary and secondary groups. But primary groups remain central to who we are. Our sense of self is intimately connected to these groups. In somewhat different sociological language, primary groups are crucial reference groups; we refer ourselves to these groups to judge who we are, what to do, how to act, and where to find validation for the people we have become. For all these reasons, our webs are held together by our thickest social ties to primary groups.

Cooley's second major contribution is his notion of the self, which is closely tied to primary groups. The key point is simply that there is no self or individual apart from our relationships with other people. "From Cooley's vantage point, then, the self is a social product, a product 'produced' largely in the primary group. It is a product best labeled a 'looking-glass self,' in that a child obtains an identity only with the realization that his or her picture, idea or image of himself or herself 'reflects' other people's picture of him or her" (Reynolds 2003, 63—64).

Imagination is crucial to Cooley's notion of the self. To say that we live in an imaginary world sounds like a put-down. But imagining involves basic processes of thought and cognition; to imagine is to think about the world, about people in the world, about our impressions of them, and about their impressions of us. In this sense, we inevitably live in an imaginary world, because we routinely try to understand the world by thinking about it. These processes are central to how we construct, maintain, or undermine our sense of self and identity.

When we combine primary groups and imagination, we can see the logic in Cooley's "looking-glass self." A crucial part of our imaginary lives involves speculation about the thoughts of others. The thoughts of others, in turn, contain impressions about who we are (and we're pretty disappointed if they don't). It is through this interactive process that we arrive at our sense of self.

This self has three components. First, we imagine how we appear to others. Second, we imagine how they evaluate our appearances. Finally, we construct a sense of self, based on our imaginary understanding of how others evaluate us (Reynolds 2003, 64). Put more succinctly: I am who I think you think I am.

Although the term *looking-glass* sounds quaint, the metaphor of a mirror still makes the point. Without others to reflect who we are back to us, we would have no reliable means of arriving at a sense of self. Common sense might dismiss this as "imaginary," but sociological insight says that this is all we have to base a self on.

We can even dispense with the metaphor. We use real mirrors when we want to assess, modify, or repair our physical appearance. The mirror is essential to get outside ourselves and see ourselves from the perspective of other people. In parallel fashion, our self only becomes known to us through the perspective of other people.

Cooley claimed we also develop strong, emotional responses to the selves that we construct through the looking-glass process. The emotions Cooley regarded as most central were pride and shame. When our judgments of others' judgments about us suggest we are viewed positively, then our self incorporates pride in who we are. When our judgments of others' judgments about us suggest we are viewed negatively, then our self incorporates shame about who we are. For Cooley, the looking-glass self was as much about emotional responses as cognitive processes (Scheff 2005).

Popular culture often tells people to "be positive" and "feel good about themselves," as if this could be accomplished by sheer will. More sociologically informed advice would say surround yourself with people who are positive about and feel good about you. Easier said than done, but if Cooley is right, our self-feelings do not arise on their own and cannot long exist in contradiction to the feelings we imagine others have about who we are.

Mead's Synthesis

Building on the work of Cooley and others, George Herbert Mead formulated a distinct perspective on self and society. Mead wrote little but was a gifted lecturer at the University of Chicago. Upon his retirement and death in 1931, his students assembled his ideas into a sociological classic titled *Mind, Self and Society* (Mead 1934).

Mead's work synthesized ideas prevalent in late nineteenth- and early twentieth-century social thought. Georg Simmel's web of group affiliations is one element. So is Max Weber's insistence that we can only understand social action if we see it from the perspective of the actor. Cooley's looking-glass sell plays an obvious role. William James had also studied the social self. Mead also drew on the work of John Dewey, who approached mind not as a physical structure but as a process of interpretation and meaning. Finally, W. I. Thomas had discussed the "definition of the situation" and demonstrated that situations defined as real will be real in their consequences. The imagery of social actors imposing definitions on the world around them and acting on those definitions was central to Mead's work.

Mead's synthesis put him at odds with other sociological approaches. Many versions of sociology analyze social structures as static entities, but Mead saw society as a dynamic process of change and fluidity. For Mead, the social world is less like still pictures and more like a movie playing at multiple frames per second. Moreover, although some versions of sociology explain the world through casual relationships of independent and dependent variables, Mead saw social elements as interrelated and interdependent. Each part gained its meaning from its relationship to others and to the whole, so it is difficult to isolate elements that can be analyzed as cause and effect.

Having said that, Mead is clearly in the sociological camp by recognizing that society precedes and shapes the individual. Although grammatically awkward, a more conceptually accurate title for Mead's book might have been "Society, Mind, Self and Society," to suggest the priority of society as a social environment in which minds and selves develop in individuals who only then become competent social actors.

Mead's exploration of minds and selves develops some of the core ideas of interactionist sociology. The first challenge is to understand the development of individual minds. Mead's concern is not with the physical structure of the brain but with the social process of the mind. The focus is not neurons and synapses but rather consciousness and meaning.

Mead begins with behaviorist logic but quickly moves from static psychological behaviorism to symbolic social psychology. He defines a gesture as any action that serves as a stimulus and provokes a response. The response becomes a stimulus for the initial actor who then responds to it, which in turn becomes a new stimulus for the second actor. In this way, a conversation of gestures is an interactive spiral of stimuli and response between two or more actors.

Whereas behaviorists applied this logic to all human behavior, Mead thought conversations of gestures were primarily found in the nonhuman animal world (which is the basis for much behaviorist research going all the way back to Pavlov's salivating dogs). Such nonhuman animal behavior is largely rooted in instincts, meaning that animals are pre-wired to act in certain ways and do not rely on symbolic interpretations to do so. Mead 's favorite example was a dogfight in which the behavior of each dog becomes a stimulus provoking an instinctive response in the other dog, leading to an escalation of barking, snarling, flattened ears, bared teeth, biting, and the like.

Mead departed from behaviorism by arguing that the vast majority of human action—and certainly the most sociologically interesting action—could not be understood as instinctual, unthinking patterns of stimulus and response. Humans differ from other animals because they formulate, interpret, and attribute *meaning to* actions and to people in their environment. This is why a boxing match is very different from a dogfight. Unlike dogs, boxers interpret, imagine, anticipate, and deceive as part of their strategy. It is this complex mental world—even in the brutality of the boxing ring—that qualitatively distinguishes human *action* from animal *behavior*.

To capture human action, Mead proposed different terminology. In contrast to the simple gestures of animals, human interaction involves significant symbols. Simple gestures become significant symbols when they meet two requirements. First, they carry a specific meaning. Second, that meaning is shared within some community of people. Although this might sound obtuse, the best example is right here on the page. Human languages are vast collections of significant symbols known as words, which in turn can be put together in larger, meaningful units like phrases, sentences, paragraphs, and even books. Physical gestures (handshakes, applause, the finger) can also be significant symbols if they carry a specific, shared meaning.

Significant symbols arise from interaction, because it is only through interaction that they achieve significance. Consider that the meaning is in the response. If you utter a phrase that elicits immediate recognition, the odds are it is a significant symbol that carries the same meaning for others as it does for you. If your phrase is met with a blank stare, the odds are it's not a significant symbol, because it is not calling up a similar meaning in those around you.

Here's a simple example. I live with a cat that freaks out when someone rings the doorbell. After an especially traumatic episode, I tried a stopgap measure of taping a small piece of paper over the doorbell. To me, the paper meant "don't ring the doorbell—knock instead." The next day, a delivery person rang the doorbell (traumatizing the cat). The day after that, someone selling something I didn't need rang the doorbell (further traumatizing the cat). Neither person interpreted the paper over the doorbell in the way I intended. It was not a significant symbol, because there was no shared meaning between me and my visitors. The day after that, a neighbor came to borrow something and gently knocked on the door. In this instant, the piece of paper became a significant symbol, because she assigned the same meaning to it that I did and acted accordingly. She did so because she had also tried to keep people from ringing her doorbell and disturbing her child's afternoon nap.

The simple example illustrates several larger points. Significant symbols are not static; they emerge through interaction only when it becomes evident that people assign the same meaning to some part of their environment. Moreover, what is a significant symbol to some people might not be a significant symbol to other people. This is most obvious when speakers of different languages attempt to communicate; it is a struggle to find even a minimal set of significant symbols so they can understand one another. But even within the same language group, there are subcultures of people who speak distinctive sublanguages known to them but not to outsiders. Indeed, the identity of many subcultures depends precisely on who "gets it" (that is, shares their significant symbols) and who doesn't have a clue. The abbreviations and shortcuts that comprise the vocabulary of texting (well understood by those who text and often impenetrable to those who don't) is merely a recent example of this long-standing aspect of human communication.

This demonstrates the social roots of individual minds. Here's the logic. "Mind" is shorthand for the process of thinking, involving consciousness and meaning. Thinking is really an internalized conversation of significant symbols. The focus of our thought could be anything: how to spend the weekend, whether we should call an elderly relative, pondering the motivation behind a friend's snide comment, or whatever. Regardless of the topic, to think is to have a silent conversation with oneself about that topic. Whereas interaction is an externalized conversation of significant symbols with others, thinking is an internalized conversation of significant symbols with ourselves.

Mead implies we cannot think without significant symbols; they are the building blocks of the internalized conversations that compose thinking. But if the symbols that comprise thinking are significant, this means they carry a shared meaning. Such shared meanings can only arise from interactions with others. The conclusion seems obvious. Humans are born with a physical brain but not a social mind. Minds are only acquired through social interaction with others. That social process provides us with the shared meanings of the significant symbols that allow us to think. When it comes to minds—as with so much else—we must first be social before we can be individual. Sociologically speaking, socialization makes us human by developing the capacities that distinguish us as a species.

Mead's argument might seem convoluted, but it resonates with common sense. Imagine encountering someone on a city street who is babbling incomprehensibly. What conclusions do we draw about their mental state? Now imagine that people who speak this person's language appear, and they have an animated discussion in Norwegian about how to find the subway station. We are likely to revise our opinion of their mental state when we recognize that they share meanings and a language with a group of people (just not us). But if no one ever comes along who understands our urban babbler, we are likely to conclude that they have "lost their mind." Even everyday language links making sense, shared meanings, and having a mind.

For Mead, the distinctive qualities of human interaction emerge from our ability to create, learn, and communicate significant symbols. They allow us to interpret stimuli and respond in meaningful ways. They allow us to develop abstract concepts that go beyond immediate experience and classify experiences into categories. This allows imaginative reflection on past experiences and future possibilities rather than learning only through trial and error. In the end, this makes intelligent action possible, as we use significant symbols, shared meanings, and abstract concepts to learn from the past, interpret the present, anticipate the future, and link them all together.

If minds only emerge through a social process, the same is true for selves. We are not born with a self but rather acquire one through socialization. Cooley's looking-glass self is an early statement of this position, and Mead builds on it.

The self has two components; one is there from the beginning. The "I" refers to impulses to act toward the world. This inborn "I" is later joined by a socialized "Me" to form a fully developed social self. Selves thereby involve interaction between the "I" and the "Me."

Although the impulses of the "I" are channeled by the socialization of the "Me," it never disappears. The "I" persists as an active subject; it is the part of us that acts in the moment. The persistence of the "I" even in the mature self means that people are always capable of spontaneous, creative, unpredictable actions. The self is never completely determined by larger social forces, because we always retain the capacity to act back upon those forces.

To have a self means to see oneself as an object. It is the capacity to be self-aware or self-conscious. The "I" can never achieve such awareness because it is always acting in the moment. It is the "Me" that provides this self-awareness. The "Me" only develops through "taking the role of the other." This is Mead's version of Cooley's looking-glass self. The underlying idea is quite similar: We arrive at a sense of self by imaginatively taking the role of other people in our social environment. From their perspective, we are an object in their world. When we imaginatively adopt their perspective, we are able to see ourselves as an object. We develop self-awareness.

Once again we must be social before we can be individual. Until we interact with others whose roles we imaginatively take, we cannot develop a concept of ourselves as an object. We need others whose roles we take to provide the mirrors that tell us that we have a self and who we are. Immersion in sustained interaction with others is the only way we develop a mind and a self; it is the way we become human.

To have a self is to be capable of observations, judgments, and feelings about the self that only become possible by taking the role of the other. If we act in ways that surprise others (and ourselves), this demonstrates the capacity of the "I" to act in novel ways. If we explain such action by saying "I'm not myself today," we are displaying a fully developed self. The statement is logically ludicrous but sociologically sensible. We are saying that some momentary action is inconsistent with a well-established sense of who we are based on a long process of role taking. Only the "Me" can offer such observations about the self.

The "Me" is thus the perspective of others internalized by the self. The "Me" is a developmental product of interaction that emerges in stages. As infants in the pre-play stage, we are incapable of getting outside ourselves and taking the role of others. Infants are all "I" and no "Me." As young children, however, we begin to develop both a mind and the ability to take the role of the other. In the play stage, we take the role of significant others in our social environment. These are specific people who are familiar to us. As we play, we model their behavior and imaginatively see the world from their perspective. This is the earliest version of seeing ourselves as an object; by imaginatively seeing ourselves through the eyes of our parents or primary caretakers, we begin to develop a sense of self.

As we become more skilled at role taking, we enter the game stage and simultaneously take the roles of multiple others in more complex situations. The famous example is playing baseball, but any team sport will do. To play such games well, each player must anticipate the actions of everyone else on the team. By anticipating their actions in different situations, good players align their actions to fit with overall team strategy. Such game playing presupposes an ability to take multiple roles that only emerges over time. This is why young children can handle some interactive play but are incapable of more complex team games.

As we progress from taking the role of significant others to multiple others, we eventually take the role of the generalized Other. This is not a particular person or group but rather the larger society and its norms and values. Returning to Cooley's language, the development of the self proceeds by switching mirrors. As very young children, it is particular, significant others who provide the mirror that tells us who we are. As older children, it is multiple others who provide that mirror. As socialization continues, the mirror becomes all of the attitudes, values, and beliefs that compose our society itself. The constant is that we look outside ourselves to know who we are. The variable is which "others" are most central in reflecting our self back to us.

The ability to take the role of the generalized Other signals a fully developed self. This "Other" is initially outside us, but it becomes incorporated inside us in the form of the "Me." The mature self combines the acting "I" and the socialized "Me." Because the self requires a "Me" and the "Me" requires taking the role of the other, the self only emerges through social interaction with others.

The development of mind and self go hand in hand. The internal conversation that comprises the mind can only occur with a corresponding self-awareness that signifies a self. Both emerge through interaction with others that provides shared meanings and role-taking opportunities. Although later sociologists have pursued many variations on these themes, Mead's synthesis provides a vital sociological understanding of the relationship between self and society.

Symbolic Interactionism

Mead's student Herbert Blumer took the lead in publishing Mead's (1934) ideas. Blumer also coined the term *symbolic interactionism* to underscore the importance of symbolic meanings in interpreting human action. The phrase sounds awkward, but conveys much about the assumptions of this approach.

Blumer (1969) subsequently claimed that symbolic interactionism could be summarized in three basic premises. The first is that human beings act toward things on the basis of the meanings things have for them. What is important is not the things but rather the meanings that we (and others) attach to them.

This seemingly subtle distinction makes a big difference. Consider the contrast between psychological behaviorism and symbolic interactionism. Behaviorists explain what we do as responses to stimuli in the environment. The environment determines behavior by providing stimuli that mechanistically lead us to seek rewards and avoid punishments. The stimuli, response, rewards, and punishments are assumed to be transparently self-evident to both the organism and the behaviorist. There is no need to explore the subjective "black box" of the mind; behaviorism rather seeks an external explanation linking behavioral responses to environmental stimuli.

This makes sense if people respond directly to things. It makes much less sense if they respond to the meanings of things, as Blumer claims. Interactionism sees action as a process of self-indication. Actors select which aspects of their environment are meaningful for them. Because they assign meanings to their surroundings, it could be said that actors determine their environment rather than the other way around. Because meanings vary across persons and situations, we must examine how minds shape meanings. Interactionism thereby seeks an internal explanation of action by linking minds, meanings, and actions.

The first premise establishes that meanings are central. The second is that meanings are derived from social interaction. This locates meanings between two polar opposites. They are not purely objective qualities attached to things in the same way in all times and places. But they are also not purely subjective choices of individuals outside interaction. Meanings are rather intersubjective accomplishments of social interaction. Like Mead's significant symbols, objects acquire meanings as a result of ongoing social interaction.

This premise explains variability in the meanings of objects over time and across groups. Why do people disagree about the appropriateness of Indian mascots for sports teams? How do people interpret the meaning of the Civil War in the South and the North? What does the word *gay* mean to different generations of people? When is graffiti a marker of gang affiliation, and when is it art? What does it mean to have a tattoo or a piercing? Such meanings are not fixed and objective; neither are they purely subjective and idiosyncratic. It is interactions in different groups that define the "same event" like the Civil War as a humiliating defeat or a glorious victory. Both meanings are "true" in different social worlds that sustain those definitions through interaction.

The variability of meanings reflects the pragmatist heritage of symbolic interaction in which things acquire meaning by how they are used or how people interact with them. Thus, a tree has different meanings and becomes a different object for the botanist, the timber company, and the poet. Take another example. A woman nursing an infant is interacting in a way that defines her breasts as nourishment and nurturance. That same woman making love with her sexual partner is interacting in a way that defines her breasts as erotic stimulation and gratification. That same woman undergoing an exam by her doctor is engaged in an interaction that defines her breasts as potential sites of disease and malignancy. Same woman, same breasts—but drastically different meanings arise from different interactions with different people.

The ways that interactions create and sustain meanings also establish the definition of the situation. Such definitions are intersubjective, cultural creations that provide cues about what to expect and how to behave in a given situation. Differing definitions of the situation create different meanings in "objectively" similar situations. A woman who bares her breast in public to nurse her infant might meet with acceptance, whereas a woman who does so in a strip joint might be condemned or even arrested (depending on local ordinances). A male doctor examining a female patient is engaging in behavior that could be construed as sexual assault in other settings, but is regarded as normal as long as the medical definition of the situation is maintained.

Blumer's third and final premise is that meanings are handled and modified through an interpretive process. This means that even when meanings are well established (and especially when they are not), people still tailor them to the specific situation at hand. This work begins with the process of self-indication in which people "create" their environment on the basis of intersubjective meanings.

The process continues because no two situations are exactly the same and general meanings must be adapted to specific settings. People are active throughout this process. "The actor selects, checks, suspends, regroups, and transforms the meanings in the light of the situation in which he is placed" (Blumer 1969, 5). This process of interpretation is a formative one in which meanings are used, revised, and modified as the actor fashions action that will be meaningful to all concerned.

Blumer's formulation of symbolic interactionism puts it at odds not only with psychological behaviorism but also with more structural approaches in sociology. Blumer insists that concepts like structure, system, function, or institution are really shorthand abstractions lor people interacting with one another. Although the shorthand is convenient, it becomes a trap when we speak as if these abstractions act or even exist apart from the interactions that sustain them. For Blumer, good sociology avoids structuralist abstractions by focusing on the meanings and interactions that create, sustain, and modify social patterns.

Identity Theory

Interactionist theory provides sociology with its best understandings of identity. The starting point is that the self is the ability to see oneself as an object, evidenced by self-awareness or self-consciousness. This awareness originally emerges from, and subsequently depends on, interactions with other people.

We move from sell to identity by asking what kind of object we see ourselves to be. If self is the object, identity is the meanings attached to that object. Identity emerges when meanings are attached to the object we call the self.

Blumer's first premise is that it is not objects but their meanings that are important. This applies to identity as follows. Everybody acquires a self. We couldn't interact with people if they didn't have a self through which to organize interaction. What is of interest in interactions is not the generic selves everyone possesses, but the particular identities or meanings of those selves. This is how we identify ourselves and others; who people are is a function of the meanings or identities linked to selves.

Blumer's second premise is that meanings arise through interactions with others. They are intersubjective accomplishments. The same applies to the meanings we call identities. Just as Mead's symbols become significant when they call up the same meaning in others as they do in us, identities become real when there is a shared understanding about who someone is. "One's identity is established when others *place* him as a social object by assigning him the same words of identity that he appropriates for himself or *announces*. It is in the coincidence of placements and announcements that identity becomes a meaning of the self" (Gregory Stone, cited in Vryan, Adler, and Adler 2003, 368; italics in original).

Take an extreme example. I might believe, and then announce to the world, that I am the second coming of Christ. If I persist in this claim, I will be dismissed as a nutcase. If I convince a small band of devoted followers of my claim, we will all be dismissed as mentally unstable (but perhaps dangerous because of our numbers). But if I somehow convince hundreds, then thousands, and finally millions of people around the world of my identity claim, and they relate to me as if I am that person, then don't I become that person? If my announcements and others' placements concur, does that not become my identity? In less extreme cases, the process is clear: identity emerges when an actor's announcements and others' placements coincide.

Blumer's third premise is that meanings are handled and modified through an interpretive process as people tailor meanings to fit specific situations. Applied to identity, this means that we continually reinterpret, select, check, regroup, suspend, and transform our understandings of who we and others are as part of ongoing interaction. For example, we understand that people (including ourselves) have different identities in different situations. When we encounter them in a certain situation, we selectively present some of our identities and expect them to do the same. If everyone enacts identities appropriate to the situation, interaction will proceed smoothly.

Each of Blumer's premises about meaning thus applies to identity itself. Interactionism also distinguishes several types of identities, including social, situational, and personal identities (Vryan, Adler, and Adler 2003, 367–372).

Social identities arise when we announce and others place us in positions within social structures. Identities based on class, race, gender, religion, or sexual orientation exemplify social identities. They are broad social categories that link us to others with similar traits and separate us from those with different traits. Social identities shape how people are enabled or constrained by social order; differing opportunities emerge from the statuses granted to or withheld from these identities.

Situational identities arise when we engage in face-to-face interactions with others and organize our action through situationally appropriate roles and definitions of the situation. Although they might be repetitive and patterned, situations are relatively short-lived. When we attend a baseball game, we become a fan; when we go on vacation, we become a tourist; when we leave for work, we become a motorist or commuter. We thus acquire a situational identity in a particular context. The ways we enact this identity are constrained by cultural norms and situational definitions, but there is always room for some individual creativity in enacting situational identities.

Personal identities arise when we construct biographical narratives about who we are. They distinguish us from others in the same positions or situations. Thus, part of my story is that when I was an undergraduate, I made my living (and more) as a drummer in a rock-and-roll band. Even though I stopped playing when I went to graduate school more than thirty-five years ago, it is part of who I am, because it is who I once was. Moreover, it helps establish my distinctiveness: not many college professors are former rock drummers, and not many rock drummers become college professors (and it's probably just as well that they don't).

Situational identities like baseball fan, grocery shopper, or wedding party member are short-lived and don't necessarily reveal much about who we are. Social identities are more permanent because they are difficult or impossible to change, although people can either embrace them or hold them at arms' length. Personal identities are more lasting in a different way, because they rest on a person's accumulated biography. Although we can distinguish different types of identity, the basic principles of identity theory still apply. Identities of all types are meanings attached to the self that emerge through announcements by self and placements by others.

Like all meanings, identities are socially constructed, maintained, and transformed. Most identity transformations are gradual, developmental transitions through the life cycle. Even though parenthood or retirement might feel sudden to the individual, they are routine in that they happen to many people and it is possible to anticipate and plan for them in advance. Other, less common identity transformations are quick and radical in nature. When prisoners of war are brainwashed, when people undergo a conversion experience, or when individuals are radicalized by extremist websites, they might renounce former identities and embrace dramatically different ones very quickly.

Another type of identity transformation involves "suspended identity" (Schmid and Jones 1991). This occurs when people must leave one identity behind while adopting another identity. If they intend to reclaim their former identity, it is not so much terminated or transformed as it is suspended. It's as if they hang that identity in the closet until they can wear it once again. When citizen soldiers are called up as army reservists or National Guard troops, they suspend their citizen identity and adopt a soldier identity. Unlike regular army troops, however, they are likely to see their citizen identity as the "real" one, which is temporarily suspended during military duty.

A classic case is people who go to prison. Before going to prison, people have a "pre-prison identity." Like the civilian anticipating becoming a soldier, these citizens anticipate becoming a prisoner as they move through the criminal justice system. A common response is self-insulation by minimizing contact with others, avoiding conflict or violence, and avoiding any situations that might undermine their preprison identity.

Despite these resolutions, inmates cannot take their pre-prison identity with them, nor can they live in complete isolation. They have to create a prison identity to relate to staff, guards, and other prisoners. Short-term inmates see this prison identity as temporary and situational, although they worry that it might displace their pre-prison identity. While serving time, inmates experience a dualistic self. They try to sustain a pre-prison identity, which is temporarily suspended, privately held, and rarely affirmed. They simultaneously enact a prison identity, which is self-consciously learned, enacted for self and others, and affirmed through prison interactions.

Toward the end of their sentence, prisoners develop a release identity that sets aside their prison identity and revives their suspended identity. Like earlier stages, this involves much self-talk about who they really are, how they might have changed, and how they can become the person they used to be. Upon leaving prison, former inmates acquire a post-prison identity that distances them from their prison experience and helps restore their suspended identity (Schmid and Jones 1991).

Prison thereby poses a particular identity challenge. Although most of us will not go to prison, all of us undergo processes of identity formation, maintenance, and transformation. Interactionist theory provides powerful tools for understanding them.

People as Reflexive Actors

Interactionist theory underscores how human action is guided by reflexivity. People are conscious of the meanings of selves, others, and objects in their world, and they use this knowledge to organize actions and pursue goals. The premise of reflexivity is shared by other theoretical perspectives as well.

[...] There is a debate in sociology over the relationship between structure and agency. Structure-based approaches emphasize large social patterns that seem to dwarf individuals. Agency-based approaches stress individual choices and seem to deny the weight of external factors. Neither approach is completely satisfactory; the challenge is to strike a balance between the two.

One attempt is structuration theory (Giddens 1984). It rejects a view of structures as merely external and constraining forces that exist on their own. Rather than structures, it speaks of "structuration processes" as a way of linking structure and action. Here, structures are no more than the outcomes of past actions and the means for organizing current ones.

Seen this way, structuration processes sometimes constrain action because they are obstacles to what we want to do. But they can also enable action when they provide resources and means to pursue goals. Rather than seeing structures as external, controlling forces, we should see structuration processes as providing opportunities to act (within certain limits). Moreover, when people act, they unintentionally reproduce (and sometimes transform) those very structures.

This approach assumes people are reflexive actors. People in society "are vastly skilled in the practical accomplishments of social activities and are expert 'sociologists.' The knowledge they possess is not incidental to the persistent patterning of social life but integral to it" (Giddens 1984, 26). In other words, people routinely use practical consciousness in daily life to monitor their actions and the actions of others and to align both. This consciousness contains much practical knowledge about how things work in a particular society and culture.

People also incorporate sociological knowledge into practical consciousness; ideas like self-fulfilling prophecies, unintended consequences, or group-think have migrated from social science to everyday consciousness. It is difficult to appreciate the importance of this practical consciousness, because it becomes second nature once were socialized. But if you've had any experiences with other cultures or languages that made you feel "dumb," it underscores how "smart" you are about your own culture and language and how unconsciously you call upon knowledge of it to do things.

Another way of describing reflexivity is sociological competence. "This seemingly native, highly practical, virtually ubiquitous capacity sustains us individually, but it also contributes mightily to our ability to form and keep social relations with others. Without it, social life would be impossible. Without it, every time we entered a new and different social situation, we would be forced to learn anew what to think of it and how to behave. But, most of the time, we understand what is going on and where we fit in" (Lemert 2008, 5). Like linguistic competence, sociological competence seems to be an inherent capacity to understand the social world. When it is matched with socialization, we use it in an almost effortless way.

Although acquiring sociological competence is *almost* effortless, it nonetheless requires practice. Charles Lemert (2008) draws on Pierre Bourdieu's (1977) notion of habitus to understand how sociological competence is sustained through practice. The concept of habitus underscores how much of social life involves habitual actions that once had to be learned but then became second nature—things that we do unthinkingly, and usually quite competently. Like Giddens's structuration, Bourdieu's habitus is where agency and structure meet and their seeming contradiction is resolved. Habitual practices simultaneously result from social rules (structures) and individual flourishes (agency) that produce action (Lemert 2008, 43).

From another angle, habitus is the intersection between actions experienced as novel by the individual while simultaneously conforming to social patterns. This is most evident when we first learn things that have yet to become habitual. The first time we drive a car, have a sexual encounter, or work at a job, the event is new to us but part of a larger pattern that happens in roughly similar ways for millions of people. The awkwardness that characterizes each of these original experiences demonstrates that these competencies must indeed be learned and practiced. At a certain point, driving, sex, or working are accomplished with much less awkwardness, signifying that we have learned and habitualized them. We have acquired sociological competence.

In everyday life, we focus on immediate concerns. We rely on sociological competence and acquired habits. It rarely occurs to us that our actions help sustain the society around us. Nonetheless, habitual actions performed by socially competent actors do precisely this. Giddens's structuration, Lemert's competence, and Bourdieu's habitus all point to the same conclusion. Social order rests upon the reflexivity of actors who use existing structures to do things while simultaneously (if unintentionally) sustaining, re-creating, and transforming those very structures. Without reflexivity, social order itself would be impossible.

Conclusion

Interactionist theory provides rich insights into mind, self, identity, and reflexivity. It is a good example of humanistic sociology. As such, it is critical in two ways. First, it is critical to an accurate understanding of the complex, dialectical connections between self and society, structure and agency, and micro and macro levels of society.

Second, it is critical by revealing that things are not always what they appear to be (Berger 1963). If we want to see beyond appearances to underlying realities, this theory is like a backstage pass in the theater of social life. Consider individualism one more time. As noted earlier, US culture is probably the most individualistic in human history. If any culture assumes we are individual before we are social, it is ours. Interactionist theory is thus critical to seeing all the ways we are unavoidably social before we can become individual (Lemert 2008).

The third sense of critical sociology explicitly examines power, domination, exploitation, and oppression. Here, interactionism has been largely silent. It critically examines US individualism, but it uncritically accepts US egalitarianism.

US culture has always emphasized its distance from European traditions, where rank, status, class, and distinction are crucial. US ideology describes a "classless" society where everyone gets a chance and no one is held back by artificial social barriers. Although not necessarily embracing these specific ideas, interactionism's image of society also downplays vertical hierarchies and emphasizes horizontal life-worlds. The interactionist image of society is multiple social worlds of distinctive meanings and identities coexisting alongside one another. It implicitly sees society as a pluralistic conglomeration of such worlds.

What is lacking in this image is the role of power in social life. Although it is true that different social worlds construct different meanings, it is also true that some worlds have the privilege and power to make their meanings normative while marginalizing others. The meanings central to interactionist theory are often hierarchically organized so that some groups benefit at the expense of others.

This is nicely captured in the notion of ideology as meaning in the service of power (Thompson 1990). Interactionism has provided a rich vocabulary for analyzing meanings in social life, but it will only reach its fully critical potential when it examines the relationships between meaning and power.

References

Berger, Peter. 1963. *Invitation to Sociology.* New York: Doubleday.

Blumer, Herbert. 1969. *Symbolic Interaction: Perspective and Method.* Englewood Cliffs, NJ: Prentice Hall.

Bourdieu, Pierre. 1977. *Outline of a Theory of Practice.* London: Cambridge University Press.

Cooley, Charles Horton. 1998. *On Self and Social Organization.* Chicago: University of Chicago Press.

Giddens, Anthony. 1984. *The Constitution of Society.* Berkeley: University of California Press.

Lemert, Charles. 2008. *Social Things.* 4th ed. Lanham, MD: Rowman & Littlefield.

Mead, George Herbert. 1934/1962. *Mind, Self and Society.* Chicago: University of Chicago Press.

Reynolds, Larry T. 2003. "Early Representatives." In *Handbook of Symbolic Interactionism*, ed. Larry T. Reynolds and Nancy J. Herman-Kinney, 59–81. Lanham, MD: AltaMira.

Scheff, Thomas. 2005. "Looking Glass Self: Goffman as Symbolic Interactionist." *Symbolic Interaction* 28(2):147–166.

Schmid, Thomas J., and Richard S. Jones. 1991. "Suspended Identity: Identity Transformation in a Maximum Security Prison." *Symbolic Interaction* 14(4):415–432.

Simmel, Georg. 1908/1955. *Conflict and the Web or Group Affiliations.* New York: Free Press.

Thompson, John. 1990. *Ideology and Modern Culture.* Stanford, CA: Stanford University Press.

Vryan, Kevin D., Patricia A. Adler, and Peter Adler. 2003. "Identity." In *Handbook of Symbolic Interactionism*, ed. Larry T. Reynolds and Nancy J. Herman-Kinney, 367–390. Lanham, MD: AltaMira.

CHAPTER 5

Deviance and Crime

Chapter 5 examines social control and the characteristics of deviance and crime. In the first section of the chapter, Plume (2017) describes theories such as cultural transmission, differential association, and labeling theory to understand how society reacts to deviant or criminal behavior. The second section explores social control, crime and punishment, crime rates, trends in crime, and the demographics of crime including gender, age, social class, and race. Additionally, it examines various types of crime such as crimes against the person, crimes against property, victimless crimes, white-collar crimes, corporate crimes, organized crimes, hate crimes, and cyber-crimes. Finally, the purpose of the criminal justice system is addressed. This section also discusses who is more likely to be in prison as well as biases against people of color and the poor.

Staying Within the Lines

Social Control, Deviance, and Crime

Mark Plume

Eternal Love

In his book *Undying Love*, Ben Harrison (1997) documents the strange case of Carl Tanzler, a Key West radiology technician who became so obsessed with one of his tuberculosis patients, Maria Elena Milagro de Hoyos, that after her death, he stole her remains and brought them to his home, where he dressed, serenaded, and made love to her. It was reported that Tanzler's love for Maria was unrequited. This fact did not deter Tanzler from visiting her grave nightly before finally stealing her remains two years after she died in October 1931. Tanzler said that the dead Maria would speak to him and beg him to take her remains. For seven years, Tanzler kept her corpse in his bed, where he applied makeup to her, dressed her, and even had sex with her. Ultimately, Maria's sister, Florinda, caught wind of the creepy behavior and had Tanzler arrested. He was charged with "wantonly and maliciously destroying a grave and removing a body without authorization." Note that he was not charged with necrophilia—having sex with a dead body. Do you consider this deviant behavior?

Have you ever told a lie? Of course you have. I asked that question in my class one time, and I actually had a student raise her hand and insist that she had never told a lie—she was in her mid-thirties. Do you think she could have made it to that point in her life without telling a lie? Could you go twenty-four hours without telling a lie? Try it! From time to time in our lives, we all commit minor transgressions—lying, jaywalking, being late for class, cheating on an exam. From the sociological perspective, we have all violated standards of conduct or social norms, making us all deviants at various points in our lives. Therefore, before you judge someone's actions as deviant, you might want to step back and use your sociological imagination and consider the social forces and circumstances that may have influenced his behavior. It is not about judging deviance; it is about exploring and understanding its complex nature.

Figure 5.1 Carl Tanzler. States have not always had laws prohibiting sex with corpses (much like Florida didn't in 1933). Currently, all fifty states have statutes that prohibit sex acts with human corpses, which illustrates the dynamic nature of deviance—as norms change, so does our interpretation of deviance. However, to this day, there is no federal law that prohibits sex with a corpse.

While we *all* violate society's rules occasionally, the vast majority of us would not rise to the extreme that Mr. Tanzler did. Necrophilia, or having sex with a dead person, is considered a violation of the norms of our culture—most Americans would find it rather disgusting. In fact, it would be considered criminally deviant. For sociologists, **deviance** refers to the violation of social norms. Therefore, strictly speaking, *all crime is deviance*, but *not all deviance is crime*. That is, **crime**—the violation of formal norms or *laws*—by its definition is deviance. However, there are a number of behaviors, traits, and beliefs that do not violate laws but are still viewed as deviant.

Take for example NAMBLA; the North American Man/Boy Love Association is a group that promotes love and consensual sex between men and boys, which the organization refers to as "intergenerational relationships." NAMBLA is a self-described political, civil rights, and educational organization that supports the rights of youth and adults to "... choose the partners they wish to share and enjoy their bodies with." Its focus is reforming age of consent laws, which it interprets as a form of ageism. It opposes these laws and "... all other restrictions which deny men and boys the full enjoyment of their bodies and control over their own lives." Furthermore, it feels that these laws unfairly criminalize men and boys who engage in consensual sexual relationships. It promotes and condones only consensual relationships, and it also clearly states that the organization does not engage in any behavior that violates the law and does not advocate that anyone else should (NAMBLA, 2011). Wow. This organization and its views would be seen by most as deviant in that its beliefs are far outside our cultural perspectives on children and sexuality. While not criminal, this organization and its beliefs are clearly deviant.

I should point out that it is not the function of sociology to make moral judgments about the beliefs or behaviors of individuals or groups, but rather social judgments. When we use the term *deviant,* we are simply recognizing that the belief or behavior violates a social norm of a particular group at a particular time. I am not using the term to indicate some flaw in one's moral character; when I refer to deviance, I am pointing out that some behavior or belief has violated a standard of conduct or a social convention. In American society, the mentally ill, those living as vampires, and people who identify as furries would all be considered deviants.

Some Characteristics of Deviance

Deviance Depends on the Social Context

While actions in one social situation may be normal, they may be seen as deviant in another. If you come home after a long day of work and school and grab some food and a beer from the fridge, sit down, prop your feet up on the table, start eating with your hands, and let out a nice, long burp, that would be completely acceptable. These same behaviors would be seen as rude and unacceptable at an upscale restaurant.

Deviance Can Be a Trait, Belief, or Behavior

Your behaviors are not the only things that may be viewed as deviant. Holding socially unacceptable views like being an atheist or a Satan worshipper can bring unfavorable reactions from others. A physical deformity, skin color, or a physical disability can also marginalize people by labeling them as deviant.

Perceptions of Deviance Can Change Over Time: The Fluidity of Deviance

It is important to remember that as sociologists, we view deviance as dynamic. That is, we understand that deviance is learned in the context of a culture; therefore, deviance is interpreted differently between cultures. We also understand that deviance changes over time within cultures.

So, why was necrophilia at one point in our history not illegal? Why is it prohibited in nearly all states now? Why is it deviant in our culture but allowed in other cultures? If deviance is defined by social norms, and norms change over time, then what we consider deviant changes over time. In addition, needless to say, deviance is viewed differently from place to place. Therefore, the violation of or deviation from social norms is bounded by culture. As social norms change over time within a culture, the definition of their violation—deviance—also changes.

For example, at one time in the U.S., you could have been diagnosed as mentally ill for being gay. The American Psychiatric Association (APA) removed homosexuality from the Diagnostic and Statistical Manual (DSM: the standard classifications for mental disorders used by mental health professionals) in 1973, but it took until 1986 to get the remaining references out of the DSM (American Psychiatric Association, 1975, 1987). No thinking person today believes that gay men or women are suffering from some sort of mental illness. Being gay has moved from marginalizing people for having a psychiatric condition to all states recognizing same-sex marriages. Being gay in America has moved from being viewed as deviant to being a widely accepted sexual orientation.

When my father went into the military, he was encouraged to smoke cigarettes; today, there are entire campuses, businesses, and cities that are smoke-free. Smokers in many parts of the country have to huddle in the cold and wet weather as they smoke their cigarettes fifty feet away from the building in which they work. Smoking has gone from being ubiquitous in our culture fifty years ago to being viewed as one of our greatest health risks. On average, 40% of adults reported being smokers during the 1970s; now, about 18% of U.S. adults claim to be smokers (Saad, 2008; Centers for Disease Control, "Current Cigarette Smoking," 2015). Fifty years ago, it was completely acceptable to smoke on planes, at work, in the classroom, on TV, and in hospitals! Smoking has moved from a mainstream behavior to one that can be viewed as deviant. Our constantly changing set of social norms creates a fluidity of deviance.

Deviance Varies Across Cultures

Our standard of normal may be very different from the standards of other cultures. What kind of society would allow women to leave their infant children with complete strangers in a non-home environment for more than eight hours a day? Well, Americans do it about 6.7 million times a day. About 33% of households with children under the age of five use non-relative childcare facilities (Laughlin, 2013). Most cultures of the world would view this practice as deviant (bordering on reprehensible); they would assume that childcare would be the duty of blood relatives, kin, fictive kin, or a known, trusted member of the community. However, in the U.S., this is completely acceptable and a practice that serves our social needs.

Food serves as another good example. Food choices in many ways help define a culture. Food is one of the most powerful ways that cultures define themselves. Some cultures do not eat meat, some see eating dogs as acceptable, and many cultures practice entomophagy (eating insects). Food can be one of the most distinguishing characteristics of a culture and what separates it from other social groups.

What if someone opened a restaurant in your town that served only animal penises? While we have quite an eclectic palate in the states, a penis restaurant would be viewed as odd and maybe a bit off-putting by many. However, if you would like some boiled, sautéed, fried, and even baked penis, all you have to do is travel to Beijing, China (Deemer, 2012). There, the Guolizhuang restaurant will serve you the penises of a variety of animals as well as stewed deer face, sheep fetus in a brown garlic sauce, and peacock claws! Eating body tokens (foods that resemble male genitalia) such as snakes and rhinoceros horns was a common practice for millennia by the people of many cultures (Orth, 2008; Zhao, 2015). Therefore, eating the actual penis or testicles of large or ferocious animals is viewed as a more potent way to imbue an individual with powers of potency and fertility as well as strength. While this is completely understandable in the context of the Chinese culture, it is deviant by our standards (Kahn, 1993; Simoons, 1990). Men in our culture simply take a little blue pill.

Figure 5.2 Bull penis with rice. Probably not something you find on restaurant menus in your neighborhood, but commonly consumed in some cultures due to its properties of male strength and virility.

Deviance Is Constructed by Dominant Groups

In society today, there are groups that have the power to label others as deviant, such as those in the judicial system, the penal system, the media, wealthy people and politicians. Sound familiar? Those who are most invested and have the most power in society have the power to decide which individuals and groups are labeled as deviant. Let's take a quick look at how black men are over-criminalized in our judicial system here in America, for example. There are more African American adults under correctional control today—in prison or jail, on probation or parole—than were enslaved in 1850, a decade before the Civil War began (Alexander, 2012). The over-criminalization of black men in the U.S. by a powerful, mainly white, justice system has acted to marginalize this population and drive into the American psyche the image of the young black male thug.

A Restaurant That Only Serves Penises

Guolizhuang is a Beijing restaurant that exclusively serves the penises of a number of animal species. You can get snake penis, yak penis, deer penis, and even seal penis. These delicacies are served in a variety of ways: in broth, stir-fried, baked, and raw. (Orth, 2008.) Food is one of the most obvious ways that cultures define themselves, and constructing food norms is part of that definition. In China, where there is a long tradition of imbuing foods with specific spiritual and physical benefits, the penises of various animals are said to be potent agents for healing an array of conditions or illnesses. (Zhao, 2015.) Would a restaurant like this fly in your neck of the woods? Why or why not? What would be the reason for resistance?

Deviance is not absolute: **There Are No Absolutes (Except that there are no absolutes!?)**

> *"No act is inherently deviant in and of itself. Deviance is defined socially and will vary from one group to another."* —Emile Durkheim

This is one of my favorite quotes because I believe it is true. If deviance were an absolute, we would see the same traits, behaviors, and beliefs labeled as deviant in every culture of the world. However, we do not. Pedophilia, bestiality, incest, and necrophilia are not inherently deviant. These acts have been and are currently practiced by a number of cultures around the world. Therefore, this variation in cultural practices shows us that deviance is relative to time and place. In a cultural vacuum, these acts are just acts like walking, running, or sleeping. However, none of us lives in a cultural vacuum; we live in cultures that have developed a set of rules whose transgressions carry consequences, such as being viewed as deviant. Deviance, then, is relative to *where* and *when* you are.

Can Deviance Be Good for Us?

When you hear the word deviance, what thought or image jumps to mind? Is it something negative? Deviance does have a negative connotation for most people, typically conjuring up images of traits or behaviors that are viewed to be annoying, disgusting, dangerous, or even immoral (Kooistra and Harrison, 2007). However, deviance can be viewed differently. Emile Durkheim (1893) saw deviance as a natural and necessary part of society. Our man Durkheim lays out four ways in which deviance and crime can act as mechanisms to reinforce social order and bring about social change:

Deviance Can Affirm Cultural Values and Norms

Understanding that deviance can result in punishment reinforces what a society views as acceptable or unacceptable. When criminals are sent to prison, our culturally held values that crime is unhealthy for society are affirmed. While we recognize that deviance will be part of our social world, we also believe that it will be dealt with appropriately so that it does not threaten or diminish our way of life.

Deviance Defines Moral Boundaries

I think most people would respect the funeral of a fallen soldier. Regardless of your political views, funerals are typically a solemn and private event. However, the Westboro Baptist Church (WBC) regularly protests the funerals of soldiers and Marines while brandishing banners that read "Thank God for Dead Soldiers," "Soldiers Die 4 Fag Marriage," "Thank God for Sept. 11," and "God Hates America." This church is filled with hate, but Durkheim sees a purpose in its madness. Most people would find all of these slogans morally reprehensible, seeing them as crossing some unspoken moral boundary.

Therefore, the deviant vitriol of this organization creates a sort of moral boundary that most Americans are not willing to cross, clearly creating two groups of people: *us*—who would not engage in hate speech and defile funerals, and *them*—deviants who are willing to defile funerals, inflict emotional injury on grieving loved ones, and spew venomous hate speech. These WBC people are whack jobs. They believe that the fallen soldiers are "... troops whom God has killed in Iraq/Afghanistan in righteous judgment against an evil nation," meaning that because we as a nation do not condemn or put gay people to death and we support gay marriage and gay rights, God will punish us by killing our troops—you read it right (Westboro Baptist Church, 2016). Moreover, they believe God is getting back at gay-loving America by killing soldiers, who deserve to die because we as a nation have chosen human rights over some vengeful God. What rock did they climb out from under?

Deviance Can Promote Social Unity or Solidarity

That is, deviance and/or criminal acts can foster the feeling of us vs. them. In our history, there have been two glaring instances of deviance that created a sense of solidarity among Americans. The attack on Pearl Harbor and September 11, 2001, were both monstrous criminal acts perpetrated against America. In the aftermath of both of these events, Americans came together in variety of ways to show their unity. In the wake of Pearl Harbor, Americans expressed their solidarity in a variety of ways, such as record numbers of men and women volunteering for military service, conserving food and needed materials, and watching what they said and whom they said it to. During World War II, many Americans would not buy any German products, and some went as far as not eating frankfurters (the German term for the hot dog).

After the 9/11 attacks, I remember seeing more American flags than I had ever seen before: people were flying them in front of their homes, some firefighters raised a flag at ground zero that very day, and it seems like everyone had American flag stickers on their cars. Some stores had a hard time keeping American flags in stock for some time after 9/11.

Deviance Can Lead to Social Change

On December 1, 1955, Rosa Parks boarded a Montgomery, Alabama, bus and headed home after another long day of work. The white section of the bus was full, and the bus driver ordered Parks to give up her seat in the colored section to a white male, but she refused. She was subsequently arrested for the violation of a local segregation code but was tried on charges of disorderly conduct as well as violating the local code. Her arrest and trial led to the Montgomery bus boycott. In fact, just over a year after her arrest, on December 21, 1956, Montgomery buses were legally integrated. Her act of defiance, her recognition that some laws are unjust, and her being just flat-out tired of being mistreated as a human, set in motion a movement that was eventually successful in striking down Jim Crow laws, and culminated in the passing of the Civil Rights Act of 1964.

How Do We Explain Deviance?

For a long time, many people have attempted to explain deviance. What have emerged are a number of discredited theories and a number that have persisted. These attempts to explain deviance can be placed into four basic categories: the supernatural, biological, psychological, and sociological.

Supernatural Explanations of Deviance

For millennia, deviant behaviors were explained by spiritual temptation or possession. The belief that spirits, angels, and especially the devil actively influenced the lives of men, women, and children and were the explanations for a host of phenomena, including crop failure, illness, and witchcraft, helped define deviance until the modern era. The Bible is filled with examples of individuals who are described as suffering a range of afflictions, and their deviance is attributed to God's wrath, blasphemy, or demonic possession—all supernatural explanations.

This supernatural or spiritual world was real and a part of everyday life for the inhabitants of 1692 Salem, Massachusetts, where twenty people were executed for being witches. Unbelievably, twenty innocent people were either hanged or pressed (stones placed on top of the person until he was crushed to death) because of fear and supernatural explanations of deviant behavior, specifically witchcraft (Wilson, 1997). People, mostly women, were routinely accused of witchcraft, and once labeled as witches, the women either confessed or denied the accusations. Oddly enough, those who confessed to being witches were not tried and lived out their lives marginalized from the community or simply moved away. Those who proclaimed their innocence (because they were) rarely escaped the hangman. (Contrary to popular belief, no witches were ever burned to death in the colonies).

Wow, glad we're done with that nonsense, right? Think again: witch-hunts are still around. In Ghana, West Africa, there a number of *witch camps* that house hundreds of women that have been accused of being witches or blamed for the death of family members or other villagers (Whitaker, 2012). They are believed to have supernatural powers that have resulted in injury, death, or the outbreak of disease. Their punishment for their perceived deviant behavior is banishment to the camps. Apparently, we still fear what we do not understand, and moreover, some still seek an irrational supernatural explanation.

Biological Explanations of Deviance

Phrenology, or the study of the shape and size of one's skull to determine character and personality, was an attempt by Victorian-age pseudoscientists to map the mind. A phrenologist would run his hands over the skull, feeling the indentations and enlargements, and from this assessment determine the relative size of the various regions of the mind and determine the temperament and character of the individual. Then, a map of one's skull would be drawn, illustrating the location and relationship between all the regions. It was further believed by phrenologists that through this process, they could determine criminal or deviant tendencies in people. Ultimately, this

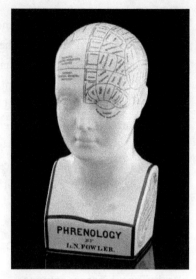

Figure 5.3 Fowler's Phrenological Head

practice was shown to be meritless and has been completely discredited. It should be noted that while they could not predict criminal intentions, phrenologists advocated rehabilitating criminals rather than warehousing them, which was a progressive idea at that time.

Body Types

In the 1940s, a psychologist named William Herbert Sheldon (1954) attempted to predict criminal or deviant behavior based on an individual's body type. That's right, he believed that for each of his designated body types, there was a set of corresponding personality characteristics—intelligence, temperament, and moral worth—that were set in genetic stone, as it were, unwavering over the life span. Basically, this guy thought he could tell who you were as a person from looking at the shape of your body. Body type as destiny? Sheldon proposed three body types (somatotypes):

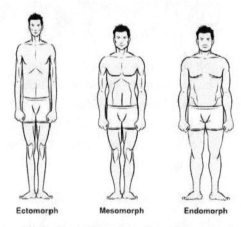

- *Ectomorph*: Tall and thin with a flat chest, lightly muscled with a delicate build.
- *Mesomorph*: Muscular, rectangular shape with thick skin and an upright posture.
- *Endomorph*: Short and corpulent with underdeveloped muscles and a round shape.

Figure 5.4 Sheldon's Three Body Types. Believed to be associated with temperament, personality characteristics and propensity toward crime. Does your body type influence your personality or world view?

Sheldon proposed that mesomorphs were far more likely to engage in delinquency and have criminal tendencies. However, there really is no sound scientific evidence to show a significant connection between one's body shape and a propensity to engage in deviant or criminal behaviors. Sheldon's longtime research assistant even went as far as to claim that Sheldon fudged his data, falsifying data to fit his theory. Sheldon held both a Ph.D. and an M.D., which seemed to legitimize his work until a female freshman complained to her parents about his data collection methods, which began his rapid descent into scientific disgrace. Fortunately, his work has been discredited and viewed by many as quackery. While his science was crap, there could be a grain of truth in it (Butler et al., 1992; Vertinsky, 2007). Do you think that body shape and attractiveness can influence how others perceive us and how we view ourselves?

Table 5.1 Sheldon's Body Types and Personality Characteristics

Body Type	Temperament
Endomorph	Sociable, fun-loving, love of food, tolerant, even-tempered, good-humored, relaxed, a love of comfort, and the need for affection. Endomorphs are gregarious and just like to chill.
Ectomorph	Self-conscious, private, introverted, inhibited, socially anxious, artistic, intense, emotionally restrained, and thoughtful. Ectomorphs are uptight, private people.
Mesomorph	Adventurous, courageous, indifferent to what others think, assertive, bold, physically active, competitive, desire to dominate and engage in risky activities. Mesomorphs are outgoing, action-oriented people whom Sheldon thought of as criminal types.

Try This

For each of your friends or other people you know well, consider what body type they would be, and then see if their personalities or temperaments match up to characteristics listed for their body type in Table 5.1 above. You really shouldn't see a strong association between the characteristics listed and your friends' personalities. You can see that many of the traits listed are vague or traits that we all possess—like the need for affection—regardless of our body type.

Take a look at the characteristics Sheldon associated with each body type. Do we hold stereotypes about certain body types? Are large people viewed as lazy and unhappy? Are mesomorphs viewed as more competent and likable? Do you think your friends or family members are stereotyped by their

Nude Posture Photo Project

How did Sheldon collect data on body types? For decades, he and a colleague, Earnest Albert Hooton, took nude photos of incoming freshmen at a number of Ivy League schools and affiliated colleges, amassing thousands of nude pics. The nude "posture photo" program began, independently of Sheldon's research, around the turn of the twentieth century. It was ostensibly designed to determine the goodness of students' posture, thought at the time to be a key indicator of health. Sheldon and Hooton hijacked that program to collect data for their body type theory. Yep, college freshmen were required to strip naked and be photographed from the front, in profile, and behind as part of freshman orientation. What would you say if you were told to strip naked for freshman orientation? Hell no! If that wasn't creepy enough, at least two past presidents, a number of celebrities, and other notable Americans whose names you would easily recognize were photographed nude during that period. The program was finally discontinued in the 1970s. For decades, rumors abounded that the photos and/or their negatives had been stolen and were being circulated. Not to worry: the nude pics were located and destroyed by either the respective colleges or the Smithsonian Institution, which mysteriously acquired some of them (Rosenbaum, 1995).

body shape? Do people come to be who they are in part because of how people perceive what they are like because of their body shape?

The Extra Y Chromosome Theory

Along similar lines, researchers looking for a connection between our biology and criminal behavior proposed the extra Y chromosome theory. This theory attempted to show a connection between men who possessed an extra Y chromosome (XYY versus XY) and a propensity for criminal behavior. The condition known as 47, XYY or so-called "supermale syndrome" was believed to be linked to violent criminal behavior due to hyper-aggressiveness. Therefore, many researchers thought these men would be found in greater numbers among violent offender populations. Well, it is not that simple. The best evidence indicates that while these 47, XYY males may be taller on average than XY males and slightly more aggressive, they do not have a higher incidence of violent behavior toward others (Beckwith and King, 1974; Beckwith, 2002; Jacobs, 2006).

While there is slightly increased criminality among 47, XYY males, it tends to manifest in crimes against property and rarely against people. The real explanation is most likely not in the simple connection between aggression in 47, XYY males and criminality (even regular XY males in prison exhibit higher levels of aggression than the general population), but rather in a more complex connection between lower IQs, behavioral issues, and criminal behavior among the 47, XYY population. Being overtly taller than their classmates and suffering from severe acne (common among 47, XYY males) may compound any behavioral or cognitive issues these adolescent males already exhibit, leading to impulse control, poor judgment, and, ultimately, to deviant or criminal behavior. However, this is very likely the same set of circumstances and characteristics that predict criminality for all populations (Gardner, Griffiths, and Hamelin, 2012; Ratcliffe, 1994; Walzer, Bashir, and Silbert, 1990). The overwhelming majority of 47, XYY males live out normal lives, oblivious to their condition. Therefore, the extra Y chromosome theory provides no real explanation for criminal behavior.

Psychological Explanations of Deviance

Unlike supernatural explanations for deviant behaviors, psychological explanations seek to understand deviance as pathology of the individual and not some spiritual or demonic force controlling the individual. There are a range of psychological theories attempting to explain deviance. Some invoke psychic struggles, others show us that missteps in developmental stages lead to pathologies, and still others reduce it to reward and punishment.

Basically, Freud argued that all humans are in a psychological struggle between two opposing forces: our *id*, or our base impulses for food, sex, and pleasure, and our *superego*, the internalized understanding of our society's rules and conduct for satisfying those impulses. Freud believed that we are all involved in this grand psychic struggle between satisfying our immediate impulses to have sex and poop and realizing that we have to wait until we get home to our partner to have sex and use a toilet. Typically, those individuals who cannot control their impulses end up engaging in any number of deviant acts such as rape, murder, or pooping on your front lawn. Many experience severe consequences of their actions, such as ending up in prison or dead.

Sociological Perspectives

Bumps on your head, your body type, and the possession of an extra Y chromosome do not provide valid or adequate explanations of deviance. In addition, while psychological approaches to deviance can be useful and provocative, observing the inner workings of the human mind is difficult, making the connection to deviance sometimes hard to establish. So, where can we look for some strong explanations of deviance? Sociology, of course! The following are some theories commonly used to explain deviance from the sociological perspective.

Cultural Transmission

A culture of deviance can be transmitted and is learned through interactions with others. Individuals who grow up and live in deviant subcultures/communities come to adopt the behaviors, beliefs, and values of those groups. If engaging in criminal behaviors are common and necessary ways for

- *The Cultural Matrix* by Orlando Patterson (2015). This work explores the complex world of urban black youths and how both structure and their crime-filled neighborhood cultures interplay with their own decisions to engage in crime. The book explores cultural transmission theory with an ear to hearing the voice of these urban youths. It's not just the environment; they make conscious choices and know that their values, attitudes, and actions are not the same as the dominant culture.

people in a particular subculture/community to survive, make a living, and provide for their families, then it will be viewed as normative for that group. Younger members are then socialized into this community of criminals and hustlers—to a certain degree, they are products of their environments; the culture of deviance has been learned through a range of experiences and interactions.

Shaw and McKay (1942) were two pretty smart cats who noticed that the high-crime areas of Chicago remained the same year after year. They found that as one ethnic group moved out of a high-crime area, another one took its place, then juvenile delinquency rates for the new group climbed, and the relocated group saw a drop in delinquency. Many young Latinos in Los Angeles grow up in neighborhoods where gang activity is bound up in the daily lives of its members. Criminal activity is a way of life, viewed as necessary for survival, and is transmitted from one generation of gang bangers to another (Parra, 2001).

Differential Association

The primary conduit for the transmission of these criminal values, beliefs, and behaviors is in peer groups. This process is illustrated by Edwin Sutherland's (1947) theory of **differential association**—association with intimate groups that are engaged in criminal behavior will result in members' conformity to the values, beliefs, and behaviors of that group. Deviant values, beliefs, and behaviors are learned in context of intimate groups. Like me, Sutherland understood that people have a basic desire to fit in. That desire to be accepted by a group leads to conformity. No one hangs out with a group of people hoping she/he will be rejected—"Oh, I can't wait until these people I like don't accept me" is not something you hear people say!

So, if you are hanging out with a bunch of people involved in computer hacking, at some point you will conform to the behavior and ultimately be accepted by that group. The *differential* in this theory alludes to the notion that if you associate with *different* crowds, you will get different results. Think about the distinctive groups that could be identified in your high school: the stoners, the jocks, band geeks, student government types. Kids who hang out with the stoners are at one point going to have to smoke pot to be accepted by them and become a stoner. However, the kid who associates with the student government kids will most likely raise her grades, run for office, and conform to the more mainstream dominant norms of the school.

Labeling Theory: Primary Deviance, Secondary Deviance, and Stigma

She's a "ho" and he's a "playa." People are often labeled by others, which can many times result in negative social consequences. Rooted in symbolic interactionism, labeling theory argues that deviance exists once the label of deviance has been applied: "… deviance is *not* a quality of the act the person commits, but rather a consequence of the application by others of rules and sanctions to an 'offender.' The deviant is one to whom the label has successfully been applied; deviant behavior is behavior that people so label" (Becker, 1963).

That is a great quote, but what is Becker saying here? Basically, that no behavior and no one is deviant until a label of deviance has been applied to the behavior or person. **Labeling theory** has three main parts: (1) people are deviant once they have been labeled as deviant, (2) deviant labels can affect the way labeled individuals view themselves and how others view them, and (3) deviant labels are applied by those with social power. Think about it in terms of our discussion earlier in the chapter about the relative nature of deviance (nothing is inherently deviant). Deviance for labeling theorists is like beauty: it is in the eye of the beholder (Simmons, 1969).

Labeling theorists believe that until the group labels a person as deviant, neither the act nor the person are deviant, but once labeled, others' negative reaction to the label, and therefore their reaction to the person, can cause the individual to alter his self-perception and continue the deviant behavior. **Primary deviance**—deviant acts that elicit little reaction from others and have little to no effect on one's self-image—are minor norm violations that we all engage in frequently (Lemert, 1972). For instance, many of us are guilty of a number of minor infractions such as speeding, littering, or jaywalking. If you are speeding and littering and not being ticketed (which happens to many of us), this is not altering your self-image, and others aren't shouting out "there goes that litterer" when you walk by. Typically, we rationalize our behavior, telling ourselves we were speeding to get to class on time and that jaywalking when no cars are approaching saves us time.

However, habitually engaging in behaviors like drug abuse, heavy drinking, or sexual promiscuity so that "others take notice" will get us labeled as a tweaker, alcoholic, or ho. Once the label of deviance has been applied, people react negatively toward the individual, which may lead the individual to adopt a deviant identity. Thus, **secondary deviance** occurs when labeled individuals accept the label as part of their own identity, which leads them to act in ways that are consistent with others' expectations (Lemert, 1951).

A **stigma** is a powerful, negative social label that leads individuals to be devalued, discredited, and socially rejected. Stigmatized individuals experience negative social treatment that greatly impacts their self-concept. While stigmas can be the result of criminal activity, such as "sex offender," "felon," "rapist," or "pedophile," many other social groups are stigmatized for just being themselves. Erving Go˙man (1963) identified three types of stigma: Physical, group identity, and character trait. *Physical stigma* refers to a physical deformity or defect, such as people with Down syndrome, amputees, and the blind. Many disabled people report a feeling of social isolation because of their physical disability. They feel as though they are irrationally stigmatized by nondisabled people, making it doubly hard to interact with others and feel socially included (Weiss, Ramakrishna, and Somma, 2006; Kittle, 2011). Stigmas, then, are labels that are so powerful they can prevent people from fully participating in society. Many times, stigmatized individuals are pushed to the margins of society, isolated, and discriminated against.

Group identity stigmas come from being a member of a particular religion, race, ethnic group, etc. Unfortunately, some people are stigmatized not for deviant or criminal behaviors, but simply being born a particular race or affiliating with a certain religion.

*Character trait stigma*s include things such as mental illness, drug addiction, alcoholism, and criminal background. Character trait stigmas might include labels such as "sex offender," "drunk" or "junkie." Stigmatized individuals come to accept their deviant identity and many times resign themselves to that identity. They experience a "self-fulfilling prophecy," assuming behaviors that are consistent with their stigma. Let's take my boy Jonathan for example.

Jonathan, who comes from a working-class family, was caught smoking pot when he was seventeen by his parents, and while they were a bit upset, they realized that he was just experimenting, and it was, after all, the 1970s. No police were involved, and it was dismissed as an innocent juvenile behavior typical of the times. At age twenty-three, Jonathan was arrested for brewing up some methamphetamines; he was tried, convicted, and sent inside for seven years. When he got out and returned to his hometown, he found it difficult to get work because he was labeled as a felon and drug dealer. As a result of not being able to find straight work, he started dealing drugs again. He figured if everyone was going to treat him like a drug dealer, he was going to be a drug dealer; besides, no one would hire him, and he had to make a living. This criminal label affected the way people reacted to and interacted with him, and it profoundly changed the way he viewed himself.

Central to the labeling perspective is the idea of power. That is, those with social power can determine what actions are labeled as deviant and who is more likely to be labeled. As painful as it may be, let's go back to high school again. Remember earlier in the chapter, we identified a number of social groups or cliques in our high schools like the jocks and geeks, etc. High schools, like human societies, have dominant cultures. In high school, those with power in the dominant culture are the most popular, high-achieving, good-looking kids. Let's call them the *pleasers*. The pleasers decide what "cool" is and what "uncool" (deviance) is. This group is the arbiter of cool and has the power to label others as uncool or deviant. For example, one of the pleasers comes to school wearing his clothes inside out, and they all think it is hilarious and creative—a statement to the absurdity of the fashion industry and how we are all just slaves to fashion.

Soon after that, a few of the stoners come to school wearing their clothes inside out, and a number of the pleasers notice and ridicule them for how stupid they look, telling them that they are so stoned they can't dress properly. Other groups will most likely join in deriding the stoners because the pleasers set the standards of deviance by having the power to label others, and members of other groups do not want to take the chance of being painted with the same brush of ridicule and embarrassment.

However, within each of the social groups we identified at our high schools, there is typically a hierarchy of power. So, even within these groups, there are members who have the power to label other members as deviant—especially if they stray from what the group considers cool. A stoner who refuses to skip school to get high one day in order to take an exam may be labeled as teacher's pet by others in the group and possibly be ostracized or given the silent treatment for a few days because he violated the expected behaviors of the group.

Social Control

Above, I discussed a variety of theories that attempt to explain how people come to be viewed as deviant and/or engage in deviant behaviors—essentially, explanations of how people come to be deviant. While that's necessary to explore, to me, it is not nearly as interesting as how most of us will not engage in any seriously deviant or criminal behavior over our lifetimes. Sure, like we discussed above, from time to time we all engage in "primary deviance," minor infractions that do not draw attention from others and do not affect our self-image: a little underage drinking here, a little littering there, and maybe a bit of drunk texting.

What is more interesting is how most people will do what I refer to as "color within the lines." Remember that as a kid, your parents and teachers would praise or reward you for coloring within the lines of the images in your coloring books. You were encouraged to color within the lines because everyone told you that was the right way to color. Moreover, most of us learned to color within the lines because we sought praise and came to believe it was the right thing to do.

Social control involves the social processes and practices that promote conformity and obedience among members of society. Social control, then, encourages all of us to stay within the lines of normative boundaries. There are a number of mechanisms at work in society that lead us to believe that we are doing the right thing and to act according to those beliefs. Social control comes both from within all of us and from influences outside of all of us. People learn how to navigate their social worlds through learning and accepting appropriate beliefs and behaviors—the process of socialization. The internalization of social values and beliefs is necessary for individuals to conduct themselves in socially appropriate ways and ultimately to be integrated, productive citizens who conform to societal norms—they *fit in*.

Like the renowned criminologist Travis Hirschi (1969), I prefer *not* to ask the criminal why she/he does crime, but why the great majority of us *do not* do crime. The answer for Hirschi can be found in the pro-social bonds we form with others and our communities. In his *social bond/social control theory*, he argued that bonds are responsible for controlling us when we are tempted to engage in criminal or deviant behavior. He said that these bonds come in four interconnected forms:

Attachment: The strong social attachments we create with others, communities, and institutions encourage conformity to social norms. Throughout our lives, we establish a number of emotional attachments to others—our parents, friends, our neighborhood, and romantic partners. These attachments, in turn, constrain our behavior because we do not want to disappoint our loved ones or lose the relationships we have with them by committing crimes. Have you ever thought to yourself, "My mom/dad would be so mad with me if I (insert deviant act/crime)"? These thoughts inform our decisions not to take part in deviant or criminal behavior. The stronger our attachments to parents, friends, and others, the greater the level of social control we experience. Alternately, weak emotional attachments leave individuals at great risk for performing deviant or criminal acts.

Commitment: The more committed individuals are to legitimate opportunities, the more likely they are to conform to social norms. Commitment can include marriage and family, jobs, mortgages, and membership in a range of organizations. People who are married with kids and have a mortgage to pay, neighbors to help, and Girl Scout cookies to sell are far less likely to engage in deviant and criminal behavior. Most of us do not want to jeopardize our marriage, employment, or standing in the community by committing deviant or criminal acts. Those with few commitments are more likely to be attracted toward deviance and crime. Again, these bonds of commitment, like attachment, serve as sources of social control.

Involvement: Attachments and commitments take up a great deal of our time. We spend most of our time living our lives, doing legitimate activities such as taking the kids to basketball practice, mowing the lawn, preparing dinner, and going to work. If we are engaged in all these legitimate, time-consuming endeavors, then we don't have the time for crime.

Belief: The stronger the belief in conventional social values and behaviors, the greater the likelihood of social conformity. Most people do not engage in deviant/criminal behaviors *not* because they are afraid of breaking the rules and being punished, but rather because they are too busy following the rules because they *believe* their behavior is appropriate. Think about it: do you struggle each day deciding whether you should rob a bank for money, or are you too busy working and going to school—behaviors that most individuals *believe* to be the socially correct thing to do?

This internalization of social values, beliefs and behaviors that lead people to engage in appropriate social interactions when no one else is around is what sociologists refer to as **internal social control**. Most societies rely heavily on internalization through the process of socialization to establish social order. If people failed to internalize this kind of self-control, then there would have to be law enforcement, paramilitary, and military personnel on every street corner to ensure that people conformed and complied with all the rules.

External social control is when others respond to one's behavior with approval or disapproval. That is, others will either approve or not approve of our behavior. This approval and/or disapproval

Police Hand Out Rewards

In early 2015, the Farmington, New Hampshire, police department struck upon an interesting idea. In an attempt to both boost the police department's image and reward good civic behavior, the police began handing out coupons for free pizza slices to law-abiding citizens (Keady, 2015). So, if you find yourself in rural New Hampshire and you use the crosswalk, keep your pooch on its leash, or pick up litter off the streets, you may have a run-in with the police—and get some free pizza.

can be thought of as rewards and punishments that strive to guide behavior toward desired social conduct. **Sanctions** are the rewards or punishments given in response to individuals' behaviors, which seek to either encourage or discourage those behaviors. **Positive sanctions** are actions that reward behaviors that are considered desirable, such as getting a raise at work for being innovative or enjoying a high credit score for being responsible with your credit, paying bills on time, and buying stuff with credit cards.

There are many programs around the country that reward designated drivers by providing them with free non-alcoholic drinks, free cover charges at clubs, and free appetizers. Obviously, these programs are designed to promote designated driving and decrease driving under the influence. These are commonly used positive sanctions. Take a look at a creative use of positive sanctions in the insert Police Hand out Rewards.

Negative sanctions are actions that punish behaviors that are perceived as socially undesirable. For example, being put on academic probation because you partied too much last semester or being arrested for hacking the school's computer system and giving yourself all A's for the last three years. Alternatively, for example, your wife withholding sex from you because you got drunk at her company's holiday party and embarrassed her by dancing around with a lampshade on your head.

Both positive and negative sanctions are used to control behavior, and these sanctions can be applied by **agents of social control**—individuals, groups, and institutions that have the official or unofficial ability to sanction deviance. Those who have power or authority, such as police, parents, umpires, deans and college professors exercise **formal social control**. It's easy to see how formal social control is exercised in the world. For example, police make arrests, judges sentence criminals to prison, deans can expel students, and parents ground their children. On the flip side, parents can reward their child with a new car for good grades, and a fraternity president could honor the pledge who drank the most Pabst Blue Ribbon. Those with the power and authority society or organizations have vested in them perform formal social control.

These *agents of social control* can take many forms; they can have positions of power and/or authority, or they can be ordinary citizens. **Informal social control** is used by ordinary people in everyday interactions to approve or disapprove of behaviors. These could include the disapproving look you get from your partner for your insensitive comments or being flipped off by the angry driver you just cut off in traffic. Getting a standing ovation for your riveting oral report on informal social control or the cheers from the crowd that has gathered to watch you rescue a cat from a tree represent positive informal social control.

Think about it this way: social control is necessary for all societies to maintain social order. Some societies, such as North Korea, are not subtle about their control mechanisms. They sustain propaganda campaigns against free Western nations, stage large, festival-like events that exalt the leadership, and starve and imprison their citizenry to maintain tight social control. Other nations use less obvious and more insidious methods like maintaining religious ideologies that constrain and control the behaviors of both men and women. Ultimately, social control is maintained through a combination of agents of social control, internalization of values and beliefs, and sanctions.

Crime and Punishment

Hacking the cloud in order to release nude photos of celebrities, shooting up an elementary school and killing more than twenty people, bilking thousands of investors out of billions of dollars, trafficking young girls around the world and forcing them into prostitution, or poaching rhinoceroses (cutting off their horns, and leaving them to die in the hot African sun). All of these are examples of crime, but all are very different types. Crime, as noted earlier in the chapter, is the violation of formal social norms or laws. However, when we think of crime, we are more likely to think of the response to it than the violation. That is, crime brings with it severe consequences for the violation of laws. Those responses vary by the type of crime, the severity of the crime, the age, sex, and race of the offender, and the prevailing social climate.

Measuring Crime

When you hear newscasts about the crime rate going up, going down, or staying the same, you probably imagine that someone, somewhere, is calculating all the crime that was committed in the last year. Is this true? Yes and no. Yes, the FBI produces the annual Uniform Crime Report (UCR), the official measure of crime in the United States. No, the UCR is not a measure of *all* crime reported. The FBI calculates the UCR by tabulating the number of crimes reported by more than 18,000 law enforcement agencies from around the country. For inclusion in the UCR, however, the FBI only counts eight types of crime that fall into two categories (see Table 5.2 below): *violent crimes* and *property crimes.*

Table 5.2 The Uniform Crime Report's Crime Index

Violent Crime	Property Crime
Murder	Burglary
Aggravated Assault	Larceny-Theft
Rape	Motor Vehicle Theft
Robbery	Arson

The violent crimes category includes murder, forcible rape, aggravated assault, and robbery. The property crimes category is made up of motor vehicle theft, burglary, larceny-theft, and arson. It's obvious that the reports you hear about are not a complete accounting of all crime committed; moreover, they are only a record of those crimes *reported* to law enforcement. However, the UCR is a useful tool in tracking both trends and patterns in crime. The UCR allows criminologists to view trends in crime over time and can locate patterns in criminal activity, such as comparing urban vs. rural crime rates.

So, how can we get a fuller picture of the number and types of crimes committed? In 1973, the Department of Justice started the National Crime Victimization Survey (NCVS) in an attempt to capture those crimes that were not reported to law enforcement. The NCVS compiles data from law enforcement agencies as well as surveying more than 90,000 households, representing about 160,000 individual responses about crimes that were not reported to law enforcement, producing national estimates of criminal victimization (Bureau of Justice Statistics, "National Crime Victimization Survey," 2015). Even with this effort, a significant amount of crime continues to go unreported. Therefore, the combination of reported crime contained in the UCR and unreported crime captured by the NCVS gives us a more accurate idea of the number and types of crimes committed nationally.

Why do you think people are reluctant to report crimes? Can you come up with at least three reasons why people are reluctant to report them? Now, take a look at Figure 5.6 and see if your choices match up with what victims had to say.

In the period from 2006 to 2010, nearly 3.4 million violent crimes went unreported; that is more than half of all violent victimizations. As you can see from Figure 5.6, most people (34%) dealt with the crime in another way, whether handling it personally or reporting it to non-law enforcement personnel such as a superior or school counselor. I think it is interesting that 16%, or more than a half-million victims, did not think the police could or would do anything about it. While Americans report a number of reasons for not reporting crime there are some categories of crime that are more underreported than others. Even though there is an underreporting of all crimes, rape and sexual assaults are grossly underreported, along with other violent crimes like assault and robbery (Truman, Planty and Langton, 2013; Wolitzky-Taylor et al., 2010). Why do you think these types of crime are so underreported?

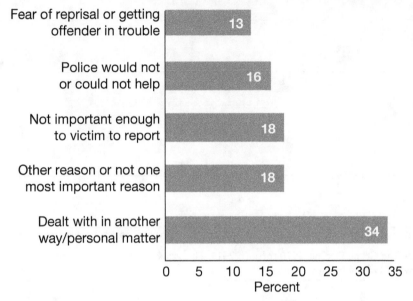

Most important reason violent victimizations were not reported to the police, 2006–2010

Reason	Percent
Fear of reprisal or getting offender in trouble	13
Police would not or could not help	16
Not important enough to victim to report	18
Other reason or not one most important reason	18
Dealt with in another way/personal matter	34

Figure 5.5 U.S. Department of Justice Special Report: National Crime Victimization Survey

Trends in Crime

A comprehensive description and exploration of trends in crime is beyond the scope of this chapter, but we can get a good look at the general trends in crime and then examine some crimes that seem to be on the rise. From about 1960 through the early 1990s, violent crime rose fairly steadily, but then unexpectedly, violent crime rates fell dramatically through 2001 and then began a general decline that continues to today (Fox and Zawitz, 2007). In Figure 5.7, the chart illustrates these general trends. Sometimes referred to as the "1990s crime decline," this dramatic fall in crime rates has been attributed to several factors that include demographics, economics, policing strategies, gun laws, and prison expansion.

Unfortunately, these explanations are woefully inadequate in fully accounting for the dramatic fall in violent crime that we have witnessed since 1991. Because of a demographic bulge of juveniles, John DiIulio, Jr. (1995) infamously predicted that millions of young men that he referred to as "juvenile super-predators" would wreak havoc on our society by creating a surge in violent crimes. This prediction was based on the belief that an increase in young males in a population is accompanied by a rise in the rates of violent crime. DiIulio, Jr. (2005) stated, "… nothing affects crime rates more than the number of young males in the population," predicting that as a result of these millions of young men being added to the population, we, as a society, will suffer waves of violent, predatory crimes over the next two decades. So much for predicting the future. The demographic bulge showed up, but there was no wave of juvenile super-predators roaming the streets, driving the rest of us indoors

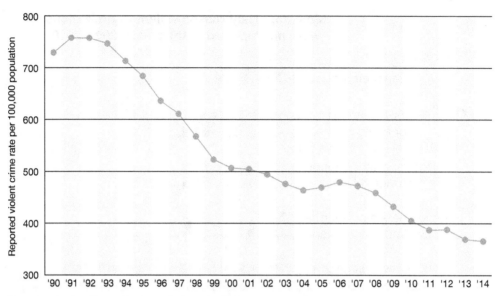

Figure 5.6 The Crime Decline, 1990 through 2014. This graph illustrates the fall of violent crime in the U.S. over a twenty-four-year period.

for fear of falling victim to testosterone-driven, violent criminals. In fact, the violent crime rate has kept on dropping during the last decade since DiIulio made his prediction, even in the face of this demographic event. Yep, more young men in the population but less violent crime (less crime overall), which does not bode well for a fully demographic explanation of violent crime rates.

So much for a strong demographic explanation. As we have seen in other chapters, economic factors seem to be instrumental in explaining various social phenomena. Let's take a look at the economic impact on crime rates. If a strong economy is associated with a decline in crime, and economic downturns are associated with increases in crime rates, then we would expect that the booming economy of the 1990s would be linked to dropping crime rates, and that is indeed what we saw. Then the argument would be that between 2008 and 2012, we would see an upswing in crime due to the severe economic downturn resulting from the mortgage debacle. However, this was not the case.

Let's take murder, the most accurately recorded and most serious crime, for example. If we look at Figure 5.8, we see that murder rates from 1990 to 2013 have dropped almost in half, and universally, murder rates have plummeted in every major American city and in every region of the country (FBI, "Crime in the United States, 2013," 2014). If we look specifically at homicide rates for the years 2008–13, we see a steady decline in murder rates even in the face of serious economic troubles. It seems that economic explanations come up short in explaining the continuing decline in crime. In fact, econometrics give researchers a number of sophisticated tools to work on the problem of crime decline, but unfortunately, econometrics consistently fail to account for most of the variation in crime rates (Manzi, 2012).

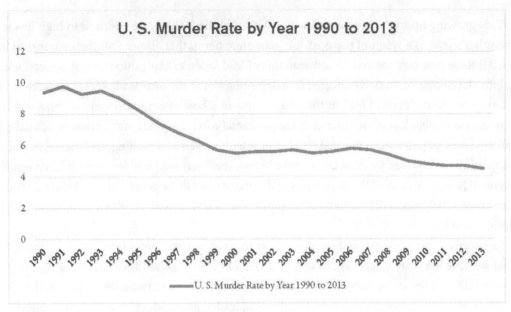

Figure 5.7 U.S. Murder Rate by Year 1990–2013

Along comes economist Steven Levitt (2004), who shows that factors commonly associated with crime decline, such as innovative policing strategies, gun control laws, increased reliance on prisons, strong economy, and demographic changes, do *not* account for the decline. Rather, he identifies four factors that account for "... virtually the entire observed decline in crime," and these include the waning crack epidemic, increased number of police, the rising prison population, and the legalization of abortion. Unlike other attempts at explaining crime decline, Levitt suggests that a specific combination of factors is responsible for the decline. These include putting more police on the streets, incarcerating more people, having fewer people involved in crime to support a crack habit, and fewer "unwanted" babies born to mothers who, he believes, will abuse and/or abandon them to the streets, where they will ultimately become the juvenile super-predators that DiIulio warned us about.

While these explanations account for some of the decline in violent crime, no single sociological theory or combination of theories adequately explains the huge drop in violent crime. I would like to show that sociological explanations account for nearly all the decline in crime so I could proudly and conspicuously strut around my college's campus, feeling secure and a bit smug in the knowledge that sociology can accurately and fully explain social phenomena, but I can't.

What does provide us with a fuller answer to this crime decline, you ask? Wait for it ... lead. More precisely, tetraethyl lead, the stuff they started adding to gasoline in the 1920s. That's right, leaded gasoline. Compelling research and arguments have demonstrated a powerful connection between the drop in lead levels and the decline in violent crimes (Needleman, 2004; Nevin, 2000; Reyes, 2007; Wright et al., 2008). Here is how the proponents of this perspective lay out their argument.

Kids growing up in the era between the 1940s and the 1970s were exposed to high levels of atmospheric lead as a result of the post-war economic boom that allowed all their parents to buy cars. All these new cars spewed record amounts of lead-laden exhaust into the atmosphere, where the kids' developing brains were affected from ingesting all the airborne lead. Recent research shows that even moderate levels of lead in the body results in a host of neuroanatomical abnormalities, including permanent loss of grey matter in the prefrontal cortex, the part of the brain associated with aggressiveness, impulsivity, emotional regulation, attention, verbal reasoning, and mental flexibility. To top off all those issues, for decades, we have known that increased lead levels in children result in lowered IQs. Breathing in all that lead affected the brains of all those generations of kids and resulted in an array of behavioral difficulties and cognitive deficits, almost all of which are associated with criminal profiles.

Fast-forward twenty years, and we see the rise in violent crime rates of the 1960s, '70s and '80s. What we have is a couple generations of lead-soaked kids with all kinds of emotional, behavioral, and cognitive issues, doing lots of crime and driving up the crime rates. Beginning in the 1970s right through 1996, when it was banned in the U.S., leaded gas production and consumption falls, dramatically reducing the amounts of lead in the atmosphere. Therefore, the crime decline we started to witness in the 1990s should just be the front edge of an overall continuing decrease in crime (Cecil et al., 2008; Drum, 2013). Perhaps most interesting is that this lead level-crime connection has been detected at the international, national, state, local, and individual levels.

Unraveling the complex nature of the crime decline is not an easy task and demands that we take into account all the variables that can help us explain this phenomenon. I am not abandoning the more traditional sociological, econometric, or demographic approaches to explaining the crime decline, but evidence from them is not adequate for any one of them to be the main cause. Including the lead level-crime connection is just good science sleuthing that will lead to a more comprehensive understanding of the crime decline. Because the crime decline was so unexpected and dramatic, sociology has been unable to produce adequate explanations for it. Ultimately, the crime decline we have been witnessing for the past two decades will no doubt only be fully understood by including all of the factors we have discussed.

The Demographics of Crime

Who is committing crime in the United States? While knowing how much crime there is and where it is most likely to happen is important, understanding what types of people are more likely to commit and be the victims of crime is essential to understanding the cause of crime. There are several variables that are involved in understanding who is engaging in crime: *age, race, gender, and social class.*

Age: Young people overwhelmingly commit more crime than any other group. This has been the case in the United States since the mid-1930s. The peak ages for criminal activity are between fifteen and twenty-four. In 2013, those aged fifteen to twenty-four made up nearly 35% of all arrests in the

U.S., while those aged fifty and older comprised just 10.7% of arrests and those sixty-five and older accounted for a mere .9% (FBI, "Crime in the United States, 2013," 2014). These age differences in criminal activity are explained in part by what criminologists refer to as *aging out of crime*. As people *age out of crime*, they take on more responsibilities and new statuses and roles such as wage earner, parent, spouse, etc. The possibility of jail time becomes a relatively more serious matter because of the impact it will have on the perpetrators' lives and responsibilities.

Other reasons we see these age differences may be that younger criminals are engaged in more visible crimes like gang activity, assault, and robbery, while older people are more likely to engage in crimes that are more difficult to detect like insider trading or embezzlement. Additionally, the belief that young people are more likely to be criminally active may motivate the police to harass (stop and frisk), accuse, and arrest young people more than seniors.

Gender: Males are far more likely to engage in crime than females, and this is a global phenomenon. In 2013, of all people arrested in the U.S., 74% were male and 26% were female. If we focus on violent crimes, males account for 88% of homicide arrests and a predictable 98% of arrests for rape. Overall, men account for 80% of all violent crimes arrests compared to 20% for women. When attempting to explain gender patterns in crime, researchers typically focus on three general areas: socialization, socioeconomic status, and differential treatment of the genders by the criminal justice system (Farrington and Painter, 2004).

In general, boys are encouraged to be more aggressive, competitive, impulsive, and rebellious, and girls are expected to be more dependent, passive, and expressive. These gendered traits become reinforced in society as children grow older, preparing girls for home life and boys for roles outside the home, affording them more opportunity for criminal activity (Lindsey, 2015). Basically, boys will be boys and be aggressive and get in trouble and that is expected, but a good girl has no business getting into trouble. However, these gender roles are changing; women have many more opportunities outside the home, and this is reflected in their economic power and crime rates.

Low crime rates among women were traditionally tied to their low socioeconomic status (SES). Traditionally, women were more financially dependent on men and they had children who depended on them. Both these factors contributed to women refraining from criminal activity. However, in recent years, there has been a surge in female arrests, convictions, and incarceration. As social change allows women more latitude in activities outside the home, finances become a driver for crime, especially when we see these increases primarily in property crimes and drug offenses.

The number of females incarcerated increased 33% between 2000 and 2008, and arrest rates for women increased 11.6% compared to a decrease of 3.1% for men in the same period. With more recent data, an alarming trend emerges: Overall arrests were down for both sexes in the period covering 2004–13, a significant decrease of 18.3% for men but only a drop of 5.2% for women. However, if we look across all UCR crimes, we find a decline in arrests for *all* crimes for men but an overall increase of 15.5% in property crime arrests for women (FBI, "Crime in the United States, 2012", 2013).

According to the *chivalry hypothesis*, police, prosecutors, and judges are reluctant to arrest, prosecute, and incarcerate women precisely because they are women: maternal, loving, caregiving, and "weak" (Embry and Lyons, Jr., 2012). There was strong support for this hypothesis in the past, but recent data shows support weakening, mainly because of the increased number of women being arrested and having more frequent encounters with the courts. Additionally, more women, like male offenders, are subject to mandatory minimum sentencing and "three strikes you're out" laws.

Race: Differences in race can be seen across the board regarding the criminal justice system. Differential treatment of people of color is reflected in arrest, conviction, and incarceration rates. While more whites are arrested each year, they represent a much smaller proportion of the total white population. Of those arrested in 2013, 69% where white and 28.3% were black. Blacks make up less than 13% of the U.S. population but represent 28% of all arrests and 39% of arrests for violent crimes.

For example, America's war on drugs is expensive, inefficient, and racially biased. Let's take smoking pot, for example. While marijuana use rates are roughly the same between whites and blacks in the U.S., if you are black and like to puff, you are nearly four times more likely to be arrested than your white pot-smoking friends are. In 2010, the black arrest rate for marijuana possession was 716 per 100,000 but only 192 per 100,000 for whites (American Civil Liberties Union, 2013).

Seeing such stark differences in arrests between races, we have to ask why this is happening. In general, cops tend to focus their attention on neighborhoods with high rates of crime. Those neighborhoods tend to be populated by members of low-income minority groups. Cops patrolling those neighborhoods are often empowered to stop and frisk residents on the slimmest of pretexts, and because of that, they are likelier to find people who are carrying marijuana (ACLU, 2013).

Here is a disturbing fun fact that influences police departments' motivation for busting people for minor drug infractions. A federal program called the Byrne Justice Assistance Grant gives money to local police departments based on the number of drug arrests they make (U.S. Department of Justice, "Byrne Justice Assistance Grant", 2016). With many local police departments struggling with thin budgets, they may see federal programs like this as necessary for their survival, providing incentive for them to keep on busting tokers.

Social Class: The same argument we used above applies to the issue of social class. Police concentrate more resources in low-income neighborhoods, and subsequently, those in poorer areas are more likely to be targeted, arrested, convicted, and incarcerated than those in middle-class, suburban enclaves. This targeting and arresting of those in lower socioeconomic areas helps foster the impression that poor neighborhoods have high rates of crime.

Surveys of prison inmates show that about 68% have less than a high school education and only 11% report having any college education (Harlow, 2003). Those with a lack of education, which translates into fewer resources like money, property, or connections, are more likely to have an overworked and underpaid public defender. On the other hand, someone with more resources could afford their own attorney, who would most likely be more invested in a client who could pay and may even be a friend. More than 90% of those on death row were represented at trial by public defenders ... and look where it got them (ACLU, 2012).

The impact of social class on public and police perceptions is well-demonstrated in William Chambliss' (1973) study *The Saints and Roughnecks*. The Saints was a pseudonym for a group of upper-middle-class boys who came from well-respected families in well-to-do neighborhoods, and society expected them to do well in life. While the Saints were perceived as "good" kids, Chambliss reported that they engaged in an array of delinquent behavior such as drinking and stealing automobiles. But they were outwardly obedient toward authority figures and therefore labeled as "good boys." The Roughnecks, however, came from less well to do families and in general members of the community didn't expect them to be successful. While both groups engaged in deviant behaviors the two groups experienced very different reactions from adults. Most adults in the community dismissed the Saints' behavior because they perceived them as decent kids just being teenagers. However, those same members of the community defined the Roughnecks as troublemakers and were more likely to label them as deviant and punish their behaviors. Both groups of boys engaged in deviant behaviors but had different labels attached based primarily on their social class, and others treated them differently based on those different labels.

This is played out day after day in less well-to-do neighborhoods all over the country. When police roll into poorer neighborhoods, they have already decided that the youth there are up to no good and are more likely to stop and frisk them than their counterparts in wealthier neighborhoods. For example, the police in Miami Gardens, Florida, a working-class, predominately African American neighborhood with a population of about 111,000, made more than 99,980 "field contacts" (stop and frisk and/or question) on citizens between 2008 and 2013 (Chappell, 2013; Brennan and Lieberman, 2014). The number of these *same types of stops* for the entire Miami metropolitan area, with a population of about 5 million, in *the same period* was 3,753. The Miami Gardens police even stopped a five-year-old black youth who was described by police as a "suspicious person."

It is important to remember that the variables we have just discussed above—age, gender, race, and class—are interrelated. Black youth in poorer neighborhoods will be treated differently by the police and courts than wealthy, white, highly educated, older men—it's never just one thing. *Intersectionality* is the perspective that seeks to understand the complex interplay of race, gender, age, class, religion, sexual orientation, education, and even our geographic and historical location (Crenshaw, 1989). This perspective is sensitive to the connections between many of the variables we examine in sociology. For example, the police do not just harass young men—they stop and frisk lower-class, young, black males with few resources in high-crime neighborhoods.

Types of Crime

We have already seen two types of crime in our discussion of the FBI's Uniform Crime Report. **Crimes against the person (violent crimes)** involve bodily harm, the threat of bodily harm, or other actions committed against the will of an individual, including, but not limited to: murder, forcible rape, stalking, kidnapping, and hate crimes.

Crimes against property are any criminal acts that destroy another's property or deprive an owner of property against the owner's will. These may include such acts as motor vehicle theft, burglary, shoplifting, arson, and vandalism. Both crimes against the person and property are included in computations for national crime rates, but there are a number of other categories of crime that are not included in national calculations yet still impact our social world.

While I believe it to be a misnomer, **victimless crimes** are those offenses that are clearly violations of the law but have no identifiable victim. Some view these offenses as victimless because those involved are adults who are willingly exchanging goods or services. Common examples of victimless crimes are prostitution, gambling and recreational drug use. The reality is there are always victims of crimes. The person's house that is burgled so an addict can cop his heroin is the victim of his drug use. Crack babies and abused and discarded children are many times the victims of drug use and prostitution. Ultimately, the offenders are the victims. In a study that looked at street prostitutes, nearly all of those who responded reported being ripped off, assaulted, or physically abused by their johns (Venkatesh, 2010). Also, think about the harm that long-term drug use has on the addict and how many times that cost is passed on to the larger community through treatment and medical expenses.

In 2008, Bernard Madoff was arrested for bilking thousands of investors out of more than $50 billion in what today is still the largest Ponzi scheme ever uncovered. He stole all this money without ever threatening a single person, without taking a single purse or wallet, and without using any violence. People, businesses, and other investors gave their money to him, some even forcing him to take their investments. His reputation of being able to produce huge returns on investments had grown over the previous two decades. However, it was all a scam designed to enrich himself at the expense of all those who had entrusted him with everything from retirement funds to life savings. Ultimately, this all came crashing down, and his scheme was exposed for what it was: a pyramid scam that left investors from old ladies to charities penniless. Madoff is the poster child for **white-collar crimes**—crimes committed by affluent individuals who hold high status occupations (Sutherland, 1949). Typically, these offenders commit crimes in the context of a business that they are familiar with—bank executives that commit bank fraud, the insurance executive who defrauds his company, or the stockbroker practicing insider trading.

Unlike crimes against persons and property, which have immediate visible effects, white collar crimes can be less obvious, but still have disastrous effects on individuals and businesses. It is estimated that white-collar crime costs Americans between $300 and $600 billion each year, and that amount is projected to increase (Kane and Wall, 2006). The costs are not just monetary; workers in companies that collapse due to criminal mismanagement can lose their jobs, like in the case of Enron Corporation in 1996, where four thousand employees were dismissed. Other non-financial fallout from white-collar crime may include such things as retirees forced back to work due to drained retirement accounts, individuals having to depend on relatives for living situations, and other unexpected, life-disrupting events. While all violent crime and property crimes are down, white-collar crimes are among a small number of crime categories that are on the rise. (The FBI's UCR data for 2013 shows all property and violent crimes are down 5% from the same period in 2012.)

A related category of crimes includes **corporate crime**—offenses committed by corporate officials and offences of the corporation itself (Clinard and Yeager, 1980). These crimes may range from polluting the environment to knowingly manufacturing and selling defective or dangerous products. A prime example of corporate crime would be the 2010 BP Deepwater Horizon oil spill, considered the largest accidental oil spill, which dumped an estimated 210 million U.S. gallons into the Gulf of Mexico, killing eleven people, and leaving in its wake dead and injured marine life and thousands of miles of oil-soaked coastline (Pollardy, 2015). Total cost for this accident now approaches $50 billion; one estimate puts losses just for Gulf Coast anglers at $585 million (Xu, 2014). However, losses are more than economic; downstream effects include continued loss of marine life and loss of livelihood among the inhabitants of coastal communities in a number of states. The fallout from this disaster has been so profound that many residents have relocated in order to find work; those who stay face economic loss and disruption of their lives.

Many times, corporate crime is committed by individuals who believe that their criminal activity is merely a means to promote their organization. Sometimes referred to more specifically as *organizational crime*, these offenses are committed by individuals who believe that their crimes with serve to further the goals of an organization or movement. Something like flying jet airliners into the World Trade Center or setting off sarin gas bombs on a crowded Tokyo subway are examples of organizational crime. Those who flew the planes into the World Trade Center did so in part to promote their cause/organization, Al-Qaeda, and to prove their allegiance to the cause to show that they were "true believers."

Extortion, controlling gambling outlets, prostitution, drug and human trafficking, and more sophisticated electronic crimes like credit card fraud and identity theft are typical criminal enterprises that describe organized crime. **Organized crime** refers to any group which possesses a formalized structure and whose primary objective is to profit from crime (FBI, "Organized Crime," 2016). The United States has experienced waves of ethnically linked criminal organizations through the centuries. As various ethnic groups settled in America, criminal organizations emerged in their communities, many times in response to the discrimination they encountered here.

Most of these organizations began in their respective ethnic enclaves, and while many remain local, such as the Cuban, African American, and Vietnamese organizations, others spread out into the larger society. The Italian mafia is a high-profile example of a criminal enterprise that eventually left the Italian neighborhoods of New York City and over the decades has gone global. In a constant search for new criminal endeavors, the ma a now has its hands in credit card fraud, identity theft, hacking financial institutions, and Internet porn (FBI, "Italian Organized Crime," 2015). Probably the most damaging to society is its involvement in government corruption. From the cop on the beat, to the local building inspector, to the judge on the bench, to the senator on the Hill, the mob has wide influence that can affect laws and social policies. This corrupting influence it has on the local government and the criminal justice system leads many to believe that it can control local officials and influence the outcome of trials. Ultimately, the criminal acts of organized crime degrade the public trust in the integrity of local government, the police, and the judicial system.

Hate crimes are defined by the FBI as any "criminal offense against a person or property motivated in whole or in part by an offender's bias against a race, religion, disability, sexual orientation, ethnicity, gender, or gender identity" (FBI, "Hate Crimes," 2016). The vast majority of hate crimes are violent crimes that have the added element of being motivated by hatred for the victim's religion, race, sex, sexual orientation, or disability. While the term hate crime is relatively new in the popular culture, hate crime laws (not titled as such) date to the end of the Civil War, and the hate crime laws in the modern era can be dated back to 1968 with an amendment to the Civil Rights Act.

California passed the first state hate crime law in 1978; now, forty-five states and the District of Columbia all have hate crime laws. Federal statutes start to catch up beginning in 1990, leading to a more comprehensive Hate Crimes Prevention Act in 2009. Unfortunately, the United States has a long and illustrious history of hate crimes represented by organizations like the Ku Klux Klan, Skinheads, the Black Panthers, and the U.S. government—yes, our own government. Take, for example, the treatment of the Native American population, Chinese immigrants, and Japanese Americans during WWII. In an attempt to reconcile past cases with current hate crime statutes, the FBI actively investigates hate crimes retroactively. That is, it investigates unsolved cold-case crimes that at the time were not categorized as hate crimes but now can be prosecuted as such. Most of this effort has been concentrated on crimes committed in the South during the height of the civil rights movement.

Crimes involving computers are extensive in their scope, but not all crimes using a computer are considered cyber-crimes. Cyber-crimes are defined as "offenses that are committed against individuals or groups of individuals with a criminal motive to intentionally harm the reputation of the victim or cause physical or mental harm to the victim directly or indirectly, using modern telecommunication networks such as Internet (Chat rooms, emails, notice boards and groups) and mobile phones (SMS/MMS)" (Halder and Jaishankar, 2011). The intent of cyber-crimes is as wide-ranging as the type of cyber-crimes. Cyber-crimes range from conning people into sending money to your long-lost uncle in Nigeria to secretly installing malware on the computers of unsuspecting users. Frequently, these criminals are pursuing financial gain by stealing credit card information, robbing bank accounts, creating bogus online charity sites, or stealing identities. However, a growing number of cyber-crimes are aimed at either infecting computer networks with malware and/or viruses in order to disable or crash a system or spreading malicious bots and viruses simply to be, well, malicious. It seems that financial gain is a much stronger motive than others are. Both the FBI and Bureau of Justice Statistics indicate that the fastest-growing crime in the United States is identity theft, mainly through cyber tactics (FBI, "Identity Theft", 2015; Javelin Strategy & Research, 2013; Harrell, 2015).

Recently, nude photos of several celebrities were distributed on the Internet without the knowledge or consent of those celebrities. Where did these pics come from? They were hacked from the iCloud, where those celebrities had stored them in what they believed to be a secure digital environment. In December 2013, Brian Curtis Hile was sentenced to five years in federal prison for interstate stalking (FBI, "Interstate Stalking," 2013). In an ironic twist, Hile was the victim of a "catfishing" cyber-romance scam in which a South African man posed as an attractive woman and maintained an online-only, two-year romance with Hile, exchanging intimate photos and letters.

When Mr. Hile discovered the true identity of his online lover, he became enraged and sought revenge, but South Africa was too far away, so he focused on the identity of the woman whose image the scammer had used as his female alter-identity. Hile discovered who the woman in all those intimate pics was and tracked her down in San Diego, where he was arrested. Apparently, Hile had determined that the woman was somehow complicit with the South African scammer and she had to pay (the woman had no idea that her photos from a hacked email account were being used to lure young men into fake relationships). The FBI determined that Hile had intended some violent end for the woman and her family when they found a knife, zip ties, and chloroform on him when he was arrested.

There's An App for That

Below I have listed some crime-fighting apps:
- *iSpotACrime* allows users to report crimes directly to their local police. The app allows you to use GPS to pinpoint the location of the crime, upload pics, text and make voice recordings. So, you can witness crimes and send photo, video and audio evidence right to the police (Vorpal Fox.com, 2016).
- *Tip Submit* allows users to snitch anonymously to a range of agencies including Crime Stoppers, police, and local school administrators (Public Engines Inc., 2014).
- *iWitness* this smartphone app lets you capture and broadcast video and audio while maintaining real time tracking of your location via GPS. The data then is retrievable only by you and with your permission law enforcement. One feature allows you to alert trusted contacts with your location if you feel endangered (iWitness, 2015)

Black Hats, White Hats, and Gray Hats

Not all hackers are the same. Black hat hackers, or black hats, as they are known, are people who hack computer systems for personal gain or other malicious reasons. They will hack a bank's computer system just to rob it or steal confidential information from a large retail organization in order to commit identity fraud. Sometimes, they merely want to inflict damage to a system or shut it down. For example, the large retailer Target was hacked in late 2013, and it was reported that the personal and credit card information from nearly 70 million customers was compromised ("Target: 40 Million Credit Cards," 2013).

White hats are typically computer security specialists who breach computer systems and networks to assess their security. Typically, they are hired by organizations to expose any vulnerabilities present in their systems in an attempt to head off malicious black hat attacks. While they may employ similar or identical techniques, white hats have permission to hack their clients' systems and many times are doing so to improve customer security. Today, many financial institutions, businesses, and even the federal government hire white hat cybersecurity firms to probe the vulnerability of their systems and report ways that their security can be enhanced.

Gray hats are hackers who fall somewhere in between black hats and white hats. While gray hats may breach a computer system or network, they will not crash it or seek to profit from the breach. Gray hats may compromise a bank's computer network and then publicly expose the flaw rather than privately notifying the organization. While they have compromised a computer system, which is illegal, they typically do not seek personal gain from the intrusion. However, there is a time lag between publicly announcing the flaw and the organization's response, which leaves plenty of opportunity for black hats to strike.

The Criminal Justice System

The criminal justice system in the United States is represented by a number of linked organizations involved in policing, adjudicating, sentencing, and jailing those involved in crime. It includes, but is not limited to, law enforcement, courts of law, and prison. Unfortunately, by any metric, the criminal justice system is seriously flawed. The chances of an individual being arrested, convicted, and sentenced in the U.S. are greatly increased if he/she is a person of color and/or poor (The Sentencing Project, 2013).

Law Enforcement

Police are the first point of contact with the criminal justice system and, therefore, are in a position to either enhance or detract from their public image. Through this daily contact with members of the community, they have the potential to escalate or deescalate volatile situations and ultimately have the ability to make decisions about who will and will not be detained or arrested. They are armed with their most powerful weapon: discretion.

Currently, police play many roles: law enforcement, peacekeeping, and public relations. However, police are only effective if they secure public trust. Police, after all, are public servants, but when they are viewed as adversaries rather than allies in achieving social goals, distrust in them grows. This may arise from changes in police practices, as was evinced in New York City in the early 1990s when the city adopted a zero-tolerance police policy (arresting people for small infractions as well as more severe ones) that has led to fear and mistrust of police (Staples, 2012). This mistrust of law enforcement has only been exacerbated by a series of high-profile, police-involved homicides during 2014 and 2015, most notably the choking death of Eric Garner, an unarmed black man, by NYPD officers and the shooting death of Michael Brown, an unarmed black man, in Ferguson, Missouri, in August 2014 (Goldstein and Schweber, 2014; Chuck, 2014). These deaths sparked both violent riots and peaceful protests that lasted for months.

In large part, this mistrust is fueled by the staggering difference in arrest rates between whites and people of color in the United States. Black men are far more likely to be arrested than white men are. Brame et al. (2014) found that by age eighteen, 30% of black males, 26% of Hispanic males, and 22% of white males had been arrested, and by age twenty-three, 49% of black males, 44% of Hispanic males, and 38% of white males had been arrested.

These are big differences. However, the question remains—why do we see such differences? Are law enforcement officers just discriminating? For example, research indicates that police training, professional socialization, stereotypes and experience, can lead police to suspect, "stop and frisk", and arrest members of certain minority groups and the poor (Alpert et al., 2005; Alpert, Dunham and Smith, 2007; Gelman, Fagan and Kiss, 2007).

In general, in the U.S., you are far more likely to be stopped and arrested if you are poor than if you appear well to do, and if you are black in America, you are far more likely to be in poverty than if you are white (Brown and Males, 2011). Unlike the wealthy, who typically commit crimes that evade police detection, the poor are more likely to commit street crimes that are more visible to the police. Moreover, political and peer pressure may make police less likely to confront and arrest more affluent citizens.

The Courts

After being arrested by law enforcement, the accused have to deal with the criminal courts system, which serves to adjudicate offenses, determine guilt or innocence, and pronounce sentences. Again, the differences in treatment between the poor and affluent and blacks and whites are present in the courtrooms of America.

From their initial contact with the courts, differences emerge. Poor people are far less likely to be able to afford bail; therefore, they have to spend their pre-trial time in jail (Justice Policy Institute,

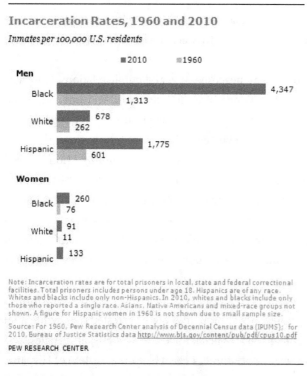

Incarceration Rates, 1960 and 2010

Inmates per 100,000 U.S. residents

■ 2010 ■ 1960

Men

Black — 4,347 / 1,313
White — 678 / 262
Hispanic — 1,775 / 601

Women

Black — 260 / 76
White — 91 / 11
Hispanic — 133

Note: Incarceration rates are for total prisoners in local, state and federal correctional facilities. Total prisoners includes persons under age 18. Hispanics are of any race. Whites and blacks include only non-Hispanics. In 2010, whites and blacks include only those who reported a single race. Asians, Native Americans and mixed-race groups not shown. A figure for Hispanic women in 1960 is not shown due to small sample size.

Source: For 1960, Pew Research Center analysis of Decennial Census data (IPUMS); for 2010, Bureau of Justice Statistics data http://www.bjs.gov/content/pub/pdf/cpus10.pdf

PEW RESEARCH CENTER

Figure 5.8 Bar chart showing incarceration rates for whites, blacks, and Latinos, 1960 and 2010

2012). This may affect their ability to aid in their own defense, they may lose their job, and they are separated from their family and friends. Imagine how being led into the courtroom by bailiffs and perhaps wearing a bright orange jail uniform could influence the judge or jury, whereas someone with more resources is able to post bail and can show up in court with his lawyer wearing a suit. Research indicates that defendants who can pay their bail and afford their own attorney are more likely to be acquitted than someone who cannot afford these things (Frederique et al., 2015).

Poor people are far less likely to be able to afford an attorney. While they may get a court-appointed attorney, most are working for lower wages or pro-bono, which can motivate them to rush the case along or, more often than not, plea-bargain the case. On the other hand, affluent defendants who can afford their own attorneys will most likely get off as a result of a number of legal maneuvers executed by their well-paid attorneys. Additionally, the reality for the poor in the United States is that on average they are more likely to receive harsher penalties and do more time than their wealthier counterparts.

Blacks are arrested far more often than whites, are more likely to do time than whites, and are more likely to be handed stiffer prison terms. Therefore, there is no question that the courts are treating black and white defendants differently. For instance, when it comes to sentencing for homicide those who kill whites are more likely to get the death penalty than those who murder minorities. The reality is that if a white man and a black man were to be arrested on identical charges, have the same criminal history, be the same age, and have similar family and employment backgrounds, the black man is more likely to be convicted and do time than the white man (Kochel et al., 2011; Walker et al., 2004).

Punishment

Ultimately, court convictions lead to some form of punishment or penalty. These punishments can take several forms: fines, restitution, probation, community service, or incarceration. Overwhelmingly, in the United States, the trend has been toward incarceration. In 1971, there were fewer than 200,000 inmates in our federal and state prisons; by 1996, we approached 1.2 million—the prison population sextupled in that twenty-five-year span. As of 2013, there were nearly 2.2 million inmates in state and federal prisons. We really like to lock people up. Is it because there is so much more crime? Well, earlier in the chapter, I showed you that all violent crime is down and only cyber-crimes and hate crimes are on the rise, but not enough to account for incarceration rates. In their book, *Why Are So Many Americans in Prison?* Raphael and Stoll (2013) show what drove up imprisonment rates was not crime—it was policy.

That's right, the public concern over the growing crime rate of the '70s and '80s led politicians, afraid of appearing to be soft on crime, into enacting minimum sentencing laws. The thinking went something like this: in order to remove criminals from society, police need to arrest all offenders, minor and major alike, and deter future crime through harsh sentencing. From 1975 through 2002, all fifty states adopted mandatory sentencing laws, specifying minimum sentences. Many also adopted "three strikes" laws to punish recidivists. Judges lost the discretion they previously had in determining sentences, their hands were tied, they had to pronounce minimum sentences. This combined with tougher policing strategies like the zero-tolerance policy adopted by the NYPD help put more and more offenders inside. For the most part, minimum sentencing guidelines have led to the swollen prison population. Unbelievably, today the United States has a greater proportion of our population in jail and prison than China, India, and Russia. Yes, while the U.S. has the world's third-largest population, the percentage of our population that is behind bars is the highest in the world! Think about it this way: The United States represents just 5% of the world's population, yet those we have incarcerated represent 25% of the world's prison population. Table 5.3 below shows the top ten countries with the largest prison populations. The United States tops the list. Take a look at the other countries that top this list; they are also countries that have long records of human rights abuses. The United States should not want to top a list like this.

Table 5.3 Top Ten Countries Ranked by Number of Incarcerated

Rank	Country	Incarcerated Population
1	United States	2,217,000
2	China	1,657,812
3	Russian Federation	649,500
4	Brazil	607,731
5	India	411,992
6	Thailand	308,111
7	Mexico	255,138
8	Iran	225,624
9	Turkey	165,033
10	Indonesia	161,692

Source: Institute for Criminal Policy Research 2015

Who Is More Likely to Be in Prison?

While there may be more white males in prison than black males, the proportion of black males imprisoned is far greater than for whites (Glaze and Herberman, 2013). Blacks in America make up less than 13% of the country's population, but they represent nearly 40% of the nation's prison inmates. As a matter of fact, all black men are six times more likely to be in prison than all white men. Estimates put the black prison population at 1 million out of 2.3 million inmates in American prisons. Take a look at Table 5.4 below for a clear picture of who is in prison in America.

Table 5.4 Inmate Race

Race	Number of Inmates	Percentage of Inmates
Asian	2,927	1.5%
Black	73,557	37.6%
Native American	3,963	2.0%
White	115,046	58.8%

Data from the Federal Bureau of Prisons, April 2016

These rates of incarceration are compounded by level of education. Figure 5.9 shows that the greatest rates of imprisonment are associated with lack of education. Low levels of education are associated with greater levels of poverty, which, in turn, are linked to criminal activity. This creates a cycle of high arrest rates for poor black men, who cannot afford attorneys, who then are more likely to be convicted and are more likely to be sentenced to prison. It seems that as a society, it would benefit us greatly to focus our resources more heavily on education to reduce poverty and crime rather than to focus on prison as a solution to crime.

Why Do We Put People in Prison?

There are four main motivations for imprisoning someone: retribution, deterrence, rehabilitation, and removal from society. Remember, these motivations represent expressions of formal social control. Each is seen as a way to reinforce social norms and promote conformity.

- *Retribution* means exacting punishment on the offender—an eye for an eye and a tooth for a tooth. This rationale goes something like this: if you commit a crime, you should be held accountable and have to "repay" society by being punished. Retribution is about society exacting its pound of flesh from the criminal o˙ender, and this may include time in jail or prison.
- *Deterrence* refers to structuring punishments in a way that the cost of crime will appear so great that would-be criminals will refrain from crime in order to avoid harsh punishments. The death penalty is, in theory, a deterrent to crime. The belief is that the threat of death is so severe that it will deter criminals from engaging in capital crimes. However, there seems to be no credible evidence to support this position.
- Those who argue for a process of *rehabilitation* seek to design prisons as institutions that have the capacity to educate and/or train inmates so they will have legitimate job skills when they re-enter society, becoming productive members of society and ultimately reducing recidivism rates. Rehabilitation programs like prison-based education and training programs

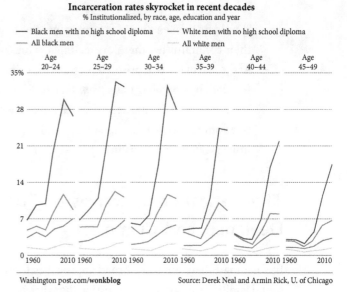

Figure 5.9 Incarceration Rates by Education Level, Blacks and Whites, 1960 and 2010.

Read More

- *Race, Incarceration and American Values* by Glenn C. Loury (2008); *Let's Get Free: A Hip-Hop Theory of Justice* by Paul Butler (2009). Both of these books explore our broken criminal justice system, putting it in a social context of racism, prejudice, and discrimination. They expose how unfairly people of color are treated by the system and how the system reproduces its practices. These books will open your eyes to the truth of how our criminal justice system treats people of color.

should be seen as a way for former inmates to gain employment and feel more integrated into their communities, therefore feeling less inclined to engage in criminal acts.

- At the end of the day, prison represents the criminal justice system's ability to take away offenders' freedom by *removing them from society*. Removing offenders from the rest of society is one of the most fundamental acts of social control a society can perform. Denying individuals their freedom to move about in society and separating them from friends and family is nearly a universal form of punishment—a sort of *time out* for adults.

Theoretical Perspectives on Social Control, Deviance, and Crime

In sociology, there are three broad approaches to understanding deviance and crime. They should sound familiar: we have been discussing them in every chapter. Remember, these theoretical approaches are attempts to explain existence and causes of deviance in society. In general, functionalism views deviance as present in all societies and the response it provokes functions to maintain social order. Functionalism recognizes that individuals within a society need to feel integrated or connected to others and society for them to contribute to the various social institutions that maintain social order. Dysfunctions occur when people do not feel connected and engage in deviant and criminal behavior, which is disruptive to social order. Some functionalists argue that there is positive value in deviance that contributes to maintaining social order, while others see it as a result of modern society's constant pressure for material success, which leads to norm violations to achieve success.

Conflict theory focuses on social inequality and how that can result in the differential definitions and treatment of deviants. Adherents to this approach see the powerful in society as having the ability to influence the passing of laws that can serve them and maintain dominance over the less fortunate. Those disadvantaged like the poor and minorities are more likely to be viewed as deviant than the affluent and, consequently, are treated differently by law enforcement and the criminal justice system, as we saw in our discussions above.

In contrast to both functionalism and Conflict theories, symbolic interactionism has a micro-sociological focus on deviance and crime. That means that deviance and crime are constructed out of the interactions between people. Nothing is inherently deviant but may become defined as such through the responses of others, the reactions of others are highly variable, and labeling someone as deviant may lead to the development of secondary deviance and deviant careers.

Table 5.5 summarizes each of the three main theoretical perspectives. For each perspective in the table, I have included a brief distillation of its main points and an example that helps illustrate the major proposals.

Table 5.5 Theoretical Perspectives on Deviance and Crime

Theoretical Perspective	View of Deviance and Crime	Example
Structural-Functionalism	Deviance and crime are a result of weak social integration—the less attached, committed, and obligated individuals are to others and society, and the less they believe in conventional social values and behaviors, the more likely they are to commit deviant or criminal acts.	Depression is most commonly associated with suicide. However, there is a large body of research that shows that most suicides are the result of a host of social factors that can lead to depressive feelings. Shortly after the collapse of the housing market in 2008, Kathy lost her job in Boston. She had recently moved there and had no real friends. She was an only child whose parents had died. She could not seem to find a job, started feeling isolated, did not have anyone to turn to, and was evicted from her apartment. Soon after, she fell down the stairs at the motel she was staying in and had to be treated as an indigent. The motel manager found her dead in her room a week later. She had taken all the pain pills she had recently been prescribed. Her note stated that it seemed the best solution given she had no friends and family and felt disconnected from the world. Such an individual act is usually seen as a result of some pathology, but deviant acts like suicide are commonly impacted by social forces and circumstances that conspire to make individuals feel disconnected from the social world.
	Deviance and crime can serve positive social functions for society, such as establish moral boundaries, create solidarity, affirm social norms and values, and promote social change.	In August 2014, an unarmed young black man was killed by a police officer in Ferguson, Missouri. The ensuing protests, riots, and looting eventually led to more protests and a dialogue between the police and community leaders, who demanded a thorough investigation. Ultimately, the protests lead to a Department of Justice investigation of that police force, which resulted in a 102-page report filled with recommendations for changes in police practices and procedures. The report highlighted rampant racism and the overcriminalization of the black community. This led to the resignation of the police chief, among other officials, and these changes will hopefully result in less criminalization and police violence against the black community. (Berman and Lowery, 2015; U.S. Department of Justice, "Investigation of the Ferguson Police Department", 2015).

(continued)

Table 5.5 Theoretical Perspectives on Deviance and Crime (*Continued*)

Theoretical Perspective	View of Deviance and Crime	Example
	Deviance and crime can be a reaction to social strain—when individuals feel like they cannot achieve social goals through legitimate means, they may turn to crime.	In the movie *Fun with Dick and Jane* (1977), Dick loses his job and can't seem to find work, and the couple have a hard time maintaining their middle-class lifestyle—keeping up with the Joneses. Exhausted from job hunting, stressed over mounting bills, and afraid they may lose their house, Dick and Jane start robbing banks and other businesses to pay the bills and keep the house!
Conflict	Conflict theory is all about inequality in society. It maintains that laws and social norms reflect the interests of the powerful in society. They can pass laws to their benefit and influence the justice system in other ways that allow them to define deviance and crime.	Take for example the CEO of an auto parts manufacturing plant who was busted for drug possession at the same time one of his machine operators was also arrested for the same offense. The CEO was able to pay a high-priced lawyer to keep moving his court date until the lawyer could work out a deal with the prosecutor (whom he went to law school with) to dismiss the charges and keep it all out of the press. Unfortunately, the machine worker could not afford an attorney, got a court-appointed lawyer, and took a plea bargain that sent him to jail (under minimum sentencing laws passed by the powerful) for five years. He lost his job, home, and family.
	The poor and minorities are more likely to engage in more visible street crimes, making them vulnerable to arrest, conviction, and imprisonment, unlike the more affluent or powerful members of society.	White-collar criminals, such as our friend Raj in the story below, are much more likely to go undetected because of the complex nature of their crimes and because many times, there is no identifiable victim. Often, the companies do not want the bad press and will try to bury the crime by not prosecuting the oꞌender. White-collar criminals are sometimes able to use their power and influence to avoid prosecution. Because of their social and economic influence, white-collar criminals are less likely to face criminal prosecution than less affluent criminals. When prosecuted, they are much less likely than members of lower social classes to receive a prison sentence. They are more likely to pay a fine as punishment for their crime.

Table 5.5 Theoretical Perspectives on Deviance and Crime (*Continued*)

Theoretical Perspective	View of Deviance and Crime	Example
Symbolic Interactionism	Deviant and criminal behaviors are a result of our need for acceptance by others—our association with criminal groups will lead to conformity with the criminal group's values, attitudes, techniques, and motives so we are accepted.	Raj was recently promoted to a special investment section at Global Bank. He worked on multimillion-dollar accounts with just five other brokers. After a few months, Raj and the others were working hard together and socializing outside of work. Raj felt privileged because he felt he was fortunate to work with who he felt were his best friends. After work one night, the others confided in Raj that they had worked out a scheme that allowed them to skim thousands of dollars each day undetected by anyone—after all, they all worked hard and never got any bonuses. Raj did not want to lose his friendships or job, and there was a lot of money to be made from a multinational company that does not recognize its employees. Within a few weeks, Raj had mastered the scheme and started filling his own oʼshore account with embezzled funds. He and his friends became even closer.
	Deviance can be the result of negative social labels—individuals are labeled as deviant, leading others to react to that label, which, in turn, can marginalize the individuals and impact their own self-perception.	People who have been labeled as sex offenders report having difficulty fully engaging with others and society. Many times, their label prohibits them from finding employment, housing, and even companionship. Others may avoid them or even recoil in disgust when they learn of their label. This ultimately affects how they interpret their value as a human.

The Bottom Line

No thought or action is inherently deviant. Therefore, what is deviant in one culture may not be in another, and what is considered deviant may change over time in any society. While deviance is typically interpreted negatively, there seem to be some clear positive functions it can serve society. For example, Martin Luther King, Jr., was arrested many times during his marches and protests in the 1950s and 1960s. He broke laws, making him a criminal and therefore deviant ("Martin Luther King Jr.—Biography," 2015). History has shown that while his past actions might have been criminal, now those actions are accepted and legal.

Moreover, his deviant actions and those of other Freedom Marchers laid a foundation for social change.

Throughout history, there have been many attempts to understand what causes deviance in humans, including the supernatural, the bumps on our heads, our body types, and the human genome. While many have been discredited and some need more investigation, sociological approaches offer promise in understanding the presence and causes of deviance. The sociological explanations for deviance center on one's social environment, the pressure to conform, desire for valuable social resources, social power, and labels that affect the way others treat us and how we view ourselves.

As we have seen, some crimes in America are at all-time lows and others are declining. Explaining this decline has tasked criminologists, economists, historians, and sociologists alike. Currently, there is still a vigorous debate about why we witnessed such a dramatic decline in violent crime from 1993 until 2010. The connection between lead and crime rate decline is highly controversial; at first glance, it seems outside the purview of sociology, but upon closer inspection, it considers variables such as social class, race, and the urban-rural divide.

Figure Credits

Bibliography

Alexander, Michelle. *The New Jim Crow: Mass Incarceration in the Age of Colorblindness.* New York: The New Press, 2012. Print.

Alpert, Geoffrey P., Roger G. Dunham, and Michael R. Smith. "Investigating Racial Profiling by the Miami-Dade Police Dept.: A Multimethod Approach." *Criminology & Public Policy* 6.1 (2007): 25–55. Web. 18 Apr. 2016.

Alpert, G., J.H. MacDonald, and R.G. Dunham. "Police Suspicion and Discretionary Decision Making During Citizen Stops." *Criminology* 43 (2005): 407–434. Web. 29 May 2015.

American Civil Liberties Union. "The Case Against the Death Penalty." American Civil Liberties Union, 2012. Web. 29 May 2015.

American Civil Liberties Union. "The War on Marijuana in Black and White." American Civil Liberties Union (2013). Web. 28 May 2015.

American Psychiatric Association. *Diagnostic and Statistical Manual of Mental Disorders.* 3rd ed. Washington, D.C.: American Psychiatric Association, 1987. Print.

American Psychiatric Association. "Minutes of the Council of Representatives." *American Psychologist* 30 (1975): 633. Web. 21 May 2015.

Becker, Howard S. *Outsiders: Studies in the Sociology of Deviance.* New York: Macmillan, 1963. Print.

Beckwith, Jon and Jonathan King. "The XYY Syndrome: A Dangerous Myth." *New Scientist* (1974): 474–476. Web. 9 Mar. 2016.

Beckwith, Johnathan R. *Making Genes, Making Waves: A Social Activist in Science.* Cambridge: Harvard University Press, 2002. Print.

Brame, R., S.D. Bushway, R. Paternoster, and M.G. Turner. "Demographic Patterns of Cumulative Arrest Prevalence by Ages 18 and 23." *Crime and Delinquency* 60 (2014): 471–486. Web. 29 May 2015.

Brennan, Alice, and Dan Lieberman. "Florida City's 'Stop and Frisk' Nabs Thousands of Kids, Finds 5-Year-Olds 'Suspicious'" *Fusion.* Fusion Publishing Media, 9 May 2014. Web. 29 May 2015.

Brown, Elizabeth and Mike Males. "Does Age or Poverty Level Best Predict Criminal Arrest and Homicide Rates?" *Justice Policy Journal* 8.1 (2011): 1–30. Web. 18 Apr. 2016.

Butler, J. Corey, Richard M. Ryckman, Bill Thornton, and Rachel L. Bouchard. "Assessment of the Full Content of Physique Stereotypes With a Free-Response Format." *The Journal of Social Psychology* 133.2 (1992): 147–162. Web. 22 Sept. 2015.

Butler, Paul. *Let's Get Free: A Hip-Hop Theory of Justice.* New York: The New Press, 2009. Print.

Cecil, Kim M., Christopher J. Brubaker, Caleb M. Adler, Kim N. Dietrich, Mekibib Altaye, John C. Egelhoff, Stephanie Wessel, Ilayaraja Elangovan, Richard Hornung, Kelly Jarvis, and Bruce P. Lanphear. "Decreased Brain Volume in Adults with Childhood Lead Exposure." *PLoS Med* 5.5 (2008): 741–750. Web. 28 May 2015.

Chambliss, William J. "The Saints and the Roughnecks." *Society* 11.1 (1973): 24–31. Web. 28 May 2015.

Chappell, Bill. "Miami-Area Police Chief Resigns Amid Charges of Racial Profiling." *The Two-Way. NPR.* Natl. Public Radio. 11 Dec. 2013. Web. 29 May 2015.

Chuck, Elizabeth. "The Killing of an Unarmed Teen: What We Know About Brown's Death." *NBC News.* NBC News. 13 Aug. 2014. Web. 23 Sept. 2015.

Clinard, Marshall B. and Peter C. Yeager. *Corporate Crime.* New York: Free Press, 1980. Print.

Crenshaw, Kimberle. "Demarginalizing the Intersection of Race and Sex: A Black Feminist Critique of Anti-discrimination Doctrine, Feminist Theory and Antiracist Politics." *University of Chicago Legal Forum* 140 (1989): 139–167. Web. 10 Dec. 2015.

Deemer, Andy. "Beijing's Single Most Horrific Meal." *Asia Obscura.* N.p., 12 July 2012. Web. 21 May 2015.

Dilulio Jr., John J. "My Black Crime Problem, and Ours." *Race, Crime, and Justice: A Reader.* Eds. Shaun L. Gabbidon and Helen Taylor Greene. New York: Routledge, 2005. 73–86. Print.

Dilulio Jr., John J. "The Coming of the Super—Predators." *The Weekly Standard.* Clarity Media Group, 27 Nov. 1995. Web. 28 May 2015.

Drum, Kevin. *America's Real Criminal Element: Lead.* Mother Jones, Jan. 2013. Web. 28 May 2015.

Durkheim, Émile. *The Division of Labor in Society.* 1893. New York: Free Press, 1964. Print.

Embry, Randa, and Phillip M. Lyons Jr. "Sex-Based Sentencing: Sentencing Discrepancies Between Male and Female Sex Offenders." *Feminist Criminology* 7 (2012): 146–162. Web. 28 May 2015.

Farrington, David P. and Kate A. Painter. "Gender Differences in Offending: Implications for Risk-Focused Prevention." *Home Office Online Report.* Home Office, Sept. 2004. Web. 11 Dec. 2015.

Fox, James Alan and Marianne W. Zawitz. *Homicide trends in the United States.* U.S. Dept. of Justice, Bureau of Justice Statistics [2007]. Web. 8 June 2016.

Frederique, Nadine, Patricia Joseph, and R. Christopher C. Hild. "What is the State of Empirical Research on Indigent Defense Nationwide? A Brief Overview and Suggestions for Future Research." *Albany Law Review* 78.3 (2015): 1317–1340. Web. 10 Dec. 2015.

Gardner, William I., Dorothy M. Griffiths, and Jeffrey P. Hamelin. "Biopsychosocial Features Influencing Aggression: A Multimodal Assessment and Therapy Approach." *The Handbook of High Risk Challenging Behaviors in People with Intellectual and Developmental Disabilities.* Ed. J. Luiselli. Baltimore: Paul Brooks Publishing, 2012. 83–104. Print.

Gelman, Andrew, Jeffrey Fagan, and Alex Kiss. "An Analysis of the New York City Police Department's "Stop-and-Frisk" Policy in the Context of Claims of Racial Bias." *Journal of the American Statistical Association* 102.479 (2007): 813–823. Web. 18 Apr. 2016.

Glaze, Lauren E., and Erinn J. Herberman. *Correctional Populations in the United States, 2012.* U.S. Dept. of Justice, Bureau of Justice Statistics [2013]. Web. 10 July 2014.

Goffman, Erving. *Stigma: Notes on the Management of Spoiled Identity.* New York: Simon & Schuster, 1963. Print.

Goldstein, Joseph, and Nate Schweber. "Man's Death After Chokehold Raises Old Issue for the Police" *New York Times.* New York Times, 18 July 2014. Web. 23 Sept. 2015.

Halder, Debarati, and K. Jaishankar. *Cyber Crime and the Victimization of Women: Laws, Rights, and Regulations.* Hershey: IGI Global, 2011. Print.

Hanson, Joyce A. *Rosa Parks: A Biography*. Santa Barbara: Greenwood Biographies, 2011. Print.

Harlow, Caroline Wolf. "Education and Correctional Populations" *Bureau of Justice Statistics Special Report* Washington: Office of Justice Programs, 2003. Web. 28 May 2015.

Harrell, Erika. "Victims of Identity Theft, 2014." *Bureau of Justice Statistics Bulletin* Washington: Office of Justice Programs, Sept. 2015. Web. 11 Dec. 2015.

Harrison, Ben. *Undying Lo`e: The True Story of a Passion That Deffed Death*. Far Hills, NJ: New Horizon, 1997. Print.

Hirschi, Travis. *Causes of Delinquency*. Berkeley: University of California, 1969. Print.

Institute for Criminal Policy Research. "World Prison Brief." *Institute for Criminal Policy Research*. Institute for Criminal Policy Research, 2015. Web. 3 Aug. 2016.

iWitness. *iWitness personal safety*. Computer software. *Apple App Store*. Vers. 2.0.7 iWitness, 6 Oct. 2015. Web. 18 Apr. 2016.

Jacobs, Patricia A. "The Discovery and History of Trisomy X and XYY Syndrome." *National Conference on Trisomy X and XYY*, UC Davis M.I.N.D. Institute. 2006. Web. 21 May 2015.

Javelin Strategy & Research. "How Consumers can Protect Against Identity Fraudsters in 2013." *Javelin Strategy & Research*. Javelin Strategy & Research, Feb. 2013. Web. 11 Dec. 2015.

Justice Policy Institute. "Bail Fail: Why the U.S. Should End the Practice of Using Money for Bail." *Justice Policy Institute*. Justice Policy Institute. Sept. 2012. Web. 23 Sept. 2015.

Kahn, M. *Always Hungry, Never Greedy: Food and the Expression of Gender in a Melanesian Society*. Long Grove: Waveland Press, 1993. Print.

Kane, John and April D. Wall. "The 2005 National Public Survey on White Collar Crime." National White Collar Crime Center, 2006. Web. 10 Dec. 2015.

Keady, Cameron. "New Hampshire Police Department Gives Out Free Pizza to Law-Abiding Citizens." *The Huffington Post*. HuffingtonPost.com, Inc., 12 Mar. 2015. Web. 8 Apr. 2015.

Kittle, Cameron. "A year after paralyzing accident, 'it could be worse' says Cooper Doucette." *The Telegraph*. The Telegraph, 31 Aug. 2011. Web. 28 Sept. 2015.

Kochel, Tammy Rinehart, David B. Wilson, and Stephen D. Mastrofski. "Effect of Suspect Race on Officer's Arrest Decisions." *Criminology* 49.2 (2011): 473–512. Web. 29 May 2015.

Kooistra, Paul, and Daniel M. Harrison. "Durkheim, Terrorism, and Positive Deviance." *International Journal of Crime, Criminal Justice, and Law* 2.2 (2007): 2–31. Web. 15 Sept. 2014.

Laughlin, Lynda. "Who's Minding the Kids? Child Care Arrangements: Spring 2011." *Household Economic Studies*. Washington, D.C.: U.S. Census Bureau, Apr. 2013. Web. 21 May 2015.

Lemert, Edwin M. *Human Deviance, Social Problems, and Social Control*. Englewood Cliffs: Prentice-Hall, 1972. Print.

Lemert, Edwin M. *Social Pathology: A Systematic Approach to the Theory of Sociopathic Behavior*. New York: McGraw-Hill, 1951. Print.

Levitt, Steven D. "Understanding Why Crime Fell in the 1990s: Four Factors That Explain the Decline and Six That Do Not." *Journal of Economic Perspectives* 18.1 (2004): 163–190. Web. 28 May 2015.

Lindsey, Linda L. *Gender Roles: A Sociological Perspective.* 6th ed. New York: Routledge, 2015. Print.

Loury, Glenn C. *Race, Incarceration, and American Values.* Cambridge: MIT Press, 2008. Print.

Manzi, Jim. *Uncontrolled: The Surprising Payoff of Trial-and-Error for Business, Politics, and Society.* New York: Basic Books, 2012. Print.

"Martin Luther King Jr.—Biography." *Nobel Prize.org.* Nobel Prize. 2015. Web. 23 Sept. 2015.

Needleman, Herbert. "Lead Poisoning." *Annual Review of Medicine* 55 (2004): 209–222. Web. 28 May 2015.

Nevin, Rick. "How Lead Exposure Relates to Temporal Changes in IQ, Violent Crime, and Unwed Pregnancy." *Environmental Research Section* 83 (2000): 1–22. Web. 28 May 2015.

"Who We Are." North American Man/Boy Love Association. The North American Man/Boy Love Association, 2011. Web. 28 July 2016. <http://nambla.org/welcome.html>.

Orth, Stephan. "Members Only: A Visit to Beijing's Exclusive Penis Restaurant." *Spiegel Online International.* Spiegel Online International, 25 Apr. 2008. Web. 28 July 2016.

Parra, Fernando. "Good, the Bad, and the Ugly: Veterano (Older) Chicano Gang Members and the (Dys) Functional Aspects of the Role." *Journal of Gang Research* 8.4 (2001): 13–18. Web. 22 Sept. 2015.

Pollardy, Richard. "Deepwater Horizon Oil Spill of 2010." *Encyclopedia Britannica.* 20 Apr. 2015. 29 May 2015.

Public Engines Inc. *TipSubmit Mobile.* Computer software. *Apple App Store.* Vers. 3.1 Public Engines Inc., 29 Oct. 2014. Web. 18 Apr. 2016.

Raphael, Steven, and Michael A. Stoll. *Why Are So Many Americans in Prison?* New York: Russell Sage Foundation, 2013. Print.

Ratcliffe, S. "The Psychological and Psychiatric Consequences of Sex Chromosome Abnormalities in Children, Based on Population Studies." *Basic Approaches to Genetic and Molecularbiological Developmental Psychiatry.* Ed. Poustka, F. Berlin: Quintessenz, 1994. Print.

Reyes, Jessica Wolpaw. "Environmental Policy as Social Policy? The Impact of Childhood Lead Exposure on Crime." *The B.E. Journal of Economic Analysis and Policy* 7.1 (2007): 1–41. Web. 28 May 2015.

Rosenbaum, Ron. "The Great Ivy League Nude Posture Photo Scandal." *New York Times.* New York Times, 15 Jan. 1995. Web. 1 Oct. 2014.

Saad, Lydia. "U.S. Smoking Rate Still Coming Down." *Gallup.* Gallup, 24 July 2008. Web. 28 May 2015.

Shaw, C.R., and H.D. McKay. *Juvenile Delinquency and Urban Areas.* Chicago: University of Chicago Press, 1942. Print.

Sheldon, William Herbert. *Atlas of Men; A Guide for Somatotyping the Adult Male at All Ages.* New York: Harper, 1954. Print.

Simmons, J.L. *Deviants.* Santa Barbara: University of California Press, 1969. Print.

Simoons, Frederick J. *Food in China: A Cultural and Historical Inquiry.* Ann Arbor: 1990. Print.

Staples, Brent. "The Human Cost of 'Zero Tolerance'" *New York Times.* New York Times, 28 Apr. 2012. Web. 23 Sept. 2015.

Sutherland, Edwin H. *Principles of Criminology*. 4th ed. Philadelphia: J.B. Lippincott, 1947. Print.

Sutherland, Edwin H. *White Collar Crime*. New York: Dryden Press, 1949. Print.

"Target: 40 Million Credit Cards Compromised." *CNN Money*. Cable News Network, 19 Dec. 2013. Web. 30 May 2015. <http://money.cnn.com/2013/12/18/news/companies/target-credit-card/>.

The Sentencing Project. "Report of The Sentencing Project to the United Nations Human Rights Committee: Regarding Racial Disparities in the United States Criminal Justice System." *The Sentencing Project*. United Nations, Aug. 2013. Web. 3 Aug. 2016.

Truman, Jennifer, Lynn Langton, and Michael Planty. *Criminal Victimization, 2012*. U.S. Dept. of Justice, Bureau of Justice Statistics [2013]. Web. 9 Mar. 2016.

United States. Dept. of Health and Human Services. Centers for Disease Control and Prevention. *Current Cigarette Smoking Among Adults in the United States*. Washington: Centers for Disease Control and Prevention, 23 Jan. 2015. Web. 28 May 2015.

United States Dept. of Justice. Bureau of Justice Assistance. *Byrne Justice Assistance Grant (JAG) Program FY 2014 Local Solicitation*. Washington: Office of Justice Programs, n.d. Web. 28 May 2015.

United States Dept. of Justice. Bureau of Justice Statistics. *National Crime Victimization Survey*. Washington: Office of Justice Programs, 2015. Web. 21 May 2015.

United States. Dept. of Justice. Federal Bureau of Investigation. *Crime in the United States, 2012*. Washington: Federal Bureau of Investigation. Sept. 2013. Web. 1 Oct. 2014.

United States. Dept. of Justice. Federal Bureau of Investigation. *Crime in the United States, 2013*. Washington: Federal Bureau of Investigation. Sept. 2014. Web. 28 May 2015.

United States. Dept. of Justice. Federal Bureau of Investigation. *Hate Crimes*. Washington: Federal Bureau of Investigation. 2016. Web. 18 Apr. 2016.

United States. Dept. of Justice. Federal Bureau of Investigation. *Identity Theft*. Washington: Federal Bureau of Investigation. 2015. Web. 11 Dec. 2015.

United States. Dept. of Justice. Federal Bureau of Investigation. *Italian Organized Crime*. Washington: Federal Bureau of Investigation, 2015. Web. 29 May 2015.

United States. Dept. of Justice. Federal Bureau of Investigation. *Organized Crime*. Washington: Federal Bureau of Investigation, 2016. Web. 3 Aug. 2016.

United States. Dept. of Justice. Federal Bureau of Investigation. San Diego Division. *Interstate Stalking Defendant Sentenced to Five Years in Prison*. Washington: Federal Bureau of Investigation, 2013. Web. 23 Sept. 2015

United States. Federal Bureau of Prisons. "Inmate Race." Federal Bureau of Prisons, 2016. Web. 3 Aug. 2016.

Venkatesh, Sudir. "Five Myths About Prostitution" *The Washington Post*. N.p., 12 Sept. 2010 Web. 29 May 2015.

Vertinsky, P. "Physique as Destiny: William H. Sheldon, Barbara Honeyman Heath and the Struggle for Hegemony in the Science of Somatotyping." *Canadian Bulletin of Medical History*, 24.2 (2007): 291–316. Web. 21 May 2015.

Vorpal Fox. *iSpotACrime*. Computer software. *Apple App Store*. Vorpal Fox, 15 Mar. 2016. Web. 18 Apr. 2016.

Walker, S., C. Spohn, and M. DeLone. *The Color of Justice: Race, Ethnicity, and Crime in America*. 3rd ed. Belmont: Wadsworth/Thompson Learning, 2004. Print.

Walzer, S., A.S. Bashir, and A.R. Silbert. "Cognitive and Behavioral Factors in the Learning Disabilities of 47,XXY and 47,XYY Boys." *Birth Defects Orig Artic Ser*. 26.4 (1990): 45–58. Web. 9 Mar. 2016.

Weiss, Mitchell G., Jayashree Ramakrishna and Daryl Somma. "Health Related Stigma: Rethinking Concepts and Interventions." *Psychology, Health, and Medicine* 11.3 (2006): 277–287. Web. 29 May 2015.

Westboro Baptist Church. "GodHatesFags." Westboro Baptist Church. *Westboro Baptist Church*, 2016. Web. 3 Aug. 2016.

Whitaker, Kati. "Ghana Witch Camps: Widows' Lives in Exile." *BBC News*. BBC, 1 Sept. 2012. Web. 21 May 2015.

Wilson, Lori Lee. *The Salem Witch Trials*. Minneapolis: Lerner Publications, 1997. Print.

Wolitzky-Taylor, Kate B., Heidi S. Resnick, Jenna L. McCauley, Ananda B. Amstadter, Dean G. Kilpatrick, and Kenneth J. Ruggiero. "Is Reporting of Rape on the Rise? A Comparison of Women with Reported Versus Unreported Rape Experiences in the National Women's Study-Replication." *Journal of Interpersonal Violence* 26.4 (2010): 807–832. Web. 9 Mar. 2016.

Wright, John Paul, Kim N. Dietrich, M. Douglas Ris, Richard W. Hornung, Stephanie D. Wessel, Bruce P. Lanphear, Mona Ho, and Mary N. Rae. "Association of Prenatal and Childhood Blood Lead Concentrations with Criminal Arrests in Early Adulthood." *PLoS Med* 5.5 (2008): 732–740. Web. 28 May 2015.

Xu, Daniel. "Total Cost of 2010 BP Oil Spill to Gulf Anglers Estimated at $585 Million." *OutdoorHub*. Outdoor Hub, 11 Sept. 2014. Web. 29 May 2015.

Zhao, Rongguang. *A History of Food Culture in China*. Trans. Gangliu Wang and Aimee Yiran Wang. New York: SCPG Publishing Corporation, 2015. Print.

CHAPTER 6

Social Stratification

Chapter 6 encompasses the elements of wealth, income, status, power, hierarchical differences, and inequalities. This chapter includes a more detailed account of the accelerating gap between the people with great wealth and the poor with little or nothing to provide their future generations. Further, this chapter paints a picture of the inequalities distressing the lives of billons of people around the world. Collins (2012) explains why unequal societies are more likely to have greater instances of heart disease, asthma, mental illnesses, cancer, and other diseases. The three core themes of this chapter are as follows:

1. Greater inequality of wealth and power undermine our democratic system, economic stability, and public trust.

2. Inequality was the foremost underlying factor of the 1929 and 2008 economic declines in the United States.

3. Poverty and inequality are the main contributing factors for poor health outcomes.

How Inequality Wrecks Everything We Care About

Chuck Collins

....

> *The reality is that U.S. society is polarizing and its social arteries are hardening. The sumptuousness and bleakness of the respective lifestyles of rich and poor represents a scale of difference in opportunity and wealth that is almost medieval—and a standing offense to the American expectation that everyone has the opportunity for life, liberty and happiness.* —Will Hutton (b. 1951)

Inequality is wrecking the world. Not just poverty, which is destroying the lives of billions of people around the planet, but also inequality—the accelerating gap between the 99 percent and the 1 percent.

The Inequality Death Spiral

According to research in dozens of disciplines, the extreme disparities of wealth and power corrode our democratic system and public trust. They lead to a breakdown in civic cohesion and social solidarity, which in turn leads to worsened health outcomes.

Inequality undercuts social mobility and has disastrous effects on economic stability and growth. The notion of a "death spiral" may sound dramatic, but it captures the dynamic and reinforcing aspects of inequality. And these inequalities were a major contributing factor to the 1929 and 2008 economic downturns. What follows is the case against inequality.

Inequality Wrecks Our Democracy and Civic Life

Inequality is disenfranchising us, diminishing our vote at the ballot box and our voice in the public square. As dollars of the 1 percent displace the votes of the 99 percent as the currency of politics, the 1 percent wins. Not every time, but enough so that the tilt continues toward the agenda of the 1 percent.

The money of the 1 percent dominates our campaign finance system, even after efforts at reform. To run for U.S. Senate—or to win additional terms in the Senate after being elected—politicians must raise an estimated $15,000 a day in campaign contributions. To do this efficiently, politicians have to spend a lot of time courting people in the 1 percent, attending $1,000-a-plate fund-raising dinners and listening to their concerns and agenda. This means less time shaking hands in front of the Costco or Cracker Barrel. We all respond to the people we are surrounded by, and politicians are no different.

Elections do matter. Politicians care about votes on Election Day, and they campaign for those votes and work to get supporters to the polls. But candidates for the U.S. Congress know that every other day of the year they have to think about money.

The corporate 1 percent dominates the lobbying space around federal and state policies. In the last thirty years, the ranks of official lobbyists have exploded. In 1970, there were five registered lobbyists for every one of the 535 members of Congress. Today there are twenty-two lobbyists for every member.[1]

Who lobbies for the 99 percent? There are impressive organizations out there, such as Public Citizen and the Children's Defense Fund, that stand up, wave their arms, and say, "Hey, what about the 99 percent?" But they are severely underresourced, outgunned, and outmaneuvered by the organized 1 percent.

Inequality Makes Us Sick

The medical researchers have said it. And now a growing body of public health research is arriving at the same conclusion: inequality is making us sick.

The more inequality grows between the 1 percent and the 99 percent, the less healthy we are. Unequal communities have greater rates of heart disease, asthma, mental illness, cancer, and other morbid illnesses.

Of course, poverty contributes to all kinds of bad health outcomes. But research shows that you are better off in a low-income community with greater equality than you are in a community with a higher income but more extreme inequalities.

Counties and countries with lower incomes but less inequality have better health outcomes. They have lower infant mortality rates, longer life expectancy, and lower incidences of all kinds of diseases. Counties with higher average incomes but greater disparities between rich and poor have the opposite indicators. They are less healthy places to live.[2]

Why is this so? According to British health researcher Richard Wilkinson, communities with less inequality have stronger "social cohesion," more cultural limits on unrestrained individualism, and more effective networks of mutual aid and caring. "The individualism and values of the market are restrained by a social morality," Wilkinson writes. The existence of more social capital "lubricates the workings of the whole society and economy. There are fewer signs of antisocial aggressiveness, and society appears more caring."[3]

Inequality Tears Our Communities Apart

Extreme inequalities of wealth rip our communities apart with social divisions and distrust, leading to an erosion of social cohesion and solidarity. The 1 percent and the 99 percent today don't just live on opposite sides of the tracks—they occupy parallel universes.

New research shows that we're becoming more polarized by class and race in terms of where we live. A 2011 report based on U.S. Census data notes, "As overall income inequality grew in the last four decades, high- and low-income families have become increasingly less likely to live near one another. Mixed income neighborhoods have grown rarer, while affluent and poor neighborhoods have grown much more common."[4] As this distance widens, it is harder for people to feel like they are in the same boat.

High levels of inequality lead to the construction of physical walls. In many parts of the world, the members of the 1 percent reside in gated communities, surrounded by security systems and bodyguards. More than 9 million house holds in the United States live behind walls in gated communities, similar to the statistics in polarized societies such as Mexico and Brazil. Over a third of new housing starts in the southern United States are in gated communities.[5]

The relationship between the 1 percent and the 99 percent is characterized by fear, distance, misunderstanding, distrust, and class and racial antagonisms. As a result, there is less caring and a greater amount of individualistic behavior. Part of how people express care is support for public investments in health infrastructure and prevention that benefit everyone. As societies grow unequal, support for such investments declines.

Solidarity is characterized by people taking responsibility for one another and caring for neighbors. But for solidarity to happen, people must know one another and have institutions that transcend differences in class, culture, and race. In communities with great inequality, these institutions don't exist and solidarity is weakened.

Inequality Erodes Social Mobility and Equal Opportunity

Inequality undermines the cherished value of equality of opportunity and social mobility. Intergenerational mobility is the possibility of shifting up or down the income ladder relative to your parents' status. In a mobile society, your economic circumstances are not defined or limited by the economic origins of your family.

For many decades, economists argued that inequality in the United States was the price we paid for a dynamic economy with social mobility.[6] We didn't want to be like Canada or those northern Europe an economies, economists would argue, with their rigid class systems and lack of mobility.

But here's the bad news: Canada and those Europe an nations—with their social safety nets and progressive tax policies—are now more mobile than U.S. society. Research across the industrialized OECD countries has found that Canada, Australia, and the Nordic countries (Denmark, Norway, Sweden, and Finland) are among the most mobile. There is a strong correlation between social mobility and policies that redistribute income and wealth through taxation. The United States is now among the *least* mobile of industrialized countries in terms of earnings.[7]

Inequality Erodes Public Services

The 99 percent depends on the existence of a robust commonwealth of public and community institutions. As Bill Gates Sr., the father of the founder of Microsoft, wrote,

> The ladder of opportunity for America's middle class depends on strong and accessible public educational institutions, libraries, state parks and municipal pools. And for America's poor, the ladder of opportunity also includes access to affordable health care, quality public transportation, and childcare assistance.[8]

Historically, during times of great inequality, there is a disinvestment in the commonwealth.[9] There is less support provided for education, affordable housing, public health care, and other pillars of a level playing field. By contrast, in 1964, a time of relative equality, there was greater concern about poverty; in fact, we launched the War on Poverty to further reduce disadvantage.

Today, as the 1 percent delinks from our communities, it privatizes the services it needs. This leads to two bad outcomes. First, because the 1 percent does not depend on commonwealth services, it would rather not pay for them. They often prefer tax cuts and limited government, which leave them more of their money to spend on privatized services.

Second, the quality of life for the 99 percent suffers when the wealthy don't have a personal stake in maintaining quality public services. As we've seen, the 1 percent has tremendous clout. Its members have the ear of elected officials, command over charitable dollars, dominance of media ownership, and networking connections that are sometimes called "social capital." In a democratic society, good government and strong public institutions require civic engagement by everyone. But when those with the biggest amount of political power, largest number of connections, and greatest capacity don't have a stake, a cycle of disinvestment occurs.

The cycle of disinvestment begins when public services start to deteriorate after the withdrawal of tax dollars and the participation of the powerful. For example, if someone doesn't use the neighborhood public swimming pool because he or she belongs to a private club or spends summers at a private beach house, that person doesn't have a stake in ensuring that the public swimming pool is open all summer, clean and well maintained, and staffed with qualified lifeguards. When services deteriorate and the powerful no longer participate, it leads to a decline in political support and resources, which in turn leads to a cycle of further disinvestment.

This lack of stake is even more visible in terms of public education, where the withdrawal of the 1 percent and even the top 30 percent of families has contributed to severe disinvestment in some school districts. This triggers a vicious circle of budget cuts, stakeholders pulling out, and declining public support for education.

The cycle of disinvestment accelerates when it becomes rational to abandon public and community services if one can afford to do so. Those who can get out do so, in a rush-to-the-exits moment. Families in the 99 percent work extra hard to privatize the services they need until there is a wholesale withdrawal from the public sphere.

If you can't depend on the bus to get to work, you buy a car. If you can't rely on the local public schools to educate your child, then you stretch to pay for private schools. If you can't depend on the lifeguards to show up at the public pool, then you join the private pool. If you can't depend on the police to protect your neighborhood, you hire a private security service or move to a gated community. The cycle of disinvestment continues and the costs of privatized services rise, trapping the remaining families in poor schools and neighborhoods lacking services.

Inequality Undermines Economic Growth

Remember the last time in history that the 1 percent had such a large share of the wealth pie? It was 1929, the eve of the Great Depression. Economic historians argue that this was not a coincidence. Too much inequality contributes to economic instability.

The corollary is that periods of shared prosperity have greater economic growth and stability. The period after World War II, 1947 to 1977, is often cited as a case study of a high-growth and high-equality period.

Making such comparisons is fraught with danger—we're not just comparing apples and oranges, we're comparing bicycles and dump trucks. The period after World War II was unprecedented in terms of the dominant and unrivaled role the United States played in the global economy. But international comparative data that look at inequality and economic performance reinforce this story. More-equal societies do better on most indicators.

The conventional wisdom, espoused in the 1960s by economists such as Arthur Okun of the Brookings Institution, was that there was a trade-off between growth and equity: policies that increased equality would slow economic growth, and aggressive pro-growth policies would worsen inequality. But this thinking is now being turned on its head.

Research by the International Monetary Fund (IMF) and the National Bureau of Economic Research point to the fact that more-equal societies have stronger rates of growth, experience longer economic expansions, and are quicker to recover from economic downturns. According to Jonathan Ostry, an economist at the IMF, trends toward unequal income in the United States mean that future economic expansions will be just one-third as long as they were in the 1960s, prior to the widening of the income divide. Less-equal societies are more vulnerable to both financial crises and political instability.[10]

In volatile markets, investors become gun-shy, even those in the 1 percent. When they perceive that financial markets are rigged in favor of insiders and the politically connected, they take their money somewhere else. "You're going to lose a generation of investors," observed Barry Ritholtz, an investor researcher with Fusion IQ. "And that's how you end up with a 25-year bear market. That's the risk if people start to think there is no economic justice."[11]

Many economists have drawn parallels between 1929 on the eve of the Great Depression and the 2008 economic meltdown. Raghuram Rajan, a former chief economist for the IMF, argues that both depressions were preceded by periods of extreme inequality. In his book *Fault Lines: How Hidden Fractures Still Threaten the World Economy*, Rajan observes that during the decade prior to both economic downturns, the 1 percent captured a gigantic percentage of income gains and wages were stagnant for the majority of Americans. Meanwhile, government policies and private corporate practices encouraged easy access to credit and borrowing among the poor and middle classes. House hold debt nearly doubled during both periods.[12]

Did inequality play a role in the 2008 economic meltdown?

Notes

1. According to the Center for Responsive Politics, there were 12,220 registered lobbyists in 2011. This is 22.84 lobbyists for every one of the 535 members of Congress. Center for Responsive Politics, "Lobbying Database," www.opensecrets.org/lobby/index.php?ql3 (accessed January 3, 2012).

2. For a good overview of health and inequality issues, see Sam Pizzigati, *Greed and Good: Understanding and Overcoming the Inequality That Limits Our Lives* (New York: Apex Press, 2004), 311–30. Also see Dr. Stephen Bezruchka's website, Population Health Forum (http://depts.washington.edu/eqhlth), for information on global and U.S. health and inequality information. Also see Stephen Bezruchka and M. A. Mercer, "The Lethal Divide: How Economic Inequality Affects Health," in M. Fort, M. A. Mercer, and O. Gish, eds., *Sickness and Wealth: The Corporate Assault on Global Health* (Boston: South End Press, 2004), 11–18.

3. See Richard Wilkinson, *Unhealthy Societies: The Afflictions of Inequality* (London: Routledge, 1996).

4. Sean F. Reardon and Kendra Bischoff, "Growth in the Residential Segregation of Families by Income, 1970–2009," Stanford University, US 2010 Project, Russell Sage Foundation, and American Communities Project at Brown University, November 2011, www.s4.brown.edu/us2010/Data/Report/report111111.pdf (accessed January 3, 2012).

5. Edward J. Blakely and Mary Gail Snyder, *Fortress America: Gated Communities in the United States* (Washington, DC: Brookings Institution Press, 1997); and Justice Policy Institute study, as reported in Jesse Katy, "A Nation of Too Many Prisoners?" *Los Angeles Times*, February 15, 2000.

6. Wojciech Kopczuk, Emmanuel Saez, and Jae Song, "Earnings Inequality and Mobility in the United States: Evidence from Social Security Data Since 1937," *Quarterly Journal of Economics* 125, 1 (February 2010): 91–128, http://ideas.repec.org/a/tpr/qjecon/v125y2010i1p91-128.html (accessed January 3, 2012).

7. OECD, "A Family Affair: Intergenerational Social Mobility Across OECD Countries," *Economic Policy Reforms: Going for Growth*, www.oecd.org/dataoecd/2/7/45002641.pdf (accessed January 3, 2012). Also see the Pew Charitable Trust's Economic Mobility Project (www.economicmobility.org) and their study "Chasing the Same Dream, Climbing Different Ladders: Economic Mobility in the United States and Canada," January 2010, www.economicmobility.org/reports_and_research/other/other?id=0012 (accessed January 3, 2012).

8. Bill Gates Sr. and Chuck Collins, *Wealth and Our Commonwealth: Why American Should Tax Accumulated Fortunes* (Boston: Beacon Press, 2003).

9. Ibid., 19–22.

10. David Lynch, "How Inequality Hurts the Economy," *Business Week Insider*, November 16, 2011, www.businessweek.com/magazine/how-inequality-hurts-the-economy-11162011.html?campaign_id=rss_topStories (accessed January 3, 2012).

11. Ibid.

12. Raghuram G. Rajan, *Fault Lines: How Hidden Fractures Still Threaten the World Economy* (Princeton, NJ: Princeton Unversity Press, 2010).

CHAPTER 7

Race and Ethnicity

Chapter 7 examines race as social phenomenon. This chapters argues established biological, physiological, and genetic differences to categorize race. Rather than viewing race as a biologically self-evident reality, it focuses on complex social, historical, political, and cultural characteristics. By examining characteristics of race and ethnic groups, Buechler (2014) views race as a powerful social fact and asserts that its categories are arbitrary. To understand the social construction of race and racism, this chapter discusses European colonization, exploitation of African slaves, and the conquests of Native people. It also encompasses the recent interpretations of racial categories and ethnic identities including Latino/a and Asian populations in the United States. Finally, this chapters describes the effects of ethnocentrism, stereotypes, unequal treatment, prejudice, segregation, racism, discrimination, assimilation, and the social construction of difference on dominant and subordinate racial and ethnic group relations. Forms of discrimination are explained as they relate to daily life in terms of income, jobs, education, political representation, life expectancy, and health.

The Social Construction of Race

Steven M. Buechler

....

T he analysis of social class has been part of sociology from the beginning. Race is different. Although scholars like W. E. B. Du Bois (1903) had crucial insights into race relations more than a hundred years ago, sociology was slow to see race as an important subject in its own right.

This gradually changed after Gunnar Myrdal's *An American Dilemma* (1944) placed racial prejudice at the forefront of public consciousness. Along with other work, it helped establish race and ethnic relations as a major subfield within sociology. Group dynamics, racial conflict, prejudice, and discrimination attracted increasing sociological attention.

What really invigorated the study of race were not academic developments but social conflict. As the civil rights movement overturned the most explicit forms of racial segregation and discrimination in the 1950s and 1960s, race became even more central in public awareness and academic study. As the movement evolved from liberal integration to black power to cultural nationalism, different understandings of race emerged. These movement-inspired analyses revealed how race was embedded in social structure.

Current sociological understandings of race thus have a dual legacy. The slowly developing academic study of race has been infused with critical insights from race-based social movements. Much the same can be said for the impact of the feminist movement in jump-starting sociology's understanding of gender issues.

What is Race?

Few things seem more obvious than someone's race. As we interact with others, we unthinkingly place them within familiar racial categories. On rare occasions, someone doesn't easily fit the categories. We might regard them as odd or unusual, but we rarely use such cases to question the categories themselves.

When we "see" race like this, we are also likely to assume race is rooted in biology. The physical differences between races (skin color, facial features, eye shape, hair texture) seem so self-evident as to be beyond question. Everyday consciousness assumes these features reflect well-established biological, physiological, and genetic differences that distinguish races. Well-meaning people might struggle to avoid prejudices and stereotypes, but they are likely to see race as a biologically self-evident reality.

This is a good time to recall Peter Berger's (1963) sociological insight that things are not always what they seem. Beneath the seemingly self-evident biology of race, there are complex social, political, and cultural forces that sustain that appearance. Put differently, race is not biologically determined but rather socially constructed. This implies two seemingly contradictory things. First, racial categories are arbitrary. They have little scientific or biological foundation. They are not "real." Second, these categories nevertheless *become real* through social definitions. As W. I. Thomas noted long ago, if a situation is defined as real, it will be real in its consequences. When the definition is embedded in centuries of institutions and interactions, then race becomes as real as any social phenomenon can be. Race is an illusory biological fiction but a powerful social fact.

There are several reasons to question the biological basis of race. Human beings share almost 99 percent of our genetic composition with higher primates. Put differently, homo sapiens are only 1 to 2 percent genetically different from chimpanzees. If the genetic margin separating two species is so small, the likelihood that there will be consistent genetic differences *within* the category of homo sapiens that sort humans into genetically distinct races is highly implausible.

A second reason to doubt the biological basis of race involves the logic of categories and classification. Such logic makes sense when things fall into mutually exclusive categories based on many relevant traits. It makes less sense if there is a lot of overlap between things in supposedly separate categories. The logic is weakest when there is more individual variation within categories than the average variation between categories. And yet it is this weakest version that applies to race. On any number of physical traits, individual variations within races far exceed average differences between them. When categories persist in such situations, it is because they are based on social definitions rather than on logically compelling reasons or scientifically verifiable data.

A third reason to doubt the biological basis of race involves the history of racial typologies. Systems of racial classification have been proposed for centuries, with none of the logical consistency, cumulative advances, or increasing specificity that define scientific progress. Throughout this history, there has been major disagreement over things as basic as how many races exist. After centuries of work, the only real lesson here is that the very idea of distinguishing races in biological terms is not scientifically feasible.

A fourth reason to question the biological basis of race involves social and legal definitions. When Southern legislators defined people as "Negro" if one thirty-second of their ancestry was African, this was a social definition and not a biological fact. When Native American tribes use similar measures to determine who is a legitimate tribal member, this is also a social definition and not a biological fact. Because racial definitions vary by place, you can change your race by flying to Brazil where an unusually complex set of racial distinctions will define your race differently from the place you just left (Henslin 2005, 327). Racial definitions also change over time; consider "how the Irish became white" (Ignatiev 1995) in nineteenth-century US history.

One final example: People sometimes defend a biological conception of race based on medical conditions. In the United States, sickle-cell anemia is considered a "black disease." In reality, a predisposition to sickle-cell anemia derives from geography and evolution and not race. In places where malaria was a big threat to human health, a few people had a natural immunity. Through natural selection, they reproduced in greater numbers. However, the same factors creating the immunity also made them susceptible to sickle-cell anemia. Thus, some but not all Africans are susceptible, and some non-Africans from Mediterranean regions and South Asia are susceptible. It is difficult to see how this qualifies as a "racial" disease (Adelman 2003).

It is not physical but social facts that make races "real." This social construction of race is a historical process. People have always noted human differences, but a new discourse of race emerged during European exploration, conquest, and colonization typically dated from the "discovery" of the "New World" in 1492. Thus, Columbus's diaries refer to the "savages" he encountered. With each subsequent encounter between European colonizers and indigenous groups, the discourse of race grew to describe these "others" in racial terms (Winant 2004).

This discourse rested on two premises. The first was that races were biological realities. The second was that races existed in a hierarchy of superiority and inferiority. In these hierarchies, whites, Europeans, or some subgroup of Europeans were inevitably located at the top of the hierarchy. Despite many variations, some races (the people doing the classifying) were always superior to others (the people being classified). The very concept of race is *racist,* because beliefs about superiority and inferiority have always been part of the concept.

The reasons are not a big mystery. European colonization was often brutal and inhumane. It contradicted many social norms, religious principles, and moral imperatives of the colonizers. It required some type of legitimation of the contradiction between humane values and inhumane behavior. Thus the invention of race/racism.

Colonialism only poses a moral dilemma if people are seen as equals. The social construction of race/racism defines the colonized group as inferior or subhuman. The more their humanity is denied, the more brutality becomes acceptable. Consider that few people have qualms about the slaughter and consumption of animals because they are seen as a different species. It hardly occurs to us that this requires a justification. Some versions of racism also suggest that "others" are a different species, so the moral code of the dominant group does not apply. The same logic operates in warfare; it is easier to kill people who are seen as less than human. It is no accident that the most extreme versions of racial thinking culminate in genocide, where others are not only seen as subhuman but as a threat that must be eliminated.

The social construction of race links biology, inferiority, and racism in fateful ways. Like race, racism has many variations. It can provide justifications for enslavement and genocide. It can seek to convert others who have not yet had the benefits of "civilization." It can portray "others" as innocent children requiring protection and guidance. In every version, however, a presumption of racial inferiority is central.

The social construction of race and racism was vital in legitimizing European colonization and conquest. The United States followed suit in the exploitation of African slaves, the conquest of Native peoples, and racist relations with Latino/a and Asian populations. The timing and groups were different, but the history of US race relations mirrors the European model quite closely.

Although race is a biological fiction, there is a social logic to why this fiction arose and how it shapes contemporary society. The challenge of seeing race as a social construction is to balance the seeming contradiction that something arbitrary has been socially constructed into something as "real" as any social fact can be.

Race vs. Ethnicity

The social construction of race also becomes evident by contrasting "races" and "ethnic groups." Common sense equates race with biology and ethnicity with culture. Although the link between race and biology is problematic, the equation of ethnicity and culture is sound.

Ethnic groups are distinguished by cultural differences in language, customs, norms, values, and religious beliefs. Although their members might be geographically dispersed, ethnic groups often trace their roots to a distinctive place. Although it is culturally learned, ethnicity "feels" natural to people. Ethnocentrism is a common expression of the "naturalness" or superiority of one's group and way of doing things.

As socially constructed categories, "races" lump together many ethnic groups in the same racial category. Each of the major races typically recognized in the United States (African Americans, European Americans, Latino/a Americans, Native Americans, and Asian Americans) includes multiple ethnicities. The most obvious expression of racism is the blatant division between the dominant racial group of European Americans and all other subordinate racial groups.

A subtler expression of racism is that ethnic variations within the dominant racial group are often recognized, whereas variations within subordinate racial groups are not. Thus, in both popular consciousness and much sociological work, ethnicity really means cultural variations among European Americans (Polish, Swedish, Italian, German, etc.) whereas race lumps others into broad racial categories (blacks, Hispanics, Native Americans, etc.). This practice obscures the fact that "white" is also a socially constructed race and that other races have internal ethnic differences.

A long history of unequal treatment has made these arbitrary distinctions into powerful realities. Consider the following contrasts. Members of white ethnic groups typically entered the United

States voluntarily, could sometimes conceal their ethnicity, were seen as variations on a common theme of being white, were eventually pressured to assimilate, and had at least some opportunities for integration and upward mobility. Members of racial minorities, by contrast, became part of the United States involuntarily, could rarely conceal their race, were seen as fundamentally different, were subject to strict segregation, and had few opportunities for integration and upward mobility until quite recently. Such differences suggest different models of ethnic and race relations.

For white ethnic groups, the main story is assimilation. However, the melting pot image of assimilation is misleading by implying that all groups change equally as they are "melted" into something new. In reality, there has always been a hierarchy among white ethnic groups. WASPs, or white Anglo-Saxon Protestants, have been at the top, followed by other Northern Europeans, and then Central and Southern Europeans. Assimilation has not meant blending but rather change by subordinate white ethnic groups. Consider that the United States did not create a new language through assimilation. Assimilating groups gave up native languages and adopted English. Assimilation involved a trade-off in which subordinate white ethnic groups sacrificed ethnic distinctiveness in exchange for admission into mainstream society.

Assimilation involves several stages that begin with cultural assimilation (Gordon 1964). This occurs when a newly arriving white ethnic group learns and adopts the culture of the dominant group. This is the only stage the subordinate group can control. Indeed, they might initially resist this stage, in which case assimilation will not occur. If and when they do initiate the process, control passes to the dominant group.

This is evident in the second stage of structural assimilation. This means acceptance of the subordinate group by the dominant group. Such acceptance initially occurs in secondary groups like the workplace and other public settings. It then involves accepting people as neighbors or in churches and voluntary organizations. It culminates with acceptance into primary groups like friendship networks. At each stage, the subordinate group can initiate contact, but the dominant group retains the power to accept or reject it.

Assimilation then proceeds through other stages that reflect still greater acceptance. Marital assimilation occurs when members of different groups intermarry with increasing frequency and decreasing disapproval. Identificational assimilation occurs when members of the assimilating group switch identities from their original ethnicity to their new nation. This could take generations. Immigrants might retain their Italian identity, while the next generation identifies as Italian American, and subsequent generations identify as American.

Subsequent stages include attitudinal assimilation, indicated by a reduction in prejudicial attitudes about the subordinate group. This often corresponds with behavioral assimilation, evidenced by a reduction in discrimination against members of the group. The process culminates with civic assimilation, signified by the elimination of ethnic conflict.

Although the story of assimilation seems to offer a happy ending, it is shaped by unequal power throughout. The dominant group provides the standard for what assimilation means (becoming like them), and it controls the pace. They retain their dominance because their culture becomes normative for all. The subordinate group pays the cost by relinquishing their ethnic heritage. When the costs seem worth the benefits, groups seek assimilation. Although abstract models oversimplify complex histories, this model accurately describes the assimilation of a number of white ethnic groups in the United States.

Given their different treatment, it is not surprising that the assimilationist model doesn't fit racial groups in the United States. Some insist that with enough time, racial minorities will also assimilate, but this is a dubious claim. The histories of these groups are different, the scope of discrimination is wider, and resistance to assimilation has been substantial. Moreover, the persistence of distinctive racial cultures suggests that many people in these groups would not seek assimilation even if it were possible.

Such differences drew many scholars to the model of internal colonialism to analyze racial dynamics (Omi and Winant 1994, 44–46). This model rests on an analogy between race relations within a single country and colonial relations between countries. In the analogy, the white power structure in a single country is like the colonial power, and racial minorities in that country are like colonies.

Several parallels lend credence to the analogy. Both relationships begin with forced contact, because colonial powers and white power structures use coercion to establish the relationship in the first place. Coercion might be resisted, but the power imbalance has allowed colonial powers and white power structures to retain dominance for centuries.

A second parallel involves cultural domination. The beliefs and practices of the colonized group or the racial minority are denigrated as primitive or uncivilized. Sometimes there are efforts to convert the subordinate group to the culture of the dominant group, but in all cases the dominant group attempts to undermine the culture of the subordinate group.

Political control is a third parallel. In the colonial situation, extensive staffs of governors and administrators were sent to the colony to run its political affairs on behalf of the colonizing power. With internal colonialism, the dominant group uses both formal and informal political mechanisms to ensure a similar degree of control by the white power structure. The underrepresentation of racial minorities in positions of political power is the tip of the iceberg of political control by the dominant group.

Perhaps the most important parallel involves economic exploitation. This is the driving motive of colonial relations, whether the resources involve cheap labor, raw materials, or commodity markets. With internal colonialism, the role of racial minorities as a secondary labor force with lower pay, fewer benefits, and higher unemployment is merely one indicator of the economic exploitation that is central to this relationship.

Both traditional and internal colonialism create institutional discrimination, as social organizations and practices are built on discriminatory principles. This creates racial inequalities and racially coded practices not just in the economy and polity, but also in housing, education, health care, and criminal justice.

A final parallel is racist legitimation. Systematic beliefs about the inferiority of the subordinate group accompany both forms of colonialism. These beliefs seek to legitimate unequal treatment. At their most powerful, such racist legitimations make colonial domination seem logical, natural, and even beneficial for subordinate groups.

No analogy is perfect, but the history of US race relations more closely approximates internal colonialism than assimilationist integration. What the colonial model underscores is that race relations are rooted in conflicting interests between dominant and subordinate groups. Dominant groups who benefit have a vested interest in maintaining such relations; subordinate groups who pay the price of these relations can be expected to change them if possible.

The question of group interests requires a closer look. The dominant group is really a white power structure of elites who make economic, political, and cultural decisions with far-reaching consequences. This group most clearly benefits from exploitative race relations. The subordinate group refers to racial minorities disproportionately located toward the bottom of class and other hierarchies of inequality. This group most clearly pays the price of racial oppression.

What is less clear are the interests of "ordinary whites." They belong to the dominant racial group but are not in positions of institutional power and do not receive the same material benefits from institutional racism that dominant whites do. This status inconsistency between race and class could lead this group to define its interests in rather different ways.

On one hand, ordinary whites may primarily identify with their race. This links them to dominant whites of the same race but of a different class and distances them from racial minorities with whom they might share similar class positions. Historically, this identification allowed even poor whites to claim status on the basis of race; no matter how economically deprived they were, they were still white in a society where that meant a great deal. Ordinary whites can thus derive a social-psychological benefit from their racial identity regardless of material circumstances. But the benefits are more than psychological. Ordinary whites might also derive material benefits from discrimination against minorities if it expands their opportunities at the expense of minorities. By this logic, ordinary whites might see their interests in alignment with powerful whites despite their class differences.

On the other hand, ordinary whites might primarily identify with their class position, which would distance them from powerful whites and align them more closely with racial minorities. This suggests a class alliance across racial lines in which the material similarities of working-class whites and minorities trump racial differences. Such an alliance could challenge racial discrimination, and there is a logic for doing so. Where racial discrimination is high, it allows employers to use a divide-and-conquer strategy that ultimately undermines living standards for both whites and racial minorities (Reich 1981). Racial discrimination thus hurts minorities directly and ordinary whites indirectly. In this scenario, the collective self-interest of ordinary whites is to align with racial minorities and oppose racial discrimination.

The colonial model remains an imperfect analogy, but it frames important questions about the future of race relations. Even without clear answers, it sensitizes us to how group interests shape the social construction of race.

Forms of Discrimination

The colonial model offers a big picture of race relations that rests on many small episodes of discrimination. It is these practices, enacted on a daily basis, that sustain the social construction of race.

Discrimination ranges across many institutions and social arenas. It obviously includes the economy, employment, and political representation. It also includes differences in health, mortality, and life expectancy as a result of differential access to physical and mental health services. It includes deeply rooted patterns of residential segregation that create other problems like unequal access to education. It includes very different probabilities of becoming caught up in the criminal justice system. The effects of discrimination are cumulative, as initial disadvantages become larger inequities over time. Acts of discrimination are the building blocks of racial inequality.

The traditional view of discrimination is that prejudicial attitudes cause discriminatory behavior (Feagin and Feagin 1978). The term *prejudice* means to "prejudge" people on the basis of their group identity. Such judgments often involve negative stereotypes about an entire category of people that are attributed to all its members.

The discrimination that results from prejudice can be explicit, as when people engage in name-calling, racist behavior, or hate crimes. But it can also be subtle or covert. If someone is advertising a job or an apartment and the "wrong" applicant appears, that applicant might be told that the job has been filled or the apartment rented. When the "right" applicant comes along, the apartment or job suddenly becomes available again. In this case, intentional harm is done to someone who might not be aware that they have been the victim of discrimination. Explicit discrimination grabs headlines, but subtle, covert forms are more common and often go undetected. Indeed, it is impossible to know the full extent of discrimination, because much of it is hidden in this fashion. The common thread is a prejudicial attitude. In the traditional model, discrimination occurs when "evil motives" are translated into action.

This model implies that reducing prejudice reduces discrimination. This was part of the logic behind social policies and court decisions favoring integration. It was thought that, with more social contact between groups, people would rethink their prejudices and treat others as individuals and not stereotypes. If prejudice melted away, discrimination would, too. Although the logic seems plausible, there's a problem. By many measures, prejudice in the United States has declined, but racial discrimination has not shown a corresponding reduction.

This prompted a closer look at the traditional view. It became clear that prejudice alone might not lead to discrimination. Prejudiced people need the power to act on prejudice if it is to become discrimination. It also became more evident that discrimination can occur without prejudice. Thus, an employer might have no prejudice against certain people but still refuse to hire them out of a belief that it would drive customers away.

More generally, discrimination limits opportunities for "others" and increases them for discriminators. In such cases, discrimination simply flows from group interest without prejudice. Such discrimination without an "evil motive" can also be an unintentional by-product of institutional policies. As the limits of the traditional model became more evident, sociologists developed another way of thinking about what causes discrimination.

The result was the institutional model in which organizational practices replace prejudice as the major cause of discrimination (Feagin and Feagin 1978). The idea is that social institutions routinely discriminate against many people. In contrast to the traditional model, the institutional model sees discrimination as a normal, routine, chronic outcome rather than a sporadic one. It recognizes that most discrimination is subtle or covert, although overt institutional discrimination still happens, too. It sees discrimination as something that affects thousands if not millions of people, because it is embedded in major social institutions like the criminal justice system or the labor market. Finally, institutional discrimination can be either intentional or unintentional.

Intentional institutional discrimination occurs when there is a conscious goal of unequal treatment. It might be rooted in prejudice, racism, group interest, or some other motive. As with the traditional model, there is an "evil motive" behind such action. Unlike the traditional model, it is not individuals but large organizations that enact these behaviors. In systems of apartheid or legalized segregation, discriminatory purposes are officially proclaimed.

When segregation becomes illegal, intentions to discriminate might no longer be publicly stated but can continue to shape institutional functioning. The redlining of certain neighborhoods as poor credit risks is one example. The use of racial profiling in police practices is another example. The purging of voter registration lists is a third example of intentional, institutional discrimination (Moore 2001). While rarer hate crimes grab headlines, more routine institutional discrimination affects many more people on a daily basis.

Institutional discrimination can also be unintentional. This is indicated by effects rather than motives. Here, we must work backward from discriminatory outcomes to identify the practice or policy that produced them. An example is "side-effect" discrimination that occurs as an unintended by-product of some other practice. Imagine a university that uses an entrance exam to screen applicants. Assume the exam contains no subtle racial biases. Nonetheless, if applicants have been unequally prepared by previous schooling to perform well on this exam, it will produce discriminatory outcomes despite the best of intentions.

A related example is "past-in-present" discrimination where a current practice unwittingly perpetuates prior discrimination. Consider a layoff policy based on seniority. This is not discriminatory in itself. But to whatever extent racial minorities or women have shorter or more episodic work histories as a result of past discrimination, implementing layoffs by seniority will benefit white males and harm minorities and women despite good intentions.

Unintentional discrimination harms many but remains elusive, because it cannot be traced back to a specific person or group with evil motives. In a final twist, it is also possible for "sophisticated racists" who *do* have evil motives to use practices that do not *appear* to intentionally discriminate, knowing that such practices are difficult to identify (Feagin and Feagin 1978).

According to the traditional model, reducing discrimination requires reducing prejudice. According to the institutional model, reducing discrimination requires changing institutions. Whereas the traditional model is "optimistic" that increased social contact will reduce prejudice and discrimination, the institutional model is "pessimistic" that institutions will not simply evolve into less discriminatory behavior. Indeed, the institutional model suggests that if nothing is done, discrimination will continue indefinitely, because institutions are self-perpetuating and because some groups benefit from discriminatory practices.

This is the logic behind affirmative action. It assumes that discrimination will continue unless affirmative action is taken to change the practices that produce it. As a policy, most affirmative action programs involve voluntary efforts to increase the diversity of a pool of qualified applicants. Such policies target informal practices whereby people tend to recruit, hire, or admit people like themselves. By creating policies that require looking beyond familiar social circles when recruiting applicants, affirmative action programs have made modest contributions to reducing discriminatory outcomes.

The persistence of racial inequality in the United States has also prompted a rethinking of the traditional focus on individual prejudice. New research has led one analyst to conclude that in the post—civil rights era, we have entered a time of "racism without racists" (Bonilla-Silva 2003). This argument downplays prejudicial attitudes by suggesting that racism rests on a material foundation of group interests and white privilege. Racism persists because whites derive substantial material benefits from it. Thus, even when whites do not have stereotypical views of minorities, they often perpetuate racism in ways that obscure its victims and beneficiaries.

Where traditional prejudice often assumed biological differences, "color-blind racism" is a more complex racial ideology emphasizing cultural differences. Four distinct frames express color-blind racism (Bonilla-Silva 2003). "Abstract liberalism" uses familiar political discourse about individual rights and equal opportunity to subtly deny structural barriers and implicitly blame victims. "Naturalism" suggests that segregation reflects freely chosen preferences of people to associate with others like them. "Cultural racism" identifies supposedly defective values, beliefs, and practices within minority cultures that are responsible for their lack of progress. Finally, "minimizing racism" acknowledges lingering problems of discrimination while emphasizing how much progress has been made. The implication is that such problems no longer require systemic solutions.

None of these frames sound overtly racist. Indeed, they sound quite reasonable by comparison. They still function, however, as an ideology legitimizing racial inequality. Color-blind racism denies or minimizes institutional barriers and uses the rhetoric of individual opportunity and cultural differences to blame minorities and excuse whites for racial inequality. The emergence of "racism without racists" illustrates how racial meanings and definitions change over time. To analyze such changes, we need to revisit the idea that race is socially constructed.

Racial Formation

The theory of racial formation sees the social construction of race as a contested process of ongoing conflict (Omi and Winant 1994; Winant 1994, 2004). "[R]ace can be defined as a *concept that signifies and symbolizes socio-political conflicts and interests in reference to different types of human bodies*" (Winant 2004, 155; italics in original). The theory of racial formation also insists on the "reality" of race despite its origins as a social construction.

The challenge is to understand the simultaneous "arbitrariness" and "reality" of race. It arises once race is decoupled from biology. This has often led social scientists to reduce race to some other kind of group and transpose their experiences onto races. This problematic response implies that if race is not about biology, then it is not about anything real. The theory of racial formation maintains that race is not about biology, but it «still about something very real. That reality, moreover, needs to be understood on its own terms and not reduced to something else.

One way mainstream perspectives have denied the reality of race is by equating it with ethnicity and using the ethnicity paradigm to analyze race relations. This inevitably turns the discussion back to assimilation. Despite the different histories of racial minorities and white ethnics in the United States, some maintain that racial minorities will eventually undergo the same assimilation as white ethnic groups in earlier decades and centuries. Rather than analyzing race on its own terms, this substitutes the history of ethnic assimilation as a goal for race relations.

This reduction of race to ethnicity is problematic, because it denies the unique features of racial formation (Omi and Winant 1994). It falsely transposes white experience onto nonwhites. It denies ethnic variations within racial groups by equating broad racial categories ("African American") with specific white ethnicities ("Italian"). The ethnicity paradigm also advocates individualistic solutions like upward mobility. The reduction of race to ethnicity thus obscures the distinctiveness of racial oppression and proposes unachievable or undesirable solutions to racial conflict.

An alternative is the class paradigm. This approach reduces race to class or sees the real meaning of race through a class lens. The class paradigm underscores how members of racial minorities are disproportionately located in the working class or lower socioeconomic levels. The logic is that their fates are determined more by their class position than by their racial identity. Moreover, race has been used to reinforce class exploitation when employers designate racial minorities as a secondary labor force, divide workers along racial lines, and play one group off the other to the detriment of both. In this paradigm, race is important for its role in a more fundamental set of class dynamics.

Although it illuminates intersections of race and class, this paradigm is not sufficient for understanding racial formation on its own terms. It simply assumes class is fundamental and race is secondary. Moreover, the equation of racial minorities with only one class oversimplifies race and implies that middle- or upper-class minorities face no racial barriers. "It would be more accurate to say that race and class are competing modalities by which social actors may be organized" (Omi and Winant 1994, 32). If so, the class model with its reduction of race to class is insufficient.

A third alternative is the nation paradigm or the internal colonialism model discussed earlier. As we saw, this model emphasizes differences between the assimilationist history of white ethnic groups and the quasi-colonial status of racial minorities. The metaphor of colonial relations has much to tell us about the history of race relations within the United States. As a viable model of contemporary racial formation, however, it has serious limitations.

In a postcolonial world of global mobility, equating races with geographically bounded nations is an increasingly implausible way to think about race relations. There is substantially more interracial contact in contemporary, racially diverse societies than in classic colonial relations. The nation paradigm also obscures increasingly important class differences among minorities by reducing them to a homogeneous, cultural nationality. Although more instructive than the ethnicity and class paradigms, this one also falls short as a way to understand racial formation.

The problem is that each paradigm—ethnicity, class, and nation—reduces race to something else. Each fails to see race on its own terms. The solution is to move beyond these paradigms to a model that sees race as an independently constructed social reality.

This means seeing racial formation as a process in which social, economic, and political forces determine the meaning of racial categories in a given historical context. To emphasize the importance of process, the term *racialization* is coined (Omi and Winant 1994) to refer to the extension of racial meanings to relationships that were previously not classified in such terms.

Consider slavery. Although US planters used African Americans as slave labor for centuries, the practice did not originate for racial reasons. It derived from the economic realities of plantation agriculture. In order to be profitable, such agriculture requires the cheapest possible labor. Planters first used white indentured servants from Europe and then captured Native Americans (Geschwender 1978). Neither group worked out well in the long run. Importing African slave labor gradually emerged as a later alternative in the search for cheap labor. Once the practice was institutionalized, slavery was racialized through racist beliefs and legitimations to justify the use of black slave labor by white,

"God-fearing" Christians. Slavery became racialized over time. In other words, "we know that racism did not create slavery, but that slavery created racism" (Winant 2004, 84).

Institutions, practices, and beliefs become "raced" when they are shaped and understood through racial categories. Consider how many urban social problems have become "raced," as poptdar consciousness and media representations link race with poverty, welfare, gangs, drugs, and crime. These issues involve many more whites than nonwhites, but their racialized nature becomes a self-fulfilling prophecy. Thus, people act on racialized beliefs about crime and who commits it, leading to highly disproportionate numbers of racial minorities being suspected, arrested, convicted, and incarcerated for "raced" definitions of crime. The differential penalties for crack cocaine used by minorities and powder cocaine favored by whites is one of the more blatant examples of such racialization.

The most important raced institution is the state. In a racially divided society, the state racializes many social dynamics. "For most of U.S. history, the state's main objective in its racial policy was repression and exclusion" (Omi and Winant 1994, 81). It commenced with the Naturalization Act of 1790 that limited citizenship to free, white immigrants. The pattern continued throughout the nineteenth century as racialized policies of repression and exclusion regulated race relations. A more recent example of state power is the creation of the category "Hispanic" in 1980, racializing a new group of people and embedding the category in state policies, practices, and institutions. States and racial formation are thus closely intertwined.

Racial formation is not just about top-down power. When a collective identity is constructed and used to dominate people, that same identity will eventually become a rallying point for resistance. Whether the identity involves race, ethnicity, gender, nationality, or sexuality, domination provokes resistance. Thus, racial formation is a contested process. People fight back, and even powerful elites cannot completely control racial formation for long. It is more accurate to see racial formation—and the social construction of race more generally—as an ongoing struggle over what race means. Authorities use race to subordinate groups, and racially defined groups use it to resist subordination.

The contested quality of racial formation is evident in recent racial politics. On the eve of the civil rights movement of the 1950s and 1960s, racial formation took the form of domination. White power was the norm, backed up by coercion, segregation, exclusion, and violence. In this period, racial formation was a top-down affair, because of the overwhelming power of whites. Collective resistance appeared futile.

Social changes nevertheless created opportunities to contest racial formation. The disruptions of World War II, the partial integration of the armed forces, the mechanization of Southern agriculture, and migration from the rural South to the urban North all undermined racial domination. When the civil rights movement appeared in the 1950s, it echoed the ethnicity paradigm with themes of individualism, opportunity, and integration. That such a modest agenda provoked such a ferocious backlash is revealing. Simply asking for what whites took for granted amounted to an almost revolutionary challenge to racial domination.

The movement soon transcended the ethnicity paradigm, in part because of the resistance it encountered to its integrationist goals. But the shift was also sparked by "the rearticulation of black collective subjectivity" (Omi and Winant 1994, 98). In other words, black activists made the redefinition of racial identity a central goal. The movement *made* racial formation a two-way street by challenging static notions of race and racial hierarchy. In effect, activists reclaimed the meaning of race from a white power structure and made it their own.

These events transformed the civil rights movement. Activists adopted multiple racial paradigms and diverse political strategies. "Entrists" argued that strategic participation in elections and mainstream institutions could transform the state. Socialists tried to build class alliances across racial lines and link struggles against racism and capitalism. Nationalists encouraged a separatist response of institution building and cultural pride within minority communities. None met with complete success. The entrist, socialist, and nationalist strategies had the same shortcomings as the ethnicity, class, and nation paradigms on which they were based. Each reduced race to something else and missed the complexity of racial formation. This activism nevertheless shattered older understandings of race and put racial formation center stage (Omi and Winant 1994).

As the movement became more complex, so did the response of the raced state. In some instances, it brutally repressed militant leaders and groups that challenged its authority. More broadly, the state shifted from racial domination to racial hegemony. This meant incorporating oppositional challenges in ways that defused their transformative potential. "Under hegemonic conditions, opposition and difference are not repressed, excluded, or silenced (at least not primarily). Rather, they are inserted, often after suitable modification, within a 'modern' (or perhaps 'postmodern') social order" (Winant 1994, 29). Although hegemony might be less violent than outright domination, it amounts to a more complex system of racial control.

Racial hegemony has sparked competing racial projects on both sides. On the reactionary side, the far right still equates race with biology and advocates violence to prevent all forms of "race mixing." The new right translates old-fashioned racism into code words that are not explicitly racist but nonetheless trigger racist attitudes and actions among those who know the code. The neoconservative right uses egalitarian language to advocate individualism and reject group-oriented solutions. They use the rhetoric of a color-blind society while ignoring the historical legacy of being a color-conscious society. This is the most sophisticated defense of the white power structure. It uses familiar, liberal ideas to argue for illiberal ends. It exemplifies "racism without racists" advocating "color-blind racism" (Bonilla-Silva 2003).

On the progressive side, pragmatic liberalism appeals to group identities to mobilize political support for racially progressive policies, including affirmative action. It advocates pluralism and tolerance and attempts a difficult balancing act between advancing minority rights and maintaining social peace. Finally, radical democrats seek full acceptance of racial difference and identities in the name of autonomy. They seek democratization of the state and redistributive policies to foster racial equality (Winant 1994).

Racial formation is thus a dynamic, contested set of social and political meanings. The current diversity of racial politics—consisting of at least five distinct and competing racial projects—testifies to the fluidity of racial formation and the social construction of race.

The Construction of Whiteness

It is intriguing that whites attribute "race" to "people of color" but don't see "white" as a "color." It's as if race applies to people who differ from the norm but not the group that is the norm. Given this, it is important to turn the microscope back on the dominant group and its construction of whiteness.

Like other socially constructed racial categories, whiteness emerged historically. Consider how "the Irish became white" over decades of conflict and eventual assimilation in the United States. More pointedly, this is the story of "how the Catholic Irish, an oppressed race in Ireland, became part of an oppressing race in America" (Ignatiev 1995, 1). When Irish immigrants first arrived in the United States, they were perceived as an inferior race by Anglo-Saxon powers on both sides of the Atlantic. However, rather than joining with other subordinate races, the Irish distanced themselves from minorities and aligned with whites. They pursued the classic assimilationist trade-off: "In becoming white the Irish ceased to be Green" (Ignatiev 1995, 3). This suggests that assimilation means moving toward the dominant group and away from minorities, because the dominant group is defined precisely by its distance from racial minorities. Until a group made both moves, assimilation was unlikely.

The Irish example fits a broader template of how whiteness was created through an amalgamation of initially diverse ethnicities. This history falls into three periods (Jacobson 1998, 13—14). From the founding of the country into the mid-nineteenth century, citizenship was confined to "free white" immigrants, implicitly meaning Anglo-Saxon and sometimes other Northern European peoples. From the midnineteenth century to the early twentieth century, immigration from Southern, Central, and Eastern Europe challenged the equation of whiteness and Northern European descent. During this period, a complex racial politics initially defined these immigrants as inferior races at the same time that they sought a broadening of the definition of "white" to include them. It has only been since the 1920s that ethnic differences were downplayed and a more generic white identity was forged. This period "redrew the dominant racial configuration along the strict, binary line of white and black, creating Caucasians where before had been so many Celts, Hebrews, Teutons, Mediterraneans, and Slavs" (Jacobson 1998, 14).

By the mid-twentieth century, whiteness became the dominant racial norm. This proved short-lived, as "it is no longer possible to assume a normalized' whiteness, whose invisibility and relatively monolithic character signify immunity from political or cultural challenge" (Winant 2004, 50). As race-based social movements recast their own racial subjectivity, white identity also became more self-conscious.

As white dominance was challenged, it triggered "grievances of the privileged." Some whites claimed they were under attack "simply for their race." Others decried a world in which minorities seemed to get advantages withheld from whites through "reverse discrimination." Still other whites lamented the lack of a distinct and vivid white culture they could identify with just as other races identified with theirs. Such defensive responses imply that although whites are still dominant, such dominance can no longer be taken for granted.

These responses also belie the ongoing privileges of the dominant group. White privilege means that despite recent challenges to the racial order, it continues to be organized in ways that benefit the dominant group. Such privilege is often invisible to those who benefit, while being highly visible to those who pay the price.

This is nicely captured in Peggy McIntosh's (2005) efforts to teach about male privilege in women's studies courses. Her female students quickly grasped the concept and readily supplied examples. Her male students conceded that women faced certain disadvantages but denied their male privilege. To understand this denial, McIntosh examined her own dual status as a white woman. As a woman, she could readily see male privilege. As a white, she had difficulty seeing her racial privilege, just as men had difficulty seeing male privilege. The broader pattern is that privileged groups rarely recognize their own privileges and perceive any challenge to them as victimization. Such complaints are not simply disingenuous; they reflect a real inability to see how whiteness and maleness continue conferring privileges even in a social order undergoing challenge and reformulation.

These privileges come in two categories. "Unearned advantages" are "positive" privileges that should not be abolished but made available to all. The privilege of not being a crime suspect simply on the basis of one's race is an unearned advantage for whites that should ideally be an unearned entitlement for all. "Conferred dominance" involves "negative" privileges that need to be abolished to create racial equality. Discrimination that benefits dominant groups at the expense of subordinate ones fits this type; it should be abolished in any society seeking racial equality (McIntosh 2005).

These are now the goals of a "new abolitionist racial project." Proponents of this movement identify white privilege as the lynchpin of white supremacy and see rejection of privilege by whites as essential to creating a just racial order. Advocates put a positive spin on the epithet "race traitor" by countering that "treason to whiteness is loyalty to humanity" (Winant 2004, 63). As this racial project unfolds alongside others described earlier, it is difficult to deny that we are in a period of highly contested racial formation.

Understanding race requires looking beyond taken-for-granted appearances. It also requires a multilayered analysis of domination. Critical sociology is tailor-made for both tasks. It illuminates both the social construction of race and the challenges seeking to deconstruct racial hierarchies in the name of a more egalitarian society.

References

Adelman, Larry. 2003. *Race: The Power of an Illusion*. Videodisc, California Newsreel.

Berger, Peter. 1963. *Invitation to Sociology*. New York: Doubleday.

Bonilla-Silva, Eduardo. 2003. *Racism without Racists*. Lanham, MD: Rowman & Littlefield.

Du Bois, W. E. B. 1903/1989. *The Souls of Black Folk*. New York: Bantam Books.

Feagin, Joe, and Clairece Booher Feagin. 1978. *Discrimination American Style*. Englewood Cliffs, NJ: Prentice Hall.

Geschwender, James. 1978. *Racial Stratification in America*. Dubuque, IA: Wm. C. Brown.

Gordon, Milton. 1964. *Assimilation in American Life*. New York: Oxford University Press.

Henslin, James. 2005. *Sociology*. 7th ed. Boston: Allyn and Bacon.

Ignatiev, Noel. 1995. *How the Irish Became White*. New York: Routledge.

Jacobson, Matthew. 1998. *Whiteness of a Different Color*. Cambridge, MA: Harvard University Press.

McIntosh, Peggy. 2005. "White Privilege and Male Privilege." In *Great Divides*, ed. Thomas Shapiro, 300–307. New York: McGraw-Hill.

Moore, Michael. 2001. *Stupid White Men*. New York: Regan.

Myrdal, Gunnar. 1944. *An American Dilemma*. New York: Harper and Row.

Omi, Michael, and Howard Winant. 1994. *Racial Formation in the United States*. 2nd ed. New York: Routledge.

Reich, Michael. 1981. *Racial Inequality*. Princeton, NJ: Princeton University Press.

Winant, Howard. 1994. *Racial Conditions*. Minneapolis: University of Minnesota Press.

———. 2004. *The New Politics of Race*. Minneapolis: University of Minnesota Press.

CHAPTER 8

Gender and Sexuality

Chapter 8 examines gender socialization. This chapter explains the meaning of gender and sex, the socially constructed roles associated with men and women, the role of parents in shaping a child's gendered behavior, the role of peers in gender socialization, and the media's part in reinforcing gender roles. This chapter discusses how gendered inequalities persevere in many fields, including social services, education, and health professions. It describes the structural forces effect of occupational roles on gender and sexuality. Hannon (2015) discusses how men and women are distinguished and categorized by culture and society. Functionalist and conflict theoretical frameworks are employed to understand gender, the roles of authority and power, and the difference in average earnings between men and women. The final issue presented in this chapter is that gender, marriage, and family are reviewed in the labor force participation rate As a final point, the important body of context examines family, gender, and marriage and this chapter provides clear criteria for the percentage of married women, achieved higher level of education, allocating social rewards, and assigned roles.

Gender

Lonnie Hannon

··

Introduction: Wonder Woman

The character traits of superhero Wonder Woman help us understand the duality that women in our society experience. As a woman, it takes the strength and power of a super heroine to overcome one of the central problems of the universe: the excesses of the masculine ego, which in comic book terms was manifest in the characters of various villains who believed that they should have total domination over the universe. In more literal terms, Wonder Woman's debut in 1941 during the height of the Nazi occupation of Europe spoke to the ego-driven desires of men like Adolf Hitler and Benito Mussolini.

If my assessment of Wonder Woman sounds like a lecture in social theory, then that is because the Wonder Woman character was created by famed social scientist William Moulton Marston. Marston was a psychologist and one of the early inventors of the polygraph machine (lie detector). Moulton based the Wonder Woman character on his wife, Elizabeth (Daniels, 2000). This is important because through his wife and his experience as a psychologist, he was able to understand the balance between strength and feminine grace that women in society are expected to exhibit even under the hardest circumstances. His creation of Wonder Woman and, ironically, the lie detector, seem to rest with his preoccupation with promoting truth and justice in society (Bunn, 1997). Indeed these were the virtues most advocated by Wonder Woman.

Wonder Woman's character is full of social meaning. She manages to fight the harshest villains without belying her feminine qualities. She sports an hourglass figure with rich flowing hair. She wears a one-piece outfit, similar to a strapless swimsuit, topped off with a tiara. Her feminine aura is reified by her link to Aphrodite and Athena. Unlike her male contemporaries who use brute physical strength and bravado to overwhelm their foes, she fights evil with the feminine qualities of truth and love. Some have examined her act of using her golden lasso to "tie men up and reel them in" in a metaphorical context related to the power of female sexuality. Others suggest that Wonder Woman's lasso of truth is more symbolic of Marston's lie detector (Bunn, 1997).

Whatever the case, Wonder Woman was an illustration of what women across the world were already experiencing. They were navigating a male-dominated world where they were expected to labor in the factories during the war, raise children, manage the household, and fulfill cultural duties within the community, all while upholding rigid standards of beauty. Wonder Woman was symbolic of these efforts. Indeed, it takes a wonder woman for us to advance as a society. Whether we call her Harriet Tubman, Joan of Arc, or mom, it seems they always defeat the worst enemies of our existence. With their formula of truth and love, they conquer all.

Gender Socialization

Gender

"Gender" and "sex" are often used interchangeably but they have different meanings. Gender refers to the socially ascribed traits that we associate with masculinity or femininity. The expectation that men are supposed to be tough is based on gender. When a man and woman are together on a date, the expectation that the man is to open the car door for the woman is an example of a gender role (the woman is perfectly capable of opening her own door, right?). The majority of the norms that revolve around gender are socially constructed. In other words, society determines what it means to be male or female. With gender being socially constructed, men and women tend to be subject to the norms and values associated with a particular culture. However, this can be somewhat tricky with gender. As we have learned, norms are usually relative to time, place, and circumstance; however, unlike other cultural phenomena, gender norms tend to be similar across different cultural contexts. Because of this, arguments have been made that a biological component is interwoven in the way we construct gender, given that biologically, humans are the same across the globe. In other words, biology plays a part in determining gender. This explains why gender roles are similar across the globe. For example, men on average have more muscle mass than women have. This makes them physically stronger. Recognizing this, society assigns to men roles that require more physical strength. Here, there may be some association between biology and social norms. Nonetheless, most of the roles we assign to gender are interchangeable. The individuals who play these roles are, for the most part, following agreed-upon social norms.

Sex

"Sex" consists of the genetic traits that make us male or female. The most salient difference concerning sex is a women's capacity to reproduce. Just as most mammals, women develop mammary glands that yield milk to their young. Women also have higher levels of the hormone estrogen. Men tend to have more of the hormone testosterone. There are other genetic traits that differentiate men from women. While it is acknowledged that some sex traits contribute to the socially constructed roles we assign to males and females, sociologists tend to leave discussion of these unique physical traits to biologists.

Roles

Men and women share different roles in society. Though society is evolving, the primary roles assigned to women involve nurturing and those of men revolve around the provision of resources. Other than the production of milk, these roles are in theory and often in practice interchangeable. Across the world, women are expected to care for children as well as others in the household and community. The first example of this involves the preparation of food. When we think about who is in charge of buying groceries and cooking, we often have a picture of women in mind. Even if the woman works outside of the home, society still looks to her as the primary agent of food production. Meanwhile men are expected to generate income either alone, or in modern contexts, in combination with woman. Whether the woman works for pay or not, the man maintains the role of primary breadwinner in the family. Men who are unable to execute this function may be viewed as inadequate by society.

There are numerous other roles associated with men and women. Nonetheless, they are all mostly related to the two mentioned above. As the primary nurturer,

Figure 8.1 The ideal of chivalry encompasses many of our expectations associated with gender. Copyright in the Public Domain.

Figure 8.2 Our perception of what constitutes the nuclear family have changed little over the years. Copyright in the Public Domain.

women are thought of as responsible for ensuring the health of family and community members. In fact according to Merriam-Webster dictionary, the word "nurse" describing a healthcare professional and the act of providing milk to a child has a common origin with the word "nurture," both signifying the provision of nutrition.

Women in our society are traditionally thought of as sources for physical and emotional comfort, cultural development, and growth. Men are typically seen as the group who exchanges their labor for resources used to finance the operation of the household. The more successfully he is able to care for the household financially, the more status he gains as a man. The male-centered attributes of physical strength, aggressive behavior, and financial acumen help solidify his expected role as bread-winner. Men are expected to exercise the power derived from these male-centered attributes to enhance the status of the entire family. His efforts are supposed to be the source of security and protection from a chaotic world.

Let us imagine some situations where gender comes into play. I will state an action, statement, or scenario and you reply by checking the box of the gender that you *expect* to see fulfilling the role(s):

Figure 8.3 Gender roles are especially robust within the context of family. Copyright in the Public Domain.

While a man or woman can fulfill any of these roles, we typically expect to see each filled by a particular gender. That is why we use the term *expectation*. The reason we expect a man or a woman in these specific roles is that we have been conditioned to associate gender with certain behaviors. Violent, aggressive, forceful, risky behaviors are typically associated with men. Communicative, gentle, accommodative, and caring behaviors are typically associated with women. If we were to see a woman walking through the woods revving a chainsaw, we would not necessarily be shocked, but a woman is not who we would expect to see in this role, either.

The stress associated with executing certain roles is referred to as role strain. Role strain is experienced by both men and women who have difficulty meeting social expectations. A man who cannot adequately care for his children and wife may become frustrated. A woman who has to work a demanding full-time job while being the primary caregiver to her children and elderly parents may experience role strain as well. Sometimes role strain leads to role exit, a situation where the strain of the role becomes too much to handle, leading the individual to completely relinquish his or her responsibilities. Humans consistently jettison roles that become too strenuous. The number of roles that one can take on without experiencing strain is unique to the individual. Some individuals have the capacity to take on many roles while experiencing small amounts of strain. Others can handle only one or two roles at a time. For example, the man who cannot adequately meet social expectations by taking care of his family financially may exit the situation and opt for weekend visits instead of being in the household full time. Likewise, a woman may decide that the role of taking care of children and a husband may be too much and she decides to exit the role of wife.

Parents

Parents socialize their children to norms and values familiar to them as participants in the social world. They teach etiquettes, ethics, and morality based on what they believe will help their children meet the expectations of society. Boys and girls are taught how to play, how to sit, how to walk, and how to laugh. They act out this socialization while playing. One study using a sample of children who played video games found that boys were more likely than girls to be motivated by competition and the desire to win (Olson, 2010). Boys are socialized to engage in competitions that determine order within the hierarchy. What we see during play is that boys and girls at an early age began exhibiting gender-based behavior. This behavior solidifies and becomes normative by the time they mature into adults, as displayed in Table 8.1. Few will question that differences between boys and girls materialize at an early age. However, there is some debate as to why. Some social scientists believe that many differences would disappear if the parental socialization process were free of bias. The idea that parental socialization plays a significant role in shaping the child's gendered behavior is expressed by Caryl Rivers and Rosalind Barnett:

> It may be that mothers in particular have internalized stereotypes about boys, even when their children are very young. Mothers of boys, research finds, often talk differently to their sons than to their daughters. Boys are often given commands and instructions—"pick up those blocks!" "come here!" while mothers more often infuse emotion into exchanges with their daughters ("Does the doll feel good today?" "Do you like Michelle and her mommy?"). Young boys may get the message that emotions are not "boy turf." (2013)

Table 8.1 Stereotype Checklist

Statement or Scenario	Male	Female
Kiss it and make it better		
Search team rescues hikers		
Cookies and milk after school		
"Break his kneecap!"		
Firing a subordinate for texting at a board meeting		
Aerobics at the gym		
"Let's have a cigar!"		
"Jerk!"		
Barroom fight		
"Welcome to Dr. Bonner's office, please sign in"		
Cutting down a tree with a chainsaw		
"I'll have a light chardonnay"		
"I want to destroy my enemies"		
PTA president		
Cleaning the gutters		
"My car is faster than yours"		
"My car is cute"		

While the authors reiterate the importance of parental socialization, it must be understood that on average, parents will not scour the available scientific literature in search of the latest findings on best practices for rearing children. As discussed earlier, most parents feel a responsibility to raise their children within the context of familiar gender norms. "I want my boy to be tough, because boys are supposed to be tough." "I want my girl to be sweet, because girls are supposed to be sweet." Although there are plenty of scientific data to back up the authors' point, challenging these and other rules of thumb often conflicts with what many parents feel is their basic role: to teach their children to adhere to the social norms that will provide them the best shot at being successful in the future. There is a reason that gender norms are so robust.

Peers

The effect of parental gender socialization is significant. Children usually develop their worldviews on gender during this process. However, peer socialization has a strong influence as well. The attitudes

Figure 8.4 Peers are enormously influential as agents of gender socialization. Copyright in the public Domain; Copyright © Xenobiologista (CC by 3.0) at http://commons.wikimedia.org/wiki/File:Kampung_Punjut_Orang_Asli_girls_playing.jpg.

toward gender that children gained from parental socialization manifest during play. However, the people whom they are playing with are other children who have also received gender socialization from their parents. A meeting of norms occurs when children first enter the social world at daycare or elementary school. Given that most will come from the same culture, most of these norms will be similar. Also of importance is that for the first time, children will have to *earn* their way into the group. During parental socialization, children are automatically accepted as part of the group known as the family. The social milieu is different in the social world. An individual is not accepted until the other members of the group approve.

Acceptance of the prevailing gender norms plays a significant role in whether or not a child will be brought into the group. If a girl is seen as aggressive, competitive, and unemotional, then other girls who were socialized under the prevailing norms may not accept her. She could try to play with the boys, but they may not accept her either because she conflicts with their understanding of how girls should act. The same is true for boys. If a boy tries to interact with other boys but he displays behaviors more associated with their perception of a girl, then he may be shunned as well, by the boys and the girls. This type of behavior is not prosocial and it is certainly not exemplary of political correctness; however, children tend to be least inclined to evoke standards of adult etiquette. Because of their honesty, they offer social researchers with perhaps the best glimpse into human behavior. Peers play an important part in gender socialization from childhood throughout adulthood.

Media

Gender socialization received from the media is ubiquitous. The images from television, music, movies, or print all play a part in reinforcing gender roles. Unlike parents, however, the media is pervasive throughout all sectors of society. The media is important because it broadcasts what many people perceive as the "ideal" image of body type and social behavior for men and women. The thought is that these people "have what it takes" to be celebrities. The media profoundly affects women and men in shaping their views of what is "in" or cool. Gender norms associated with physical beauty are strongly impressed upon women through the media. Many of the images of beauty presented by the media are incongruent with the physical attractiveness possessed by average women. Women who are not confident in themselves could develop problems with self-image if they feel they are not measuring up to what the media suggests they should look like. Also of note is the sexual objectification of women in the media. Sex sells. Women are often over-sexualized to sell products or to increase viewership of certain shows. For instance, the infamous video vixens in male rap videos were an example of an egregious over-sexualization of black women. What this does is reduce the human who possesses thoughts, emotions, and goals to a material object—a possession like a car or a boat. No wonder we refer to so many material objects with the feminine pronoun "she."

Effect of Socialization on Career Choice

On an aggregate level the gender norms learned as children appear to influence the career choices of adults. Careers that involve nurturing, caretaking, emotional and psychological wellbeing, and support tend to be dominated by women. Jobs that require aggression, risk-taking, and spatial reasoning tend to be dominated by men. Table 8.2 demonstrates these trends. It provides a list of occupations derived from the United States Census (2014). The data reflect the percentage of males and females who work in each occupation and the median earnings.

Table 8.2 reveals that occupational fields such as community and social services (social workers and counselors), education, health professionals (nurses and doctors), home healthcare providers, and office support were dominated by women. These are all important jobs that must be fulfilled; however, the problem is that even in the job fields dominated by women, the median salary for female workers is less than that for the men who work in these fields. In fact, the average salary for men is higher in every occupation category. Pay close attention to the "health diagnosing and treating practitioners" field. These are the healthcare professionals such as doctors and nurses. While women are the majority in this field, their male counterparts make substantially more money. The median annual salary for males in this field is $97,321, while their female counterparts earn $57,392. That is a difference of $39,929. Much of the discrepancy here is due to the gender hierarchy within the field. In terms of physicians, male doctors tend to focus on high-paying specialties, such as neurosurgery and cardiology, while women tend to focus on specialties that pay less. Elianne Riska (2011) maintains that women focus on specialties that will allow them to balance home and work. They also report that structural forces, such as the lack of female mentors, may be at play in preventing women from obtaining higher-ranking positions. In 2005, only 25% of surgery residents were women (Riska, 2011). The desire to balance the intense workload of practicing medicine with home responsibilities shows the power of gender socialization.

Table 8.2 Occupation and Median Earnings by Sex 2012

Occupation	Percent of Males in Occupation	Percent of Females in Occupation	Median Annual Earnings for Males 2012	Median Annual Earnings for Females 2012
Management	61.1%	38.9%	71,986	52,210
Computer and mathematical	73.6%	26.4%	74,061	62,165
Architecture and engineering	85.6%	14.4%	73,849	59,889
Life, physical, and social science	54.1%	45.9%	59,962	49,875
Community and social services	36.1%	63.9%	38,846	36,495
Legal occupations	48.7%	51.3%	101,725	51,838
Education, training, and library	27.0%	73.0%	46,712	35,262
Arts, design, entertainment, sports, and media	52.8%	47.2%	41,071	30,012
Health diagnosing and treating practitioners and other technical	26.7%	73.3%	97,321	57,392
Health technologists and technicians	22.5%	77.5%	40,719	34,030
Healthcare support	13.3%	86.7%	24,849	21,509
Protective service	78.1%	21.9%	42,777	31,002
Fire fighting and prevention, and other protective service workers including supervisors	76.3%	23.7%	31,467	20,746
Law enforcement workers including supervisors	80.4%	19.6%	56,433	44,286
Food preparation and serving related	45.5%	54.5%	14,917	11,668
Building and grounds cleaning and maintenance	60.2%	39.8%	21,054	13,788
Personal care and service	22.8%	77.2%	19,725	13,638
Sales and related	50.0%	50.0%	38,197	17,100
Office and administrative support	27.5%	72.5%	30,015	27,946
Natural resources, construction, and maintenance	95.5%	4.5%	33,850	21,458
Farming, fishing, and forestry	79.8%	20.2%	20,510	12,048
Construction and extraction	97.3%	2.7%	31,879	26,661
Installation, maintenance, and repair	96.1%	3.9%	40,269	34,160
Production	71.9%	28.1%	35,259	22,080
Transportation	86.4%	13.6%	34,356	21,749
Material moving	79.6%	20.4%	22,426	17,507
Total for employees age 16 years and older	52.4%	47.6%	38,968	27,352

Source: United States Census (2014). American Community Survey. Occupation by Sex and Median Earnings in the Past 12 Months (in 2012 inflation-adjusted dollars) for the Civilian Employed Population 16 Years and Over.

Figure 8.5 Gender norms are often associated with occupational roles. Copyright in the Public Domain.

Males dominated the fields that required spatial reasoning such as those dealing with computers, mathematics, engineering, and architecture, as well as in fields that required risk-taking behavior, such as law enforcement, fire-fighting, construction, and extraction (mining). Again, this speaks to the differences in gender socialization received by males and females. The median male earnings for all occupations amounted to $38,968, while that of females came to $27,352.

Theoretical Explanations

Functionalist Approach

Social scientists employ a variety of theories to advance our understanding of gender. Those that fall under the functionalist framework argue that gender roles are an important part of a balanced society. Women carry and nurture babies during pregnancy. After birth, they have the biological capacity to nurse their children. Therefore, they have the natural capacity to care for children. Because of their responsibility as primary caretaker, their base of operation will be the home, given that small children are not yet ready to be active participants in the external social world. In general, women have developed, whether genetically or socially, a deeper capacity to nurture and provide support. Even women who work outside of the home are expected to fill jobs that require such skills.

The competitive and forceful nature of men, on the other hand, helps them survive in a cutthroat world, according to the functionalists. Moreover, men are better suited for physically and mentally demanding work. Their strength and accelerated metabolism help them excel in labor-intense jobs such as coal mining and construction. Their lack of emotional connectedness and their competitiveness help them focus on the rational goal of work, which is to procure resources for the household. The economy tends to favor men with the benefit of higher pay because they are expected to be the breadwinners. Because they are the breadwinners, they tend to take jobs that require more intense sacrifices such as long hours, risk, and intense study.

These sentiments are based on broad generalizations. Certainly, there are women who are just as rugged as the stereotypical man. There are women who work on cars and construction sites. Women fight crime and extinguish fires. The functionalists are examining the aggregate population. That is, the population as a whole. The functionalists go on to argue that jobs have to be filled. The most productive societies fill these positions with the most capable people. Why they are more capable is inconsequential. In fact, if the roles were reversed, say, it was the men who had children, then they would be the group with domestic responsibilities. If women had the traits of men, then they would be the ones with the primary responsibility of breadwinning. Of course, the functionalist argument suggests that men and women are structured into the roles that most benefit society. Girls are given dolls and Easy-Bake Ovens to prepare them for their primary future roles. Boys are given Tonka trucks, Lego blocks, and toy lawnmowers to prepare them for their future roles (we in the sociology community are not quite sure what Hot Wheels are preparing boys for). Functionalists would argue too that women are called into the labor force in greater numbers when men are absent (World War II), when labor is needed to keep up with demand (as was the case in the 1920s), or when the economy can no longer support most single-earner households (as is the case today). So the functionalists are not implying that women are genetically incapable or that it is their lot in life to be subordinate. They simply maintain that every society self-adjusts to its needs. The roles of women and men are manifestations of these needs.

The institutions that structure men and women are robust because a well-run society depends on a high degree of adherence. Schools make sure that girls do not play rough on the playground. Boys are forgiven for poor manners. Girls, on the other hand, are expected to sit with crossed legs and exhibit politeness. Churches are similar. The leadership roles of most churches tend to be filled by men. This is not just the case for the local church, but men tend to dominate national and international leadership roles

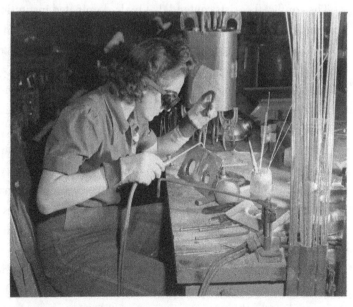

Figure 8.6 Women have always answered the call of duty. Copyright in the Public Domain.

as well. Nonetheless, a glimpse into many local churches will reveal that women do most of the actual work in the church. In fact, most of the congregants in the church, regardless of denomination or faith, are women. Furthermore, top government officials and the titans of the economy are also predominantly males.

Functionalists argue that society has a way of selecting the most qualified group or individual for each role. Likewise, it weeds out those who are not equipped for such roles. According to hardcore functionalist theories, men are in these positions because they are the most qualified; if they were not, then they would occupy another role. Functionalists suggest that the institutions in society such as schools, churches, government, and economics structure individuals into their roles. The fact that men tend to dominate these roles ensures that the social order will remain static. In other words, society has functioned well under the status quo, so it is important that individuals who are likely to further the current order remain in power.

Conflict Approach

As we have learned by now, the conflict approach offers a perspective based on the idea that the institutions of society structure individuals into hierarchical positions. While the conflict theorists agree that women and men are structured into roles, they argue that these roles are the source of the social and economic inequality. Unlike the functionalists, they do not believe that each role has worth and thus provides a benefit to society. Some roles are clearly unhealthy, unproductive, demeaning, and poverty inducing.

The conflict theorists contend that male-dominated institutions are simply "good ole boy" clubs that confer benefits unfairly to other men. Women do not even get a chance to compete, in many instances. Men in leadership positions groom other men for esteemed positions. The difference in median earning between men and women presented in Table 8.2 is a good example of the effect this transfer of power has on economic standing. The institutions encourage the current form of gender socializations because it keeps women in subordinate roles, while elevating males to roles of authority and power.

Because of this uneven distribution of power and the probability that they will be the primary caretaker of children, women are far more likely to live in poverty during their lifetime. This trend is illustrated in Table 8.3. Women have higher poverty rates than males in every category. Unemployed and employed males have lower rates of poverty. Married couples have relatively low rates of poverty. Poverty rates become most pronounced when examining single mothers with children. Of this group, 36.2% of single mothers with only one or two children live beneath the poverty level. The rate increases with additional children. The combination of being underpaid in the workforce and having to care for children often leads to the feminization of poverty. The concept was developed by Diana Pearce to describe the poor economic conditions that many women experience due to unjust gender disparities.

Table 8.3 Poverty Levels for Selected Groups 2012

Group	Percent with Income Below Poverty Level
Females Total	17.2
Males Total	14.6
Single Mother Total	41.5
Single Mother 1 or 2 Children	36.2
Single Mother 3 or 4 Children	61.3
Single Mother 5 or More Children	77.2
Married Couples	8.7
Employed Female	8.5
Employed Male	6.4
Unemployed Females	36.6
Unemployed Males	30.6

Source: United States Census. (2014). Poverty Status in the Past 12 Months of Families. American Community Survey. 2012, One-Year Estimates.

Like with other social phenomena, most explanations of gender inequality use one of many theories derived from the conflict perspective. Unlike many fundamental components of functionalism, conflict theory is testable because it identifies an objective cause and effect as well as a culprit and a victim. Using a conflict theoretical framework, researchers can assess the following example: A company has become concerned that it is not keeping up with demand for its products because its labor is not producing at maximum capacity. It finds that if it cuts back on the number of sick days employees are given, then labor can be more productive and the company can meet demand. Women at the company are more prone to take off work because of illness and childcare responsibilities. Men miss fewer days that are attributable to those reasons. Company management becomes concerned and instructs the human resource department to reevaluate their sick-leave policy. The company will now allow only five sick days per year, down from fifteen. Psychologically, HR, knowing management's new stance on attendance, becomes more reluctant to hire women. The conflict theorists will suggest that this is an act of "war on women." The company should be accommodating to the outside responsibilities of women. Society expects women to be great mothers but, on the other hand, they have to be great employees too because the same society that expects women to be domestic has produced an economy that requires both parents to work. It is the proverbial catch-22.

If states were to mandate a standard minimum of sick days regardless of what that number would be, employees, especially parents, would know exactly what to expect. If employees know up front how many sick days they will be allowed to take, then they can plan ahead for issues that may occur. A mandated minimum also helps parents balance work and emergencies without compromising job performance. States that do not have such regulations leave these decisions up to the company. In this case, the companies are free to change the policy in a way that penalizes women. Conflict theorists could therefore hypothesize that the median salary of women will be higher in states that mandate a minimum amount of sick time for full-time employees than in states with no such regulations. Researchers have conducted many investigations that test the effectiveness of women in the workplace when the rules are fair and visible. In almost every case, they have found that women tend to be as productive as men when working under fair conditions. These studies suggest that institutions that favor male dominance tend to create uneven results between men and women. When the playing field is even, however, it becomes clear that women are able to meet production demands.

Gender Marriage and Family

Economic and Social Trends

It was stated in the last section that many functionalists maintain that society self-adjusts to its needs. A look at the data trends in Tables 8.4 and 8.5 suggests that U.S. society is evolving to fit an environment that continues to transition. There is no question that women are working more, marrying less, and having fewer children. Table 8.4 reveals that the labor force participation rate has more than doubled for married women in the United States since 1960. This is the percentage of married women who are employed or unemployed but looking for a job. Although in 1960 we were in the last stages of the baby boom era, the participation rate for women was still 31.9 percent. The rate for women increased substantially between 1960 and 1990 before leveling off in 2000. For married males, the story is the opposite. Their rates have actually been falling for the last 50 years. The major dynamics at play here are the drop in manufacturing jobs that men have depended on for the last century and the rapid expansion of the healthcare industry, in which females tend to be highly represented.

While employment among married women has increased, the overall number of men and women who marry is decreasing. The marriage rate has dropped to its lowest recorded level in a century to 6.8 marriages per 1,000 residents of age. Birth rates have also followed this trend. Births have dropped from almost 24 babies per 1000 women in 1960 to 13 in 2010. All of these trends speak to a changing economy and subsequent changes in social norms. While the cost of living has steadily increased over the last 50 years, median household income over this period has risen at a much slower pace. Thus, the economy has increasingly required women to be employed outside of the home. Stagnant incomes and the evaporation of blue-collar jobs equate to fewer resources for marriage and child

Table 8.4 Selected Gender Trends in Marriage, Births, and Employment 1960–2010

Year	Labor Force Participation Rate		Marriage Rates per 1000 residents of age	Birth Rate per 1000 women
	Married Females	**Married Males**		
1960	31.9	89.2	8.5	23.7
1970	40.5	86.1	10.6	18.4
1980	49.8	80.9	10.6	15.9
1990	58.4	78.6	9.8	16.7
2000	61.1	77.3	8.2	14.4
2010	61	75.8	6.8	13

Sources: United States Census. (2012b); National Center for Health Statistics. (2014); Grove, Robert D. and Hetzel, Alice M. (1968); National Center for Health Statistics. (1995); Centers for Disease Control. (2014).

Table 8.5 Highest Degree Attained for Males and Females over the Age of 25 (percentages)

	Females	**Males**
High School Diploma	27.5	28.6
Associate's Degree	8.8	7
Bachelor's	18.3	18
Professional Degree	1.5	2.4
Master's Degree	8.3	7
Doctorate Degree	.9	1.6
Bachelor's and Above	29	29

Source: United States Census (2014c). Sex by Educational Attainment for the Population 25 Years and Over. American Community Survey

bearing. While more women have entered the labor force, this is not to suggest that they have achieved equality in job status and pay. As we have discussed, many discrepancies in pay and status still exist.

Women are achieving higher levels of education. According to the U.S. Census, there is an equal percentage of men and women in the United States over the age of 25 who have a bachelor's degree or higher. Actually more women have bachelor's degrees than men have, while men tend to slightly outpace women in professional and doctorate degrees. Women are projected to pass men in the near future in terms of achieving higher education. In fact, the growth of women in education is a trend that has been occurring for the last 40 years. Whether the functionalist argument for why women have made

Figure 8.7 Women receive bachelor degrees at a higher rate than men. Copyright in the Public Domain.

such advances is true or not, the changes in our society are a credit to the hard work put forth by women to balance the demands placed on them by our culture. The combination of higher educational achievement and increased labor force employment for women are positive signs that our society is evolving. In light of the data on college graduation rates and labor participation rates, the question must be asked: Are men becoming the next disadvantaged group?

Discussion Questions

1. Take a look at Table 8.3. Notice how the labor participation rate for women increased by 9 points or more for each decade from 1960 to 1990. Then it leveled off in 2000 and actually decreased by one tenth of a point during the next decade. In your opinion, what caused this leveling of rates after decades of steady growth?

2. Women will soon outpace men in terms of college graduation rate. How, specifically, will this affect the job market and overall economy?

3. Will the role of nurturer for mothers change as we move further into the Digital Age? Why or why not?

4. Describe some adjustments that we can make in society to prevent poverty among single mothers.

5. How have gender roles or expectations (A) changed and (B) stayed the same in your lifetime?

Key Terms

Gender   The societal expectations that we associate with males and females.

Sex   The genetic traits that make us male or female.

Role Strain   The stress associated with executing certain roles. Role strain is experienced by both men and women who have difficulty meeting social expectations.

Role Exit   A situation where the strain of the role becomes too much to handle, leading the individual to completely relinquish his or her responsibilities.

Feminization of Poverty   A concept developed by Diana Pearce to describe the poor economic conditions that many women experience due to unjust gender disparities.

References

Bunn, Geoffrey. (1997). "The Lie Detector, Wonder Woman and Liberty: The Life and Work of William Moulton Marston." *History of the Human Sciences*, 10:91–119.

Centers for Disease Control. (2014). Table 3 (page 1 of 3). "Crude Birth Rates, Fertility Rates, and Birth Rates, by Age, Race, and Hispanic Origin of Mother: United States, Selected Years 1950–2012." Retrieved on May 28, 2014 from <http://www.cdc.gov/nchs/data/hus/2012/003.pdf>.

Daniels, Les. (2000). *Wonder Woman: The Complete History*. Chronicle Books: San Francisco.

Grove, Robert D. and Alice M. Hetzel. (1968). "Vital Statistics Rates in the United States 1940–1960." National Center for Health Statistics. U.S. Department of Health, Education, and Welfare. Public Health Service. Retrieved on May 27, 2014 from <http://www.cdc.gov/nchs/data/vsus/vsrates1940_60.pdf>.

National Center for Health Statistics. (1995). Monthly Vital Statistics Report. Marriages and Marriage Rate. Centers for Disease Control. 43(12S) retrieved on May 28, 2014 from <http://www.cdc.gov/nchs/data/mvsr/supp/mv43_12s.pdf>.

National Center for Health Statistics. (2014). National Marriage and Divorce Rate Trends. Provisional Number of Marriages and Marriage Rate: United States 2000–2011. Centers for Disease Control. Retrieved on May 27, 2014 from <http://www.cdc.gov/nchs/nvss/marriage_divorce_tables.htm>.

Olson, Cheryl. (2010). "Children's Motivations for Video Game Play in the Context of Normal Development." *Review of General Psychology*. 14(2):180–187.

Riska, Elianne. (2011). "Gender and Medical Careers." *Maturitas*, 68(3):264–267.

Rivers, Caryl and Rosalind Barnett. (2013). *The Truth About Girls and Boys: Challenging Toxic Stereotypes About Our Children*. Columbia University Press: New York.

United States Census Bureau. (2014a). American Community Survey. Occupation by Sex and Median Earnings in the Past 12 Months (in 2012 Inflation-adjusted Dollars) for the Civilian Employed Population 16 Years and over. United States Department of Commerce.

United States Census Bureau. (2014b). Poverty Status in the Past 12 Months of Families. American Community Survey. 2012 One-Year Estimates. United States Department of Commerce.

United States Census Bureau (2014c). Sex by Educational Attainment for the Population 25 Years and Over. American Community Survey. United States Department of Commerce.

United States Census Bureau. (2012b). Table 597. Labor Force Participation Rates by Marital Status, Sex, and Age: 1960 to 2010. The 2012 Statistical Abstract. United States Department of Commerce. Retrieved on May 28, 2014 from <http://www.census.gov/compendia/statab/cats/labor_force_employment_earnings/labor_force_status.html>.

CHAPTER 9

Marriages and Families

Chapter 9 examines marriage and family from macrosociological and microsociological standpoints. For many societies, family is titled as the backbone of society and is one of the most important social and universal institutions around the world. It is impossible to look at marriage alone, however, as marriage is intertwined with race, class, culture, financial stability, sexual orientation, family, and social harmony. Plume (2017) explains diversity of families, changing family patterns, balancing work and family, the decline in marriage rates, changes in the family household, the effects of poverty on family life, divorce, remarriage, and the graying of divorce. This chapter also applies theoretical perspectives on marriage and family. The chapter raises important questions such as: What types of families are there around the world? What are the structural and functional changes in the family and marriage? How have they changed across time and space?

Marriages and Families

Mark Plume

The Ghost Marriage Ritual and Grave-Robbing in China

In 2013, in China, four men were arrested, convicted, and imprisoned for exhuming the bodies of recently deceased women in order to sell them on the "ghost marriage" black market. They were apparently going around the countryside digging up female corpses for the purpose of trafficking in corpse brides. Each man was sentenced to at least two years in prison for digging up more than ten corpses over a two-year time period. After digging up the bodies, they cleaned them and altered their medical records in order to fetch higher prices. Their entrepreneurial endeavors were fueled by the millennia-old Chinese belief that an unmarried man who dies and is buried alone will be lonely in the afterlife, his spirit being so restless that he may even haunt his own family. In hopes of soothing the dead man's spirit, and to avoid any unwanted visits from the angry, unmarried dead, families are willing to pay large sums to find a corpse bride to bury next to their bachelor relatives.

The fate of these men is just a recent example of corpse bride trafficking. More recently, the body of a woman who died in February 2012 was sold by her family to the family of a young man who had recently died. Not long afterward, police discovered a corpse purveyor selling her now twice-exhumed body to another family. The belief that these men need a bride to lie next to them for eternity in order to rest peacefully is so powerful that it compels families who can afford it to purchase corpses, which promotes grave-robbing.

However, the buying and selling of corpse brides is not driven only by deep-rooted, long-held cultural beliefs; economic and class issues are also at play. China's superheated economy has created a surge in coal-mining activity and accidents, sending unmarried men to their graves with some frequency. An influx of coal money to some rural regions in China, populated by less sophisticated and more superstitious locals, has led to a significant increase in the area's underground corpse trade. Armed with coal cash, these Chinese hill folk can now afford to pay premium prices, some even

Mark Plume, "Marriages and Families," *Revealing Our Social World: A Brief Introduction to Sociology*, pp. 335-349, 350-354, 357-366, 461-510. Copyright © 2017 by Cognella, Inc. Reprinted with permission.

buying freshly dead corpse brides from local hospitals; these just-dead brides are highly desirable and much more expensive (Xiao, 2013).

The practice of ritual ghost marriage is believed to date back to the seventeenth century BCE and was outlawed decades ago, but it has been on the rise due to China's booming economy. This perfect storm of deeply held beliefs coupled with newly found economic resources has led to a surge in the demand for corpse brides, which has re-invigorated the grave-robbing business. This belief and ritual underscore the importance of marriage and family in Chinese culture. One's eternal soul is linked to marriage and family; it is more important to find an unmarried dead son a bride than to find his killer if he was murdered. Ghost marriage is not only found in China; it is a fairly widely practiced ritual, which underscores the importance of marriage and family across many cultures and beyond the grave.

What is Marriage?

Marriages

Will you get married someday? Are you already married? Well, whether you are married or you want to be, you are in good company. The vast majority of Americans who are not married say that they would like to marry at some point in their lives. And for what reason will you marry? For companionship? A lifelong commitment? To have children? For financial stability? If you are like most people, you will choose love over any other factor (Cohn, 2013).

Marriage is an essential institution in most, but not all, societies. In many cultures, marriage marks the transition from childhood to adulthood. Frequently, marriage is the first step in building a family, and it is instrumental in forming familial and kin networks. The current heated debate in the United States and worldwide about same-sex marriage highlights the importance of marriage. Marriage is seen as such a central part of a person's life that many societies currently restrict or previously restricted people from marrying outside their group or marrying a partner who was not approved of by the family. Children have been disowned by their families for marrying the "wrong" person (Beattie, 2014; Fox, 1967; Faruqui, 2010). I think the number of ways people around the world come together to form families would surprise most of you; however, you would probably be less surprised to know that some form of the family is found in all societies.

As we saw in the story above, marriage is so important in some cultures that people will go to extremes to find a mate for a loved one, even if he is dead. In Nepal, among the *Nyinba* people, women are allowed to be married to several men at the same time; in fact, the men are brothers. It is customary for Nyinba brothers to take a single wife, and if the brother's parents have another son, the wife is expected to help raise her future husband. The *Mosuo* minority group of China practice *axia* (visiting marriage), a system in which there is no formal marriage. Mosuo couples simply engage in romantic relations until the woman decides to end things by boarding up her *azhu* house, indicating to her lover the affair is over. If children are produced in a relationship, they live with the mother, and the father is not expected to maintain any ties with the child ("Mosuo: A Mysterious Matriarchal Group", 2003).

In the United States, we practice **monogamy**, a marriage between two individuals. Worldwide, this is the most common type of marriage. At one time, this type of marriage was designated as a union between one woman and one man. However, as of 2015, more than fifteen counties recognize same-sex marriages, and as of June 2015, same-sex marriage is legal in all fifty states and the District of Columbia. Due to the high rates of divorce and remarriage in many postindustrial nations, such as the United States, some sociologists have labeled the pattern of engaging in a number of monogamous marriages over one's lifetime **serial monogamy** (I'm using marriage in the definition, but the term also applies to a series of monogamous romantic relationships over one's lifetime). Some notable serial monogamists include Martin Scorcese, who married five times; Larry King, who married eight times, twice to the same woman; Billy Bob Thorton, married five times and, Elizabeth Taylor who walked down the aisle eight times, twice with Richard Burton. While monogamy is the most commonly practiced form of marriage globally, there are many types of marriages found in a variety of cultures. Table 9.1 below shows a number of marriage forms.

Polygamy is the general term for having multiple spouses at the same time. This type of marriage is illegal in all fifty states and the District of Columbia despite that there are television shows that depict it like *Big Love* and *Sister Wives*. How do you think the marriages in these shows get around the law? Even though polygamy is illegal in the U.S., there are an estimated 30,000 people involved in polygamous marriages, mostly associated with breakaway sects from the Mormon Church, specifically The Fundamentalist Church of Jesus Christ of Latter-Day Saints (Giddens, 2006). Additionally, an estimated 50,000 to 100,000 Muslim Americans are secretly involved in polygamous marriages in the U.S. (Hagerty, 2008).

Polygamy may be gaining some popularity here in the United States. The Polygamists Rights Organization argued that when the Supreme Court struck down the Defense of Marriage Act in 2013, it was a step in the right direction for recognizing alternate marriage forms like polygamy (Vorwerck, 2013). In her 2014 Daily Beast article "Is Polygamy the Next Gay Marriage?" Sally Kohn (2014) wonders if, in light of widespread acceptance of gay marriage, our society will be open to other marriage patterns like polygamy. Regardless of its recent popular exposure, polygamy is probably not coming to a church near you soon, as it remains outlawed in about 75% of the world's nations.

More specifically, **polygyny** refers to one man having more than one woman at the same time. In many cultures of the world, polygyny is practiced as a secular custom, and it is encouraged in nearly all Muslim nations as a religious expectation. Even though it is the most common form of polygamy, it is legal or tolerated in only about one-quarter of the world's countries. A variant of polygyny is **sororal polygyny**, in which one man takes two or more wives who are sisters. It is believed in some cultures that sisters are more agreeable and cooperative, which makes for a more harmonious

Table 9.1 Marriage Forms Found Around the World

Type of Marriage	Description	Function (Rationale)	Region(s) Where Practiced
Child Marriage	A marriage form in which one or both partners are under the age of eighteen.	Deeply rooted in tradition, the practice is most prevalent among the poor. These are usually arranged or forced marriages. One purpose is to ensure the bride is a virgin. Other reasons include creating bonds between two families or villages, economic survival, and debt repayment.	The Middle East, Africa, Asia, Bangladesh, India, Papua New Guinea, and Guatemala
Group Marriage (Also referred to as Polygynandry and Polyamory)	Marriage arrangement where several men are married to several women at the same time—mostly expressed as more of a household arrangement consisting of several married couples and their children.	Mostly seen as a way to communally raise children, pool resources or maintain peace by uniting rival groups.	Caingang people of Brazil, ancient Hawaiians, Melanesia, Europe, North America, and Australia The Oneida community in upstate New York 1848–1878 The Kerista Commune in San Francisco, California, between 1971 and 1991
Same-Sex Marriage	A marriage type in which both partners are of the same sex.	Affords same-sex couples the same marriage rights as heterosexuals in many Western industrialized nations including the U.S. Among the Lovedu of South Africa, the "Rain Queen" (the highest recognized social position) is presented with many "wives." The custom of "bride-giving"—offering young women as symbolic brides—ensures loyalty from local chiefs. Male "two-spirit" people from many Native North American nations can take a same-sex spouse. Among the Nuer people of South Sudan, a barren woman can be married o˙ as a "husband" to another woman, who is then impregnated by a secret boyfriend. The infertile women are socially recognized as the father.	Legal or recognized in approximately twenty-two countries, including the United States Third-gender marriages among Native North Americans. South Africa (symbolic)

Table 9.1 Marriage Forms Found Around the World (Continued)

Type of Marriage	Description	Function (Rationale)	Region(s) Where Practiced
Levirate Marriage	The practice of a widow marrying her dead husband's brother.	The brother is considered a proxy for his dead brother—therefore, any offspring from the new union are considered that of the first husband (dead brother). This allows for the continuation of the bloodline and keeps wealth within the family. It also maintains the existing ties between the two families.	Americas, Africa, India, and Australia
Sororate Marriage	A type of marriage in which a woman marries her dead sister's husband.	Like levirate marriage, this type of marriage is used to maintain existing bonds between the two families. In some sororate societies, that husband may have sex with his wife's sister if the wife is infertile.	Native North Americans, India, Africa
Ghost Marriage	A marriage in which one or both partners are dead	In Chinese culture, it is necessary for dead unmarried men to have a wife buried next to them to ensure a peaceful afterlife. Also in Chinese culture, families may tempt a living woman to marry their dead unmarried son so that the mother will have a daughter-in-law as her servant. Among the Nuer people, a woman may marry the "ghost" of a deceased man to keep her wealth and power. She is seen as married, but there is no one she has to share her wealth and power with.	Asia, Africa, Europe
Line Marriage (Fictional)	A form of group marriage in which spouses are constantly being added so the marriage never ends.	So that the marriage and all its attendant benefits never end.	In the fictional writings of Robert A. Heinlein (on a lunar penal colony)

Source: "Oneida Community", 2014; Jones, 2001; Evans-Pritchard, 1990; Graburn, 1971; Heinlein, 1966

Figure 9.1 While monogamy is the most commonly recognized and practiced marriage pattern globally, there are many cultures and religions that practice polygyny.

home. Polygyny has a distinct advantage for producing many children, which are often needed in agrarian cultures where it is practiced. Additionally, having many children provides a sort of "social security" for the husbands and wives, as they have someone to care for them in their advanced years. Regardless of which version is allowed, nearly all cultures that practice polygyny insist that the man treat each wife *equally* and that he must able to financially *afford* multiple wives.

Today, nearly all organizations that oppose polygyny do so on the basis of human rights; they view the practice as a violation of women's rights. Citing that it violates the dignity of women, the United Nations has called on all nations to outlaw the practice. However, there is tremendous variation in the way polygyny is practiced, and this view may not fit the reality in all societies.

The flip side of polygyny is **polyandry**—one woman married to two or more men at the same time. Once believed to be extremely rare, practiced mainly by groups living in India, Nepal, China, and the Marquesas, research by Starkweather and Hames (2012) has identified an additional fifty-three societies that permit polyandry. The Nyinba people of Nepal and the Toda of Southern India both practice **fraternal polyandry**—when two or more brothers marry one woman. This is an infrequently practiced marriage form; most times, it is used to preserve family-owned land so that it can sustain a family. Imagine a married couple has three sons; the couple is getting too old to farm the family land, so it splits the family farm into three equal portions, one for each son. While the size of the original family farm was large enough to sustain a family, each of the three parcels is not. If each son were to take a wife and have a family, his one-third share of the family farm is not large enough to support his new family. However, if all three sons inherit the entire farm jointly, and they all take one wife, now there is enough land to support a growing family. In addition, this family will grow slower than three families with three wives. Other advantages of polyandry include allowing one husband to be away from the family without necessarily disrupting the family and providing economic security for the wife if one husband were to die.

Same-sex marriages—in which two people of the same sex marry—are now legal in all fifty states and the District of Columbia, and twenty-one countries recognize same-sex marriages. The fact that so many societies of the world resist recognizing same-sex marriages indicates how strong the link is between marriage, family, and reproduction. However, same-sex marriages are viewed by advocates as a human rights issue; people should not be denied the right to marry just because of their sexual orientation. This position has been successful in changing marital laws in more than twenty countries. Some societies allow symbolic same-sex marriages to maintain family lineage, wealth, power, or to preserve bonds between families. Some societies like the Omaha Nation, for example, allow "two-spirit" or third-gender individuals to take same-sex marriage partners.

All societies enforce a number of rules about marriage, both prescriptive and proscriptive, in order to control who marries whom. Here in the United States, we have few rules that would restrict anyone from marrying whomever he or she wants. However, many cultures of the world strictly enforce rules of endogamy and exogamy. **Endogamy** refers to social rules that require individuals to

---

Do You Have to Marry a Person?

When people tell you they were just married, you may not know what gender, how old, what religion, or how rich or poor their spouse is, but you do assume they married another human. Below is a short list of people who found their soulmates in objects or animals.

- An American woman, Erika Eiffel, married the Eiffel Tower in a 2007 ceremony.
- Eija-Riitta Berliner-Mauer has been married to the Berlin Wall since 1979.
- A Japanese man who goes by the name Sal-9000 married a video game character named Nene Anegasaki from the Nintendo game "Love Plus" in 2009.
- A Korean man, Lee Jin-Gyu, married his "dakimakura," a kind of large huggable pillow, usually bearing the image of an anime character.
- A woman in India's state of Orissa married a cobra in 2006.
- In 2007, Liu Ye of China married himself. In a simple ceremony, he married a foam board cutout of himself in a stunning red dress.
- In the Sudan, if you are caught sleeping with an unmarried woman, you must marry her immediately. In 2006, Sudan applied this law to goats. Subsequently, Charles Tombe was caught *in flagrante* with a goat and had to marry it.
- In some parts of India, if your partner leaves you at the altar on your wedding day, you may marry a clay pot in his or her absence. In 2005, a young Indian woman named Salvita couldn't wait for her fiancé, who was late to the wedding, so she placed a picture of him on a clay pot and continued the ceremony.

Source: Snow and Brady, 2009; Alleyne, 2008; Lah, 2009; Phillips, 2010; Thompson, 2014; Landin, 2015

marry someone from within their group. Religion, race, ethnicity, class, caste, tribe, or language can define that group. Marrying within one's family was widely practiced by royalty throughout history. Royals believed they could keep their bloodlines pure by keeping it all in the family. In fact, Cleopatra's parents were brother and sister. Traditionally, in the caste system of India, you must marry within your own caste; Orthodox Jews still require members to marry only other Orthodox Jews. Can you think of any rules of endogamy in the United States? Are Americans, in general, required to marry within a certain group? Other than those who practice religious endogamy, the only endogamous requirement in the U.S. is to marry within our own species.

For example, we can show that people in the United States are far more likely to marry someone of the same race. Of all those who married in 2013, the most recent data available, only 12% married someone of a different race. Moreover, if we look at all marriages in the United States, about 6.3% are between spouses of different races (Wang, 2015). While interracial marriages represent a small number of all U.S. marriages, the practice is on the rise. In 1970, only 1% of all marriages in the U.S. were interracial. I use this as an example to show that people overwhelmingly marry those of the same race, but the same can be said of religion and social class. Research from 2014 indicates that nearly seven in ten (69%) people reported being married to someone who shares their religion (Murphy, 2015). Similarly, people from the same socioeconomic background marry more frequently than those from different social classes.

Exogamy, on the other hand, is the requirement of individuals to marry outside of some designated group. At one time in the U.S., you were required to marry outside your sex; that is, a woman had to marry a man and a man had to marry a woman. Until 1967, when the United States Supreme Court ruled them unconstitutional, anti-miscegenation laws prohibited individuals from marrying outside of their race. These laws criminalized interracial marriage and, in some cases, sexual activity between people of different races.

Common exogamy practices include the prohibition of marrying family members; in nearly all cultures, people are required to marry outside their family. This reinforces the **incest taboo**—a cultural rule that prohibits sexual activity between closely related persons. However, in the U.S., twenty-six states allow first cousins to marry, and despite the stereotypes, West Virginia is *not* one. Does your home state allow first cousin marriages?

Even the looming specter of divorce is not a deterrent to marriage in the U.S.; most Americans either are married or plan to marry at some point. When I ask students in my classes if they are married or plan on marrying, almost every hand goes up. Even though people are staying single longer and delaying first marriage (the average age for men is twenty-nine and twenty-seven for women), most will marry. Marriage in the U.S. is a $70 billion industry, which is more than we spend on coffee, childcare, toothpaste, and toilet paper combined (The Week Staff, 2013; IBISWorld, 2015; Franchise Direct, 2014). In addition, you really need those things. Do you really need to be married? And what about starting that family? Pushing off marriage has led to delaying birth of the first child, and that late start has resulted in families having far fewer children.

Courtship and Mate Selection

When most of us think about courtship and mate selection, we imagine meeting that someone special, falling in love, and marring him or her. That's usually the way it goes in the United States and many Westernized cultures. However, in many societies, you may have little to no input into whom you will marry. Your marriage partner may be selected for you or you may have to steal your mate. There are three types of mate selection processes that are generally recognized: free choice, arranged, and marriage by capture.

In the United States, our marriage partners are typically not selected for us—we choose our own. This is commonly referred to as a "participant-run" mate selection process; the participants run the show. This process is also called **free-choice** mate selection. Some have called the mate selection process in the U.S. a "marriage market" due to the practice of comparing the positives and negatives of potential partners, then choosing the best mate. Regardless of which label you apply the process serves several important functions. It gives participants socially acceptable ways to experience a number of partners for fun, explore sexual expression/intimacy, find companionship, and ultimately decide with whom they are most compatible. We have the ability to test drive as many makes and models as we want before we buy.

Even with all this freedom of choice, most people end up marrying someone similar to themselves. **Homogamy** is the tendency for individuals with similar backgrounds to marry. Similar backgrounds may include religion, race, ethnicity, social class, or geographical region. Homogamy is not a social rule, ritual, or custom; it is merely a descriptive concept. Why do "likes" marry "likes"? Researchers have proposed a number of factors that explain who marries whom, and I cannot cover all of them.

Tinder

There are many different ways to meet a potential mate: through family and friends, at work, school, church, or running on the beach. However, if your life is too busy for any of that nonsense, try Tinder. If you are not familiar with Tinder, it is a hook-up app that uses location-based profile matching with text chatting. You are presented with a series of photos of possible matches. Think about the set of pictures like a stack of cards: for each pic, you either swipe left (discard, not interested) or swipe right (interested) as you work your way through your "stack" of photos. If you both swipe right, it's a "match." The match leads to conversation, which leads to meeting in person, which may lead to a hook-up. Whether this techno-sexual app is or isn't the wave of the future, using technology to meet others is a growing practice and industry. Tinder, for example, has tens of millions of users that say they find the app fun and no different from real life. You usually approach someone you initially find attractive; if he or she chats you up, fine, and if he or she blows you off, oh, well. This is not really any different from swiping right or left. Even though this app can broaden your potential mate horizons, geography rears its ugly head. *Propinquity* (remember that from above?) still reigns supreme. Users on Tinder were 54% more likely to hook up if they were within one mile of each other; that percentage drops in half for every two miles they move out from where they are (Gazibara, 2015). The digital world is wonderful, but people still have to meet, and apparently, the closer you are, the better.

So, I will briefly discuss the factor I think is the most intuitive and convincing in explaining the tendency toward marital homogamy—propinquity.

Propinquity is geographical closeness, being close to someone or something. The people we have frequent contact with are people who tend to share our beliefs and activities: those we run into at the gym, school, work, coffee shops, and church share similar backgrounds and attitudes. Take the TV sitcom *How I Met Your Mother*, for example. The characters are all white, college-educated, middle-class professionals of which two have married. The others end up dating each other or people similar to themselves (usually meeting at their local bar). We tend to date and marry people we bump into in our social circles.

According to sociologists Michael Rosenfeld and Reuben Thomas (2012), 30% of heterosexual married couples met through friends, and another 10% met their spouse at work. A very interesting 2013 study by Facebook Data Sciences found that 28% of their members married college sweethearts. Interestingly, the top three schools for men to meet their spouses, according to the study, were all religiously affiliated colleges. The study also showed that the top three colleges for women to meet their future husbands were all technical schools. You really can't avoid running into someone who is similar to you in social class, religious background, or interests at those schools.

I know what you are thinking: the Internet blows the idea of propinquity out of the water. Remember our man Rosenfeld from the paragraph above? Well, he found that the Internet has only partly displaced traditional meeting places like school, work, neighborhood, and family. His research indicates that about 20–24% of people make initial contact with their spouses online. Even if you live in the U.S. and meet your soulmate online, and he or she happens to live in Bhutan, one of you has to move so you can get married. You really cannot start a family over the Internet. At least I don't think you can.

In contrast to the free-choice model of mate selection is the arranged marriage. The partners in **arranged marriages** are chosen by parents, community leaders, matchmakers, or clergy. The bride and groom typically have little or no say in the matter. Arranged marriages are still commonly practiced today in Iran, Iraq, Afghanistan, and India. Arranged marriage was once an extremely common practice, but it has since fallen out of favor in many societies like China and India. This is due to the diffusion of Western cultural practices and the liberalization of social customs.

Often in cultures, whom one marries is far too important a decision to be left to someone so young and inexperienced. Marriage, in these societies, is the union of two families, not two individuals. Marriages should be the result of careful negotiations, not from young people following impulses of the heart. These decisions are a common way of securing alliances so that families can enjoy increased status, political power, economic gain, or to clear a debt. It is commonly believed that while they do not know each other, their love will grow for each other as time passes. This process of choosing a mate is difficult for many of us to understand because it is at odds with our values, beliefs, and customs. Would you want your marriage arranged? Who would you trust to arrange it?

Arranged marriages are many times secured with either a bride price or dowry. *Bride price* is the price paid by the groom's family to the bride's family for the loss of her services. This can be paid in the form of livestock, shells, money, services, years of labor, or other valuables. A *dowry*, on the other hand, is an incentive for a man to marry a woman and relieve her family of the burden of having a daughter. This is paid by the bride's family in the same forms as bride price. In fact, a Kenyan lawyer offered President Obama fifty cows, thirty goats, and seventy sheep as a bride price for the his daughter Malia (Leopold, 2015).

Arranged Child Marriages

Although now illegal, arranged child marriages are common in the Rajasthan region of northern India. Children as young as five years old are forced to accept their parents' choice of whom they will marry. In 2011, three young girls, aged fifteen, thirteen, and five, were all secretly married on a hilltop in northern India. National Geographic reporter Cynthia Gorney (2011) describes the scene and circumstances as three young Indian girls are married to boys they have never even seen.

There's an App for That

While I mentioned Tinder above there are a number of alternatives to this popular app. Below I have listed and briefly described some alternative mate-finder apps.

- *Hot or Not.* I don't think I have to say more (Or Not Limited, 2016).
- *Clover.* Like Tinder this is a location based profile match app that lets you sift through potential mates/hook-ups by the type of relationship they are looking for. You can also sort by things like ethnicity and height (Clover Inc., 2016).
- *Wingme.* Find a mate with the help of your friends, they have input on each of your selections. You can be the dater or act as a wingman for your friends (Wingme, 2014).
- *Stitch Companionship.* Tinder for older adults (Stitch Holdings Pty Ltd, 2016).
- *Grindr.* The all gay version of Tinder, for finding a lasting relationship or a casual hook-up (Grindr LLC, 2016).
- *3nder.* Meet like-minded people who want three-ways. This is an open minded app where trios are made easy and discretely, your friends and family will never know (3nder Ltd, 2015).

"Because the wedding was illegal and a secret, except to the invited guests, and because marriage rites in Rajasthan are often conducted late at night, it was well into the afternoon before the three girl brides in this dry farm settlement in the north of India began to prepare themselves for their sacred vows. They squatted side by side on the dirt, a crowd of village women holding sari cloth around them as a makeshift curtain, and poured soapy water from a metal pan over their heads. Two of the brides, the sisters Radha and Gora, were 15 and 13, old enough to understand what was happening. The third, their niece Rajani, was five. She wore a pink T-shirt with a butterfly design on the shoulder. A grown-up helped her pull it off to bathe. The grooms were en route from their own village, many miles away. No one could afford an elephant or the lavishly saddled horses that would have been ceremonially correct for the grooms' entrance to the wedding, so they were coming by car and were expected to arrive high-spirited and drunk."

This scene is not that uncommon. The practice of child marriage crosses many continents, languages, religions, and cultures. It is a common practice in parts of India, Yemen, Afghanistan, Nepal, Bangladesh, Nicaragua, and more than fifteen African nations. In fact, in Niger, 75% of women were married before they turned eighteen (United Nations, "Motherhood in Childhood", 2013; International Center for Research on Women, 2015). Whether the child bride is married off by her family to unite communities, resolve a feud, or to repay a debt, the results are the same: she is exploited by the husband's family, and her health and safety are put at risk. Essentially, her future is stolen.

A 2013 report from the United Nations Population Fund (UNFPA) indicates that between 2011 and 2020, more than 140 million young girls will be exploited through arranged child marriage. Of these 140 million child brides (girls under eighteen years), fully 50 million of them will marry under the age of fifteen. While both young boys and girls may be involved in child marriage, the practice is far more common among young girls. These young brides are frequently married off to men who are five, ten, or even thirty years older than they are. Most importantly, child brides are a far greater risk for a range of health and social issues. Their education is effectively ended, opportunity to gain vocational skills is blocked, and they are at increased risk for intimate partner sexual violence. Moreover, they are exposed to the "risks of too-early pregnancy, childbearing and motherhood before they are physically and psychologically ready". In addition, this population is at an increased risk of HIV infection. Child marriage is recognized by most international health and economic assistance organizations as a violation of the rights of girls.

Marriage by capture is the practice of taking a wife by force or deceit. This is almost always performed without the consent of the woman or her family. Unfortunately, it is practiced in many places, such as Asia, Africa, the Middle East, the Caucasus and even the Americas. While there is some variation in methods, the practice goes something like this: A frustrated man waits until the woman he wants is alone, grabs her, and takes her back to his place, where he quickly marries her, therefore claiming her as his property. Sometimes, the bride's family is able to dissuade the kidnapper to let her go but more often they must fight, or pay for her safe return. Many times, men who marry by capture are the least desirable members of their society: poor, of low status, and without resources. Therefore, for these men, the capture is viewed as their only access to a mate (Barnes, 1999).

Another common technique is to rape the woman, attempting to impregnate the "bride," which allows the "groom" to lay claim to her. Historically, and on a larger scale, this practice is common during times of war. Think the rape of the Sabine women, the French during the Napoleonic Wars, the Russians in WWII—basically, any and every war. You can even find marriage by capture in the Bible (Deuteronomy 21:10–14). More recently, for example, Boko Haram, a Jihadist terrorist group operating mainly in Nigeria, kidnapped more than two hundred schoolgirls in April 2014. Some of

---

Read More

- *I am Nujood, Age 10 and Divorced* by Nujood Ali and Delpine Minoui (2010). This book recounts the story of Nujood, a ten-year-old Yemeni girl who found the strength and courage to travel alone to a courthouse seeking a divorce. She wanted a divorce from her husband, a man in his thirties her father had forced her to marry. I also highly recommend Stephanie Sinclair's photographs and accompanying stories of the sorrow, abuse, and bravery of child brides.

the girls managed to escape, but most were beaten, executed, or forced into marriage by their captors ("Nigeria frees dozens", 2015; Oduah, 2015).

Fortunately, marriage by capture in most countries is considered a crime. The practice of marriage by capture, in many cultures, has evolved into the custom of bride price. Apparently, it seems more civilized to pay for your wife rather than kidnap her. Either way, these practices perpetuate the treatment of women as objects to be bought and sold or taken by force.

[...]

What Is Family?

Family has variously been labeled the basic unit of society, the backbone of society, and the universal social group. These terms imply that family is instrumental in organizing societies, important to holding societies together, and found in all societies. While some form of the family is found in all cultures, its form varies widely across societies and over time. We often talk about "the family" as if there was just one type, yet we know there are many types of families around the world and in our own society. Those types may include some with children, some without, some with two parents, and some with just one. Other families may include grandparents, uncles, cousins, nieces and nephews, or same-sex parents.

There are many definitions of family, and I really haven't found one that I like. However, I know there are students who need definitions. The U.S. Census Bureau defines a **family** as a group of two or more people related by birth, marriage, or adoption and residing together. As of 2013, only 66% of Americans fit this definition, down from 81% in 1970 (Vespa, Lewis, and Kreider, 2013). What do you think about this definition? Is it inclusive enough? It does cover many living arrangements, but it may exclude some that many people consider to be their "family." Think about the family you were raised in. Would this definition include the household in which you grew up?

When we discuss change and family in sociology, we consider both its structure (shape) and its function (purpose). That is, we examine what families look like—nuclear, blended, single parent—and what society expects the family to do—provide support, raise children, etc. Moreover, in sociology, we study the family as both a social institution and as a system of intergenerational relationships. We analyze the family from both a macrosociological and a microsociological perspective.

Change in the Family: Structure and Function

- Structure: The shape of marriage and family
  - What do marriages and families look like?
  - How and why have they changed?
- Function: The social and cultural purpose of marriage and family
  - What purpose do marriage and family serve in society?
  - How and why have they changed?

Family Forms

Family is embedded in culture; therefore, so are our perceptions of family. What family is changes across time and space; what did you think family was when you were ten years old, what do you think family is now, and what will you think family is when you are much older? Our perceptions of family have changed and will continue to change as our society embraces the growing number of alternate family forms. The events in your life such as marrying, having children, divorcing, remarrying, and becoming a stepparent will no doubt influence your thoughts on what family is. Most people will move through several family types over the course of their lives. Let's take a look at what families look like in today's society and how they have changed.

Perhaps the most salient feature of change in society in the past one hundred years has been the family. Some lament that the "family" is disappearing. Politicians and pundits alike bemoan the decline of the American family. Statements like "The American family is at its worst state in the history of the country," "... the nationwide decline of the family unit," and "The American family is no more" all seem to indicate there is no more "family" in the U.S. (Ginsborg, 2005; Dodrill, 2013; Bidwell, 2013). What family are they referring to? Nearly all are referring to a family that was present in the U.S. as a majority family type for less than twenty years: The *Leave It to Beaver*, nuclear, "traditional" family of the 1950s and '60s.

However, this is just a longing for a "family" that never was. In her book *The Way We Never Were: American Families and the Nostalgia Trap* (1992), Stephanie Coontz presents a compelling argument that shatters our image of the family from "the good old days." Neither the 1950s nor any other time in our past lines up with the mythical image of the "traditional family." The historical evidence shows that families were always complex, dynamic, and sorting through crises like many families today, just trying to make things work. This nostalgia for a mythical past is a dangerous obsession that hinders our ability to embrace the ever-changing landscape of modern family arrangements.

The **nuclear family**—married parents and their biological or adopted children sharing a common residence—is a waning family type. In 1960, the nuclear family—the *Leave it to Beaver* version of mom, dad, and two kids—accounted for about 44% of households; now that number is around 19% (Laughlin, 2013). Many times, politicians and others point to the nuclear family as the "normal" family, which we should all strive to achieve. In fact, the nuclear family was a relatively new type of family springing up mostly after WWII. For decades, it was common for Americans to live in families comprised of several generations. For the great number of rural farming families, these large, multigenerational families made sense. Before 1935, there was no Social Security, and the elderly counted on their children and grandchildren for housing and support, a sort of all-in-the-family social security. Additionally, The Great Depression forced many family members to come together for economic reasons. In 1940, just before the outbreak of WWII, extended families accounted for one-quarter of all U.S. households (Taylor et al., 2010).

The **extended family**, as the name suggests, extends the nuclear family by including additional family members. This is a common family type found in many societies. *Vertical extended* families include grandparents, their children, and their grandchildren. Imagine you, your parents, and your grandparents all sharing a residence. *Horizontal extended* families usually include two or more siblings living together with their families, so you get a mix of uncles, aunts, nieces, nephews, and cousins. Try this out: you, your brothers and sisters, mom and dad, mom's no-good brother, his wife, their five kids, and a goat all in the same house, with one bathroom. Many times, extended families are cultural expressions of reverence for older generations, consolidation of labor, or economic necessities. When they first come to the U.S., many immigrant groups live in extended family arrangements to pool their resources, and some are continuing cultural patterns.

While a common family pattern at one time in America's past, its popularity bottomed out in 1980 with only 12% of households reporting extended family living arrangements. However, the extended family has made a resurgence in the past decade. Between 2000 and 2010, those living in extended family households increased from 15% to 16.7%, spiking after the Great Recession of 2008. While the increase has been across all age segments, millennials (those born between 1982 and 2000) are the major contributors to the rise in extended family households. They are part of what sociologists call the boomerang generation—because they leave home and come right back, like a boomerang. Some of the factors contributing to the boomerang generation include the Great Recession, increased cost of college, and an inclination to postpone marriage (Pew Research Center, "A Portrait of Stepfamilies," 2011).

Figure 9.2 Extended families are found more frequently among certain ethnic groups in the U.S. However, in recent years the overall number of extended family households has been on the rise.

The **blended family** (stepfamily) is a family in which at least one spouse has children from a previous marriage or relationship. Blended families are quickly becoming one of the most common family patterns in the U.S. Currently, blended families comprise about one-third of all U.S. families. Why do you think there are so many blended families? Why are their numbers increasing? The majority of blended families are formed when parents decide to remarry. Divorce is the driving force behind the large and growing numbers of blended families. However, some blended families can be formed by previously unwed parents who have decided to marry.

The number of single parent families has nearly doubled since 1960, according to the U.S. Census. **Single parent families** are living arrangements that involve one parent and his or her dependent children. These families make up just over 30% of all U.S. families. Fully one-quarter of all U.S. households are single female-headed, and 6% of single households are male-headed. This represents a tripling of single parent households since 1960. I think by now you are getting the sense that single parent families are growing, and growing fast. In fact, the fastest-growing family form in the U.S. is the single parent-headed household. Let's break it down. Single parent-headed families are formed in a variety of ways like divorce, desertion, death of a spouse, or by choice. Below, I present a brief overview of the structure of single parent-headed households.

- Of all single parent-headed families, 84% are headed by a woman, and only 16% are dad-only households.
- Births to teenage unwed mothers have dropped in half since 1991. Today, unmarried single moms are more likely to be in their twenties or thirties.
- Education level is a factor: about 90% of women with a college degree marry before giving birth to their first child. However, of women with some college education, 40% are unmarried when they have their first child. In addition, for women with a high school diploma or less, 57% are unmarried at the birth of their first child.
- About 46% of female-headed households are at or below the poverty line, which is over four times that of married families.
- Non-marital births vary by race. It is highest for black women at 72%, followed by Hispanic with 53%, whites with 29%, and Asians with just 17%.

(*Sources:* U.S. Census, 2012; Department of Health and Human Services, "Information on Poverty", 2014; Livingston and Cohn, 2010)

Cohabitation

In the past, it has been referred to as "shacking up" or "living in sin," but **cohabitation**—unmarried couples living together in a committed, non-marital relationship—is on the rise. Between 1990 and

2007, the number of unmarried cohabiting partners increased 88% (Kreider and Elliot, 2009). While cohabitation is more popular than ever, who is doing it is changing. More and more, the age of those who cohabitate is on the rise. Fully half of those aged thirty to forty-nine have cohabitated at some point in their lives; those twenty-four and younger make up only 20% of people living together (Fry and Cohn, 2011).

Some people are not ready for marriage, some do not want to marry, and some just want to take a committed, long-term relationship for a spin. Others just want to share the cost of running a household. Whatever the reason, Americans like to cohabitate. Many view cohabitation as a viable alternative to marriage. Of all married women in the United States, 60% cohabitated with someone at some point in their lives before they married (Manning, 2013). Cohabitation, apparently, is a gateway drug to marriage.

Does cohabitation bode well for marriage? Two years ago, I would have written an emphatic no. Recent research by Arielle Kuperberg (2014) has cast some doubt on decades of research that showed cohabitation leads to divorce. Her research showed no correlation between cohabitation before marriage and divorce. Why? Well, we know that those who marry young are at considerably greater risk for divorce than those who marry at older ages. Therefore, she adjusted for age of cohabitation. That is, young people who live together and then marry are at greater risk for divorce. It's not that cohabitation leads to divorce; it's that young people establish their marital roles during their cohabitation and carry those roles over into their marriage, essentially dooming them. So, the younger that a couple who eventually marry begin cohabitation, the greater their risk for divorce. If you are going to shack up with someone while you are young, do not marry him or her. You could always wait until your mid-twenties to live with someone before marriage, which dramatically reduces your risk of divorce.

Those with lower education levels and lower incomes are more likely to cohabitate. Moreover, working-class and poor cohabitating couples are more likely to have children. More educated, wealthier live-in partners are more likely to marry their partner than their less educated, poorer counterparts. Educated live-ins with higher incomes are more likely to use cohabitation as a *launching pad* for marriage, while those with less education and income are more likely to use cohabitation as an *alternative* to marriage.

[...]

Work and Family

We have discussed a number of changes in marriage and families, but our discussion would not be complete without a look at how work, especially women's employment, has influenced those changes. Below, I have indicated the factors that have been most influential on families over the past few decades.

- Women make up nearly half of the workforce. Fully 47% of all workers are women, up from 38% in 1970. Additionally, women are increasingly becoming the household breadwinners.

Nearly all the growth in family incomes in the past several decades can be attributed to women's increased earnings. For all households, more than 40% of moms are now the sole or primary source of income. In 1970, only 7% of working women earned more than their husbands; today, 24% do. In fact, since the 1970s, nearly all the rise in family income has come from women's earnings (Bureau of Labor Statistics, 2014).

- Education is linked both to earnings potential and to likelihood of employment. Over the past few decades, women's college attendance and graduation rates have approached and then surpassed that of men. Today, substantially more women graduate from college than men. Therefore, they will soon be the majority of college-educated workers, positioning them to be the bulk of the highest wage earners in the workplace.

- This increase in women's earnings and presence in the workplace has affected the caregiver roles in families. Fathers are playing larger roles in caregiving. In households where mom is employed, one in five dads are primary caregivers. Stay-at-home dads with working moms have doubled since 1990. This trend in dad as the primary caregiver is reflected in the number of father-only families, which have tripled in the past forty years (The Council of Economic Advisers, "Nine Facts", 2014).

- With the decades-long increase in both dual-earner homes and working single parents, 60% of children live in homes where all parents work. In addition, it's not just childcare that can strain families: with more people living longer, more families are facing issues surrounding elder care. This has created what some have called "the sandwich generation," those sandwiched between care for their own children and care for their aging parents (Bureau of Labor Statistics, 2011; Bureau of Labor Statistics, 2012).

- Searching for flexibility in the workplace: Workers who are struggling to balance work and family are looking for employers that understand the changing needs of families in relationship to workplace flexibility and are willing to respond to those needs. Almost half of parents with kids under eighteen at home have passed up a job because it conflicted with their family obligations. Women, research indicates, are seeking career paths that offer more autonomy and flexibility (The Council of Economic Advisers, "Work-Life", 2014; Goldin, 2006). Not coincidentally, careers that can accommodate childcares needs and offer both high levels of autonomy and flexibility require more education, which more women are pursuing.

- Balancing work and family: Both men and women report they are increasingly pressed for time. Frequently, this creates conflicts between managing work and home responsibilities. Men and women are increasingly likely to report that work interferes with family, not the other way around. A 2011 study revealed that 60% of men in dual-earner families reported some form of work/family conflict, which was an increase from just 35% in 1977. In 2010, 46% of working men and women reported that work interfered with some family obligation, which was an increase over reports from 2002 (Galinsky, Aumann, and Bond, 2011; King, 2005).

Divorce and Remarriage

No chapter on marriage and family would be complete without a discussion on divorce. Divorce is nearly as popular as marriage is in the U.S. **Divorce**—the legal dissolution of marriage—is not recognized in some cultures and perhaps a little too recognized in others. The Philippines and the Vatican do not allow divorce, and in just the last twenty years, Ireland, Chile, and Malta have allowed divorce.

You have probably heard that 50% of all marriages in the U.S. end in divorce. It's not true. The cumulative percentage of those divorced from a first marriage in the U.S. is just about 41% (Goodlight, 2012). However, the percentage of those who seek a divorce from a second marriage is over 60%. Moreover, divorce is not on the rise; in fact, it has been on the decline since around 1981.

Let's take a quick peek at divorce rates and their slow decline over the past thirty years. A **divorce rate** is measured as the number of divorces per one thousand people. That number was 5.3 divorces per thousand people when divorces peaked in 1981. By 1990, that rate had dropped to 4.7 divorces per thousand people. In addition, by 2012, the divorce rate hovered right at 3.4 divorces per thousand people (Centers for Disease Control, "National Marriage", 2015). Clearly, the divorce rate in the U.S. is falling.

More people who married in the 1990s were still married at the fifteen-year mark than couples married in the 1980s. In addition, so far, those who married in the 2000s are divorcing at even lower rates. According to economist Justin Wolfers, if current divorce rate trends continue, nearly two-thirds of those who marry will never experience divorce (Miller, 2014).

In Figure 9.3 below, you can see the historical pattern of divorce in the United States. In 1950 just after the end of WWII, divorce rates were relatively low, declining steadily until 1960. Divorce rates then climbed steadily until they peaked in 1980. Since then, divorce rates have been falling slowly but remain high.

Given these patterns, we have to ask two things. Why the dramatic rise in divorce from 1960 to 1981? In addition, why have divorce rates been slowly declining in the past thirty years? Led mostly by the baby boomers, the 1960s and 1970s were times of tremendous social upheaval in the U.S. and many Western nations. Not only were the previous generations' marital and sexual norms being challenged, but so was nearly all institutional authority. Positions on the war in Vietnam, civil rights, censorship, and educational policies were being revised as many institutions experienced a general liberalization. During these decades the United States emerged from a sort of social and cultural dark ages. Drugs, music, and the sexual revolution played a key role in transforming society, altering many long-held views on social arrangements like marriage and family. Think about it this way: there were 76 million baby boomers coming of age in a very short time period. It was as though the United States was a house filled with millions of teenagers and twenty-somethings. Moreover, like many adolescents, in order to establish their own identities, they felt they must reject the conventional moral beliefs of their parents.

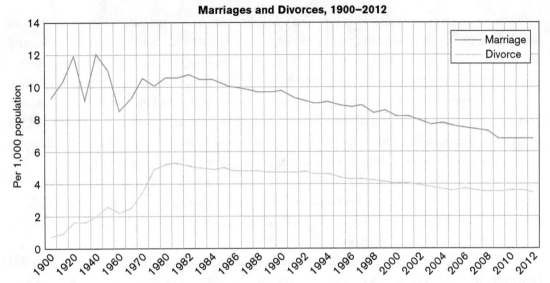

Marriages and Divorces, 1900–2012

Figure 9.3 Divorce rates climbed steadily after 1960, but peaked in 1980. Since then divorce rates have slowly dropped.

As the baby boomers vocalized their opposition to and rejection of their parents' institutional view of marriage, they adopted a more "self-fulfillment" model of marriage (Coontz, 1992). Rather than view marriage as a duty to spouse, offspring, community, and, ultimately, country, this generation looked to find love, self-fulfillment, and gratification in marriage. Also, the women's movement had increased educational and economic freedoms that allowed women to exit unfulfilling marriages. The rise of "no-fault" divorce laws made divorce less expensive, easier to obtain, and unilaterally exercised (one spouse could divorce another even if he or she did not want a divorce). Additionally, the more it was practiced, the less stigma was connected to divorce, making it more socially acceptable. These and several other social factors led many to believe in the disposability of marriage.

Understanding what elements have converged to produce both a decline in marriages and divorces is a complex task and well beyond our discussion here. Therefore, let's take a look at just a few factors that have contributed to the thirty-year slide in divorce rates. Much interest has focused on the delay of first marriage, increased average age at first marriage, cohabitation, and the increasing view by younger cohorts that marriage is not that important. Obviously, as more people choose not to marry, the potential for divorce is reduced. However, even taking into account the decrease in the number of marriages, divorce is still declining. Additionally, as people, specifically women, pursue more education, they tend to delay marriage. The median age at first marriage for men is nearly twenty-nine and almost twenty-seven for women (U.S. Census, "Decennial Censuses, 1890 to 1940", 2014). This increase in age at first marriage bodes well for success in marriage.

Today, couples are increasingly more likely to cohabitate before marriage. More than 65% of married people report cohabitating with someone of the opposite sex before marrying (Donevan, 2014). Cohabitation is quickly becoming the "gateway relationship" to marriage. Previous research suggested that cohabitation was a likely predictor of divorce. Recent analyses have speculated that divorce-prone people cohabitate rather than cohabitation causing divorce. Flipping the once commonly held idea that cohabitation increases likelihood of divorce on its head, Stevenson and Wolfers (2007) suggest that without cohabitation, divorce may be more likely. Experimenting with various elements of a relationship through cohabitation may better prepare couples before they marry.

Divorce rates, however, vary across groups in the United States. African Americans have the highest divorce rates. Whites run a close second, followed by Hispanics, and Asian Americans have the lowest divorce rates. The differences in rates are tied to a number of social variables, including income, education levels, religion, and cultural influences.

While it is clear that divorce is on the decline in the United States, it is still a part of the marital landscape. Research has identified a number of factors that put some at greater risk for divorce than others. Here are some factors that seem to increase the risk of divorce:

- Marrying young. Those who marry for the first time young (as teenagers) tend to have high divorce rates. Those rates decrease as age increases for first marriages. Marriage can be challenging without the necessary life skills, education, and employability. The high divorce rate among young couples tends to be associated with education, which is linked to income levels and economic stability (Lehrer, 2008).

- Education levels. Those with college degrees are less likely to divorce than those with a high school diploma or less. Those who attend college tend to be older at the time of first marriage and have a greater range of dating, courtship, and sexual experiences. Their college degree is also associated with higher incomes and better benefits, which may translate to more stable households (Martin, 2006).

- Income. Those married couples with higher incomes tend to experience lower divorce rates. Income is highly correlated with education. Research indicates that those households with annual incomes of $50,000 or more run a lower risk of divorce than those with incomes of $25,000 or less (Lewis and Kreider, 2015).

- Parents' divorce. You cannot control all risk factors for divorce. However, if your parents divorced, that doubles your risk of divorce, and if your partner's parents were divorced, that can just about triple the risk (Dennison, 2014).

- Childless marriages. Married couples without children are more likely to divorce than those with kids. With fewer reasons to remain in an unhappy marriage, those without children can find divorce easier. The divorce laws in many states make dissolution of the marriage easier if there are no children involved (Bronson, 2006).

- Religious affiliation. Those who report belonging to a religion are slightly less likely to divorce than those who claim no religious affiliation. Moreover, if you and your spouse share a common religious affiliation, risk of divorce is further reduced (White, 1990).

The Graying of Divorce

Divorce rates in the United States are on an overall downturn except for one group: those over age fifty, our beloved baby boomers. In 1990, a mere 10% of all divorces were among those fifty and older. Today, those calling it quits with their marriages over age fifty make up 25% of all divorces. In addition, those who do divorce after age fifty are far more likely to hold at least a bachelor's degree (Brown and Lin, 2012). We don't know exactly why we are seeing this rise in divorce among older people, but researchers have speculated that this rise in "gray divorce" is due in part to an increase in life expectancy—believing you have enough years left to do marriage one more time. Perhaps it is due to increased financial stability for both spouses, which translates to a greater financial ability to divorce. Other reasons may include a shift in marital expectations. Marriage was once expected to simply provide stability and security; now, the added expectations of self-fulfillment and personal satisfaction may be deal-breakers. Now that the nest is empty and couples being to "recouple" they may find that through the years they have drifted too far away from their partners or they simply realize they no longer like them. After decades of distractions from intimacy as a couple like juggling careers, childrearing, and keeping the household together, couples may realize they don't like the person on the other side of the breakfast table. Whatever the reasons, make no mistake: just as boomers have driven other economic and social changes, they could be reshaping divorce.

Remarriage

Along with both first marriages and divorce, **remarriage**—any marriage in which at least one spouse was previously married—is also on the decline. The remarriage rate in the U.S. has declined by 40% since 1990. Men are twice as likely to remarry as women; either they are more eager to remarry or have greater resources to help them find a new spouse (Payne, 2015). Interestingly, about 6% of those who remarry do it with their ex-spouse (Kalish, 2005). People are also taking longer to remarry than in past decades; today, most remarry within four years, although on average, women take longer to remarry than men. Why do you think women take longer than men to remarry?

Often, remarriage means the formation of complex families. Nearly half of all remarried couples already have children in the home. Overall, men are more likely than women to be the stepparents in newly formed blended families, which makes sense given the greater likelihood of women retaining custody of children. Therefore, women are more likely to bring children to the marriage than men. While blended families have become far more common, evidence suggests that the children in those families do not fare as well as those raised by two biological parents or a single parent (Stewart, 2007).

Why do you think children in blended families don't do as well as those raised by either one or both of their biological parents?

Even though remarriage is on the decline, people are still taking a second, third, or fourth ride on the marriage-go-round. Americans love the idea of marriage. However, these remarriages are forming complex blended families with a mixture of step, half, and biological siblings, many of whom are in variety of custody situations. This can create a sense of impermanence or transience, which can undermine the stability of the new family. In addition, unfortunately, this is evident in the divorce rates among second and third marriages. There is a 67% divorce rate among second marriages, and 73% of third marriages end in divorce.

Theoretical Perspectives on Marriage and Family

The structural functionalist view emphasizes the importance of social institutions and the particular functions they perform in maintaining social stability and keeping society chugging along. Therefore, a functionalist understanding of the family stresses how the family, as a social institution, performs several important functions that contribute to social order. Functionalists see the family as the primary agent of socialization, responsible for the development and social adjustment of its members. Families help their younger members understand and internalize acceptable social values, beliefs, and behaviors, which are central to maintaining social solidarity and stability. Functionalists also view the family as a source of a range of support, from physical to financial to emotional. Not only do we expect families to provide food, shelter, and clothing for their members, but we also expect families to provide love and comfort—to care for us and be there when we need them.

Families also provide their members with a social identity. When children are born, they assume their families' social status, race/ethnicity, religion, etc. While for some this can bring advantage, for others it can mean lifelong deprivation. Whatever a family's status, functionalists expect it to transmit to each new generation the central social values, beliefs, and behaviors that will help duplicate social statuses, roles, and, ultimately, social structure, all with the aim of promoting social order. Consequently, functionalists see family types that vary from the conventional as a threat to the well-being of children, the family, and, by extension, society itself.

Like functionalists, conflict theorists recognize that the family as a social institution serves many functions. However, while functionalism focuses on reproduction of social statuses and roles for the maintenance of social stability, the conflict approach sees families as a locus of the reproduction of inequality and patriarchy. Primarily, the conflict perspective focuses on how the capitalist system maintains inequality between the powerful and less powerful classes, which, in turn, shapes other institutions such as the family.

For instance, families with the resources to do so pass their wealth from one generation to the next. This concentration of wealth in a small number of families reinforces existing social and wealth inequality. Family, for conflict theorists, is essentially an institution that reproduces social class. Patterns of inequality affect families across the social class spectrum. Poor families experience a deprivation of social resources, while advantaged families enjoy social privilege. The lack of social resources becomes a source of stress and contention within poor families, which can impair family functioning and relationships. On the other hand, wealthier families have access to better schools, extracurricular activities, and travel, therefore enhancing their children's social and human capital.

The family is also seen as replicating patterns of patriarchy. The family is a microcosm of the capitalist system in which power is directly related to earnings. Historically, men have been the top wage earners in most households; therefore, they exercise the most power over other family members. This has led to the control of women and children by men. Some feminists suggest this power imbalance and control leads to domestic violence when family members resist. The conflict approach maintains that the capitalist system creates family relations that mirror inequality in the large society.

The interactionism perspective examines the family at a more microsociological level than either functionalism or the conflict approach. Rather than seeing family roles as automatically adopted by family members as part of preexisting social structure, this approach contends that families and households operate on a system of expected behaviors that have been constructed from their day to day interactions (McLennan et al., 2000). Much work by symbolic interactionists focuses on socialization and gender roles. For example, symbolic interactionists might examine how gender role conceptions influence the boundaries of spousal responsibilities or how male and female children may be treated differently. Also, socialization is viewed as a reciprocal process in which parents guide children's social development and adjustment while they are socialized into the role of parent. These daily interactions between family members are how each individual family is formed and maintains its internal order.

The Bottom Line

It is clear that the family is an essential thread in our larger complex social fabric. For many societies, the family is formed through marriage. We have seen that there are a variety of marriage patterns available in many cultures, but monogamy is the preferred marriage form worldwide. There is tremendous variation in how the cultures of the world define marriage and structure their families. In the United States, there have been profound changes in the arrangement of families and even considerable debate about marriage and how that is defined.

Shifts in demographics, economic conditions, and social attitudes have given rise to a number of different, flexible, and practical family patterns. While some lament the bygone days of "the family" and fear that its changing complexion is a harbinger of the end of civilization, others see these changes as necessary adaptations to a changing society. Families are not in danger: they are thriving, and they are as meaningful as ever. American households have never been more diverse, more baffling,

Table 9.2 Theoretical Perspectives on Marriage and Family

Theoretical Perspectives

	Structural Functionalism	**Conflict Approach**	**Interactionist Approach**
Marriage	The social value of marriage encourages couples to marry. Marriage is the foundation of the family unit, which is needed to fulfill its social functions. Therefore, marriage should be encouraged. Other institutions reinforce the value of marriage by offering cooperative rules and practices. There are more than 2,000 legal benefits marriage in the U.S. including tax advantages.	The institution of marriage is designed to replicate the larger social economic conditions. A man essentially takes a wife as chattel—his possession. He puts a ring on her finger to show is possession and she will take his name at marriage further solidifying his control.	Marriage is a social reality negotiated between two people using symbols. Engagement parties and engagement rings act as highly visible symbols that establish the social acknowledged relationship between the engaged couple.
Family	The family is an important social institution for socializing younger members of society and reproduction. The family is necessary for the transmission of social values, beliefs, and norms, which are key factors in stabilizing society and maintaining social order.	Families are arrangements that reproduce the economic relations in the larger society. This is played out within the family as patriarchal control. The father-husband has his wife and children adhere to family "rules" and "ideology" that reinforces his dominance.	Through daily interactions, family members create a negotiated reality—a shared understanding of what your "family" is—which sets boundaries for each family member's roles, fostering social regularity in the context of the family.

or more accepted. Because there are so many different living arrangements, most people will pass through several different types in the course of their lives.

The last sixty years have brought about significant change in family patterns. Specifically, the second wave of the women's movement has had a profound influence on the complexion of the family. Women seeking more education and career stability have been delaying age at first marriage, age at birth of first child, and are having fewer children. The increased economic power of women along with changes in no-fault divorce laws make exiting a bad marriage easier. While divorce rates peaked in 1981, they have been falling steadily ever since, but not terribly fast.

There was also a shift in our attitudes toward marriage. Those of the boomer generation transformed the meaning of marriage away from duty and obligation to an institution in which one finds self-fulfillment and gratification, from the marriage of *we* to the marriage for *me*. Some social critics have pointed out that among past generations, spouses felt an obligation to the marriage and the larger community. Now, they say if one spouse or both don't find personal happiness in the marriage, they just divorce. These changing attitudes toward marriage and divorce have led some to speculate that many see marriage as disposable.

The changing face of the American family is evident from just these few statistical profiles I have presented below. Today, we are:

- Marrying later, staying single longer
- Choosing not to marry at all, even when there are minor children involved
- Cohabitating in record numbers
- Forming a greater variety of family arrangements
- Having smaller families (the average number of people per household dropped from 3.1 in 1970 to 2.5 in 2013)
- Having fewer children (average number of children per family in 1970 was 1.3; that dropped to 0.9 children per family in 2013)

While divorce is slowly declining, it is still a common event, leaving many to remarry. While the number of first marriages is at a low point, remarriage is still as popular as ever. Fully 84% of those who divorce will remarry. Most of them remarry in five years or less; men are faster to return to the altar than are women. Even though divorce rates are down overall, they are on the rise for those fifty and older. Older, better-educated, wealthier Americans are experiencing a gray divorce boom.

In the historical long view, the functions of the family have changed. We no longer expect the family to be a unit of economic production *and* consumption. The family is no longer responsible for educating the young, and even religious instruction is conducted largely in the community. However, if we look at the great many changes in the demographics of the family in the past sixty years, we still expect the family to perform some basic functions. We certainly expect the family to socialize the young, provide physical, emotional, and financial support for its members, and provide us with a place in the world. While there may still be the expectation of having children within the context of a marriage, this requirement of the family is becoming increasingly less important.

Figure Credits

Figure 9.2: Henry M. Trotter, "Extended Family," https://commons.wikimedia.org/wiki/File:Coloured-family. jpg. Copyright in the Public Domain.

Figure 9.3: Copyright © Rcragun (CC BY-SA 4.0) at https://commons.wikimedia.org/wiki/File:Marriage_and_ Divorce_Rates_1960-2011.png.

Bibliography

3nder Ltd. *3nder*. Computer software. *Apple App Store*. Vers. 3.3.0 3nder Ltd, 13 Nov. 2015. Web. 26 Mar. 2016.

Ali, Nujood, and Delpine Minoui. *I am Nujood, Age 10 and Divorced*. Trans. Linda Coverdale. New York: Three Rivers Press, 2010. Print.

Alleyne, Richard. "Woman 'married' to Berlin Wall for 29 years." *The Telegraph*. The Telegraph, 27 May 2008. Web. 24 Sept. 2015.

Barnes, R.H. "Marriage by Capture." *The Journal of the Royal Anthropological Institute* 5.1 (1999): 57–73. Web. 24 Sept. 2015.

Beattie, Tina. "Sex, marriage and the Catholic Church." *The Guardian*. The Guardian, 8 Oct. 2014. Web. 20 Apr. 2016.

Bidwell, Allie. "Study: The American Family is No More." *U.S. News*. U.S. News, 11 Sept. 2013. Web. 24 Sept. 2015.

Bronson, Po. *"Why Do I Love These People?": Understanding, Surviving, and Creating Your Own Family*. New York: Random House, 2006. Print.

Brown, Susan L. and I-Fen Lin. "The Gray Divorce Revolution: Rising Divorce Among Middle-Aged and Older Adults, 1990–2010." *Journals of Gerontology Series B: Psychological Sciences and Social Sciences* 67.6 (2012): 731–741. Web. 25 Sept. 2015.

Clover Inc. *Clover Dating App*. Computer software. *Apple App Store*. Vers. 5.0 Clover Inc., 22 Feb. 2016. Web. 25 Mar. 2016.

Cohn, D'vera. "Love and Marriage." Pew Research Center, 13 Feb. 2013. Web. 29 Aug. 2015. <http://www. pewsocialtrends.org/2013/02/13/love-and-marriage/>.

Coontz, Stephanie. *The Way We Never Were: American Families and the Nostalgia Trap*. New York: Basic Books, 1992. Print.

Dennison, Renée Peltz. "Are Children of Divorce Doomed to Fail?" *Psychology Today*. Psychology Today, 2 Aug. 2014. Web. 26 Mar. 2016.

Dodrill, Tara. "The Downfall of the American Family." *OffTheGridNews*. OffTheGridNews: Better Ideas for Off the Grid Living, 17 July 2013. Web. 24 Sept. 2015.

Donevan, Connor. "Millenials Navigae the Ups and Downs of Cohabitation." *All Things Considered. NPR*. Natl. Public Radio. 1 Nov. 2014. Web. 25 Sept. 2015.

Evans-Pritchard, Edward. *Kinship and Marriage Among the Nuer*. Oxford: Clarendon Press, 1990. Print.

Faruqui, Fahad. "Saudi Arabia's cruel marriage laws." *The Guardian*. The Guardian, 3 Apr. 2010. Web. 14 Apr. 2016.

Fox, Robin. *Kinship & Marriage: An Anthropological Perspective*. Cambridge: Press Syndicate of the University of Cambridge, 1967. Print.

Franchise Direct. "Food Franchise Industry Report 2014: Industry Segment Overviews." *Franchise Direct*. Franchise Direct, 9 July 2014. Web. 25 Mar. 2016.

Fry, Richard and D'vera Cohn. "Living Together: The Economics of Cohabitation." Pew Research Center, 27 June 2011. Web. 24 Sept. 2015.

Galinsky, Ellen, Kerstin Aumann, and James T. Bond. "Times are Changing: Gender and Generation at Work and at Home." *Families and Work Institute*. Families and Work Institute, 2011. Web. 26 Mar. 2016.

Gazibara, Steve. "10 Crazy Facts from the Indiana University Tinder Study." *10Worthy*. 10Worthy, Feb. 2015. Web. 11 Dec. 2015.

Giddens, Anthony. *Sociology*. 5th ed. Malden: Polity Press, 2006. Web. 29 Aug. 2015.

Ginsborg, Paul. *The Politics of Everyday Life: Making Choices, Changing Lives*. Bury St. Edmunds: Yale University Press, 2005. Print.

Goldin, C. "The Quiet Revolution That Transformed Women's Employment, Education, and Family." *AEA Papers and Proceedings* (2006): 1–21. Web. 25 Sept. 2015.

Goodlight, Sandra. *Why Marriages Do Not Last*. Bloomington: Author House, 2012. Print.

Gorney, Cynthia. "Child Brides." *National Geographic*. National Geographic, June 2011. Web. 24 Sept. 2015.

Graburn, Nelson H.H. *Readings in Kinship and Social Structure*. New York: Harper & Row, 1971. Print.

Grindr LLC. *Grindr—Gay chat, meet & date*. Computer software. *Google Play*. Vers. 2.3.3 Grindr LLC, 22 Feb. 2016. Web. 25 Mar. 2016.

Hagerty, Barbara Bradley. "Some Muslims in U.S. Quietly Engage in Polygamy." *All Things Considered*. NPR. Natl. Public Radio. 27 May 2008. Web. 29 Aug. 2015.

Heinlein, Robert A. *The Moon is a Harsh Mistress*. New York: Tom Doherty Associates, 1966. Print.

IBISWorld. "Wedding Services in the US: Market Research Report." *IBISWorld*. IBISWorld, Sept. 2015. Web. 25 Mar. 2016.

International Center for Research on Women. "Violence Against Women." International Center for Research on Women. 2015. Web. 24 Mar. 2016.

Jones, Ann. *Looking for Lovedu: A woman's Journey Through Africa*. New York: Vintage Books, 2001. Print.

Kalish, Nancy. *Lost and Found Lovers: Facts and Fantasies of Rekindled Romances*. Lincoln: iUniverse, Inc., 2005. Print.

King, Jacque L. "Research Review: Work-Family/Family-Work Conflict." *International Journal of Leadership Studies* 1.1 (2005): 102–105. Web. 25 Sept. 2015.

King James Bible, Deuteronomy 21.10–14. Web. 24 Sept. 2015.

Kohn, Sally. "Is Polygamy the Next Gay Marriage?" *The Daily Beast*. The Daily Beast, 12 Sept. 2014. Web. 24 Sept. 2015.

Kreider, Rose M. and Diana B. Elliott. *America's Families and Living Arrangements: 2007.* Washington: U.S. Census Bureau, Current Population Reports, Sept. 2009. Web. 24 Sept. 2015.

Kuperberg, Arielle. "Age at Coresidence, Premarital Cohabitation, and Marriage Dissolution: 1985–2009." *Journal of Marriage and Family* 76.2 (2014): 352–369. Web. 24 Sept. 2015.

Lah, Kyung. "Tokyo Man Marries Video Game Character." *CNN.* CNN, 17 Dec. 2009. Web. 24 Sept. 2015.

Landin, Kathy. "15 of the World's Weirdest Marriages, 'I Now Pronounce You … What?!'" *TheFW.* TheFW, 2015. Web. 24 Sept. 2015.

Laughlin, Lynda. "Who's Minding the Kids? Child Care Arrangements: Spring 2011." *Household Economic Studies.* Washington, D.C.: U.S. Census Bureau, Apr. 2013. Web. 21 May 2015.

Lehrer, Evelyn L. "Age at Marriage and Marital Instability: Revisiting the Becker-Landes-Michael Hypothesis." *Journal of Population Economics* 21.2 (2008): 463–484. Web. 26 Mar. 2016.

Leopold, Todd. "Kenyan Lawyer oˇers Cows, Goats, Sheep to Marry Malia Obama." *CNN.* CNN, 28 May 2015. Web. 25 Mar. 2016.

Lewis, James R. *The Encyclopedia of Cults, Sects, and New Religions.* Amherst: Prometheus Books, 2002. Print.

Lewis, Jamie M. and Rose M. Kreider. *Remarriage in the United States.* Washington: U.S. Census Bureau, American Community Survey Reports, Mar. 2015. Web. 26 Mar. 2016.

Livingston, Gretchen and D'vera Cohn. ˙"The New Demography of Motherhood." Pew Research Center, 6 May 2010. Web. 23 Sept. 2015.

Manning, Wendy D. "Trends in Cohabitation. Over Twenty Years of Change, 1987–2010." National Center for Family & Marriage Research, 2013. Web. 24 Sept. 2015.

Martin, Steven P. "Trends in Marital Dissolution by Women's Education in the United States." *Demographic Research* 15.20 (2006): 537–560. Web. 26 Mar. 2016.

McLennan, Gregor, Allanah Ryan, and Paul Spoonley. *Exploring society: Sociology for New Zealand students.* Auckland: Pearson Education New Zealand Unlimited, 2000. Print.

Miller, Claire Cain. "The Divorce Surge is Over, but the Myth Lives On." *New York Times.* New York Times, 2 Dec. 2014. Web. 25 Sept. 2015.

"Mosuo: A Mysterious Matriarchal Group in China."*ChinaCulture.org.* ChinaCulture.org, 2003. Web. 29 Aug. 2015.

Murphy, Caryle. "Interfaith marriage is common in U.S., particularly among the recently wed." Pew Research Center, 2 June 2015. Web. 24 Sept. 2015.

"Nigeria frees dozens from Boko Haram captivity." *Aljazeera.* Aljazeera, 31 July 2015. Web. 24 Sept. 2015.

Oduah, Chika. "Women held by Boko Haram in Sambisa Forest describe abuse, crippling fear." *Aljazeera America.* Aljazeera America, 8 June 2015. Web. 24 Sept. 2015.

"Oneida Community: Utopian Religious Community." *Encyclopedia Britannica Online.* Encyclopedia Britannica, 9 Dec. 2014. Web. 29 Aug. 2015. <http://www.britannica.com/topic/Oneida-Community>.

Or Not Limited. *Hot or Not.* Computer software. *Google Play.* Or Not Limited, 23 Mar. 2016. Web. 26 Mar. 2016.

Payne, Krista K. "Median Age at First Marriage, 2013." *National Center for Family & Marriage Research*. 2015. Web. 25 Sept. 2015.

Pew Research Center. "A Portrait of Stepfamilies." Washington, DC: Pew Research Center, 13 Jan. 2011. Web. 26 Mar. 2016.

Phillips, Tom. "Man Marries Pillow." *Metro*. Metro, 9 Mar. 2010. Web. 24 Sept. 2015.

Rosenfeld, Michael and Reuben J. Thomas. "Searching for a Mate: The Rise of the Internet as a Social Intermediary." *American Sociological Review* 77.4 (2012): 523–547. Web. 24 Sept. 2015.

Snow, Kate and Jonann Brady. "Woman Proves Love for Eiffel Tower with Commitment Ceremony." *ABC News*. ABC News, 8 Apr. 2009. Web. 24 Sept. 2015.

Starkweather, Katherine E. and Raymond Hames. "A Survey of Non-Classical Polyandry." *Human Nature* 23.2 (2012): 149–172. Web. 24 Sept. 2015.

Stevenson, Betsey and Justin Wolfers. "Marriage and Divorce: Changes and their Driving Forces." *National Bureau of Economic Research: Working Paper No. 12944*. 2007. Web. 25 Sept. 2015.

Stewart, Susan D. *Brave New Stepfamilies: Diverse Paths Toward Stepfamily Living*. New York: SAGE Publications, 2007. Print.

Stitch Holdings Pty Ltd. *Stitch Companionship*. Computer software. *Apple App Store*. Vers. 0.1.6 Stitch Holdings Pty Ltd, 23 Mar. 2016. Web. 26 Mar. 2016.

Taylor, Paul, Jeffrey Passel, Richard Fry, Richard Morin, Wendy Wang, Gabriel Velasco, and Daniel Dockterman. "The Return of the Multi-Generational Family Household." Pew Research Center, 18 Mar. 2010. Web. 24 Sept. 2015.

The Council of Economic Advisers. *Nine Facts About American Families and Work*. Executive Office of the President of the United States, June 2014. Web. 25 Sept. 2015.

The Council of Economic Advisers. *Work-Life Balance and the Economics of Workplace Flexibility*. Executive Office of the President of the United States, June 2014. Web. 25 Sept. 2015.

The Week Staff. "The Wedding Industrial Complex." *The Week*. The Week, 15 June 2013. Web. 25 Mar. 2016.

Thompson, G. Deon. *Standing Under the Wrong Rainbow*. Bloomington: Abbot Press, 2014. Print.

United Nations. Population Fund. *Motherhood in Childhood: Facing the challenge of adolescent pregnancy*. United Nations, 2013. Web. 24 Sept. 2015.

United States Census Bureau. *Decennial Censuses, 1890 to 1940, and Current Population Survey, Annual Social and Economic Supplements, 1947 to 2014*. Washington: U.S. Census Bureau, 2014. Web. 24 Sept. 2015.

United States Census Bureau. *U.S. Census Bureau Projections Show a Slower Growing, Older, More Diverse Nation a Half Century from Now*. U.S. Census Bureau, Newsroom Archive, 12 Dec., 2012. Web. 28 Sept. 2015.

United States. Dept. of Health and Human Services. *Information on Poverty and Income Statistics: A Summary of 2014 Current Population Survey Data*. Health and Human Services, 16 Sept. 2014. Web. 24 Sept. 2015.

United States. Dept. of Health and Human Services. Centers for Disease Control and Prevention. *National Marriage and Divorce Rate Trends*. Washington: Centers for Disease Control and Prevention: National Vital Statistics System, 2015. Web. 25 Sept. 2015.

United States. Dept. of Labor, Bureau of Labor Statistics. *American Time Use Survey—2010 Results*. Bureau of Labor Statistics, News Release, 2011. Web. 25 Sept. 2015.

United States. Dept. of Labor, Bureau of Labor Statistics. *American Time Use Survey—2011 Results*. Bureau of Labor Statistics, News Release, 2012. Web. 25 Sept. 2015.

United States. Dept. of Labor. Bureau of Labor Statistics. *Women in the Labor Force: A Databook*. Bureau of Labor Statistics, BLS Reports. Dec. 2014. Web. 26 Mar. 2016.

Vespa, Jonathan, Jamie M. Lewis, and Rose M. Kreider. *America's Families and Living Arrangements: 2012*. Washington: U.S. Census Bureau, Current Population Reports, Aug. 2013. Web. 24 Sept. 2015.

Vorweck, Molly. "Polygamists find promise in Supreme Court Decisions." *USA Today*. Gannett, 2013. Web. 24 Sept. 2015.

Wang, Wendy. "Interracial marriage: Who is 'marrying out'?" Pew Research Center, 12 June 2015. Web. 24 Sept. 2015.

White, L.K. "Determinants of Divorce: A Review of the Research in the Eighties." *Journal of Marriage and the Family* 52 (1990): 904–912. Web. 25 Sept. 2015.

Wingme. *Wingme*. Computer software. *Apple App Store*. Vers. 1.23 Wingme, 5 Aug. 2014. Web. 25 Mar. 2016.

Xiao, Kaijing. "'Ghost Marriages' Prompt Grave Robbing as Men Dig Up Brides." *ABC News*. ABC News, 6 Mar. 2013. Web. 29 Aug. 2015.

CHAPTER 10

Education

Chapter 10 examines education in contemporary society. It discusses the goal of education as well as how the educational process is related to an informal and formal process including schooling, socialization, modernity, and employment. Three major goals include democratic equality, social efficiency, and social mobility. These goals are analyzed to understand dynamics of educational systems in the United States. Viewing education in terms of its contribution to the social system, this chapter focuses on the macrosocial level by adopting functionalist and conflict perspectives to analyze educational systems in modern society. The interactionist perspective, such as labeling theory, is employed to view microsocial level analyses. To understand the climate of achievement and educational efficiency among poor and minority children, cultural deprivation theory is also discussed. Opportunities and performance of minority students are compared with white students as evaluated in the Coleman Report. Finally, academically challenging subjects in modern society, increased educational choices, social mobility prospects, and online education are also addressed.

Education

Jeffrey C. Alexander and Kenneth Thompson

....

T he livin' promises to be anything but easy this summertime for Lindsay Rosenthal, 17. With senior year and college application season looming, the aspiring doctor from Burlingame, California, plans to shadow two Bay Area rheumatologists on their rounds. She will volunteer to buy groceries for AIDS patients, spend hours being tutored for SATs and, if there's any time left over, look for a paying gig. After a frenzied junior year filled with Advanced Placement courses, standardized exams and varsity tennis matches, what's wrong with whiling away the summer at the beach with a good novel? It just wouldn't wow admissions directors. "I really want to go to a school on the East Coast, and they're really competitive," Lindsay said. Getting into Ivy League and other elite schools has long been tough, but the bar keeps rising as competition intensifies. For stressed-out teenagers in the final throes of high school, that means more testing, more AP classes, more community service—in short, more resume-building. (Groves 2000: 1)

What are the goals of education, and how are they achieved? For some students, like Lindsay Rosenthal and other "stressed-out teenagers," education is about working hard to achieve the goal of reaching a good social position in an increasingly competitive race. School District Superintendent Thomas Doluisio has another take on the subject. From his perspective, as summarized in the box titled "BASD Superintendent Links Academic, Societal Decline," the main goal of education should be to train workers so that America can compete successfully in world markets. And for the two African-American students whose stories are told in the box titled "Dispositions Toward (Collective) Struggle and Educational Resilience in the Inner City," the goal of education should be to promote democratic equality, although they differ about whether that goal is attainable.

These three views correspond to three different goals that American education has been expected to serve over the years: democratic equality (schools should focus on preparing citizens), social efficiency (schools should focus on training workers), and social mobility (schools should enable individuals to compete for social positions) (Labaree 1997). These goals represent the issue of education from the perspective of three different social roles, respectively: the citizen, the consumer, and the taxpayer. Sometimes these competing visions and goals come into conflict.

One trend marking the gradual transition from a modern society to a postmodern, consumer society is the growing domination of the social mobility goal, which has reshaped education into a commodity for the purpose of gaining social status. This outcome has strengthened the popular belief that education is a matter of individual choice, and that success is determined solely by talent and motivation. It is widely believed that if individuals are motivated to work hard, provided that they have sufficient intelligence, they will acquire the qualifications that will bring them the rewards they deserve.

An Individual or a Social Story?

In the twentieth century, sociologists focused on the goal of **democratic equality** and investigated whether it was true that educational success is just a matter of individual talent and motivation or more a result of social position. They found evidence that certain aspects of social structure have an effect on the distribution of educational opportunities and achievement. For example, children from the poorer social classes with fewer material resources at home, such as a good diet and space to study, are likely to be educationally disadvantaged. Schools in poorer districts often have fewer facilities and fewer qualified teachers than those in more affluent areas, and the amount of public money invested per student is up to four times higher in affluent suburban areas than in poorer areas (Ballantine 1997; Carroll 1990). The conclusion might seem obvious: that differences in educational achievement are due to differences in resources.

However, the sociological story does not end here, with a social structural explanation of educational patterns replacing the individualist story. Even when economic and educational resources are improved or more evenly distributed, students vary in their educational achievements. Sociologists have examined factors such as family and group cultures that might account for this variance. For example, James Coleman, the author of *Equality of Educational Opportunity* (Coleman et al. 1966), found inequalities in schools' resources but concluded that the home environment affected students' achievement more significantly than the schools themselves. The family's educational and social background was most important, followed by the backgrounds of other children in the school. It was on the basis of this finding that Coleman recommended the integration of schools so that lower-class students, who were disproportionately black, could share an education with middle-class students and thus be in a **value climate** more conducive to learning. In a later study, Coleman compared private (mainly Catholic) and public schools and concluded that the value climate in private schools was more favorable to achievement. However, other studies have shown that value climate is also influenced by principal leadership, staff cooperation, student behavior, teacher control over school and classroom policy, and teacher morale (NCHS 1987: 74; Smith et al. 1995: 47, 57).

How we frame the story of what is happening to education in contemporary society depends on the focus we adopt. Early sociologists, such as Émile Durkheim, saw education as a morally unifying force that could counteract the negative effects of social divisions in modern society. But the question now is whether postmodern society is becoming so fragmented into different cultural groupings that the goal of a common education as a source of unity is increasingly difficult to attain. Addressing this issue involves looking at the ways in which post-modernity seems to offer the possibility of greater variety and choice in education, but at the risk of transforming it into just another form of consumption. Indeed, educational institutions are losing some of their old authority, such that they have to sell themselves in the market and be sensitive to consumer demands. Likewise, students and their parents must act like critical consumers. Even knowledge itself is being transformed. You may have seen advertisements that promise to turn the consumption of information into a pleasurable, entertaining pastime. Could it be that all the hard work and discipline associated with learning will become more like playing computer games? And that the organization of education will be radically changed? Already there are signs that information technology, such as online courses, is making it possible for education to break out of the constraints set by conventional educational organizations and to create "virtual" schools and colleges for lifelong learning.

It is certainly the case that the former goals of the education system—to prepare citizens, train future workers, and enable individuals to compete for positions—are being reassessed and redefined in postmodern society. Before trying to answer these questions about what is happening to education in postmodern society, we need to review how education developed as a central feature of modern society.

Education and Modernity

We tend to use the terms **education** and **schooling** interchangeably, often forgetting that much education has always taken place outside the walls of schools and colleges (and not just in the form of homework!). Informal processes at home and between friends are a major source of information and training in life skills, ranging from how to behave toward others to how to work appliances. In more traditional societies, the greater part of education took place through such processes, in the absence of a specialized institution devoted to schooling. The various forms of school that we are familiar with came into being at different times and for a number of reasons. In Western societies, primary schools were invented from the early eighteenth century onward by modernizing kings and emperors who wanted to teach basic literacy to their subjects, while at the same time building an identification of young people in distant realms with the language and national heroes associated with the political center. The predecessors of our modern secondary schools can be found in the ancient Greek academies, where the teaching of philosophy and rhetoric was rooted in the life and ideals of the aristocracy, who wished to prepare their sons for public life. And modern universities can find their predecessors in the colleges of the Middle Ages, which prepared young men for the "learned occupations," most of which had some connection to the church: the clergy, medicine, law, and teaching itself (Brint 1998: 18–19).

A key factor in the development of a separate and specialized institution devoted to education was the rise of the nation-state in the Middle Ages, whose rulers frequently sought to assert their power independent from that of the church. The interests of the state included instilling, through education, a sense of shared identity and loyalty, as well as equipping sufficient numbers of people to carry out such tasks as administration and legal adjudication. Similar social goals—"reasons of state"—influenced the development of modern American schools.

Democratic Equality and Citizenship

When, in 1779, Thomas Jefferson first devised a system for free education based on intellectual merit, it was conceived less as a means for facilitating social mobility than as a vehicle for ensuring democratic representation (Jefferson 1950).

Aside from facilitating citizenship in a general sense, education affects voting behavior. Education has been shown to be positively and directly related to voter participation in the United States. The more education people have, the more likely they are to register to vote and to cast their vote in a presidential or congressional election.

In the 2000 presidential election, 70 percent of the voting-age citizen population (18 and older) was registered to vote, and 60 percent voted. However, from the perspective of levels of education, we find that only 52 percent of those with less than a high school education were registered to vote compared to 83 percent of those with a bachelor's degree or higher. Moreover, of those who did not complete high school, 38 percent reported voting in 2000 compared to 78 percent of those with a bachelor's degree or higher. Table 10.1 shows similar effects for elections in 1994, 1996, 1998, and 2000.

The goal of training children and young people for citizenship grew out of the process of nation-building—a fact that offers one of the best explanations for the founding and spread of common schools in mid-nineteenth-century America. The new American republic was thought to be at risk from the spirit of individualistic economic striving and cultural fragmentation due to large-scale immigration, unless future citizens could be educated into a common sense of citizenship and devotion to the public good. We can still see the results of this concern in the curriculum of American schools—specifically, in courses such as social studies, civics, government, and American history. The concern for preserving the republic also lay behind the pursuit of equal treatment in the school system, irrespective of religion, race, and ethnic background (although some states would have preferred to keep schools racially segregated, and there was some argument about gender—whether girls and boys should receive different but equal treatment). However, from an early stage, the ideal of providing a common experience for all school students was compromised by tendencies toward

Table 10.1 Percentage of U.S. Citizens Ages 18 and Older Who Reported Being Registered to Vote and Voting, by Educational Attainment, Type of Election, and Year, 1994–2000

	Presidential Election		Congressional Election	
Education	**1996**	**2000**	**1994**	**1998**
Reported being registered to vote				
Total	**70.9**	**69.5**	**67.1**	**67.1**
Less than high school	54.2	52.2	51.5	51.2
High school diploma or equivalent	65.5	63.9	62.4	61.9
Some college	76.1	73.3	71.7	71.4
Bachelor's degree or higher	85.3	83.2	81.5	80.3
Reported voting				
Total	**58.4**	**59.5**	**48.3**	**45.3**
Less than high school	38.8	38.4	30.7	29.6
High school diploma or equivalent	51.7	52.5	42.9	39.2
Some college	63.1	63.1	51.5	48.3
Bachelor's degree or higher	77.0	77.5	67.4	61.1

Note: The survey sample includes the civilian, noninstitutionalized population. A presidential election includes those years in which a president is elected as well as congressional, state, and local officials. A congressional election is one that takes place in years when a president is not elected but when congressional, state, and local officials are elected. In this study, information was collected from respondents two weeks after each election. These estimates may differ from administrative data or data from exit polls.

Source: U.S. Department of Education (2003).

stratification on the basis of age, academic achievement, divisions between academic and vocational curriculum tracks, institutional prestige, and social class. These stratifying tendencies were often a response to pressures to promote the goals of social efficiency and social mobility.

Social Efficiency

It was in the context of **social efficiency** that the modern economy was believed to require sufficient numbers of suitably qualified workers, leading to the expansion of educational provision to the level of "mass education." In the late nineteenth and early twentieth centuries, there developed a movement called **vocationalism,** formed by an alliance of leaders from business, labor, and education devoted to moving the curriculum away from academic learning and toward training in skills necessary for carrying out job roles. This shift was noted by the school board president of Muncie, Indiana, who, in the 1920s, told sociological researchers Robert and Helen Lynd: "For a long time all boys were trained to be President. ... Now we are training them to get jobs" (Lynd and Lynd 1929: 194). To some extent vocationalism was manifested in vocational courses at the secondary school level and, later, at the community college level; it was also stratified along gender lines, with boys taking courses relevant to jobs such as lathe operator and mechanic whereas girls were encouraged to develop secretarial skills. However, such specialized courses were never more than a minority part of the curriculum, inasmuch as the main thrust of the social efficiency argument was that future workers should have acquired basic intellectual skills as a result of disciplined effort.

The social efficiency goal came into prominence again as a result of increasing economic competition in the 1980s. An influential National Commission on Excellence in Education report, *A Nation at Risk* (1983), found that only one-fifth of 17-year-olds could write an adequate essay and only one-third could solve mathematical problems requiring several steps. The level of **functional illiteracy** (reading and writing skills inadequate for everyday living) was higher in America than in most comparable countries. The report stated: "Our nation is at risk. Our once unchallenged preeminence in commerce, industry, science, and technological innovation is being overtaken by competitors throughout the world. ... We report to the American people that ... the educational foundations of our society are presently being eroded by a rising tide of mediocrity that threatens our very future as a nation and a people" (National Commission on Excellence in Education 1983: 5).

This anxiety gave rise to a concern with raising educational standards by specifying testable competencies and skills that should be attained by students at different levels—an approach that has been very appealing to politicians, public officials, and taxpayers, who like to be able to see value for the money expended on education (often amounting to one-third of all state and local revenues). But the results have not always been encouraging. Scores on the Scholastic Aptitude Test (SAT) declined between 1967 and 1998, from a median score of 516 down to 505 in mathematics and from 543 down to 512 in verbal ability. Compared with their counterparts in other countries, U.S. eighth graders ranked only seventeenth in the world in science and twenty-eighth in mathematics in 1996 (Bennett 1997).

Another aspect of standardized testing is that it facilitates comparisons of the achievements of individuals and schools, thereby intensifying the sense of competition. It also leads to further stratification. Indeed, the educational system has become a kind of obstacle race in which some students fall behind or drop out at each level. Dropout rates are highest in large, urban school systems and for schools with large numbers of African-Americans or Hispanics. This results in a pyramid-shaped educational achievement structure, with percentages decreasing on the way to the top at the higher degree levels (see Figure 10.1). Since this structure reflects the verticality of the job market and its rewards, it seems perfectly logical from the viewpoint of those advocating the social efficiency goal. In

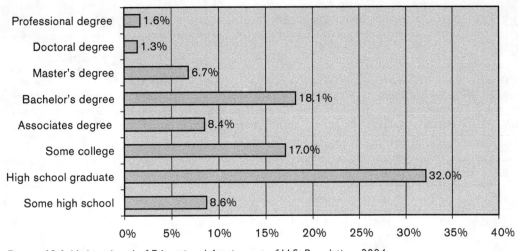

Figure 10.1 Highest Level of Educational Attainment of U.S. Population, 2004

Note: Data pertain to persons 25 years and older, with N = 187 million.
Source: U.S. Census Bureau (2005).

principle, the best-qualified candidates should get the best jobs, but in practice it seems to be more a question of where you come from.

Social Mobility

Whereas the social efficiency goal pertains to the collective needs of modern society for trained workers, the **social mobility** goal concerns the needs of individual educational consumers to improve or maintain their social status. The former can be thought of as a top-down view, the latter as a bottom-up one. Both exert pressure toward stratification of education. In the case of the social mobility goal, the individual seeks to gain competitive advantage over others by scoring higher grades and gaining higher qualifications from more prestigious institutions. In fact, there is evidence that much of the upward expansion of education in the United States over the last 150 years has resulted more from consumer demand for this kind of educational distinction than from pressure to meet the needs of society (Brown 1995; Labaree 1988). As the enrollment of students becomes almost universal at one level—grammar school, then high school, and, recently, even college—the demand for educational distinction shifts to the next level.

The downside of the influence of the social mobility goal is that it can have negative effects in terms of the other two goals of education: democratic equality and social efficiency. Democratic equality is made more difficult by the increasing demand for distinctions and hierarchy, and social efficiency is compromised when the scarcity of a particular qualification is what determines how much it is valued, rather than how much usable knowledge it represents. According to some critics, the social mobility goal ultimately results in **overcredentialing** (the overproduction of academic qualifications relative to the

Table 10.2 Educational Attainment by Race and Hispanic Origin, 1940–2000[1]

	White[2]			Black[2]			Hispanic		
Year	Less Than 5 Years of Elementary School	High School Completion or Higher[3]	4 or More Years of College[4]	Less Than 5 Years of Elementary School	High School Completion or Higher[3]	4 or More Years of College[4]	Less Than 5 Years of Elementary School	High School Completion or Higher[3]	4 or More Years of College[4]
1940	10.9	26.1	4.9	41.8	7.7	1.3	—	—	—
1950	8.9	36.4	6.6	32.6	13.7	2.2	—	—	—
1960	6.7	43.2	8.1	23.5	21.7	3.5	—	—	—
1970	4.2	57.4	11.6	14.7	36.1	6.1	—	—	—
1980	1.9	71.9	18.4	9.1	51.4	7.9	15.8	44.5	7.6
1990	1.1	81.4	23.1	5.1	66.2	11.3	12.3	50.8	9.2
2000	0.5	88.4	28.1	1.6	78.9	16.6	8.7	57.0	10.6

Notes: (—) = data not available.

[1] Data pertain to percentage of population 25 years and older, by years of school completed.
[2] Includes persons of Hispanic origin for years prior to 1980.
[3] Data for years prior to 1993 include all persons with at least four years of high school.
[4] Data for 1993 and later years are for persons with a bachelor's or higher degree.

Source: Adapted from U.S. Department of Commerce (2005).

occupational need for advanced skills) and **credential inflation** (the rising level of educational attainment required for jobs whose skill requirements remain largely unchanged) (Labaree 1988: 55; Shelley 1992).

Since educational credentials play a role in social stratification and social mobility, we need to look closer at who achieves what. Indeed, as Table 10.2 and Figure 10.2 demonstrate, differences among people based on race and ethnicity are significant and need to be taken into consideration. Consider, for example, the racial and ethnic backgrounds of students who have completed four or more years of college. In 2000, this educational level was attained by 28.1 percent of whites but only 16.6 percent of blacks and 10.6 percent of Hispanics.

As illustrated in Figures 10.3–10.7, educational attainment also varies on the basis of income. In particular, these figures show how earnings in the United States increase with education: Workers with at least a bachelor's degree earn more than those who have had less education. Note, however, that within the various categories of earned-education credentials, there are significant differences by gender. In 2002, for example, males with a bachelor's degree or higher earned $48,955 on average, compared to their female counterparts, who earned only $40,021. This gender gap holds across all categories of education. How have these trends shifted over time?

Historical Summary

As detailed above, we can think of American education's development from modernity toward postmodernity in terms of the changing balance among the three major goals of democratic equality, social efficiency, and social mobility (Labaree 1997):

1. In the *mid-nineteenth century*—the era of the common school—democratic equality was the dominant goal. The main outcome expected from education was that it should maintain social stability in the face of social and economic changes. By 1850 half of the U.S. population aged 5 to 19 were enrolled in schools.

2. During the *late nineteenth century and early twentieth century,* social efficiency and

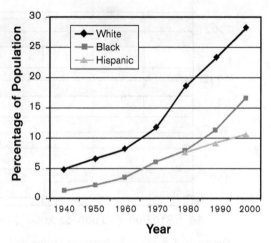

Figure 10.2 Four or More Years of College Completed by Race and Hispanic Origin, 1940–2000

Note: No separate data exist for Hispanics prior to 1980.

Source: U.S. Department of Education (2004).

social mobility goals became more prominent. Growing numbers in upper elementary grades created consumer demand for distinctive credentials in high school and college, and educational and business leaders were concerned about how to prepare students for an increasingly differentiated workforce. By the mid-1960s a majority of U.S. adults had a high school diploma.

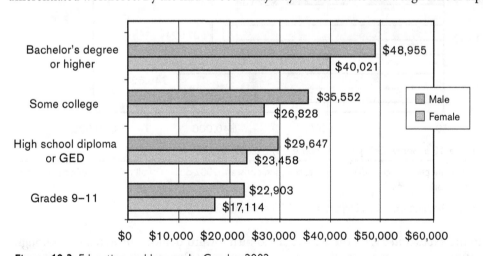

Figure 10.3 Education and Income by Gender, 2002

Note: Data pertain to median annual earnings in constant 2002 dollars of all full-time, full-year wage and salary workers ages 25–34.

Source: Adapted from U.S. Department of Education (2004).

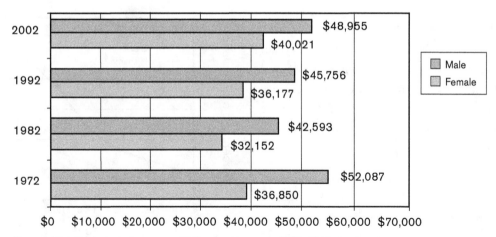

Figure 10.4 Bachelor's Degree or Higher and Income, 1972–2002, by Gender

Note: Data pertain to median annual earnings in constant 2002 dollars of all full-time, full-year wage and salary workers ages 25–34.

Source: Adapted from U.S. Department of Education (2004).

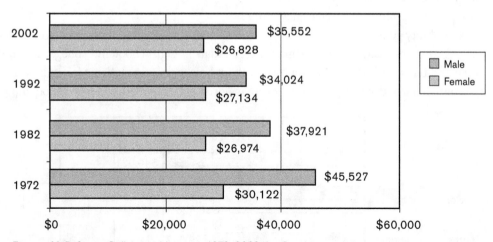

Figure 10.5 Some College and Income, 1972–2002, by Gender

Note: Data pertain to median annual earnings in constant 2002 dollars of all full-time, full-year wage and salary workers ages 25–34.

Source: Adapted from U.S. Department of Education (2004).

3. In the *1960s and 1970s*, the tide began to turn toward democratic equality (although it was still linked to social mobility). This trend was tied into the more general movements for racial and gender equality—the civil rights movement and the feminist movement. Sociologists focused on questions of social inequality and educational opportunity in relation to class, race, and gender. Educational opportunities policies were introduced, including

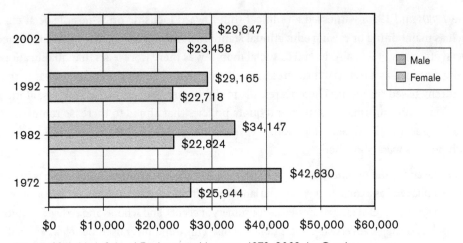

Figure 10.6 High School Diploma and Income, 1972–2002, by Gender

Note: Data pertain to median annual earnings in constant 2002 dollars of all full-time, full-year wage and salary workers ages 25–34.

Source: Adapted from U.S. Department of Education (2004).

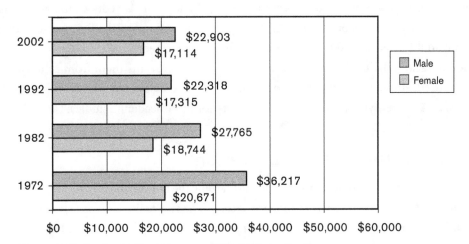

Figure 10.7 Grades 9–11 and Income, 1972–2002, by Gender

Note: Data pertain to median annual earnings in constant 2002 dollars of all full-time, full-year wage and salary workers ages 25–34.

Source: Adapted from U.S. Department of Education (2004).

busing of students to schools outside their own neighborhood and setting quotas for minority students in colleges. And there was a massive increase in enrollments in higher education, especially in community colleges, which tripled student numbers between 1966 and 1976.

4. The *1980s and 1990s* witnessed a political shift toward focusing on issues of social efficiency, such as maintaining or raising educational standards. Although this move was concerned with social efficiency, it was also linked to social mobility, as there were fears that qualifications were being devalued as a result of their greater availability—an outcome seen as a threat to the social hierarchy based on merit. There were calls to tighten up educational standards, along with a reaction against affirmative action and quota policies that aimed to increase representation of ethnic minorities in higher education. The result was that, in California and some other states, such policies were abolished.

5. From the *end of the twentieth century and into the twenty-first century,* education has increasingly been emphasized as a consumer good. The language of the market is more and more common among educators, students are being addressed as consumers or clients, and schools and colleges are promoting themselves through advertising and public events. This trend has raised people's expectations, as consumers, and they are now demanding that schools satisfy many and various functions.

The problem for postmodern society in trying to satisfy all these demands and goals is that they often come into conflict. The goal of producing citizens with a common educational experience is not helped by an emphasis on achieving a social position by acquiring an education that is somehow "better" than that of other people. And while the goal of increasing social efficiency and educating people only to the level required to fill available jobs may have been served by the introduction of a vocational track, individuals may feel that such education prevents them from achieving social mobility. Indeed, ethnic minorities have complained about being steered into vocational tracks on the basis of racial stereotypes about their unsuitability for more academic studies.

Different Perspectives on Education

In the twentieth century, sociologists were divided regarding the best perspective to adopt in analyzing the educational system and its goals in modern society. The two main competing approaches were **functionalism** (sometimes referred to as *structural-functionalism*) and the **conflict perspective.** Functionalism concentrated on the functions that education performed in maintaining social integration by passing on shared values and norms and preparing members to take up roles in society, whereas the conflict perspective assumed the existence of a tension in society created by the competing interests of individuals and groups.

Functionalism and Social Integration

Not just one of the founders of sociology, Émile Durkheim laid the basis for the sociological study of education—clearly believing that education was central to the development and maintenance of modern society. Three of his major works were about education: *Moral Education* (1925), *The Evolution of Educational Thought* (1938), and *Education and Sociology* (1956). In the last of these he gave a definition of education and described its functions: "Education is the influence exercised by adult generations on those that are not yet ready for social life. Its object is to arouse and to develop in the child a certain number of physical, intellectual and moral states that are demanded of him [*sic*] by both the political society as a whole and the special milieux for which he [*sic*] is specifically destined" (Durkheim 1956: 28).

In short, Durkheim saw education mainly in terms of preparing children and young people to take up their positions as citizens and workers. Primarily concerned with the role of schools in transmitting values that would preserve stability in society, he did not consider possible conflicts between the need for stability and the values and skills necessary for living in changing, emerging industrial societies. Later functionalists, such as Talcott Parsons (1959), continued this approach. The functionalist approach was criticized for disregarding conflicts over values and interests, such as those between rival educational goals and different classes.

Conflicts and Interests

Like the functionalist approach, the conflict perspective attempted to explain how education contributes to the maintenance of the status quo in modern society. However, the latter did so from a critical standpoint, seeking to reveal how education functioned to mold individuals to fit the needs of an unequal society and a capitalist economic system. Its basic premise was that there are conflicting group interests and goals in society.

Max Weber's studies of power in society and the ways in which groups seek to maintain their status inspired one version of the conflict approach to education (Collins 1971). Weber also used cross-cultural examples to shed light on the role of education in different types of society (Weber 1958a). During the preindustrial era, education served the primary purpose of training people to fit into a particular status ("station") in society, whereas in the modern industrial era, pressures were put on education from upwardly mobile members of society competing for higher positions in the economic system.

Another version of the conflict perspective derived from Marxism. Advocates of this perspective view mass education as a tool of the capitalist class for producing the disciplined workers needed by the economy and for making them think that the system is fair. Specifically, they see the culture and knowledge passed on in education as ideologically biased in favor of maintaining the status quo and preventing workers from developing a class consciousness that would cause them to take collective action to change it (Bowles and Gintis 1976).

American education, in particular, has been portrayed as promoting an ideology that emphasizes individualism and competition, obscuring the fact that only a limited number of individuals can better themselves in the competition, while the majority lose out. According to Samuel Bowles and Herbert Gintis (1976), schools prepare children for the unequal stratification system in society in a way that corresponds to their family background. In other words, schools predominantly attended by blacks and working-class children emphasize behavioral control and rule following, in contrast to schools in the well-to-do suburbs, which employ relatively open systems that favor greater student participation, less direct supervision, and more student choice.

Interaction

The functionalist perspective and the conflict approach have tended to focus on the "big picture" or **macrosocial** level, viewing education in terms of its contribution to maintaining the social system. A completely different approach that became popular in the second half of the twentieth century focused on individuals in interaction at the **microsocial** level, such as students and teachers in the classroom. The most influential version of this interactionist perspective is **labeling theory** (Becker 1963), which maintains that students who are given the impression that they are dumb and not expected to succeed academically may incorporate this label as part of their self-concept and behave as the label suggests. Studies have found plenty of evidence that this was a common occurrence in schools (e.g., Rosenthal and Jacobson 1968)—particularly in cases involving a division between vocational and academic tracks, leading students to see themselves as either less or more intelligent, depending on which track they were put in.

The interactionist perspective inspired a great deal of research into small-scale interactions in educational settings, providing valuable insights into how students and teachers took their cues from others in developing their self-concepts and ideas about how they should behave. The main criticism of this perspective was that it often failed to show how such interactions linked into the larger structures of the social system.

Other Perspectives

Beginning in the 1970s, attempts were made to create new syntheses of the macrosocial and microsocial approaches. One effort at synthesis focused on the difference between the speech of working-class students and that of middle-class students (Bernstein 1971). Students from working-class families were found to employ a "restricted speech code," whereas middle-class students exhibited an "elaborated speech code" in addition to a restricted code (as did their middle-class teachers). The restricted code is a kind of shorthand speech whose meanings are limited to a particular social group; they are bound to a specific social context and are not readily available to outsiders. In contrast, the elaborated code explicitly verbalizes many of the meanings that are taken for granted in a restricted code. Its meanings tend to be "universalistic," in that they are not tied to a particular context. It follows that, because schools are concerned with the transmission of universalistic types of meanings, working-class students are at a disadvantage in the educational system.

There is also a relationship between occupations and speech codes. Routine occupations provide little variety, offer few opportunities to participate in decisionmaking, and do not require elaborate verbal skills. By comparison, professional occupations involve more discussion and negotiation in reaching decisions and therefore require elaborate speech patterns.

Speech codes are part of culture, and it is by turning to cultural factors that sociologists of education have attempted to link the microsocial and macrosocial levels. In some cases, however, these cultural factors seem little more than a kind of "message system" through which the macrostructure determines what happens at the microlevel of families, schools, and individuals. This is the criticism leveled at the writings on education by French sociologist Pierre Bourdieu, especially his concept of **cultural capital** (Bourdieu 1977; Bourdieu and Passeron 1977). Bourdieu correctly notes that children of middle-class families arrive at school already possessing many of the cultural qualities that are prized in the educational system, including the "right" language (linguistic capital) with which to unlock the categories used in formal education. Underlying this language are rules that function something like a grammar; they constitute what Bourdieu calls "habitus," the rules of the game necessary for success. But, although Bourdieu accepts that schools have a certain amount of autonomy relative to the economy, he seems to suggest that little choice is available—that the education system mainly functions to reproduce the established social order and to make it appear legitimate. And yet he himself is a teacher and presumably thinks he and other teachers like him could make a difference.

The attempts to link the microsocial and macrosocial levels in the sociology of education were based on the assumption that the most important structural feature of modern society was the division between social classes. And social class position was determined by a person's occupation in the system of economic production. In postmodern society, however, other factors have become equally important, if not more so; these are cultural in nature, and they include gender, ethnicity, sexuality, and the consumer lifestyle. Studies of education have begun to focus on these other cultural factors.

Education in a Multicultural, Postmodern Society

Cultural Deprivation

The focus on class divisions and the cultures associated with them remained a feature of much of the sociology of education until late in the twentieth century. Theories of cultural deprivation were first developed in connection with social class. The argument was that working-class students were being held back by aspects of their culture that were not conducive to academic success. For example, as we discussed earlier, one sociological study found that many working-class families use a restricted code of speech (Bernstein 1971), reliance on which makes it difficult for their children to undertake abstract analytical work. Other studies targeted additional cultural factors, such as lack of self-discipline, lack of parental interest, and a lack of ambition. And when attention was broadened to encompass not just class but also ethnic minorities and educational achievement, similar arguments were made about cultural deprivation or deficiencies in the culture of their families.

Among the studies attempting to evaluate the opportunities and performance of minority students compared with white students, the best known was the Coleman Report (Coleman et al. 1966). It attributed the lower educational achievement of minority students (with the exception of Asian-Americans) to their family background and suggested that one way to improve the academic achievement of poor and minority children would be to integrate the schools, putting minority children in the same classes as white children to produce a climate of achievement and to provide educational role models. This report provided a major impetus for increased efforts to integrate schools in the 1960s and later, especially through the use of busing. In a later study, however, James Coleman and his colleagues (1975) concluded that school desegregation contributed to "white flight" from big cities and was fostering resegregation of urban districts. In fact, the policy of busing and its effects on educational achievement have remained controversial and unresolved. Programs of compensatory education, dating from the Elementary and Secondary Education Act of 1965, have also been subjected to criticism; some detractors alleged that they showed small results for the billions of dollars spent on them, while others thought they institutionalized a "deficit" view of minority cultures. (On the other hand, some compensatory programs—such as Head Start, aimed at helping disadvantaged children achieve "readiness" for first grade—have been shown to be beneficial.)

The problem with the cultural deprivation or "deficit" view is that it explains the failure of certain groups as the result of their failure to conform to a single model of the good, "educable" student—usually white and middle-class. But it could also be argued that the fault lies in the educational system, which is not sufficiently responsive to different cultures. Accordingly, we need to consider differences between cultures and how they might be reflected in the curriculum and the processes of schooling.

Originally, standardized tests like the SAT were adopted as a means of sorting students and helping college admissions officers select the best candidates. Questions have been raised, however, about what exactly these tests measure: Is it aptitude and potential, or merely knowledge of the mainstream culture? If the latter, such tests are clearly weighted against students who come from disadvantaged backgrounds.

Consider, for example, the test scores on the SAT I for the class of 1999. As shown in Figures 10.8 and 10.9, there is a consistent difference between male and female test takers, with males scoring higher across all racial/ethnic categories, except for African-Americans in the verbal section. (At the college level, however, females excel at skills requiring verbal aptitude.) The differences across race/ethnicity are also quite stark, with white students scoring significantly higher (verbal: 527, math: 528) than black students (verbal: 434, math: 432). Note as well that, as shown in Figure 10.10, Asian test takers score slightly higher (math: 560) than whites in the math section.

A number of researchers have demonstrated that certain questions on tests such as the SAT are biased against students from nonwhite and non-middle-class backgrounds (e.g., Freedle 2003). The proposed movement toward eliminating affirmative action policies for higher education has raised additional concerns because, in this event, the SAT would be even more heavily relied upon

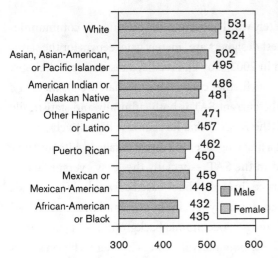

Figure 10.8 Class of 1999, SAT I Scores by Race and Gender: Verbal Scores

Source: Adapted from Hoff (1999), citing College Board data.

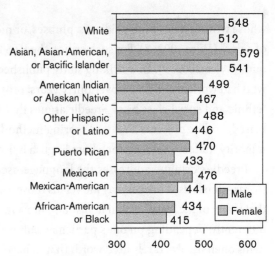

Figure 10.9 Class of 1999, SAT I Scores by Race and Gender: Math Scores

Source: Adapted from Hoff (1999), citing College Board data.

for admissions. At the same time, several large state institutions of higher education—most notably, the University of California system—have threatened to drop the SAT as a measure for admissions. Both the Educational Testing Service (ETS) and the College Board National Task Force on Minority High Achievement maintain that the gap in student performance is based not so much on the structure of the test as on the gap in student family incomes and resources, on cultural differences, on racial and ethnic prejudice, and on variations in educational policies at the K–12 level (College Board n.d.). Nonetheless, the College Board and the Educational Testing Service have been attempting to revise the SAT to eliminate racial, ethnic, gender, and class bias. The ETS, in

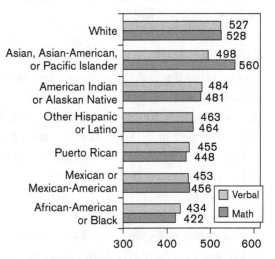

Figure 10.10 Class of 1999, SAT I Total Verbal and Math Scores by Race/Ethnicity

Source: Adapted from Hoff (1999), citing College Board data.

particular, announced in 2002 that it would "revamp" the SAT to make it more relevant, in part by replacing the "culture-bound" analogies section with a "writing" section.

However, some critics still believe that a cultural bias will reemerge, inasmuch as "[test] graders no doubt will emphasize stylistically and grammatically Standard English, marking students down whose writing style employs idioms, phrases, or merely word patterns more common to communities of color" (Wise 2002: 7). For such critics, the ETS test designers are "merely gatekeepers for the status quo" (Wise 2002: 9). In a striking study published in 2003, Roy O. Freedle, a research psychologist who had worked at ETS for over thirty years, proposes further corrections to what he calls the SAT's "ethnic and social class bias." Freedle argues that the current SAT is both culturally and statistically biased, and he presents a revised scoring method (the R-SAT) that he claims will positively impact minority students, students for whom English is not a first language, and disadvantaged white students.

Freedle's critique addresses the language used in the SAT, especially the "easy" versus "hard" words—those used in everyday life versus those learned through school-based curricula. He contends that many of the "easy" verbal items "tap into a more culturally specific content and ... are perceived differently, depending on one's particular cultural and socioeconomic background. ... Hard verbal items often involve rarely used words that ... have fewer potential differences in interpretation across ethnic communities" (Freedle 2003: 5). As a result of their different perceptions and life experiences, "whites tend to score better on easy items and African Americans on hard items" (Freedle 2003: 3). Freedle's revised test, the R-SAT, would give thousands of students an additional 100–200 points, which could mean the difference between getting into a selective college or not, or being qualified for a range of scholarships.

Multiculturalism

It is easy to imagine that, as the American population becomes more heterogeneous as a result of immigration, education will automatically change to reflect that structural fact and become multicultural. However, in doing so we would underestimate the struggles and controversies involved. The civil rights movement of the 1960s had to fight hard to gain acceptance of its demands for desegregation of the nation's schools and for changes in the curriculum to recognize and value the contributions of African-Americans. In the decades that followed, other minority groups have been able to build on that hard-won success and to press their claims for cultural recognition in education under the banner of multiculturalism.

The United States has always been a nation of immigrants, but their numbers and origins have varied over time. In the last half-century the demographic composition has changed dramatically, with the proportion of whites dropping from 90 percent in 1950 to 75 percent in 1990. Today, most immigrants come not from Europe but from Asia and Latin America. By the late 1980s, many U.S. states (beginning with California in 1987) had added principles in their curriculum guidelines requiring "multicultural and gender-fair" perspectives (Rosenfelt 1994). The transformation was most noticeable in primary schools, where the customs of different lands are studied and walls and hallways are decorated with pictures illustrating the diverse cultures. High schools have added minority writers to the English syllabus, and in some history courses the contributions of minorities are featured. And in higher education, more than half of colleges and universities surveyed have reported efforts to introduce multicultural themes into departmental offerings, although these are largely add-ons to existing curricula rather than replacements for traditional courses (Levine and Cureton 1992: 29). Such moves toward multiculturalism in education have met with resistance, giving rise to ideological controversy that some refer to as the *culture wars*. There has even been a backlash against multiculturalism, with conservatives accusing liberals of introducing a policy of "political correctness"; this, they allege, entails requiring college faculty to follow a political agenda rather than using their own academic judgment in deciding what to teach. An example of a critical account of the introduction of a multicultural policy into a university is Dinesh D'Souza's description of events at Stanford University, California, in 1997–1998 (see the box titled "Multiculturalism at Stanford").

Why has multiculturalism been so controversial? Although the dominant ideology in the United States is market-oriented individualism, it has not been a very unifying ideology in this nation of immigrants. Not surprisingly, there has always been a subtheme of cultural pluralism in the American creed (de Crevecoeur 1783). Multiculturalism could be regarded as simply extending this cultural value to include those who have previously been neglected or excluded. However, some critics take it to be attempting more than that. They accuse its supporters of wanting to jettison the cultural heritage of Western civilization. In defending the core books and authors (the canon) of the traditional curriculum, they quote figures such as the great African-American novelist Ralph Ellison, who wrote that he found mental "freedom" by reading such books as a boy in Macon County, Alabama.

The advocates of multiculturalism in the curriculum respond with two arguments. The first is that we are now living in an age when culture changes so rapidly that the idea of a canon—a set of required great books—is outmoded. Clayborne Carson, professor of history and Afro-American studies at Stanford, has been widely quoted as saying: "What's one generation's standard canonical text is the next generation's pulp" (quoted in D'Souza 1991: 62, reprinted in Thompson 1997: 196).

The other argument is that the existing canon is unrepresentative of the various groups who make up the population. This was the view of members of the campus Rainbow Coalition at Stanford, which included black, Hispanic, Asian, and Native American groups:

> "Western culture does not try to understand the diversity of experiences of different people," charged Alejandro Sweet-Cordero, a member of the Movimiento Estudi- antil Chicano de Aztlan, the Hispanic group on campus. "If you think American culture is centered on the Constitution and the Founding Fathers, then you're going to exclude a major part of what this country is," remarked Stanford student activist William King, calling for non-Western alternatives to provide students with "a different picture." King added, "It was painful to come to Stanford and find that no member of your race was in the required curriculum." Stacey Leyton, a student member of Students United for Democracy in Education ... remarked, "It's a strong statement you're making when the only required readings are by

whites and males. You're saying that what's been written by women and people of color isn't worthy of consideration." Freshman Joseph Green wrote in the *Stanford Daily,* "I get tired of reading the thoughts of white men who would probably spit on me if they were alive to face me today. ... Stanford is sending many students into the world with no knowledge of the challenges facing people of color." And Black Student Union activist Amanda Kemp protested that the implicit message of Western culture is "Nigger go home." (Quoted in D'Souza 1991: 63, reprinted in Thompson 1997: 197)

Since Stanford took the lead in the late 1980s, many colleges have attempted to make their core curriculum more representative of the cultures of their students. Those critics who claim that multiculturalism goes beyond simply expanding cultural pluralism to include minorities accuse it of adding a dimension of **cultural relativism** and a new ethnocentrism. Cultural relativism sees all cultures as equally valuable and rejects any ranking of cultures and their products in terms of quality. And ethnocentrism occurs when a group wishes to make its own culture the central focus of study. Clearly, the occurrence of such tendencies is an ever-present danger, but they are not inevitable aspects of multiculturalism.

As a nation of immigrants, modern America could establish and maintain its unity only if the various cultural groups merged in the "melting pot," and one of the main goals of education was to promote that process. But postmodern society is more like a "salad bowl" in which different cultures coexist. Multiculturalism is a recognition of that fact. Of course, the nation-state is still important, and it still requires education to serve social functions such as preparing young people to become responsible citizens and to take up work roles. But other institutions now contribute to those processes: The mass media, political parties, and organized social movements are engaged in informing people about their rights and duties as citizens, and training for work roles is available through a variety of sources, including self-instruction media packages and resources on the Internet. In short, schooling in postmodern society has become less distinct, in time and space, from education in general. If this trend continues, postmodernity will come to resemble premodernity more than it resembles modernity.

Consumers and Choice

We have suggested that education in postmodern society might be breaking out of the constraints set by formal schooling. The possibilities opened up by online courses, virtual schools and colleges, and the development of lifelong learning could make conventional schooling, as we have known it, less crucial in determining individuals' opportunities to experience social mobility. At present, however, there is often still a lack of options and choices for students and their parents, particularly for poorer or more disadvantaged groups.

Several schemes have aimed at increasing choice. For example, some districts have set up **magnet schools.** This policy is intended to distribute students and desegregate schools on the basis of special interests or talents, such as science, mathematics, art and music, and vocational education. Research shows that they achieve a certain amount of success, provided they are well resourced and are not simply the same old schools with a new name (Blank and Archibald 1992). Another scheme involves **charter schools,** which are similar to magnet schools except that they focus on a particular method, theme, or curriculum; they are publicly funded but give parents and students a degree of autonomy in school government (Ballantine 1997: 356, Bennett de Marrais and LeCompte 1995: 298).

An even more market-oriented move toward developing consumer choice has been the introduction of the **voucher system.** Families with school-aged children are given money vouchers that are valid for a year of education at the school of their choice. Toward this end, the school district is required to establish a variety of schools with different educational programs and, at times, different philosophical and discipline approaches. Parents, in turn, are encouraged to become involved in the selection and operation of the schools. In some cases, corporations have sponsored "model" schools, providing money for programs, equipment, and teacher training (Rist 1990; Weisman 1990). A more radical departure from the public school system is schooling for profit. Some school districts have issued contracts to private, profit-making companies to run their schools. The results have been mixed, with some large school boards expressing disillusionment over what has been achieved by the companies to which they gave contracts. Taken together, these various initiatives of the "school choice" movement constitute a departure from the "common school" as well as from the shared-experience goal of education in the earlier stage of modernity. Indeed, there has been a shift toward diversity and cultural fragmentation in the postmodern age.

This increasing diversity in education may be advantageous for the other two goals of education—namely, social efficiency and social mobility. It contributes to social efficiency by providing a wide range of differently equipped newcomers in the employment market, thus fitting the needs of the flexible, postindustrial economy. And for individuals looking for opportunities to improve their social mobility prospects, the increase in educational choices is something to be welcomed. It looks like a "win-win" development.

However, there are problems with the consumer approach to education. First, it often ignores the fact that consumers have varying resources, even if it tries to compensate for these inequalities through schemes such as giving poorer students state-funded vouchers or scholarships. In practice, such subsidies are seldom sufficient to produce equality. Second, it assumes that people make their choices on the basis of full and equal knowledge about the possible rewards and costs involved. In fact, poorer people are usually less well informed and thus have fewer educational choices. The educational system has been likened to a shopping mall in which consumer information is vital to making the right choices. Students with parents who have insider access to the needed information have an important advantage over those who do not.

The social inequalities reproduced by the educational system in modern society seem likely to persist (and perhaps even to widen) in the postmodern age. As research has shown, the various schemes to increase school choice only perpetuate the gap between wealthy and poor youth (Manski 1992: 1).

Postmodern Education: A Virtual Revolution

Signs that we may be entering a postmodern educational era are not difficult to find. Every day seems to bring announcements of new online courses and virtual colleges. Some of these involve consortia of prestigious universities and libraries on a global scale, indicating the extent to which information technology is bringing about a globalization of cultural products. A typical example was the October 2000 announcement of the creation of a virtual college by an alliance of Oxford University with Princeton, Yale, and Stanford. Named *The University Alliance for Lifelong Learning*, it aims to provide online courses in the arts and sciences in a distance learning venture for the institutions' 500,000 alumni and, eventually, to make the courses available to the general public.

Despite the potential benefits of globalization, of the revolutions in information and communications technology, and of increased access to education, some people are still being left behind, especially women and students in less developed countries. Literacy, on a global scale, is a key measure of a society's progress and promise. As a United Nations Educational, Cultural, and Scientific Organization (UNESCO) official has noted, "a lack of literacy skills limits the potential for societies to deal with issues such as discrimination, poor health, social exclusion and powerlessness. Literacy is at the heart of the social, political, cultural, economic and political well-being of individuals, communities, societies and nations, indeed of the world" (UNESCO 2004: 8).

Statistics for literacy on a worldwide basis differ: *The World Factbook* (Central Intelligence Agency 2005) claims that 82 percent of the world's population is literate (87 percent of males and 77 percent of females), whereas UNESCO (2005a: 2) cites data showing 67 percent literate and 33 percent illiterate. (The term *literacy* is loosely defined as referring to those members of the population over the age of 15 who can read and write.) Both organizations nonetheless agree that two-thirds of the world's illiterate population (771 million adults) are women and that the highest rates of illiteracy are concentrated in three regions: South and West Asia, sub-Saharan Africa, and the Arab states. In these regions, only 60 percent of adults are estimated to be literate, of whom two-thirds are men and only half are women (UNESCO 2005b) (see Figure 10.11).

If you are spending long hours in the classroom in order to get an education, you may be skeptical about this book's claims that the world is entering a postmodern age. To you it may seem that nothing much has changed in the system of education that was established to satisfy the needs of modern society for responsible citizens and educated workers. But you would be wrong to underestimate the enormous changes that are taking place. What was once regarded as a futuristic dream—the classroom without walls—is now becoming widely established. As detailed in the box titled "A Virtual Revolution in Teaching," computers are making it possible for students to receive schooling without entering a

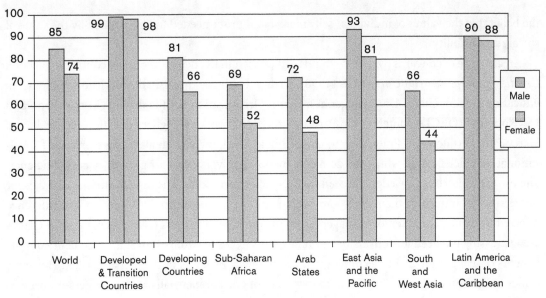

Figure 10.11 Adult Literacy Rates by Gender, 2000 (percentage)

Source: Adapted from UNESCO (2004).

building or meeting their teachers face-to-face. But does this mean the end of the distinction between schooling and education?

Clearly, much is changing, yet there are limits to what can be discarded. It is likely that postmodern education will be less spatially confined within the walls of the classroom and that teacher-student communications will be mediated by new technologies. But some functions of schooling can be satisfied only through extensive face-to-face contact between teacher and student. This is particularly the case with socializing young people for their future roles, which will require that they are able to work with others within an organization. So it is at the higher education level, rather than in the earlier grades, that we are likely to see more emphasis on "distance education," especially as the previously limited period of formal schooling gives way to "lifelong learning." The postmodern economy will necessitate that workers are able to retrain to adjust to rapid changes in the job market and to use advancing information technologies. Within the home and at leisure, technological developments will also require that people have the capacity to learn to operate new systems.

As with the "school choice" movement, the development of "distance education" holds out the promise of widening opportunities for individuals to achieve social mobility and could also have favorable implications for the goal of increasing social efficiency. Less clear, however, is whether these developments will serve the educational goal of promoting democratic equality and citizenship. It is a question about which cultural values are most influential in shaping education. Are they values mainly concerned with individual self-interest or with social responsibility? Bear in mind that education was developed in the public sphere and not left to the private sphere in modern society because of the belief that the values of individual self-interest and profit needed to be balanced by the value of social responsibility.

An example of concerns over these trends can be seen in the debate about the controversial book *Creating Entrepreneurial Universities* (1998), written by the distinguished American sociologist of education Burton Clark. One speaker at a recent Organization for Economic Co-operation and Development (OECD) conference in Paris described this work as "higher education's equivalent of Harry Potter" (quoted in Pratt 2000: 9). In his book, Clark invokes an alarming scenario of "institutional insufficiency" in which the demands made of universities—for growth, access, efficiency, and the explosion of knowledge—exceed their capacity to respond. The only solution, he says, is for universities to transform themselves and become more entrepreneurial. At the OECD conference referred to earlier, some senior managers from universities in various countries supported Clark's view, stressing the need for university autonomy, the virtues of strong central management, and the benefits of using information technology to reach new consumers in the global market. However, critics at the conference spoke of the "seamy side" of entrepreneurialism, the dangers it posed to quality, and the need for ethical considerations and consumer protection. A warning also came from Brown University's Frank Newman, who reported research "showing that there are key aspects of higher education that profit-making organizations will not undertake, notably socializing students for their responsibilities in society, contributing to social mobility and maintaining disinterested scholarship and unfettered debate" (quoted in Pratt 2000: 9).

Conclusion

In this chapter we have framed the story of what is happening to education in contemporary society by focusing on three of the competing goals of American education: democratic equality, social efficiency, and social mobility. As we have seen, the balance between these goals and the means for achieving them has varied over time. It has been suggested that the balance is shifting in favor of the goal of social mobility in the emerging postmodern era. However, this goal, like the other two, is being reassessed and reshaped. It is particularly affected by the development of the ideology of individualism in the direction of seeing ourselves, and our identities, as consumers in a market. Education itself is also increasingly being viewed as a market in which we should be able to exercise individual choice—choosing how we are educated and for what purposes.

A central feature of modern society in the nineteenth and twentieth centuries was the involvement of government (at the federal, state, and local levels) in the institutionalization of education. Schooling was thought to be too important to be left to voluntary bodies or the market; it had to be located in approved forms of organization and subjected to governmental regulation. (Even the several thousand church schools and nonreligious preparatory schools in this country, which together educated fewer than 15 percent of American children during this time period, were subjected to external rules and standards.) It is precisely this capacity of government to occupy the central position in education and to regulate it that may be weakened by postmodern developments.

Changes in education necessitate corresponding changes in the perspectives that sociology has brought to bear on it. Twentieth-century sociologists of education, in considering the macrosocial level, tended to adopt either a functionalist or a conflict perspective. The first approach was concerned with how efficiently education was serving its social functions, such as socializing youth to take up adult roles as parents, citizens, and workers, and attempting to secure social integration by molding a diverse population into a unified society sharing the same norms and values. The second approach, the conflict perspective, focused on revealing how schooling perpetuated inequalities by giving the children of better-off families the best education and assigning students from working-class and minority families to schools and tracks that fitted them for only the most routinized jobs. In addition to these inequalities in education, advocates of the conflict perspective criticized the ideology of individualism and competition, which left students believing that the system was fair and not socially or culturally discriminatory. Other approaches focused either on social interaction at the microsocial level, such as that between teachers and students, or on cultural factors, particularly language.

What these various perspectives had in common was a concern with the social functioning of schooling in modern society and with ways in which government could act to improve it. They addressed such questions as can schools be made more socially efficient through better organization and regulation? and is it possible to achieve greater fairness and equality of opportunities in schooling?

Although the various themes that characterize postmodern sociology have a different focus, concerns about social efficiency and equality remain important. Among these themes are three significant trends in education that have attracted the interest of sociologists and might be said to mark the passage from modernity to postmodernity. The first is the increasing sense of our being "productive" consumers—that is, being able to pick and choose what we want from education. The second is the gradual acceptance of multiculturalism within society, which involves a decline in the dominance of a particular ethnic culture (e.g., WASPs) and the construction of new cultural identities. And the third is the revolution in communications and information technology that is breaking down the walls of the classroom and making lifelong learning possible. Taken together, these trends could bring about a significant "deinstitutionalization" of education—freeing it from some of the narrow constraints of organized schooling and making it more a part of everyday life.

However, there is another way of interpreting these trends. They can be seen as raising more problems. For example, talking about students as customers in a market is viewed by some as a threat to certain educational values and to the goal of preparing students to be responsible and equal citizens. Others argue that multiculturalism is a threat to the educational goal of promoting national efficiency, on the grounds that it reduces the amount of time available in the curriculum for academically challenging subjects. And online education has been accused of undermining the hierarchy of prestige according to which colleges and their qualifications are ranked, making it difficult for "virtual" students to achieve the goal of upward social mobility.

These are just a few of the concerns that we need to consider in assessing what is happening to education in postmodern society.

Key Terms

Democratic equality   A goal of education that refers to the function of education to prepare good citizens.

Value climate   The atmosphere in a school. Value climate is influenced not only by the individuals in the student body but also by factors such as principal leadership, student behavior, and teacher morale. The assumption is that if these factors are positively balanced, the value climate will improve, and the school will provide a better learning environment and be more favorable to achievement.

Education   A term that refers broadly to the processes by which individuals develop their capacities by acquiring knowledge and receiving training in life skills, varying from how to behave toward others to how to use particular technologies. Education is both an informal and a formal process; it can occur at home and between friends as well as in schools.

Schooling   A term that refers to the time spent in formal educational institutions, such as elementary and high schools, as well as in colleges and universities.

Social efficiency   A goal of education suggesting that the purpose of education is to train workers.

Vocationalism   The shift in educational curriculum away from academic learning toward providing training for skills necessary to carry out job roles.

Functional illiteracy   The inability to read or write at a level sufficient for everyday living.

Social mobility   A goal of education pertaining to the ability of individuals or groups to change their social position or status within a social hierarchy. While societal myths such as the "American Dream" imply that society is open and meritocratic and that social mobility for the better is simply the result of hard work, long-standing inequalities suggest that this is not the case.

Overcredentialing   The overproduction of academic qualifications relative to the occupational need for advanced skills.

Credential inflation   The rising level of educational attainment required for jobs whose skill requirements remain largely unchanged.

Functionalism   The functionalist, or structural-functionalist, perspective focuses on the contribution of the parts of a structure to the maintenance of the whole. It rests on the assumption that there is no fundamental conflict between the demands of the parts.

Conflict perspective   The view that education contributes to maintaining the status quo by revealing how education molds individuals to fill the needs of an unequal society. The conflict perspective rests on the assumption that there are conflicting groups and interests in society, and that education reflects these conflicts.

Macrosocial   A term describing an approach that looks at the "big picture"—that is, at social structures and their role in the maintenance of a whole social system.

Microsocial   A term describing an approach that focuses on individuals, such as students and teachers in the classroom. Microsocial perspectives tend to be interactionist, as they address social relationships and everyday interactions.

Labeling theory   A microsocial attempt to explain differences in educational attainment. Labeling theory maintains that students who are given the impression that they are dumb and not expected to succeed may incorporate this label as part of their identity and behave accordingly.

Cultural capital   A concept introduced by Pierre Bourdieu referring to cultural qualities that are prized in the educational system as well as by society overall. These qualities include the "right" language, access to books, and exposure to cultural forms such as art, music, and theater.

Cultural relativism   In contrast to ethnocentrism, a perspective whose advocates see all cultures as equally valuable and reject any ranking of cultures and their products in terms of quality.

Magnet schools   Schools whose aim is to distribute students and desegregate schools on the basis of special interests or talents, such as science, mathematics, art and music, and vocational education.

Charter schools   Schools that focus on a particular method, theme, or curriculum. Charter schools are publicly funded but give parents and students a degree of autonomy in school government.

Voucher system   A market-oriented approach to education in which families with school-aged children are given money vouchers that are valid for a year of education at the school of their choice.

Exercises

Exercise 1

On a personal level, you might find it useful to compare your own education with that of your parents and then try to imagine what current trends might mean for education during the rest of your lifetime. Can you imagine what "lifelong learning" might entail—bearing in mind that the proportion of American adults taking courses is growing rapidly and that new online courses are increasingly available? Will this mean that in postmodern society everybody will be consuming education as just another aspect of everyday life?

Exercise 2

What recent developments in your own college or university seem to be aimed at making it more entrepreneurial? In what ways have such developments affected the balance among the three educational goals discussed in this chapter?

Study Questions

1. Which of the three examples related in the first paragraph of this chapter is most consistent with the concerns of the functionalist perspective?

2. Which of these examples corresponds most closely to the Weberian conflict perspective?

3. Which example offers evidence supporting the Marxist conflict perspective?

Further Reading

Anderson-Levitt, Kathryn, ed. 2003. *Local Meanings, Global Schooling: Anthropology and World Culture Theory.* New York: Palgrave Macmillan.

Brantlinger, Ellen. 2003. *Dividing Classes: How the Middle Class Negotiates and Rationalizes School Advantage.* New York: Routledge Falmer.

Brint, Steven. 2006. *Schools and Societies,* 2nd ed. Stanford, CA: Stanford University Press.

Central Intelligence Agency. 2005. *The World Factbook.* Entry for category "World," subcategory "Literacy." Last updated March 29, 2006. Available online at http://www.cia.gov/cia/publications/factbook/geos/xx.html (accessed April 15, 2006).

College Board.com. 2005. "National Task Force on Minority High Achievement Report." College Board Office of Academic Initiatives. Available online at http://www.collegeboard.com/about/association/academic/taskforce/task force.html (accessed December 28, 2005).

Freedle, Roy O. 2003. "Correcting the SAT's Ethnic and Social-Class Bias: A Method for Reestimating SAT Scores." *Harvard Educational Review* 73: 1–43. Available online at http://gseweb.harvard.edu/hepg/freedle. html (accessed April 15, 2006).

Hodges, Larry V., and Barbara Schneider, eds. 2005. *The Social Organization of Schooling.* New York: Russell Sage.

Hoff, David J. 1999. "ETS Creating Demographic Index for SAT." *Education Week* 19, no. 1: 1–2. Available online at http://search.epnet.com/login.aspx?direct=true&db=aph&an=2280301 (accessed April 15, 2006).

MacLeod, J. 1995. *Ain't No Makin' It: Leveled Aspirations in a Low-Income Neighbourhood.* Boulder, CO: Westview Press.

Patchen, Martin. 2004. *Making Our Schools More Effective: What Matters and What Works.* Springfield, IL: C. C. Thomas Publishers.

Thernstrom, Abigail, and Stephan Thernstrom. 2003. *No Excuses: Closing the Racial Gap in Learning.* New York: Simon and Schuster.

UNESCO (United Nations Educational, Cultural and Scientific Organization). 2004. "The Literacy Decade: Getting Started 2003–2004." Part of the *United Nations Literacy Decade (2003–2012) Report.* Paris: UNESCO. Available online at http://unesdoc.unesco.org/images/0013/001354/135400e.pdf (accessed April 15, 2006).

UNESCO Institute for Statistics (UIS). 2005a. "Literacy Assessment and Monitoring Programme (LAMP)." Pamphlet. Montreal: VIS. Available online at http://www.uis.unesco.org/TEMPLATE/pdf/LAMP/LAMP_EN_2005.pdf (accessed April 14, 2006).

UNESCO Institute for Statistics (UIS). 2005b. "Women Still Left Behind in Efforts to Achieve Global Literacy." Fact Sheet 6, September. Available online at http://www.uis.unesco.org/template/pdf/literacy/UIS_factsheet_06_EN.pdf (accessed April 15, 2006).

Wise, Tim. 2002. "Failing the Test of Fairness: Institutional Racism and the SAT." *Z Magazine Commentary,* August 12. Available online at http://www.zmag.org/sustainers/content/2002-08/12wise.cfm (accessed April 15, 2006).

Bibliography

Ballantine, Jeanne H. 1997. *The Sociology of Education: A Systematic Analysis.* Englewood Cliffs, NJ: Prentice-Hall.

Becker, Howard Saul. 1963. *Outsiders: Studies in the Sociology of Deviance.* New York: Free Press.

Bennett, William J. 1997. "School Reform: What Remains to Be Done." *Wall Street Journal,* September 2, 18.

Bennett de Marrais, Kathleen, and Margaret D. LeCompte. 1995. *The Way Schools Work: A Sociological Analysis of Education.* New York: Longman.

Bernstein, Basil. 1971. "On the Classification and Framing of Educational Knowledge." In *Knowledge and Control: New Directions for the Sociology of Education,* edited by Michael F. D. Young, 47–69. London: Collier-Macmillan.

Blank, Rolf K., and Douglas A. Archbald. 1992. "Magnet Schools and Issues of Education Quality." *Clearing House* 66, no. 2: 81–86.

Bourdieu, Pierre. 1977. "Cultural Reproduction and Social Reproduction." In *Power and Ideology in Education,* edited by A. H. Halsey and Jerome Karabel, 487–511. New York: Oxford University Press.

Bourdieu, Pierre, and Jean-Claude Passeron. 1977. *Reproduction in Education, Society, and Culture.* London: Sage.

Bowles, Samuel, and Herbert Gintis. 1976. *Schooling in Capitalist America: Educational Reform and the Contradictions of Economic Life.* New York: Basic Books.

Brint, Steven. 1998. *Schools and Societies.* Thousand Oaks, CA: Pine Forge.

Brown, David K. 1995. *Degrees of Control: A Sociology of Educational Expansion and Occupational Credentialism.* New York: Teachers College Press.

Carroll, Ginny. 1990. "Who Foots the Bill?" *Newsweek*: 81–85.

Central Intelligence Agency. 2005. *The World Factbook*. Washington, DC: U.S. Government Printing Office.

Clark, Burton R. 1998. *Creating Entrepreneurial Universities: Organizational Pathways of Transformation*. New York: Pergamon.

Coleman, James S., Ernest Q. Campbell, Carol J. Hobson, James McPartland, Alexander M. Mood, Frederic D. Weinfeld, and Robert L. York. 1966. "Equality of Educational Opportunity." Washington, DC: U.S. Department of Health, Education, and Welfare, Office of Education.

Coleman, James S., Sara D. Kelly, and John A. Moore. 1975. "Trends in School Segregation, 1968–1973." Washington, DC: Urban Institute.

Collins, Randall. 1971. "Functional and Conflict Theories of Educational Stratification." *American Sociological Review* 36, no. 6: 1002–1019.

de Crevecoeur, Hector St. John. 1783. *Letters from an American Farmer*. New York: Dutton. Reprinted in 1912.

D'Souza, Dinesh. 1991. "Travels with Rigoberta: Multiculturalism at Stanford." In *Illiberal Education: The Politics of Race and Sex on Campus,* edited by Dinesh D'Souza, 59–93. New York: Free Press.

Durkheim, Emile. 1925. *Moral Education: A Study in the Theory and Application of the Sociology of Education*. Glencoe, IL: Free Press. Reprinted in 1961.

———. 1938. *The Evolution of Educational Thought: Lectures on the Formation and Development of Secondary Education in France*. Boston: Routledge and Kegan Paul. Reprinted in 1977.

———. 1956. *Education and Sociology*. Glencoe, IL: Free Press.

Freedle, Roy O. 2003. "Correcting the SAT's Ethnic and Social-Class Bias: A Method for Reestimating SAT Scores." *Harvard Educational Review* 73: 1–43.

Groves, Martha. 2000. "Rivalry for Top Colleges Equals Stress for Students; Education: Teenagers Face Tougher Competition, Crushing Workloads, and High Expectations." *Los Angeles Times*, June 22, 1.

Hoff, David J. 1999. "ETS Creating Demographic Index for SAT." *Education Week* 19, no. 1: 1–2.

Jefferson, Thomas. 1950. *Papers of Thomas Jefferson*. Edited by Julian P. Boyd. Princeton, NJ: University Press.

Labaree, David F. 1988. *The Making of an American High School: The Credentials Market and the Central High School of Philadelphia, 1838–1939*. New Haven, CT: Yale University Press.

———. 1997. "Public Goods, Private Goods: The American Struggle over Educational Goals." *American Educational Research Journal* 34, no. 1: 39–81.

Levine, Arthur, and Jeanette Cureton. 1992. "The Quiet Revolution: Eleven Facts About Multiculturalism and the Curriculum." *Change* 24, no. 1: 24–29.

Lynd, Robert Staughton, and Helen Merrell Lynd. 1929. *Middletown in Transition: A Study in Cultural Conflicts*. New York: Harcourt, Brace. Reprinted in 1937.

Manski, Charles F. 1992. "Educational Choice (Vouchers) and Social Mobility." *Economics of Education Review* 11, no. 4: 351–369.

National Commission on Excellence in Education. 1983. "A Nation at Risk: The Imperative for Educational Reform." Washington, DC: U.S. Department of Education.

Parsons, Talcott. 1959. "The School Class as a Social System: Some of Its Functions in American Society." *Harvard Educational Review* 29: 297–318.

Pratt, John. 2000. "How Will Our Soul Be Saved?" *New York Times*, September 29, 9.

Rist, Marilee C. 1990. "Angling for Influence." *American School Board Journal.*

Rosenfelt, Deborah Silverton. 1994. "'Definitive' Issues: Women's Studies, Multicultural Education, and Curriculum Transformation in Policy and Practice in the United States." *Women's Studies Quarterly* 22, nos. 3–4: 26–41.

Rosenthal, Robert, and Lenore Jacobson. 1968. *Pygmalion in the Classroom: Teacher Expectation and Pupils' Intellectual Development.* New York: Holt, Rinehart, and Winston.

Shelley, Kristina J. 1992. "The Future Jobs of College Graduates." *Monthly Labor Review* 115, no. 7: 13–21.

Smith, Thomas M., Marianne Perie, Nebeel Alsalam, Rebecca Pratt Mahoney, Yupin Bae, and Beth Aronstamm Young. 1995. "The Condition of Education." Washington, DC: National Center for Education Statistics.

Thompson, Kenneth. 1997. *Media and Cultural Regulation.* Thousand Oaks, CA: Sage.

UNESCO (United Nations Educational, Cultural, and Scientific Organization). 2004. "The Literacy Decade: Getting Started, 2003–2004." In *The UN Literacy Decade (2003–2012) Report.* Paris: UNESCO.

———. 2005a. "Literacy Assessment and Monitoring Programme (Lamp)." Montreal, Canada: UNESCO Institute for Statistics.

———. 2005b. "Women Still Left Behind in Efforts to Achieve Global Literacy (Fact Sheet 6)." Montreal, Canada: UNESCO Institute for Statistics.

U.S. Census Bureau. 2005a. "Historical Income Tables: People; Table P-2—Race and Hispanic Origin of People by Median Income and Sex, 1947–2003." Washington, DC: U.S. Department of Commerce.

———. 2005b. *Current Population Survey.* March and Annual Social and Economic Supplements, 2004 and Earlier. Table MS-2. Washington, DC: U.S. Department of Commerce.

U.S. Department of Education, National Center for Education Statistics. 2003a. "The Condition of Education 2003 (NCES 2003–067)," Table 15-2. Washington, DC: NCES.

———. 2004. "The Condition of Education 2004 (NCES 2004–077)," Indicator 14 and Table 14-1. Washington, DC: NCES.

Weber, Max. 1958a. *From Max Weber: Essays in Sociology*, edited by C. Wright Mills and H. H. Gerth. New York: Oxford University Press.

Weisman, Jonathan. 1990. "$25,000 Bonuses for Exemplary Teachers Include One String—Their Donor, Milken." *Education Week* 10, no. 11: 1–18.

Wise, Tim. 2002. "Failing the Test of Fairness: Institutional Racism and the SAT." *Z Magazine* (August 12).

CHAPTER 11

Politics and Globalization

Chapter 11 examines globalization within the context of ongoing political changes, erosion of social capital, and hegemonic power in the globalized economy. In the first section of the chapter, Buechler (2014) describes critics of modernization theory, methods of modernization, and power differences among societies. In the second section of the chapter, global inequality is explained by world system theory. The main argument is whether globalization is an alternative to the world system in the rise of growing transnational corporate power. Finally, economic divisions between rich and poor, the financial meltdown, the negative effects of a rapidly globalizing work-economic system, cultural imperialism, the recipients of massive benefits, and alternatives to the dominant model of globalizations are addressed.

The Challenge of Globalization

Steven M. Buechler

In our day, the shrinking of time and space links the personal and the global. Our lives are now intertwined with peoples and processes across the planet. So we move from identity questions to global issues.

There are many global connections. Here's one. Baseball is "America's game." Although played elsewhere, it originated here and is distinctly "American" in the same way as jazz music. Whereas only a few thousand players make it to the big leagues, millions of kids play in Little Leagues every year. Participation provides important lessons about team dynamics, personal identity, and competitive pressures.

Playing baseball requires little equipment. Most obviously, it requires a baseball. Here's where the globe shrinks and America's game rests on a global connection. Every baseball used in the major leagues is made by hand in a baseball factory in Turrialba, Costa Rica. It takes a skilled baseball maker about fifteen minutes to hand-sew 108 stitches along the seams of the ball. It's the seams that give the ball its action. Along with grip, speed, and rotation, the seams turn pitches into the curveballs, sliders, and sinkers that almost magically elude even the best hitters. But without the workers of Turrialba, there would be no baseballs, and no game.

A closer look reveals a familiar globalization story. The factory is owned by Rawlings Sporting Goods, which has an exclusive contract to supply baseballs to the major leagues. Rawlings came to Costa Rica in 1988 when it was awarded free trade zone status by the Costa Rican government. This means Rawlings pays no taxes and can import cores, yarn, and cowhide duty free. The labor isn't free, but it's very cheap. The baseball workers earn less than $3,000 a year. An experienced worker who has been there thirteen years makes a little more than $50 a week, barely above the Costa Rican minimum wage. It costs about 30 cents to produce a baseball, and Rawlings sells them for $14.99 each. The steady supply and high quality of baseballs made by people earning less than $3,000 a year sustains a professional sport in which the average player earns more than $2 million.

The owners and managers of the baseball factory are satisfied. They say that the workplace is a good one and that the work is not very demanding. They have high praise for the workers and refer to them as a team or a family. They deny that there are any problems at the plant or that workers are harmed by the work they do.

The workers see it differently. They acknowledge that without the plant, their economic opportunities might be even worse. They acknowledge that although their wages have not increased in sixteen years, the plant has made improvements in workplace safety and brought in a less abusive manager. But they also speak of the difficulty of the work. A typical workday runs from 6 a.m. to 5 p.m. In summer, the temperature inside the plant approaches 100 degrees. One worker claims, "It is hard work, and sometimes it messes up your hands, warps your fingers, and hurts your shoulders." In contrast to management claims, a third of the workforce has developed carpal tunnel syndrome and up to 90 percent of the workers experience chronic pain from the exacting detail, precise standards, and rapid pace of the work.

The workers are also aware of the economic disparities. One notes that during a week in which he might produce 250 baseballs, the retail price of the first two or three balls pays his salary for the week; the return on the other 247 or 248 baseballs goes to the company. Another worker notes that "[w]e sacrifice a lot so they can play. It's an injustice that we kill ourselves to make these balls perfect, and with one home run, they're gone" (all information and quotes from Weiner 2004).

Even if you are a player or a fan, you were probably unaware of these global connections. Few of us are, because it's not in the interest of the large institutions that benefit to publicize them. They would prefer that we not connect these dots. But critical sociology is all about connecting such dots. By looking beyond appearances and asking who benefits, critical sociology is tailor-made for analyzing a globalizing world.

The Rise and Fall of Modernization Theory

Sociology is not always critical. Like any form of knowledge, it sees the world from a certain standpoint. Before discussing globalization directly, an overview of modernization theory will show how unexamined assumptions distort understanding.

Sociology emerged with modernization in Europe. Although classical sociologists had differences, they had three similarities. First, they shared a broadly European identity. Second, they focused on rapid changes occurring in their own societies. Third, they brought a Eurocentric standpoint to their understanding of the modernization process.

Such Eurocentrism is evident in the typologies these sociologists created to capture the differences between modernizing and traditional societies. They described traditional societies as preindustrial ones, in which most people worked in horticulture or agriculture for survival. Such societies had small populations and low population density. People had ascribed statuses; their position in life was largely determined by birth and not subject to much change. Mythical, magical, or religious belief systems prevailed, and science and technology were minimally developed. There was also little development of social institutions. Instead, the kinship system fulfilled social, economic, and political as well as family functions.

In contrast, European societies were seen as modern (or at least modernizing). Modern societies have industrial rather than agricultural economies. They experience rapid growth, high population density, and urban development. People in modern societies occupy more achieved statuses; their position in life depends on their own efforts or experiences rather than being determined by birth. Scientific and secular worldviews displace mythical and religious ones. Most important for social structure, the multifunctional kinship system shrinks to the nuclear family, and separate institutions emerge to fulfill economic, political, educational, and social functions.

These contrasts were the basis of much classical sociology. Durkheim traced how traditional societies with mechanical solidarity and little differentiation developed into modern ones with organic solidarity and a complex division of labor. Marx traced the transition from feudalism to capitalism in which the cash nexus of capital tore apart the motley threads that bound traditional societies. Weber revealed how the Protestant ethic and the spirit of capitalism overcame traditional barriers to profit making and launched the modern world of rational-calculative capitalism, rational-legal authority, and the disenchantment that results when science displaces myth.

Such studies revealed how modernity emerged on the European continent. They also reinforced biases about the backwardness of people in traditional societies while Europe was modernizing. There were deeper problems as well.

During the first half of the twentieth century, questions of modernization were on the back burner. At mid-century, the conclusion of World War II, the Marshall Plan to rebuild Europe, the founding of the United Nations, the rise of national independence movements, and the beginning of the Cold War brought questions of modernization back to a full boil. But the focus shifted from Europe's past to the Third World's future.

This spurred a new version of modernization theory that revived the distinction between traditional and modern societies (Apter 1967; Bernstein 1971; Kuznets 1965; Lerner 1958). But now, "traditional society" referred not to predecessors of modern Europe but rather to societies in Africa, Asia, and Latin America. Modernization theory thus transposed Europe's modernization in the past into a model of how the rest of the world might do so in the future.

Most simply, the theory understood modernization as moving from a traditional society with its interrelated characteristics to a modern society with a different set of characteristics. Modernization was seen as a holistic, universal process of societal evolution and development (Bernstein 1971, 141). The West had already done it, and now it was time for the rest to catch up. The fact that they had not yet done so supported unflattering judgments that these societies and the people in them were primitive, backward, and underdeveloped.

Some versions of the theory identified institutional barriers to economic growth. Others cited Weber's work to suggest that the impediments were primarily cultural. Underdeveloped societies were seen as trapped in traditional orientations to the world that did not provide much stimulus for achievement. In this view, they needed cultural transfusions of competitive individualism and an achievement ethic to overturn tradition and foster modernization (McClelland 1973). If not the Protestant ethic or the spirit of capitalism, some similar cultural impetus was required for these societies to "take off" on the path of modernization.

This theory was plausible to its advocates, but this had less to do with its validity than with its standpoint. After all, modernization theory presented Western-style development as the only game in town (and it implied that others would be crazy not to want to be like us anyway). When ideas portray their advocates in a flattering light, it is important to look for the flaws behind the flattery.

The flaws quickly emerged, as critics of modernization theory found multiple targets. One was the goal of modernization. By taking their own societies as the point of reference, these theorists implied that the only logical goal of modernization was a carbon copy of already developed societies. Given their highly disproportionate use of the world's resources, this goal now appears economically dubious and ecologically disastrous. Moreover, this logic denied any voice to people in "underdeveloped" societies about whether and what type of modernization they might want.

A second target of critics concerned methods of modernization. Advocacy of competitive individualism and an achievement orientation implied that there was only one way to develop. Like the goal, it just happened to be the way of the West, so once again a theory of past development in Europe was repackaged into a normative model of future development elsewhere. Such prescriptions didn't recognize how the remedies clashed with prevailing cultural practices in traditional societies.

A third target of the critics involved historical context. When the West modernized, it was the first to do so. There were no predecessors. The context is different now. Underdeveloped societies face a world of already developed societies. The unspoken assumption of modernization theory was that developed societies would provide capital investment, technology transfers, and foreign aid to spur development across the globe. Critics turned this assumption on its head. They argued that the developed world was an obstacle to global development, because developed nations benefited from ongoing underdevelopment elsewhere.

These are serious flaws, but there was a more basic problem. It was implicit in the classical typologies and became explicit in modernization theory. Consider an alternative story: Human societies have always been more diverse than the rigid dichotomy of "traditional" vs. "modern" recognizes. In addition, there have always been important connections among societies. External relations are often more critical for development (or underdevelopment) than internal factors. And finally, power has always shaped relations among societies. Where power differences exist, some societies benefit at the expense of others.

This alternative story adds a crucial insight absent from modernization theory. It is this. European modernization was made possible by domination of other societies. Colonialism, imperialism, the slave trade, and the exploitation of raw materials, agricultural products, and cheap labor from other places were essential to European modernization.

This alternative story downplays internal factors and emphasizes external ones. There is certainly a place for both. Weber could be right that the Protestant ethic and spirit of capitalism were necessary to make profit making an ethical duty rather than a greedy undertaking. But internal, cultural meanings were accompanied by external, economic relations that produced the actual profits that fueled Europe's development. Western modernization was underwritten by exploitation of non-European societies. If Europe was the beneficiary, the colonies were the victims. Colonial peoples saw their resources depleted, their labor exploited, their cultures oppressed, and their societies reshaped to serve colonial powers.

Recognizing colonialism drives the last nail in the coffin of modernization theory. "Underdevelopment" is not a natural, initial condition of all societies; it is a set of disadvantages *created* by colonialism. When Andre Guilder Frank (1969) spoke of "the development of underdevelopment," he meant that underdevelopment is a socially created condition arising from colonial exploitation (Chew and Denemark 1996).

The development of the West and the underdevelopment of the rest are thus two sides of the same coin; both derive from a single process that benefited some at the expense of others. The resulting underdevelopment of much of the world persists in the postcolonial era. The problem is not traditionalism, backwardness, or underdevelopment; it is rather the dependency that has been created between underdeveloped societies and former colonizers. As long as that dependency benefits Western powers, they will pose obstacles to global development.

There is a major irony here. If "underdeveloped" societies were to follow the *real* history of Europe, they would colonize others to fuel *their* development (at the expense of *their* colonies). Something like this has happened in some regions of the globe, but it is hardly the lesson modernization theorists had in mind. Modernization theory illustrates how certain standpoints and assumptions can generate plausible but seriously flawed understandings of the social world.

It is a further irony that even though modernization theory has been widely discredited in academic circles, it still provides rhetoric and imagery for politicians and policy makers. When discredited ideas live on, it often means they are serving powerful interests. Modernization theory does so by obscuring the colonialism that fueled Western development and the neocolonialism that still inhibits global progress.

The Global World System

The greatest flaw of modernization theory was that it ignored relations *among* societies and their impact on development or underdevelopment. The greatest strength of world system theory is that this insight is its starting premise.

World system theorists assume that a cohesive, global, economic system transcending national boundaries has existed for several centuries (Hall 2000; Shannon 1989; Wallerstein 1974, 1980, 1989). This system relies on a global division of labor incorporating numerous cultures and nation-states. This capitalist economy organizes global activities through the institution of private property, the process of commodification, and the practice of exploitation. Although global, this system has distinct economic zones. Core states are economically and politically dominant nations and leaders of the world system. They use sophisticated technologies in capital-intensive, high-wage economic production. Peripheral states are weaker economically and politically, and they use less-advanced technologies in labor-intensive, low-wage production. Semi-peripheral countries are located between core and periphery and exhibit some combination of both elements.

These economic zones also differ in their conditions of labor. In core countries, most workers are "free" to seek the best wages and working conditions the market has to offer. In peripheral countries, they are more likely to be coerced into providing labor, whether this involves outright slavery, indentured servitude, or other restrictive forms of labor. The differences between free and coerced labor create another challenge to working-class organization on a global scale, because workers in different zones confront very different working conditions, political rights, and economic opportunities.

Although the world system is economically unified, it is politically fragmented into competing nation-states. Like capitalism, the nation-state system now encompasses every region of the globe. Not surprisingly, core states are more powerful than peripheral ones, and this political power is often a tool by which the core maintains control over peripheral regions.

If capitalism is a world system, it follows that its classes are international. Hence, class analysis must recognize the global dimensions of class interest, organization, consciousness, and struggle. In terms of class formation, the capitalist class is rapidly becoming an international network without regard to nationality.

The working class is also an international class whose labor-power is sold on a global market. In terms of class formation, however, there are national, cultural, and linguistic barriers obstructing international working-class mobilization. Even so, organization within a single country is not enough, because capitalists can play workers of different nations against one another. As a world system, capitalism thus combines a global economy and class structure with diverse nation-states and status groups based on culture, language, and citizenship.

The system is driven by capital accumulation, as owners of private property seek to maximize profits through the exploitation of labor and the extraction of surplus value. These processes are increasingly acted out on a global stage, resulting in a flow of wealth from periphery to core. Historically, this exploitation underwrote development of the core and retarded development of the periphery. These economically driven processes are paralleled by political ones, as states compete for predominance in a global interstate system. The result is a symbiotic relationship between state managers and national capitalists where each group pursues its interests by facilitating those of the other.

This system has existed for approximately five hundred years, with different regions playing different roles over time. In the contemporary period, the core includes the United States, Western Europe, and Japan. As advanced capitalist societies, these regions are economically wealthy, politically dominant, and relatively stable. The periphery includes much of Africa and South Asia as well as parts of Latin America. Peripheral states are still dominated by a legacy of colonialism and forms of neocolonialism that constrict their economic and political options. Peripheral areas exhibit extreme economic inequality and less stable states.

The remainder of the globe composes the semi-periphery, including much of Latin America, some of Africa and the Middle East, parts of East Asia, China, and the former Soviet Union and its satellites. The semi-periphery is perhaps the most diverse zone of the world system, with newly industrializing countries experiencing rapid growth rates standing alongside relatively stagnant economies. The semi-periphery resembles the periphery more than the core, but these states do establish their own exploitative relations with peripheral countries, even as they remain exploited by core countries.

The world system has cycles of economic expansion and decline that are loosely correlated with turnover in core states known as cycles of hegemony. During rare periods of full hegemony, a single core state will monopolize advantages over others in production, commerce, and finance. World system theorists generally recognize three such periods of full hegemony by a single country: Elolland in the mid-1600s, Britain in the mid-1800s, and the United States in the mid-1900s. More often, no one state monopolizes power; it is rather shared among core states that nevertheless maintain their dominance over the world system.

In the ascending phase of a hegemonic cycle, a rising state takes advantage of economic opportunities for which it is better positioned than any of its rivals. Building on new technologies or forms of organization, it achieves a productive advantage, accumulates multiple resources, and acquires commercial and financial power. Such rising powers often benefit from strong states and military power.

The decline of a hegemonic power follows a similar sequence. It loses its productive advantage first, creating a downward spiral in which commercial, financial, and military powers also erode. The initial loss of productive advantage occurs when competitors copy manufacturing techniques, when dominant producers lose their competitive edge, and when militarism drains off productive resources. Although there have been long periods without a single hegemonic power, sooner or later a new ascending core state attains dominance and follows the same cycle.

Different points in the cycle have different effects on domestic stability. During prosperous periods of hegemonic maturity, economic growth can blunt class conflict and encourage moderate reform. In a relatively open political climate, diverse viewpoints might be heard and popular struggles for rights and resources might succeed. In a context of domestic prosperity and global dominance, a consensus on foreign policy is often relatively easy to forge, and nationalism can become a potent force.

This political climate changes with the transition from hegemonic maturity to hegemonic decline. The latter typically fosters economic and political inequality, greater state repression, and stagnant or declining economic resources. Political options narrow to sustain a beleaguered national capitalist class. The state is likely to cut expenditures that do not serve these interests, undermining the living standards of many people.

The United States has experienced at least three stages of the rise and fall of a hegemonic power. During ascending hegemony (1897–1913/1920), there was ongoing conflict between rival powers, as the United States challenged previously hegemonic states. In the phase of hegemonic victory (1913/1920–1945), the United States consolidated productive and military advantages over rival core states and became the newly hegemonic power. In the phase of hegemonic maturity (1945–1970), the United States exercised full control in all major spheres of economic, political, and military power, and there were no comparable rival powers within the world system. In the final stage of declining hegemony (since the 1970s), the United States has seen partial erosion of its economic advantages and the appearance of strong challengers for hegemony.

Recent conditions in the United States typify a hegemonic power struggling against decline. Consider the political climate of the past forty years. Since the mid-1970s, the US economy has undergone domestic crises alongside challenges to its international predominance as well. This resulted in increasing inequality and poverty, accelerated concentration of capital assets, attacks on the wages and living standards of workers and welfare recipients, and pressure on government to cut expenditures and reduce corporate taxes. The long-term erosion of social capital investments in education and research further weakens the competitive position of the United States. These events suggest that even powerful core countries are strongly affected by their relationships with other nations.

If even the most powerful nations are affected by external pressures, imagine their impact in the rest of the world system. Remember the baseball makers of Turrialba? Their situation exemplifies world system theory quite nicely. Although belonging to a distinct nation, culture, and status group, their labor is part of a global economy. The low cost of their labor also reflects their position in the world system. Paying workers 30 cents for a product that sells for $15 suggests the degree of exploitation at the heart of the world system. The products have changed, but the economics of baseball making in Turrialba have been part of the world system for five centuries.

Globalization: What's New?

World system theory was the dominant sociological perspective on global development from the mid-1970s to the mid-1990s. Its focus on relations among nations corrected the major flaw of modernization theory. It also provided a powerful explanation for the development of core countries and the underdevelopment of peripheral countries within a single theory. Finally, it offered a compelling explanation for persisting global inequality.

Since the mid-1990s, references to "globalization" have been increasingly frequent. Some argue that globalization has made world system theory outdated. Such discussions see globalization as an inevitable, technologically driven process beyond human control. Such claims need to be carefully evaluated through the lens of critical sociology.

At least three changes are central in the debate over whether globalization is creating an alternative to the world system. The first is the dissolution of the socialist bloc and its incorporation into the global economy. During the Cold War, the Soviet Union, its Eastern European satellites, and other socialist countries resembled the semi-periphery of the world system, but they were also disconnected from it. They were not open to foreign investment, and their production and trade were dictated more by political bureaucracies than market forces. With the breakup of the socialist bloc, these nations became more integrated into the semi-periphery as foreign investment increased, public goods were privatized, markets emerged, and trade expanded.

A second change involves the relative decline of (some) nation-states in the face of growing transnational corporate power. Historically, core nation-states were dominant or equal partners with national corporations in the world system. Corporations needed governments to make rules, stabilize currencies, negotiate treaties, and maintain order. With the rise of transnational corporations that dwarf many governments, nation-states have lost some of their ability to constrain corporate behavior. Core states still have considerable political and military power, but even here transnational corporate mobility gives them leverage. In the periphery and semi-periphery, former colonies have only recently become independent nation-states at precisely the time when the power of nation-states is declining relative to global corporate entities that can often dictate national policy and development options.

The third change involves new information and communication technologies. The ability to communicate instantaneously around the globe certainly appears to shrink the world and create a global village. The same technologies make it possible for financial transactions to occur instantaneously. The newfound ability to rapidly move currency around the global economy can enhance profits for some at the same time that it can potentially destabilize national and regional economies.

There is no denying that things have changed with globalization. Economically, globalization means a tighter integration of the world into a single market. Politically, it means the rise of supranational organizations that have partly displaced some functions of national governments. Culturally, globalization means the standardization and homogenization of world cultures, as mass media supplant indigenous cultures with Western consumer capitalism. Some conclude that globalization is replacing hierarchy with a world that is interconnected, leveled, flattened, or equalized—at least in comparison with the past. Such conclusions require critical scrutiny.

Rather than vague metaphors of leveling or equalizing, globalization is better seen as a tighter integration of social spaces into a hierarchical structure in which the center still dominates the periphery. This hierarchical relation between center and periphery has always characterized the world system, and globalization has done more to enhance than to undermine these dynamics. Seen this way, the undeniable facts of globalization are better seen as an intensification of dynamics that have been part of the world system for centuries. Put differently, globalization is the latest stage in the evolution of the world economic system rather than a departure from it.

There are several reasons for interpreting globalization in this way. Consider the changes cited as responsible for creating a supposedly new globalized world. The demise of socialism was among the most dramatic geopolitical events of the late twentieth century, but it hardly counts against world system theory. If anything, the socialist bloc was an anomaly for world system theory, because it meant that a vast portion of the globe was only loosely linked to the world system while trying to create an alternative to it. The integration of the former "second world" into the world system is more a confirmation than a refutation of world system theory. More broadly, the integration of all regions of the globe into a world market is less a departure than an intensification of world system patterns. By this standard "globalization" has been occurring since the origins of the world system in the 1500s.

The relative decline of national power does not necessarily undermine world system theory either. This system did not begin with powerful nation-states but rather in a stew of city-states, feudal principalities, and disputed regimes. In many cases, colonial exploitation fueled the consolidation of the nation-state system we take for granted today. Powerful economic interests have always sought to manipulate state power to advance their interests. In the past, this promoted state power. Today those same interests are embodied in transnational corporations that seek to limit state power. These developments might signify a relative shift in the power of states and corporations, but not the demise of the world system itself. It emerged and survived alongside weak and strong states in different historical periods, and there is every reason to believe that it will continue in an era of shifting state powers.

The third indicator of globalization is cultural homogenization in the form of Western consumer capitalism. Once again, these developments are better seen as an intensification of world system dynamics than a departure from them. Marx himself noted that capitalism creates a world in its own image. Moreover, the world system of the past five centuries has always included cultural imperialism alongside economic exploitation and political domination. The technical capacity for cultural control might have changed, but these new technologies should not blind us to older patterns of cultural domination in the world system.

The point is not to deny that globalization has recently accelerated. The point is to challenge an interpretation that says these changes constitute a qualitative break from the operation of the world system over the past five centuries. Such changes are better seen as an intensification or new stage of world system dynamics than as a departure from them.

Recent World System Dynamics

Recent developments in the world system provide the best evidence for its continuity. In 1944, the United States hosted an international conference in Bretton Woods, New Hampshire, "that more or less invented globalization" (Derber 2002, 98). Bretton Woods established the International Monetary

Fund (IMF) and the World Bank (WB). More broadly, it promoted new understandings of world finance, trade rules, and open markets as cornerstones of the global economy. Despite the international veneer, the conference was an assertion of US power on a global scale.

Under traditional colonialism, core countries exercised complete control over colonies. As colonies gained independence, the empire system of explicit, coercive control was replaced with an "umpire system" (Derber 2002), in which the United States created rules ensuring that the world system worked in its favor. It also created international institutions firmly under its control to establish policy and settle disputes. Bretton Woods was thus a transition from control by the British Empire to control by the US "umpire." It can be described as the beginning of modern globalization, but it was really a new phase in the long-standing exercise of power by the core over the periphery.

The system was refined in the 1950s, with trade rules known as the General Agreement on Tariffs and Trade (GATT) that further entrenched US power. GATT created a highly regulated global economy serving the economic and political interests of core states. In the periphery, it was another story. With few exceptions, peripheral nations did not benefit from these trade arrangements, and some saw declines in standard measures of national development and well-being. Thus, at the very time that academics were promoting modernization via the Western model, new global institutions were creating "underdevelopment" in the periphery.

Under these arrangements, investment in the Third World increased and the world economy became more densely intertwined. Core countries profited from the same dynamics that caused problems in the periphery. The development advice offered by the IMF and the World Bank often contributed to the problem. The advice went something like this. Third World nations with stagnant economies were advised to identify some raw material, resource, or type of production where they had a competitive advantage. They were urged to reorient their economies to maximize production of this commodity. Through this strategy, peripheral nations were expected to sell lots of their commodity to the world market and earn back enough revenue to fund development.

This advice sounds logical in the abstract; in reality, it was less so. The advice promoted export economies specializing in one crop or product. Such a strategy of "putting all your eggs in one basket" was risky; it violated another standard piece of economic wisdom to diversify investment and production for long-term stability. The strategy backfired in several ways. If internal problems hampered production, or if global demand declined, or if new competitors appeared, the country was in serious trouble. The strategy benefited core countries that could sample a rich supply of global commodities, but it was often destructive for poor nations struggling to develop. Such conflicts of interest and outcome between core and periphery are precisely what world system theory would predict.

This development strategy also undermined customary means of subsistence. In many regions, people had long survived through traditional agricultural methods that required access to land. When countries implemented IMF-style development plans, people were displaced and land was devoted to export crops or livestock. Many formerly self-sufficient people lost their means of economic survival. This created a brutal irony. Many countries with severe problems of hunger and malnutrition are actually exporting significant amounts of food to the world market in keeping with a dubious development strategy. Such instances illustrate how "underdevelopment" is less an initial state of backwardness than an emergent problem created by relations between different parts of the world system.

By the late 1970s, the periphery was in crisis. While old problems of poverty, hunger, and disease persisted or worsened in many places, new problems of massive debt owed to First World lenders were added to the mix. In yet another irony, the IMF and the World Bank that helped create the problems were now enlisted to solve them. Once again, there was a standard prescription, but it was backed up with more explicit coercion. To get assistance with debt relief, Third World countries had to adopt "structural adjustment programs" that imposed austerity measures and slashed social spending to save money to repay debts. Such programs cut (already inadequate) spending on health, education, and welfare. They also undermined workers' rights and environmental protections as further strategies to cut costs and reduce debt.

Just when formally independent governments were emerging in much of the Third World, these developments undercut any real national independence. "As the world s designated loaner of last resort, the IMF became a 'government within the government' in more than seventy-five desperately indebted poor countries. ..." Harvard economist Jeffrey Sachs called the IMF a "permanent 'neocolonial' force in scores of countries, drastically eroding their sovereignty" (quoted in Derber 2002, 116). The mechanisms changed from empire-driven colonialism to umpire-regulated neocolonialism, but the basic dynamic of core states' benefiting from exploitation of peripheral states remained.

The economic instability of the 1970s was a catastrophe for many poor nations, but it also destabilized core countries and the larger world system. Led by the United States, core countries responded with deregulation, privatization, and relentless promotion of global "free" markets. These strategies intensified practices dating from the Bretton Woods conference and subsequent refinements through GATT, the IMF, and the World Bank. In the name of "deregulation," older constraints on trade and capital flows were overthrown, and new rules and regulations were carefully crafted to once again favor the strongest players in the world system.

These developments created the World Trade Organization (WTO) at the conclusion of the 1994 GATT negotiations. The WTO is explicitly dedicated to defending property rights, expanding investment options, and privatizing global resources. It is the latest institutional expression of the interests of core countries and transnational corporations in the world system.

Such interests frequently conflict with popular interests at home and abroad. Hence, they must be cloaked in ideologically acceptable language. The advocacy of "free trade" and the equation of capitalist markets with "democracy" are two standard methods. The "language of free trade ... [is] largely rhetorical, because the United States, Japan, and Europe all remain selectively protectionist"

(Derber 2002, 121). Put differently, "free" trade is a politically constructed outcome of years ol negotiations and thousands of pages of regulations; it is anything but "free." It is the US umpire (and other core countries) who define "free" trade.

These efforts led to international trade agreements such as the North American Free Trade Agreement (NAFTA), the Central American Free Trade Agreement (CAFTA), and the proposed Free Trade Area of the Americas (FTAA). Alongside the WTO, such agreements have consolidated the power of international trade bodies and transnational corporations at the expense of national governments. In yet another irony, conservatives who have always feared a "world government" in the guise of a more powerful United Nations have largely welcomed the economic equivalent of a world government in the WTO.

The WTO not only makes rules about international trade; it also has the power to enforce them and impose sanctions. One model is the NAFTA provision "that sets up a court allowing corporations to sue governments for passing environmental or labor laws that 'infringe' on property rights and profits" (Derber 2002, 125). The WTO has created similar judicial tribunals to defend property rights.

With such mechanisms, transnational corporations can undermine national standards protecting workers or the environment. The strategy uses the less-rigorous standards of some nations against the stronger standards of other nations. The weakest protections to be found anywhere thus become the baseline for attacking stronger protections everywhere else. Even core states have been disciplined in this fashion. The long-term prospect is thus that the WTO will enable transnational corporations to impose Third World labor and environmental standards on First World nations in the name of defending property rights and profits (Derber 2002).

Globalization: An Assessment

Proponents of globalization claim that it will level the playing field, equalize competition, and create "win-win" situations. The bulk of the evidence to date suggests otherwise. It supports world system theory's claim that conflicting interests and exploitative practices remain central to the world system. Globalization intensifies these dynamics, so that heightened conflict and exploitation produce bigger winners and bigger losers in a more globalized world system.

Consider the startling admission by James Wolfensohn, a former World Bank president, that while globalization has greatly enriched powerful interests, it has been a failure "at the level of people" (cited in Brown 2004, 202). By "people," Wolfensohn presumably means the great majority of the world's population who are victims rather than beneficiaries of globalization. Indeed, a summary of recent evidence on the neoliberal policies of globalization concludes that, "the poorest people on Earth are poorer than before, everyday workers of the developed world have lost ground, and a small cadre of the rich have grown phenomenally richer" (Brown 2004, 202).

Although this assessment might sound extreme, the evidence is compelling. Globalization has sparked a race to the bottom that pits poor nations against one another to see who can lower workers' wages, dismantle safety nets, outlaw labor unions, and scrap environmental protections fast enough to attract capital investment. It is not surprising that global poverty has increased during the past two decades. Moreover, nations that used to be good at attracting foreign investment (like Mexico) are now losing the race to others (like China) who are playing the game even more effectively. As investors moved from Mexico's cheap labor to even cheaper labor elsewhere, and as Mexico has been fully integrated into the North American Free Trade zone, its poverty rate increased from 49 percent to 75 percent in a mere twenty years (Brown 2004, 202–203).

In much of the world, increased poverty stems from the debt Third World nations owe First World lenders. These debts now dwarf other economic indicators. Third World debt has more than doubled since 1980, and some poor countries spend five times more on debt payments than they have received in new loans over the past two decades. In some poor nations, debt payments exceed all other national spending on health, education, and welfare. In the most dire cases, total debt per capita exceeds gross domestic product per capita (Brown 2004, 203). Far from a "win-win" situation, globalization has been a failure for a great many of the world's people.

"People" also includes workers in core countries whose position has deteriorated with globalization. When the United States was the undisputed hegemonic power in the world economic system, benefits flowed to both capitalists and workers. Unions successfully fought for well-paying jobs with significant benefits, including health care and generous pensions. As global competition from other core countries challenged US economic hegemony in the 1970s, the benefits workers derived from living in a core country began to evaporate.

The capitalist response is now familiar. Deindustrialization, runaway shops, capital Hight, and downsizing combined to eliminate many well-paying manufacturing jobs and replace them with service jobs, lower wages, and fewer benefits. As jobs changed, so did government policies. For the past forty years, US domestic policy has resembled a softer version of the structural adjustment programs imposed on Third World countries. Social spending on health, education, and welfare has come under attack, leading to caps, cuts, and the complete elimination of some programs (ending "welfare as we know it"). In the name of privatization, Social Security has come under attack, and many workers have been moved from secure, "defined benefit" pensions to risky "defined contribution" accounts. Broader attacks on unions and environmental protections also follow the logic of structural adjustment programs.

The "race to the bottom" is not just a Third World sport. In industries that play on a global stage, lower standards abroad are used to undercut domestic wages, fringe benefits, worker safety, union status, health care, retirement security, and environmental protections. This amounts to the "deterritorialization" of the periphery of the world economy (Derber 2002). After centuries when the periphery was geographically separate from the core, we are now seeing "peripheral" zones within core countries in chronically depressed urban areas and pockets of extreme rural poverty. Detroit's recent declaration of bankruptcy provides a poignant example of how the periphery of the world system is coming home to roost even in core nations. Given this, it is little wonder that "in the United States, 75 percent of the workers are worse off economically now than in 1980" (Brown 2004, 202).

So much for the evidence about who loses in a globalized economy. The evidence about who wins is even more dramatic. In the first few years of the twenty-first century, corporate profits were at record levels in many industries. The gap between the pay of CEOs and ordinary workers was at an all-time high. The distribution of wealth and income in the United States was more unequal than it had been in almost a hundred years (Wysong, Perrucci, and Wright 2014). Such inequality was enhanced by government policies that subsidized profitable industries and cut taxes for wealthy interests.

The most significant disruption to these trends was the financial meltdown of 2007 that triggered a "Great Recession" whose effects still loom over millions of people in an otherwise-privileged core country like the United States. The crisis had devastating effects on Wall Street as well as "Main Street." At its height, unprecedented amounts of wealth evaporated, upper-class living standards took major hits, and the growing differential between executive compensation and employee salaries briefly shrank.

While wealthy interests suffered significant short-term losses, the most striking outcome has been a "jobless recovery" that has restored those unprecedented levels of wealth on Wall Street alongside a persisting recession on Main Street. In the words of an old blues classic, it's been "Five Long Years" of ongoing foreclosures, sustained unemployment, and downward mobility for many formerly middle- and working-class people. The tune on Wall Street sounds more like "Happy Days Are Here Again," as the portfolios of wealthy investors have recovered virtually all of their previous value and the stock market has reached unprecedented heights as a result of carefully orchestrated, pro-investor Federal Reserve policies.

Thus, the economic divisions between wealthy and mainstream Americans that temporarily shrank during an economic crisis have been restored and show every sign of growing. The pattern of austerity measures has also been restored. Consider one telling example. In the summer of 2013, the House of Representatives deviated from a decades-long pattern of farm bills. Historically, these bills offered subsidies to farmers and nutritional aid to needy Americans. Over the years, the "subsidies became a fraud-ridden program that mainly benefits corporations and wealthy individuals. Meanwhile, food stamps became a crucial part of the social safety net" (Krugman 2013, 8). In a context of recovery for the few and joblessness for the many, the House increased the subsidies for wealthy farmers and corporations and eliminated food stamps from the bill.

The Great Recession reveals that no one is immune to the negative effects of a rapidly globalizing world-economic system. It also reveals, however, that powerful elite interests are much better positioned to recover from those effects than ordinary people in all the zones of the world economic system. In the last analysis, the problem with globalization is not that there are no winners. It is rather that such a small proportion of the world's population derives such massive benefits, while the vast majority who do the work that creates the profits reap so little. Recall, one more time, the baseball makers of Turrialba, who earn less than 30 cents producing baseballs that sell for $15.

Mainstream rhetoric speaks of globalization as inevitable, unstoppable, and irreversible. The implication is that globalization is a genie that has gotten out of a bottle and can't be put back. We're told that the new technologies driving globalization have an intrinsic momentum that cannot be stopped. The further implication is that resistance is futile. In this rhetoric, opponents of globalization are sadly misguided folks who mistakenly think you can turn back the clock and reverse history.

Like many problematic ideas, this one has grains of truth. Barring a major nuclear, ecological, or economic catastrophe, many aspects of globalization are surely here to stay. But there are two assumptions behind this view of globalization that make it deeply flawed and politically dangerous. One is that there is only one way to carry out globalization (like the older, and equally flawed, image of "development" in modernization theory). The second is that this process has so much momentum that no one is, or could be, in charge of it.

The sociological term for these flawed assumptions is *reification.* It means seeing a socially constructed process as if it were a naturally determined inevitability. It means depicting one alternative as the only game in town. It means seeing trends or tendencies as predestined to unfold. A reified view further benefits those who already benefit from globalization by making it appear inevitable.

Critical sociology offers two correctives to this reified view. First, it insists on identifying agency behind globalization. That is, globalization is happening in a particular way because certain powerful groups are acting on their interests to ensure it happens in this way and not other ways. They are using their resources to create a kind of globalization that maximizes their profits and enhances their power, even if it comes at the expense of other people and their interests.

Put differently, there is someone in the driver's seat, and they are taking us to places that aren't good for most passengers on the bus. This does not mean that elites are in complete control or that there aren't unanticipated consequences that backfire on them. But it does mean that someone is responsible for the kind of globalization that is unfolding, including its negative impacts on ordinary people.

Second, critical sociology insists that there are alternatives to the prevailing model of globalization. The issue is not whether to globalize or turn back the clock. The issue is what kind of globalization is preferable. The current model is a top-down, elite-driven, profoundly authoritarian process imposed on people against their interests and without their consent. This description suggests alternative forms of globalization that could be bottom-up, people-driven, and democratically implemented. Such alternatives are actively supported by millions around the world.

Correcting the reified view of globalization requires recognizing which interests have orchestrated it and the existence of alternatives that would serve broader interests.

References

Apter, David. 1967. *The Politics of Modernization*. Chicago: University of Chicago Press.

Bernstein, Henry. 1971. "Modernization in Theory and the Sociological Study of Development." *Journal of Development Studies* 7(2):141–160.

Brown, David. 2004. *Social Blueprints*. New York: Oxford.

Chew, Sing C., and Robert A. Denemark, eds. 1996. *The Underdevelopment of Development*. Thousand Oaks, CA: Sage.

Derber, Charles. 2002. *People before Profit*. New York: Picador.

Frank, Andre Gunder. 1969. *Latin America: Underdevelopment or Revolution?* New York: Monthly Review Press.

Hall, Thomas, ed. 2000. *A World-Systems Reader*. Lanham, MD: Rowman & Littlefield.

Krugman, Paul. 2013. "Hunger Games, U.S.A." *New York Times Digest* (July 15): 8.

Kuznets, Simon. 1965. *Economic Growth and Structure*. New York: Norton.

Lerner, Daniel. 1958. *The Passing of Traditional Society*. Glencoe, IL: Free Press.

McClelland, David. 1973. "Business Drive and National Achievement." In *Social Change*, ed. Eva Etzioni and Amitai Etzioni, 165–178. New York: Basic Books.

Shannon, Thomas. 1989. *An Introduction to the World-System Perspective*. Boulder, CO: Westview Press.

Wallerstein, Immanuel. 1974. *The Modern World-System*. New York: Academic Press.

———. 1980. *The Modern World-System II*. New York: Academic Press.

———. 1989. *The Modern World-System III*. New York: Academic Press.

Weiner, Tim. 2004. "Low-Wage Costa Ricans Make Baseballs for Millionaires." *New York Times* (January 25): 3.

Wysong, Earl, Robert Perrucci, and David Wright. 2014. *The New Class Society*. 4th ed. Lanham, MD: Rowman & Littlefield.

CHAPTER 12

Population and Urbanization

Chapter 12 examines urban society. It describes how the growing urbanization of the world's population is related to one of the primary functions of industrialization. Hannon (2015) explains migration with push and pull factors to point out social and economic conditions. According to Hannon (2015), migrants moved from rural areas to urban areas in the United States for a better life, employment opportunities in manufacturing, and freedom from war, poverty, famine, and political and religious persecution. This chapter demonstrates that America's transition from a rural society to growing urban centers is the consequence of industrialization. This chapter provides urbanization trends from 1970 to 2010 to explain what changed from the industrial to the digital age that prompted urban to suburban moves in the United States. Finally, post-industrial urban society, the demise of the industrial era, the development of the suburbanization process, urban poverty, white flight, redlining, and social problems surrounding urban and suburban areas are discussed in detail.

Urban Society

Lonnie Hannon

Introduction: The Urban Blues

The Urban Blues floats on airy channels, as it blows
through sentient cityscapes,
through streetscapes, through project alleys
stirring candy wrappers to circulate
and dance in the wind.
Aqua blue breezes,
wet with the tears of bastard little boys,
ruffle a little girl's kinky-permed hair.
Together they attempt to fly a stringless kite.

On sails the urban blues, and on sails the urban blues
As it gusts through the city on midnight avenues,
Curls around apathetic towers of glass and steel,
howles around "nighthawk" cafes
into gory ghettos.

And the urban blues floats on airy channels
Laying siege to sentient cityscapes.
As the eyes of an old man
and the eyes of an old woman
dot the nighttime streetscapes.

Though their sunrise lay dormant
In shadowy project alleys.

And their visions drag on the sidewalk
Like a sagging "heavy load"
As streetlights form frightening silhouettes
that whistle a urban blues melody.
A tune that circulates and dances in the wind
Laxly floating on airy channels.

Copyright © 2001 Lonnie Hannon III. "The Astronomy of Urban Streetscapes"

Urban Society: The City as a Marketplace

All industrialized societies are becoming increasingly urban in terms of where people live and work. In fact, industrialization and urbanization are typically in concert with one another. Industrialization requires a diverse combination of people collectively contributing to the social and economic functioning of a society. The city is where this collection of innovators, skilled workers, laborers, financiers, idea creators, and consumers typically share their diverse contributions. The city provides a centralized place for people to exchange their expertise or labor and in turn, it provides a place for people to buy the necessities and desires of life. Thus, cities are large marketplaces with geographically defined boundaries. The primary reason people live in the city is to participate in this market.

Figure 12.1 Meager economic opportunities in rural areas drove many to migrate to the city in search of work. Copyright in the Public Domain.

Migration

Cities did not arise by spontaneous generation. Most cities grew over time via the migration of people from other places. The growth of an urban society is a result of most migrations being of the rural-to-urban or urban-to-urban variety. These urban migrations are a function of economic or social push and pull factors. Push factors are unique to the place where an individual or group originates.

They include the reasons unique to that place that compel people to leave. The 17th-century Puritans were pushed out of Britain because of the religious intolerance they experienced during that time. Many of them were pulled to Boston by the opportunity to practice freely. Presently, push factors for Mexican immigrants include poor economic conditions limiting the availability of jobs in their home country, while pull factors include an opportunity to compete for jobs in the U.S. Not all migrations are purely by choice. Many Jews migrated to escape political and religious persecution in Europe. Many 18th-century Irish emigrated to escape famine.

African Americans were pushed out of the rural South by draconian race laws that truncated their life chances. The Great Migration was not simply African Americans moving from the South to the North. It can be better described as a move from the rural South to urban areas in the South and North. Many such migrants moved to Southern cities like Birmingham to work in the booming steel industry, Atlanta to work in manufacturing, Mobile to work in the factories that supplied goods for the war efforts of World War II, and Houston to work on the ports or in its expanding energy industry. It is a fact that after the Great Migration the majority of African Americans lived in urban areas, but few romanticized versions of the migration point out that a large percentage of African Americans moved to cities in the South. At the dawn of the great migration in 1920, African Americans

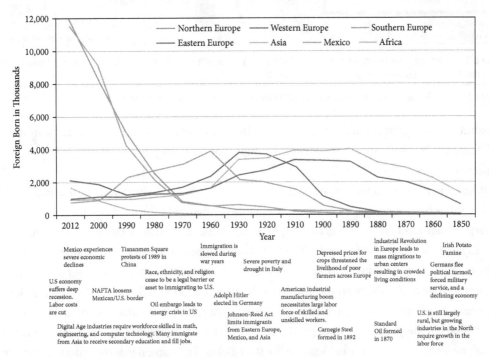

Figure 12.2 Foreign Born Population U.S. Selected Years 1850–2012. U.S. Immigration Trends and Corresponding Push and Pull Factors.

Source: U.S. Census Bureau. (1999). Region and Country or Area of Birth of the Foreign-Born Population, with Geographic Detail Shown in Decennial Census Publications of 1930 or Earlier: 1850 to 1930 and 1960 to 1990. U.S. Census (2014). Place of Birth for the Foreign-Born Population. American Fact Finder.

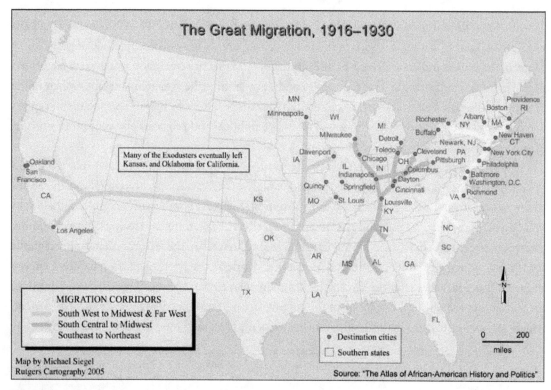

Figure 12.3 African Americans left the rural areas of the South in huge numbers at the turn of the century. They landed in urban areas in the North and South.

Source: http://lewishistoricalsocierty.com/wiki2011/tiki-read_article.php?articleId=29

constituted 26.9% percent of the population in the South and 4.6% of the population in the North and Midwest. By 1960, toward the end of the migration, these figures equated to 20.6% and 13.5%, respectively (U.S. Census, 2002).

While push and pull factors are determined by social and economic conditions, the place of destination is based largely on what migrants have to exchange in the marketplace. Despite the many cultural attractions that a city has to offer, people move to a particular city to participate in market exchange—to work, in other words. The fact that everyone is bringing different expertise is what makes the city diverse. Museums have curators, baseball teams have owners and announcers, and restaurants have cooks. Every product that an individual brings to market—whether it is physical labor, engineering skill, or wholesale foods—has an exchange value. That value determines the associated pay. Moreover, the professions that people bring to the market are diverse but interconnected. The builder needs the architect, the banker, and the steel maker. The nurse needs the orderly, the paramedic, and the medical doctor. The lawyer needs the business-person, the clerk, and the bartender. The city brings all these people together into one centralized, geographically defined place.

Industrialization and Migration

America's transition from a rural society to an urban society is a function of industrialization. The Industrial Revolution in Western Europe and the U.S. pushed people off the rural farms and into rapidly growing urban centers. The process began with mechanization. Mechanization involves using machines to do the work of humans. Mechanization was made possible when humans discovered how to generate power from natural, nonliving resources. Specifically, the discovery of steam and oil byproducts such as kerosene and gasoline were vital, powering the new machine that drove the revolution. Instead of using a horse or ox to plow land, humans could now use a gas-powered plow Instead of using a horse-drawn stagecoach for long-distance travel, one could now use a steam locomotive.

Mechanization had two major effects in 18th-century America. First, it reduced the number of workers needed on a farm. New machines that operated on steam at first and then gas could plow and reap more land in less time. The use of machines was also much cheaper than employing a gang of people to plant or harvest crops, so large farms that needed more than a hundred field hands could be operated with just a few people using machines. The need for labor in rural areas was drastically reduced.

Secondly, mechanization was taking a different form in urban areas. The introduction of the factory system of production meant that companies could produce quantities in large portions like never before. The profits available to those who developed capital led to significant investments into research and development. This engendered a wave of inventions that facilitated the factory production process, such as the piston, which ignites the revolving motion of most engines. Before the factory system, products were typically hand made one by one in a workshop by only a few individuals. Mechanization allowed companies to produce more in less time, which lowered the price of the product. This mass production meant that products that used to take weeks to make by hand could now be developed by the dozen in a day. Cheaper pricing was a key component to creating a consumer culture. Also, cheaper prices meant that companies could buy more supplies and raw materials, which meant they could also be more productive.

Unlike rural farms, the urban factory system created a tremendous need for more labor. Maximum efficiency on a farm required one or two people to do the plowing, sowing, and harvesting. Maximum efficiency

Figure 12.4 The steam engine like the one used in locomotives helped engender wide scale mechanization on the farms and in the factories. Later, the invention of the gasoline powered internal combustion engine also intensified mechanization. Copyright in the Public Domain.

in a factory, or steel mill, in this example, required many people doing one or two tasks at low wages. One person fed the furnace with coal. Another monitored the temperature of the furnace. Several people loaded iron ore onto a conveyer belt that fed the furnace. After melting the ore, the impurities had to be separated. The pure steel then had to be poured into a cast. Then the finished product had to be loaded for transport. This was not a job that could be completed by a few people. As you can see, doing so would have actually compromised efficiency, as this person would have to go from machine to machine doing different tasks. Thus, mechanization pushed people away from the farm and into the city where factories were located.

The need for labor produced by the factory system led to huge migrations of people. During the heart of the Industrial Revolution, booming American cities such as Pittsburgh, Detroit, Birmingham, Cleveland, St. Louis, Milwaukee, and Buffalo teemed with migrants, many of whom were African American or from several countries of Eastern Europe. In fact, many cities, whether they had a large manufacturing presence or not, benefited as railroads and telegraphs allowed them to become just as interconnected as individuals. Pittsburgh's impressive steel industry benefited from financing from banks in New York and Philadelphia. Cleveland's and later Houston's refinery industry benefited from the mass production of the automobile in Detroit. The result is that cities grew in population and urban society as we know it today, with its consumer culture, ethnic diversity, art, and leisure also took shape.

Transition to Urban Society

According to the first U.S. Census in 1790, only 5.1% of the U.S. population lived in urban areas compared to 94.9% living in rural areas. By 1920, the majority of Americans lived in urban areas with 51.2% of residents residing in and around cities compared to 48.8% living in rural areas. By 1990, the number of residents living in urban areas had swelled to 75.2%. Table 12.1 lists the urban/rural population changes from 1790 to 1990. In fact, the percentage of residents living in rural areas has declined every year from 1820, near the beginning of the Industrial Revolution in America until the present (U.S. Census, 2000).

The transition from a rural to an urban society brought former farmers and field hands into a vastly different world. First, they had to adjust to the organization of time. In rural societies, time was governed largely by the day cycle and seasons.

Figure 12.5 There was a higher degree of familiarity in rural society. Copyright in the Public Domain.

Table 12.1 U.S. Urbanization Trends from 1970 to 2010

Year	Urban Population	Rural Population	Percent Urban	Percent Rural	Urban Growth Rate
1790	201,655	3,727,559	5.1	94.9	
1800	322,371	4,986,112	6.1	93.9	19.6%
1810	525,459	6,714,422	7.3	92.7	19.7%
1820	693,255	8,945,198	7.2	92.8	−1.4%
1830	1,127,247	11,733,455	8.8	91.2	22.2%
1840	1,845,055	15,218,298	10.8	89.2	22.7%
1850	3,574,496	19,617,380	15.4	84.6	42.6%
1860	6,216,518	25,226,803	19.8	80.2	28.6%
1870	9,902,361	28,656,010	25.7	74.3	29.8%
1880	14,129,735	36,059,474	28.2	71.8	9.7%
1890	22,106,265	40,873,501	35.1	64.9	24.5%
1900	30,214,832	45,997,336	39.6	60.4	12.8%
1910	42,064,001	50,164,495	45.6	54.4	15.2%
1920	54,253,282	51,768,255	51.2	48.8	12.3%
1930	69,160,599	54,042,025	56.1	43.9	9.6%
1940	74,705,338	57,459,231	56.1	43.9	0.0%
1950	96,846,817	54,478,981	64	36	14.1%
1960	125,268,750	54,045,425	69.9	30.1	9.2%
1970	149,646,617	53,565,309	73.6	26.3	5.3%
1980	167,050,992	59,494,813	73.7	26.3	0.1%
1990	187,053,487	61,656,386	75.2	24.8	2.0%
2000	222,360,539	59,061,367	79	21	5.1%
2010	249,253,271	59,492,267	81	19	2.2%

Sources: United States Census. (2000). Population: 1790–1990. United States Department of Commerce. Retrieved on May 13, 2014 from <http://www.census.gov/population/www/censusdata/files/table-4.pdf> and (2010). Summary File 1. American Fact Finder

Farmers woke at the break of dawn and they worked until sunset. Only certain types of work could be done in the rain or winter. In urban societies, time was governed by the clock. Work started and ended at a scheduled time every day, regardless of the weather or season. The short days of winter had no influence on the number of hours one was scheduled to work.

Secondly, the concept of familiarity was different in urban society. The geographic isolation of rural areas facilitated familiarity with neighbors, even if they lived a mile down the road. In rural areas, people had a high degree of familiarity with those with whom they interacted. This is not the case in urban society. In the city, the majority of people whom you come in contact with are bodies with faces, just "other people" whom you will never see again in your life. Imagine your own life in urban society. Think about the last time you went to the mall or the movies. Other than the employees or your friends, how many of the people who were there have you seen since? The odds are that you will not see the majority of them ever again. We certainly have valued friends and neighbors in the city, but our degree of familiarity and our interactions with others is limited. It is impossible to get to know everyone we come in contact with in the city. Many argue that this degree of familiarity with one another is still declining. In *Bowling Alone,* Robert Putnam (2000) used the concept of social capital to measure the influence of modern social norms on our level of connectedness. Social capital is defined as network ties that can be applied to some useful purpose. Putnam emphasized connectedness mainly through our affiliations with various organizations. He found that since the mid-20th century, we have become less engaged in community, neighborhood, and civic organizations.

The Decline of Industrial Urbanization and the Rise of the Digital Age

The mid- to late 20th century saw a significant decline of the manufacturing of heavy goods in the U.S. Manufacturing could be done cheaper overseas. Foreign countries like Japan and South Korea became more competitive in the automobile industry. American blue-collar labor became more expensive. These are just some of the factors associated with the ongoing demise of the industrial era. Cities that were built on the manufacturing economic model went into decline. The very places that benefited the most from the industrial period suffered the heaviest losses. Today these places are referred to as the Rust Belt. Just as huge migrations occurred with the transition from agrarian to industrial modes of production, society also witnessed a major shift when it changed from the industrial to the digital era. However, this transition promoted moves to the suburbs and cities in the South and Southwest. Thus, the Digital Age prompted urban-to-urban and urban-to-suburban moves.

Table 12.2 illustrates this trend by providing a comparative glance at the fifteen largest cities in 1920, the first decade that the U.S. population was greater in urban areas than rural. Classic Rust Belt cities such as Baltimore, Detroit, Cleveland, and St. Louis that were in the top ten in population in 1920 are no longer in the top ten in 2010. Instead, they have been replaced by cities prominent in the Digital Age technology arena. Austin, Texas, for example, was a dusty town in the American Southwest known primarily as the Texas state capital and home to the University of Texas Longhorns until the Digital Age brought technology jobs and investment into the area. In fact, the technology and service industry has spread throughout the American Southwest and West. Now Austin is the eleventh largest city in America, and the fourth largest in Texas. The rapid population growth exemplifies how Texas, along with the rest of the American Southwest and West, has taken

Table 12.2 Population of Largest Cities in U.S. 1920 and 2010

1920			2010		
Rank	City	Population	Rank	City	Population
1	New York	5,620,048	1	New York	8,175,133
2	Chicago	2,701,705	2	Los Angeles	3,792,621
3	Philadelphia	1,823,779	3	Chicago	2,695,598
4	Detroit	993,078	4	Houston	2,100,263
5	Cleveland	796,841	5	Philadelphia	1,526,006
6	St. Louis	772,897	6	Phoenix	1,445,632
7	Boston	748,060	7	San Antonio	1,327,407
8	Baltimore	733,826	8	San Diego	1,307,402
9	Pittsburgh	588,343	9	Dallas	1,197,816
10	Los Angeles	576,673	10	San Jose	945,942
11	Buffalo	506,775	11	Austin	790,390
12	San Francisco	506,676	12	Jacksonville	821,784
13	Milwaukee	457,147	13	Indianapolis	820,445
14	Washington	437,571	14	San Francisco	805,235
15	Newark	414,524	15	Columbus	787,033
16	Cincinnati	401,247	16	Charlotte	731,424
17	New Orleans	387,219	17	Fort Worth	741,206
18	Minneapolis	380,582	18	Detroit	713,777
19	Kansas City	324,410	19	El Paso	649,121
20	Seattle	315,312	20	Memphis	646,889

Sources: United States Census. (1998). Population of the 100 Largest Urban Places: 1920 and United States Census Bureau. (2012). Top 20 Cities Highest Ranking Cities, 1790 to 2010.

advantage of the economic opportunities associated with the changing economy. One third of America's highest populated cities are in the American Southwest (shaded). Nine out of fifteen are either in the Southwest or West. Two, San Francisco and San Jose, are located in the home of the Digital Age, Silicon Valley.

The growth of San Jose due to the development of digital technology has a unique story. Investment in technology by private and public institutions, notably Stanford University and the Federal Telegraph Company, transformed the rural Santa Clara Valley in California into the world's largest center for software, chip, and web development, known today as Silicon Valley (Adams, 2011). In the ten-year span from 1950 to 1960 that marked the beginning of the chip boom in Silicon Valley, San Jose grew from 95,280 residents to 204,196. By the time of the dot-com era of the 1990s, its population had grown to 782,248. Today, San Jose with a population of 945,942, is one of the largest cities in the

United States. Importantly, it has the highest per capita income of any large city in the country (U.S. Census, 2010).

Suburbanization

Another key feature of post-industrial urban society was the migration of people from the central city to the suburbs. The phrase "metropolitan statistical area" (MSA) or metro, for short, refers to the area covering the suburbs and the central city. Over the last half century, the percentage of people and jobs moving to the suburbs has steadily increased. Because of

Figure 12.6 Detroit is the de facto capital of the Rust Belt. Copyright © no body atoll (CC by 2.0) at http://commons.wikimedia.org/wiki/File:Russell_Industrial_Complex,_Detroit,_Michigan.jpg.

the influx of people and capital that have moved to the suburbs, the metro area has become the primary reference point when examining a city. For example, if someone says she lives in Atlanta, chances are she lives in the suburbs and not the actual city. The population of the principal city of Atlanta is 420,003, which would make it a midsized city in terms of population; however, its metro population is 5,268,860, which makes it one of the largest in the U.S. (U.S. Census, 2010). This trend is consistent throughout the U.S. Ironically, most people today live in urban society, but few actually live in the city.

During the infant stages of the Digital Age in the 1950s, 57% of metro residents and 70% of metro jobs were located inside central cities. By the dawn of the dot-com era in the early 1990s, those numbers had shrunk to 37% and 45%, respectively (Mieszkowski and Mills, 1993). Today a majority of urban residents live outside of the city center. What were the causes of this exodus from the city center?

Figure 12.7 The suburbs provided the middle class a geographic class barrier, more space, and an opportunity to disconnect from the work environment of the central city. Copyright © Andrew Bossi (CC by 2.5) at http://commons.wikimedia.org/wiki/Category:Suburbia#mediaviewer/File:2008_04_03_-_Beltsville_-_Old_Gunpowder_Road_at_Sinope_Way.JPG.

Peter Mieszkowski and Edwin Mills (1993) addressed this question in their classic study of suburbanization.

One explanation put forward by the authors is that during the industrial period, jobs were located near key transportation hubs, which were typically located inside the city. Specifically, ports and railroad stations were key to moving heavy manufactured goods. As a means of increasing efficiency, factories tended to be located nearby. The proximity to transportation reduced the cost of moving goods from the factory to distant markets. Then more so than now, people tended to live relatively close to their jobs. In those days, many people commuted to work by means of

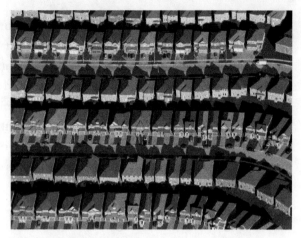

Figure 12.8 Standardization, a hallmark of the digital age, is often visible in suburban housing design. In fact, the issue of "sameness" has been a consistent criticism of the suburbs. Copyright © IDuke (CC by 2.5) at http://commons.wikimedia.org/wiki/File:Markham-suburbs_id.jpg.

walking, streetcar, subway, or in later cases, a car or bus. Automobiles became a favorite for many Americans, but the inadequacy of roadways made long-distance travel to work cumbersome. The creation of the interstate system was a major infrastructural change in the American landscape that engendered changes in how we travel long distance and commute to work. The interstate system, funded by the federal government under President Eisenhower, provided viable means of traveling by automobile. Freeways stretched beyond the central city into the metro area. The freeways, in combination with more affordable automobiles, made traveling longer distances easier.

An increase in living space was another factor that led people to the suburbs. The availability of cheap land on the outskirts of cities enticed many residents of the central city to move. This, along with the availability of home financing through banks supported by the Federal Housing Administration, made it possible to build bigger homes on larger tracts of land. The increase in land size was attractive because it provided a means for private leisure. It also provided an opportunity for people to disconnect from the workspace. Central cities that engaged in heavy industry were often crowded and polluted. The suburbs provided a way for people to escape the fast pace and grime of the industrial city.

Furthermore, the suburbs offered an opportunity for people to solidify their class status by living among those who share the same socioeconomic status (Mieszkowski and Mills, 1993). Because of the intense need for labor and the division of such labor, central cities tended to be ethnically and economically diverse. The suburbs offered an opportunity for middle-class and affluent residents to develop exclusive towns and bedroom communities consisting of people from the same racial, ethnic, and socioeconomic class. There they could develop cultural norms befitting their ilk.

The outmigration of jobs also played a role in suburbanization. The places where people work in the Digital Age are different from those of the industrial era. Far fewer people today are employed in large factories or mills. Automation has reduced the number of people needed to work on docks, in warehouses, or in factories. Today, people are engaged in service industries. Healthcare is one of the fastest growing industries in America. Hospitals or clinics can be located anywhere in the metro area. Many of them are located on the outskirts of the central city. Furthermore, an increasing number of people are able to work from home or in satellite offices located near home. The spread of jobs throughout the metro area has placed more emphasis on beltway communities—areas adjacent to a freeway that circles the outer boundaries of a city.

White Flight and Redlining

The rush to the suburbs was largely a racially homogenous phenomenon. The initial decline in central city population was characterized by an influx of white residents migrating to the suburbs. As described, many of these residents were simply leaving in search of a more comfortable and productive life. Even before suburbanization, cities were typically divided by race. However, the migration of whites from the central city led to a multitude of political and economic consequences still felt today. As stated above, the move to the suburbs was characterized by the affluent and middle class migrating beyond the city center. The loss of economically viable residents had an adverse impact on the local tax base.

There is solid empirical research suggesting that property values within central cities' neighborhoods tend to decline as African Americans began moving into predominantly white areas (Emerson et al., 2001; Harris, 1999). The perception of African Americans as threats to property value may have prompted some whites to leave the city, even though the first wave of African Americans who moved into white neighborhoods were themselves middle class. The suburbs offered whites an opportunity to protect their property values while reifying their class status.

The outmigration of "preferred" residents to the suburbs and the inmigration of residents whose presence caused property values to decline led to an overall drop in revenue collected by the principal city. Further, declines in revenue followed as property and sales taxes suffered from the loss of economically viable residents. Such revenue is vital for funding public goods, such as

Figure 12.9 With the outmigration of middle class residents to the suburbs, central cities were less able to raise the necessary revenue to function at their previous levels.

parks, schools, and libraries. As neighborhoods progressively lost financial value, they began to attract lower-income residents whose cultural values did not always correlate with the current generation of residents who were, incidentally, mostly African Americans, but middle class. This prompted middle-class African Americans to outmigrate. The process can be expressed in this manner: Middle-class and affluent whites left when middle-class African Americans arrived. Middle-class African Americans left when lower middle-class African Americans arrived. Lower-middle-class African Americans left when the poor African Americans arrived. Thus, a vicious circle was created, expediting turnover to the point where neighborhoods that were once middle class had become fully disadvantaged.

Cities became increasingly black and poor. In several instances, the principal city became associated with crime, blight, and disinvestment. The remaining residents were socially isolated from valuable resources that facilitate social mobility. For the past thirty years, Paul Jargowsky and Douglas Massey have examined the causes and effects of urban poverty. Massey (1990) argues that the social and economic isolation from being systematically excluded from the U.S. opportunity structure is a fundamental cause of persistent poverty in principal cities. What were specific policies that brought about this systematic exclusion?

The federal government, real estate elite, and banks played a role in promoting segregation through suburbanization. Through a practice called redlining, they were able to ensure that suburbanization was a mostly white phenomenon. In their estimate, it was the best financial practice, given the inverse association between African Americans and property values. Many African American neighborhoods were affected by these exclusionary policies because they limited the ability of residents to purchase high-quality housing (Hannon, 2012). From the Great Depression until the late 1960s, the institutions above participated in the systematic practice of denying loans and insurance to African Americans (Freund, 2007; Hillier, 2003). This practice included identifying African American neighborhoods as risk hazards by using red lines (redlining) to chart these areas (Freund, 2007; Hillier, 2003).

The Federal Housing Administration (FHA), created by Franklin Roosevelt in response to the housing crisis emanating from the Great Depression, refused to underwrite

Figure 12.10 Redlining of minority neighborhoods in Philadelphia. Copyright in the Public Domain.

loans in red areas. Because of this, lenders were hesitant to provide financing to homebuyers without FHA support. Gail Radford (1996) maintains that a two-tiered system was enacted to ensure racial homogeneity in low-risk areas where white middle-class residents received loans underwritten by the FHA or VA (Veterans Administration) to purchase homes. Potential homeowners who were African American were steered toward public housing and government rental programs (Johnson, 2010; Hoffman, 2007; Radford, 1996).

The practice of discriminatory commerce by government policymakers and private business leaders effectively excluded many African Americans from homeownership and helped ignite the mass migration of white residents to low-risk designations, primarily in suburban areas. The outmigration to the suburbs that followed became known as white flight. The process of redlining contributed to race-based geographic segregation. This form of institutionalized racism limited the opportunities for African American homeownership, curtailing opportunities for tax credits, wealth-building, and neighborhood stability (Hannon, 2012; Johnson, 2010).

Downtown Revitalizations

While suburbs across the United States are still growing today, a concerted effort by policymakers and urban dwellers to revitalize the downtown districts of many cities is underway. The new loft districts capitalized from policies dating back to the late 1980s. In an attempt to mitigate high-poverty areas in principal cities, the National Commission on Severely Distressed Housing suggested that a decade-long program be established to address the problem of public housing in America. The program would cost $750 million per year and was initially titled the Urban Revitalization Demonstration. The name was later changed to HOPE VI (Housing Opportunities for People Everywhere). HOPE VI won Congressional approval in 1992 and came into existence the following year during the Clinton Administration (Popkin et al., 2004). With research on the poor living conditions of public housing projects, deteriorating downtowns, and reports on

Figure 12.11 Loft districts are a nationwide trend that reflect gentrification efforts in the central city. Copyright in the Public Domain.

the negative effects of concentrated poverty in hand, HOPE VI became the panacea for distressed housing and urban blight. According to Popkin and others (2004), policymakers wanted to help citizens "relocate to better neighborhoods" and "create healthier, mixed income communities in place of the distressed public housing developments."

The HOPE VI program was a part of a much larger focus on healing urban areas devastated by globalization, the absence of manufacturing jobs, and suburbanization. The Empowerment Zone program was a broad attempt to bring together public and private capital with the purpose of eliminating the causes and outcomes of concentrated poverty. The Empowerment Zone program invested billions of dollars of government aid to eligible cities through block grants and tax incentives (Rich and Stoker, 2014). To become eligible, applicants had to develop a strategy for helping such areas become self-sufficient through the use of public and private investment. The Empowerment Zone program encouraged collaboration among investors, community groups, and local governments. Importantly, the initiative required participants to establish employment networks between those living in Empowerment Zones and opportunities existing in affluent parts of the metropolitan area. This type of cooperative regionalism was intended to distribute economic opportunities from areas of concentrated affluence to those of concentrated poverty (Rich and Stoker, 2014).

Programs like HOPE VI and the Empowerment Zone initiative created a wave of gentrification in urban neighborhoods. Gentrification is the process of applying investment capital to an economically disadvantaged area in an effort to raise its overall financial value. This process involves the development of new or renovated homes, shops, and the built environment. The fact that these areas are disadvantaged makes land and property relatively inexpensive. If the investment is successful, then the developers stand to profit. Relics of the industrial era such as abandoned warehouses and factories have been renovated for private use as meeting spaces, lofts, or restaurants. Locations such as Washington Avenue in St. Louis and Water Street in Cleveland have benefited from these opportunities.

Urban revitalization efforts are often intended to entice educated, middle-class residents to move into areas that were once blighted. In turn, the middle-class residents will attract amenities like bars, coffee houses, Panera Bread and Chipotle restaurants, strip malls, and BMW dealerships. While this strategy has seen various rates of success around the country, we are still left to wonder about the fate of the poor residents who lived in the area before the revitalization. The HOPE VI plan called for mixed-income housing. That is, a percentage of the revitalized housing had to be reserved for poor residents. In other cases, low-income homeowners may have been compelled to sell their property at basement rates and move to other parts of the city, specifically inner-ring suburbs. They are described as "inner ring" because they tend to be located right outside the city and they were the first location of migrants who fled the city. Many within the first wave of migrants have long abandoned the inner-ring suburbs for many of the same reasons they originally abandoned the city. Many of them have now moved to more remote locations in the suburbs or exurbs.

Discussion Questions

1. Why in your opinion were certain cities able to profit during the industrial era, but not during the Digital Age? What cities prospered during both periods and why?

2. Do you see the mass migration to the suburbs as a natural process in human development as we continuously seek to make improvements in life quality? Why or why not?

3. The technology associated with mechanization led people away from the farms and into the factories. Then technology played a role in the decline of manufacturing. What effect will the next wave of technology have on the job market?

4. Many inner-ring suburbs are struggling today as the original middle-class residents have been replaced by lower-income residents. How does the relationship between jobs, residence, and infrastructure affect the migration into an area?

5. What specific traits will be needed for cities to thrive in the future? Remember, cities are marketplaces.

Key Terms

Push Factors   Factors unique to the place where an individual or group originates that compel them to migrate to another place.

Pull Factors   Factors of an area different from the current residence of an individual or group that compel them to migrate to that area.

Mechanization   The use of machines to do the work of humans.

Social Capital   Network ties that can be applied to some useful purpose.

Rust Belt   American cities that once thrived on heavy industry and manufacturing that now experience some degree of decline due to their failure to transition to digital-age modes of production.

Beltway Communities   Areas adjacent to the beltway freeway that circles the outer boundaries of large cities.

Gentrification   The process of applying investment capital to an economically disadvantaged area in an effort to raise its overall financial value.

Exurbs   The areas extending beyond the suburban communities.

References

Adams, Stephen B. (2011). "Growing Where You Are Planted: Exogenous Firms and the Seeding of Silicon Valley." *Research Policy*, 40(3):368–379.

Emerson, Michael O., George Yancey, and Karen J. Chai. (2001). "Does Race Matter in Residential Segregation? Exploring the Preferences of White Americans." *American Sociological Review*, 66(6):922–935.

Freund, D. M. P. (2007). *Colored Property: State Policy and White Racial Politics in Suburban America.* University of Chicago Press: Chicago.

Hannon, Lonnie. (2001). "The Astronomy of Urban Streetscapes." Self-published: Birmingham, AL.

Hannon, Lonnie. (2012). "Housing, the Neighborhood Environment, and Physical Activity Among Older African Americans." *Journal of Health Disparities Research and Practice*, 5(3):27–40.

Harris, David, (1999). "Property Values Drop When Blacks Move In, Because ..." Racial and Socioeconomic Determinants of Neighborhood Desirability. *American Sociological Review*, 64(3):461–479.

Hillier, Amy E. (2007). "Redlining and the Home Owners' Loan Corporation." *Journal of Urban History*, 29(4):394–420.

Hoffman, Alexander Von. (2000). "A Study in Contradictions: The Origins and Legacy of the Housing Act of 1949." *Housing Policy Debate*, 11(2):299–326.

Johnson, Marcia. (2010). "Will the Current Economic Crisis Fuel a Return to Racial Policies That Deny Home-ownership Opportunities and Wealth?" *The Modern American*, 6(1):25–46.

Massey, Douglas S. (1990). "American Apartheid: Segregation and the Making of the Underclass." *The American Journal of Sociology,* 96:329–357.

Mieszkowski, Peter and Edwin S. Mills. (1993). "The Causes of Metropolitan Suburbanization." *The Journal of Economic Perspectives*, 7(3):135–147.

Popkin, Susan J., Bruce Katz, Mary K. Cunningham, Karen Brown, Jeremy Brown, Jeremy Gustafson, and Margery A. Turner. (2004). "A Decade of Hope VI: Research Findings and Policy Challenges." Washington, DC: Urban Institute.

Putnam, Robert. (2000). *Bowling Alone: The Collapse and Revival of American Community.* Simon and Schuster: New York.

Radford, Gail. (1996). *Modern Housing for America: Policy Struggles in the New Era.* University of Chicago Press: Chicago.

Rich, Michael J. and Robert P. Stoker. (2014). *Collaborative Governance for Urban Revitalization: Lessons from Empowerment Zones.* Cornell University Press: Ithaca.

United States Census Bureau. (2000). Population: 1790–1990. United States Department of Commerce. Retrieved on May 13, 2014 from <http://www.census.gov/population/www/censusdata/files/table-4.pdf>.

United States Census Bureau. (2002). Demographic Trends in the 20th Century. United States Department of Commerce. Retrieved on May 15, 2014 from <http://www.census.gov/prod/2002pubs/censr-4.pdf>.

United States Census Bureau. (2010). Summary File 1. American Fact Finder. United States Department of Commerce.

United States Census Bureau. (2012a). Top 20 Cities Highest Ranking Cities, 1790 to 2010. United States Department of Commerce. Retrieved on May 13, 2014 from <http://www.census.gov/dataviz/visualizations/007/>.

CHAPTER 13

Social Change and Social Movements

Social change is inevitable in every aspect of characteristics related to globalization, consumption, art, leisure, and the Internet. Chapter 13 examines social change by focusing on revolutionary and evolutionary development of social structures. This chapter is expanded with Marx and Weber's views on social change in society. Post-modernity is a useful term used in this chapter to argue links between new localism, reestablishing traditional cultural practices, and fundamentalism. Episodes of collective identity and behavior are discussed in the information society or network society to understand why people participate in social movements. Resource mobilization theory and new social movement theory are employed to demonstrate distinction between social movements.

Social Change, Collective Action, and Social Movements

Jeffrey C. Alexander and Kenneth Thompson

....

Thereare two main ways of looking at social change: We can focus either on major shifts of a *revolutionary* kind or on steady *evolutionary* development. A phenomenon related to the former perspective was the media hype surrounding the so-called digital revolution, illustrated by stories about get-rich-quick, dot-com millionaires in Silicon Valley. These enterprising individuals, it was said, had faith in themselves and their ability to succeed, and thereby brought about a revolution. Bill Gates's success story is the most famous example. It was only after the crash in technology shares in 2000 that commentators began to ask whether the reality of social change might be more complex. Before that, in 1999, a typical bullish story about Silicon Valley would have had the same breathless quality as the opening lines of the box titled "Generation Equity." Yet only a short time later this sunny vista was clouded over.

Taken together, the two items in this box raise questions about the nature of social change, especially change referred to as revolutionary. The first is an excerpt from a story that originally appeared in *Wired*—a glamorous story about the digital revolution. Pictured on the cover are five young entrepreneurs dressed in fashionable black, with glowing faces and a "deal with it" pose, framed against a clear blue sky—with no clouds on the horizon. They resemble the crew of *Star Trek*. They believe their mission has "historical implications." This, it is said, is no gold rush or mass mania, unlike many earlier episodes of irrational collective behavior. The media assure them that they are part of something bigger and historic—a revolution.

By 2001, less than two years after the *Wired* magazine story appeared, their dream lay in tatters. As detailed in the box's second item, they were now being informed that they had been victims of a "naïve delusion," a "classic bubble," or an "elaborate con job."

An Individual or a Social Story?

One possible lesson to be learned from this 2001 follow-up is that we should be wary of media stories of dramatic change brought about by individuals who, at the same time that they are transforming society, are themselves being transformed from "rags to riches." The belief in individual enterprise—the optimistic conviction that the individual is capable of making a difference—is part of the **American dream** (sometimes also referred to as the *American ideology*). But it is counterbalanced for many people by an awareness that, in their own lives, things may not be so simple. Meanwhile, on the larger stage of society and history, bringing about major social change is usually a complex process involving gradual institutional transformations—some the result of technological inventions and individual innovations, others the result of social movements or collective efforts over a long period of time. The question is especially pertinent today: Are we living through a **social revolution,** a transformation of the social order from one type of society to another?

Analyzing Social Change

The **evolutionary view of social change** is the one favored by most sociologists. However, sociologists have also recognized that the accumulation of changes may eventually result in a transformation that amounts to a *revolution*—that is, a change from one type of social order to another type. For example, the great theorist of revolutionary change, Karl Marx, believed there would eventually be a revolutionary change of the capitalist social order to a socialist society (albeit one that would occur only after capitalism had developed through all its possible stages). He even suggested that in some countries, such as America and England, there would be a peaceful revolution, owing to their particular cultures and institutions (cited in Tucker 1978: 523). But in most countries, Marx argued, revolution could be expected to occur as the result of a final violent struggle by workers to overcome the resistance of the capitalist class, which, in turn, would fight to defend its wealth and power.

Usually, when sociologists talk about a social revolution, they are referring to a phenomenon different from the one that political commentators mean when they describe the overthrow of one type of political regime by another. A *social revolution* involves a fundamental change in social practices. So, when a revolution is described as a change in society as a whole, the word *society* is often included in the identifying phrase—such as *information society*. Some contemporary writers on the theme of social revolution, especially the digital revolution (also known as the *information revolution*), echo their nineteenth-century predecessors in presenting a picture that is a mix of long-term developments and revolutionary change. A typical example is the work of the famous "futurologist" Alvin Toffler, who has written over a dozen best sellers, starting back in 1970 with *Future Shock*. Toffler presents, in a popular form, ideas about stages of social development that can be traced back to the founders of sociology (e.g., Auguste Comte and Herbert Spencer) and have been elaborated by their successors to take account of the complexity of contemporary changes. The central premise is that human history, though complex and contradictory, can be seen to fit a pattern. According to Toffler, this pattern has manifested as three great advances or waves:

- The first wave of transformation began about 10,000 years ago when someone, probably a woman, planted a seed and nurtured its growth. That was the beginning of the *agricultural age*, and its social significance was that people moved away from nomadic wandering and hunting and began to cluster into villages and develop an elaborate culture. Wealth was land.
- The second wave, the *industrial age* or machine age, was based on machine power; commencing in the eighteenth century, it gathered momentum after America's Civil War. People began to leave the peasant culture of farming to work in city factories. This wave culminated in World War II, during which machine-age juggernauts clashed and atomic bombs exploded over Japan. Wealth diversified into three factors of production: land, labor, and capital.
- The third wave, the *information age* or knowledge age, is said to characterize our current era. Based on mind rather than muscle, it is powerfully driven by information technology. Wealth is increasingly contingent on the possession of knowledge/information.

This three-stage model of historical development has a long history. Sociologists in the nineteenth century (including Comte) could not have anticipated the development of the computer, but they did have a futuristic view that encompassed a vision of the increasing importance of scientific knowledge and associated social changes. Contemporary analysts such as Toffler have the advantage of being able to contrast some of the emerging characteristics of the computer age with aspects of the earlier industrial age.

A central characteristic of the industrial age was centralization and **standardization.** At its height, everything was "mass," from mass production to mass destruction. The task of factory workers was to turn out the longest possible line of identical products. This was one point on which there was agreement between the assembly-line capitalist Henry Ford and the leader of communist Russia (then called the U.S.S.R.) Joseph Stalin. The bureaucracy and pyramid power structure of the industrial age had many faults, but at its best it was efficient at turning out large quantities of standardized goods. One drawback was the sameness of the goods. As Henry Ford explained, "They can have a car any color they like, so long as it's black."

The pressures of competition led the giant producers of standardized goods to seek to *differentiate* their products and to satisfy (or create) different tastes. The arrival of computer technology brought about a period of transition in which the massive corporations were able to begin to provide more differentiated products for "niche markets." The large manufacturers of automobiles increased their range of vehicles to satisfy different market segments—sports utility vehicles (SUVs) for families with small children to ferry around, sports cars for affluent young singles, and saloon cars with varying engine sizes and accessories to suit different income levels. Even the humdrum cup of coffee underwent this series of changes. In the 1920s, towns still varied in terms of the kind of coffee they had available, but by the 1970s it was the likes of Maxwell House and McDonald's that made sure you had the same limited choice of coffee everywhere you went. In the 1990s many small coffeehouses sprang up, offering a rich variety of choices to satisfy consumer preferences, with ingredients and combinations that would have seemed exotic only a decade or two previously. Today, you can have industrial-age McDonald's-style standardization combined with information-age product choice simply by walking into one of the thousands of Starbucks coffee shops nationwide (soon to be worldwide). If anything, people are beginning to complain about too much choice—choice overload!

As the coffee example makes clear, it wasn't just cars, furniture, and other household goods that were standardized in the industrial age. Many forms of culture and entertainment were also standardized for sale to mass markets. The Marxist sociologists in the famous Frankfurt Institute, founded before World War II in Germany, were fierce critics of the capitalist "culture industry"—especially that of Hollywood, which they accused of providing standardized culture for the masses. Whether mass culture had the kind of degrading ideological effects on working people that the Frankfurt critics imagined has been disputed. However, mass culture did not vanish with the arrival of the information society. Hollywood blockbusters, million-selling popular music recordings, and TV soap opera series are still very much around. But alongside these are many demassified niches. The Internet, for example, boasts thousands of special-interest newsgroups. This is the "plus side" of the current era. On the "negative side," however, it should be noted that the Internet has promoted a surge in hate groups. In March 1998, the *Los Angeles Times* ran an article reporting an all-time high of 474 hate groups in the United States; in just three years, 163 new websites had appeared on the Internet to preach hatred (Serrano 1998).

Inequalities of opportunity are also being reported. Access to the Internet is still markedly unequal among ethnic and income groups in the United States; in 2000, for example, 77 percent of white non-Hispanic children were living in homes with computers, compared with only 43 percent of African-American children and 37 percent of Hispanic children (U.S. Department of Education 2003). Indeed, determining the presence of a computer and the Internet among households is an effective way of measuring the digital divide in the United States. Table 13.1 illustrates this divide as a function of race/Hispanic origin, education, and family income.

The digital divide at the global level can be cal calculated using measures such as access to information and communications technology (ICT). Table 13.2 lists Digital Access Index values for the twenty highest-ranked and twenty lowest-ranked countries based on five variables: "availability of infrastructure, affordability of access, educational level, quality of ICT services, and Internet usage" (International Telecommunication Union 2003). The original study analyzed a total of 178 economies.

Returning to the "plus side" we find that the information age has witnessed a welcome increase in the number and variety of radio stations, offering music to suit all tastes, from classical to zydeco, and catering to different ethnic groups. In 1980 there were only 67 Spanish-language stations in the

TABLE 13.1 Presence of a Computer and the Internet Among U.S. Households, by Race/Hispanic Origin, Education, and Income, 2001

Characteristics	Total Households*	Presence of a Computer		Presence of the Internet	
		Yes Percentage	No Percentage	Yes Percentage	No Percentage
Total Households	109,106	56.3	43.7	50.4	49.6
RACE/HISPANIC ORIGIN					
White	90,680	58.6	41.4	52.7	47.3
White not Hispanic	80,734	60.9	39.1	55.2	44.8
Black	13,304	37.3	62.7	31.1	68.9
Asian/Pacific Islander	4,081	72.3	27.7	67.5	32.5
Hispanic (of any race)	10,476	40.0	60.0	32.2	67.8
EDUCATION					
Less than high school graduate	17,463	23.2	76.8	18.0	82.0
High school graduate or GED	33,469	46.4	53.6	39.7	60.3
Some college or associate's degree	29,410	64.5	35.5	57.7	42.3
Bachelor's degree	18,457	78.4	21.6	73.8	26.2
Advanced degree	10,308	82.2	17.8	77.7	22.3
FAMILY INCOME					
Total Families	**74,044**	**64.6**	**35.4**	**57.9**	**42.1**
Less than $5,000	1,322	27.9	72.1	20.5	79.5
$5,000–$9,999	2,287	24.6	75.4	18.0	82.0
$10,000–$14,999	3,656	31.6	68.4	23.5	76.5
$15,000–$19,999	3,034	36.0	64.0	24.9	75.1
$20,000–$29,999	8,274	46.2	53.8	36.7	63.3
$30,000–$39,999	7,891	59.3	40.7	50.9	49.1
$40,000–$49,999	6,307	71.5	28.5	63.1	36.9
$50,000–$59,999	6,334	76.3	23.7	68.7	31.3
$60,000–$74,999	6,727	82.7	17.3	76.8	23.2
$75,000 or more	16,472	90.8	9.2	87.0	13.0
Not reported	11,740	53.6	46.4	48.2	51.8

Note: Numbers in thousands.
Source: U.S. Bureau of the Census (2001b: Table 1A).

TABLE 13.2 Access to Information and Communications Technology (ICT), by Country, 2002

Highest Access	DAI*	Lowest Access	DAI*
Sweden	0.85	Gambia	0.13
Denmark	0.83	Bhutan	0.13
Iceland	0.82	Sudan	0.13
Korea (Rep.)	0.82	Comoros	0.13
Norway	0.79	Côte d'Ivoire	0.13
Netherlands	0.79	Eritrea	0.1
Hong Kong, China	0.79	D.R. Congo	0.12
Finland	0.79	Benin	0.12
Taiwan, China	0.79	Mozambique	0.12
Canada	0.78	Angola	0.11
United States	0.78	Burundi	0.10
United Kingdom	0.77	Guinea	0.10
Switzerland	0.76	Sierra Leone	0.10
Singapore	0.75	Central African Rep.	0.10
Japan	0.75	Ethiopia	0.10
Luxembourg	0.75	Guinea-Bissau	0.10
Austria	0.75	Chad	0.10
Germany	0.74	Mali	0.09
Australia	0.74	Burkina Faso	0.08
Belgium	0.74	Niger	0.04

*On a scale of 0 to 1, where 1 = highest access. Digital Access Index (DAI) values are shown to hundreds of a decimal point. Countries with the same DAI value are ranked by thousands of a decimal point.
Source: International Telecommunication Union (2003).

United States, but by 2000, according to the Arbitron ratings service, at least 559 of the nation's 12,800 stations were broadcasting in Spanish. Chronicling the long march of Spanish-language radio from Miami and Los Angeles to the rural towns of the Rocky Mountains, the Southeast, and the Great Plains, the *Los Angeles Times* reported: "Every month, it seems, another station gives up its English format—oldies or talk—in favor of what's known in the business as 'regional Mexican.' From one night to the next, the airwaves switch from farm reports and Howard Stern to the oom-pah-pah beat of the *norteña* and the wailing ballads of the *ranchera* and the *corrido*" (Tobar 2000).

Also on the rise, however, are "shock talk" radio programs, in which aggression and intolerance are worrying features. Some media sociologists even argue that the trend toward increasing diversity of radio content has begun to reverse direction. The evidence they cite is the massive consolidation that occurred following deregulation of ownership in 1996, with just a few giant media companies owning hundreds of radio stations. This "huge wave of consolidation," the trade publication *Variety* observed in 1999, "has turned music stations into cash cows that focus on narrow play lists aimed at squeezing the most revenue from the richest demographics" (Stern 1999: 8).

According to the media watchdogs at the Project for Excellence in Journalism, the degree of consolidation in radio is not only greater than that in other media, such as television, but also more insinuating—in particular, because "technology has made it ever easier to seamlessly splice pieces of local information into a generic broadcast to give the appearance that the programming is local." Accordingly, "radio listeners may not give a second thought to what company might stand behind their local radio station. They may be aware of the presence of corporations like Clear Channel or Infinity Broadcasting, but they might not understand how large their presence is. More than that, they might not know what impact the ownership question has on what they listen to" (Project for Excellence in Journalism 2004: 8). In fact, Clear Channel has the largest ownership of radio stations by a wide margin (see Figure 13.1).

The changes that have occurred in the economy and culture of the United States—from the massification and standardization of industrial society to the diversity said to be characteristic of the information society—have certainly not been clear-cut. Some features of the old order exist alongside those of the new, suggesting that the present period may be one of transition. In some areas there may even be reversals of trends, as in the context of radio-content diversity, which we discussed earlier, or in the economic sphere where corporations seek to maintain profits by taking over competitors or reducing the variety of products. Toffler regards such reversals as merely temporary setbacks in the inevitable development of the information society. He is less optimistic, however, about certain other social changes associated with the information society, such as the proliferation of family types that are replacing the standard industrial-age nuclear family, which had a working father and a stay-at-home mother. These new family types include the remarrieds, the adopteds, the blended family, the single-parent family, the same-sex family, the zero-parent family, the family of convenience, and the virtual family. Toffler expresses concern about the effects of this fracturing

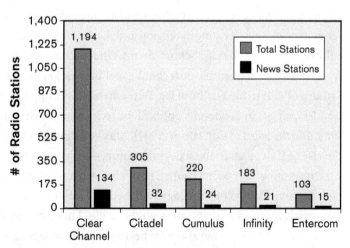

Figure 13.1 Number of Stations Owned by Top Five Companies, 2004

Source: PEJ (2005).

of the American family that has occurred in the past thirty years, but it is, after all, in keeping with other recent social changes, especially the demands for greater individual freedom and choice.

Toffler's sweeping view of history, divided into three waves, is reminiscent of the work of nineteenth-century theorists such as Comte, Spencer, and Durkheim, as we will see. Other contemporary sociologists have not been quite so ambitious. When they do talk about *postindustrial society* or the *information age*, they are likely to specify contradictory developments and a limited range of changes. This point is well illustrated by Daniel Bell's theory of postindustrial society and Manuel Castells's theory of the information society (or *network society*, as he now calls it), both of which we consider later in the chapter.

How have sociologists attempted to develop precise accounts of social change?

Defining Social Change

Admittedly, it may not be very profitable to attempt a precise definition of **social change,** because the term refers to so many different phenomena that such a definition would likely end up being too broad or omitting something important. Nevertheless, we can recommend the usage offered by Wilbert Moore, who defines *social change* as the "significant alteration of social structures" and by *social structures* means "patterns of social action and interaction" (Moore 1967: 3). Moore's definition has the advantage of focusing on observable patterns of social action, such as changes in family and work patterns; however, it gives little specific attention to various cultural elements, such as values, norms, and beliefs, which may not be so easily observable. This is not to say that culture is less relevant to social change than are structures. But it is important to stress that culture should not be seen as a static set of norms, values, and beliefs, contrasted with the more dynamic social structures. Culture is a dynamic dimension of social practices or social actions. Being a member of a culture involves being engaged in a variety of practices that are distinguishable from those of other cultures and other times, ranging from ways of eating to religion and family life (Calhoun 1992: 280). It is true that elements of culture may sometimes lag behind changes in structure, as when religious beliefs and rituals change more slowly than scientific or technological innovations—a phenomenon that sociologist William Ogburn (1964) termed **cultural lag.** But sometimes the opposite is the case, such that cultural changes lead to changes in economic, political, or technological structures. For example, in *The Protestant Ethic and the Spirit of Capitalism* (1904), Max Weber illustrated how changes in religion—specifically, the rise of Calvinism in the sixteenth century—influenced the development of capitalism.

Questions about social change have always been central to sociology. The social thinkers who laid the foundations of sociology in the nineteenth century were concerned about the impact of industrialization and urbanization on social life. They not only faced upheaval in their own societies in Europe and America but also were hearing reports of seemingly "primitive" tribal and clan societies in Africa and the indigenous peoples of America and Australasia. There was talk of cannibalism, polygamy, totemism, and magic.

Increased information and curiosity about less developed "primitive" societies raised questions about the nature of "modernity" and the direction of human development. The early sociological theories of social change focused on the stages of social development over long periods of time and throughout whole societies or even civilizations. In other words, they tended to be macrosocial, historical theories of development. "Modernization" and "progress" were the key motifs common to most of these theories. However, the early theorists diverged over whether to explain these developments in terms of social evolution or social revolution.

Social evolutionary theories viewed social change as advancing gradually through certain basic stages of development, such as from "military society" to "industrial society," and from simple agrarian forms to more complex industrial-urban ones. They were developed in the nineteenth century by some of the first thinkers to refer to themselves as sociologists—Auguste Comte, Herbert Spencer, and Émile Durkheim. In the mid-twentieth century, aspects of this evolutionary view were still to be found in *functionalism*, which regarded social change as the adaptation of a social system to its environment through **differentiation** (specialization of the parts) and increasing structural complexity (Parsons 1951b). For example, the institution of the family became more limited in its functions, and some of its former functions were taken over by institutions in other spheres such as education and the economy. By contrast, *theories of revolutionary change*, such as those deriving from Karl Marx, emphasized increasing *conflict* among different parts of society—particularly different economic groups (classes)—as the fundamental source of social change. The distinction between these two sets of theories can be illustrated in terms of the different images they favored: A typical functionalist image was that of society evolving gradually like the human organism from infancy to maturity, whereas Marx's conflict theory of revolutionary social change led him to prefer metaphors such as the sudden and sometimes violent emergence of the new baby from the womb, preceded by a period of painful labor.

These all-encompassing, macrosocial theories of development—sometimes referred to as **metanarratives**—began to come under sustained criticism in the second half of the twentieth century. They seemed to be attempting to explain too much—to be claiming to have discovered a kind of universal pattern of development. For example, Comte's social evolutionary theory of human development maintained that all humankind passed through three stages of intellectual development—theological reasoning, metaphysical thought, and positive (scientific) reasoning—and that these corresponded to three stages of social development—primitive military society, an intermediate stage of defensive military organization and a gradual switch of emphasis to production, and finally, modern industrial society.

One early twentieth-century theorist who warned against generalizations of this sort was Max Weber. Although he talked about long-term changes similar to those described by the other theorists, he emphasized the limited and specific historical character of social forms, such as Western capitalism and the modern form of bureaucratic organization. This approach proved attractive to professional sociologists in the second half of the twentieth century, who preferred "bite-sized" or "middle-range" theories (Merton 1949) over the sweeping generalizations that had suited the theorizing appetites of their predecessors.

It was only toward the end of the twentieth century that theories of macrosocial, historical change began to come back into prominence, with references to shifts from industrial to postindustrial society or information society, and from modernity to postmodernity. In contrast to the reception given to the earlier theories, these new theories have been challenged to specify the criteria and empirical evidence against which they can be judged. For example, some sociologists argue that it is misleading to talk about a change from industrial to postindustrial society because many service jobs are devoted to assisting manufacturing, as in the case of administrative staff in a factory. Furthermore, service jobs vary in type, some of which are still basically manual jobs, as is true of many cleaning and catering operations. Other sociologists, such as Manuel Castells (1996), prefer to use *information age* to emphasize the growing importance of information technology in the economy; this term, they say, is not only more specific than *service* but also allows for the fact that manufacturing may still constitute a major part of the economy. *Postmodern*, however, is even less clear-cut, as it is used to refer to a variety of social and cultural changes, not just to postindustrialism. Nevertheless, the theorist remains obligated to try to specify the criteria as clearly as possible. And, indeed, it might be easier to be specific if one links the term *postmodern* to certain changes in culture before going on to speak more generally of postmodern society—especially as *postmodernism* was originally the name of the cultural style that succeeded *modernism*.

Industrial Society

Both Karl Marx and Max Weber viewed modern industrial society as a socioeconomic system in which the *manufacturing firm* was central. For Marx, the factory was important as a prime example of the methods used by capitalists to make a profit out of combining machinery and workers to produce goods for sale; it was a means of concentrating and organizing labor. For Weber, the manufacturing firm typified the modern form of organization, which was highly rational and bureaucratic. The question to consider is: Have the changes implied by such terms as *postindustrial society* or *information society* been so revolutionary that they constitute a break with the modern society analyzed by Marx and Weber?

In addressing this question, let us consider Marx's theory of capitalism, which has been summarized as follows:

- Capitalism is a historically transient form of society—it emerged out of the constraints of a previous form of society (feudalism) and was destined to eventually give way to socialism once it had exhausted all its possibilities.

- It contains a distinctive way of producing goods, a *mode of production* that is (1) built around the production of commodities, (2) where human labor itself is commodified, and (3) where profit is created by the extraction or "exploitation" of surplus value from the workers.
- It is based on a division of ownership of the *means of production*, so that those who own the means of production (factories, machine tools, land, etc.)—the *capitalists*—are separated from those who work in or with them—the *working class*.
- It is a dynamic process, involving (1) technological progress—the incorporation of science [into] the production process in order to constantly develop methods of production through the use of increasingly complex and efficient machinery and (2) increasing the scale of production—to pay for more complex and expensive machinery, more commodities must be produced and sold to generate the profits that the enterprise requires. (Hamilton, 2002: 101, adapted from Bottomore 1985)

It is clear that, for Marx, what defines capitalism is neither the factory nor technology but rather the **social relations of production.** These are the relationships between the main groups engaged in the production of goods for sale—workers and those who supervise them on behalf of the capitalist owners. The factory, on the other hand, simply represented a way of concentrating workers within one space, working for a given period of clock time at a specific rate sufficient to yield a profit for the owner. Profit, in turn, represented the *surplus value* available to the owner once he or she had met all the costs of labor and machinery. From this point of view, the use of computerized information technology does not fundamentally alter the relations between workers and capitalist owners. And thus the introduction of such technology would not in itself indicate the emergence of an information society that could be regarded as a revolutionary change in the socioeconomic structure of capitalist industrial society.

Weber's approach to capitalism differed from Marx's in that he saw the emergence of the capitalist economic system in the West as one element of a wider socioeconomic phenomenon that he called **rationalization.** The process of rationalization entailed the replacement of traditional institutions and values by those based on principles of rational calculation regarding the most efficient means to achieve empirical ends. The process was exemplified in two main areas of modern social life: the *market economy* and the *modern bureaucracy.* The "free" market—unfettered by traditional customs and sentiments—represented an arena in which the formal, technical, calculative rationality of supply and demand operated. And the modern bureaucracy—whose performance could be checked and rechecked against quantifiable criteria—functioned on the basis of explicit, standardized, and calculable rules.

In the light of these two major components of modernity—rationalization and bureaucratization—we can see that Weber would have had no difficulty in regarding information and communications technology (ICT) as simply a continuation of such processes. Indeed, computerized financial data systems are an asset to the kind of accountancy practices that Weber regarded as typical of rationalization; for example, the personal computer (PC) achieved preeminence in the mid-1980s because of its ability to deliver standardized accounting techniques and word processing. ICT has also been a means of extending the technical rationality of bureaucracy by manipulating stored data and distributing them via **networks.** Bureaucrats no longer need to refer to written rules or to interpret them; rather, computers store the rules in application programs and apply them in standardized ways to all cases.

Weber regarded the bureaucratic administration of the state as the epitome of the rationalizing process at the heart of modernity, and computers have become its tools. The early form of the computer, the punch card machine, was invented in 1890 for the specific purpose of making the processing of U.S. Census information more rapid and efficient. Similarly, the Internet had its origins in linking federally funded defense researchers. It appears that ICT will continue to have close links with the formal and technical rationality of both the modern state and commercial organization. Thus, even though the PC offers individuals the promise of expanding human possibilities, computers continue to be used by government and corporations to exercise greater control over individuals. It is this kind of bureaucratic control that Weber described as the "iron cage" of modern society. From a Weberian perspective, then, the emergence of contemporary forms of ICT represents not a revolutionary change in society but simply an extension of rationalization and bureaucratization.

This pessimistic view of the capacity of ICT to transform society—to give individuals greater freedom and control over their lives—contrasts with the more optimistic view of those contemporary "futurologists" who, like Alvin Toffler, believe we are witnessing the dawn of a new, postindustrial society. A more mixed message is presented by the sociologist Daniel Bell.

Postindustrial Society

For Bell, who popularized the concept of *postindustrial society* in the early 1970s, the term signifies an intermediate stage between industrial society and a future form of society, the precise nature of which was still to be established. In his book *The Coming of Post-Industrial Society* (1973), Bell divided society into three spheres: social (or technoeconomic) structure, polity (the state and political institutions), and culture. The coming of postindustrial society, he argued, primarily involves changes in social structure, especially in the economy and in areas such as work, science, and technology. Although his focus in the book was directed to these structural changes, he was aware that they had implications for the polity and culture as well.

The main changes involved in the transition to postindustrial society are as follows:

- A shift occurs from the predominance of goods production to that of services. Among the various types of services (including banking and retail, for example), health, education, research, and government service are the ones most important to postindustrial society.

- In the occupational realm, knowledge workers such as those in professional and technical work, especially scientists and technologists, rise to prominence. Assembly-line workers and other manual occupations become less central.
- The type of knowledge central to postindustrial society is theoretical knowledge, in contrast to the empirical knowledge valued in industrial society. In the transition to postindustrial society, science as well as research and development (R&D) work grows exponentially, catalyzed by the codification of theoretical knowledge.
- Given postindustrial society's orientation toward the assessment and control of technology and its impact, there is reason to hope that new forecasting and mapping techniques can be developed, making possible the planned advance of technological change and reduced economic uncertainties.
- Decisionmaking involves the creation of a new intellectual technology to handle the large-scale complexity of postindustrial society, the components of which include information theory, cybernetics, decision theory, game theory, utility theory, and stochastic processes. (Adapted from Bell 1973: 29)

Bell's account resembles some of the earlier grand theories (metanarratives) of social development, inasmuch as it comprises a narrative of change from preindustrial to industrial and finally postindustrial society. At the time he was writing, only the United States had reached the postindustrial stage; Western Europe, the (former) Soviet Union, and Japan had reached the industrial stage; and Asia, Africa, and South America were largely still stuck at the preindustrial stage. Bell drew out a number of distinctions among these three types of society or stages of development. In particular, he claimed that they differed with respect to dominant occupations: In preindustrial society, the central figures were farmers, miners, fishermen, and unskilled workers; in industrial society, they were semiskilled workers and engineers; and in postindustrial society, they are professionals and technical scientists. (One outcome relating to the transition under discussion has been the decline in U.S. manufacturing jobs, which is mapped in Figure 13.2.) The key power groups changed correspondingly: They comprised landowners and members of the military in preindustrial society, industrialists and politicians in industrial society, and scientists and researchers in postindustrial society.

Many criticisms can be made of this grand narrative of development. The most obvious one is that there is little sign that power has shifted from business to scientists. Similarly, although service jobs have increased in number and variety, many of them are routine and relatively unskilled, rather than technically and scientifically advanced. Furthermore, many service jobs are still devoted to servicing manufacturing and production processes—design, marketing, finance, and administration. However, when considering the validity of arguments about the coming of postindustrial society, we should note that the thesis was developed on the basis of research carried out in the 1960s. The emergence of new information technologies from the 1980s onward, including the World Wide Web, was still

THE STATE CRISIS: MANUFACTURING JOBS LOST

June 1998–February 2005*

WA −102,400
OR −28,000
MT −3,500
ND +1,700
MN −60,500
ID −10,600
WY −1,000
SD −5,100
WI −101,500
MI −210,000
NV +5,500
UT −12,700
NE −17,400
IA −32,100
IL −224,000
IN −91,700
OH −216,600
CA −353,700
CO −42,500
KS −28,000
MO −65,500
KY −43,800
WV −16,300
VA −79,400
NY −222,000
PA −199,600
AZ −37,300
NM −7,900
OK −35,000
AR −41,500
TN −92,900
NC −228,000
SC −77,900
TX −201,100
MS −57,400
AL −74,900
GA −107,600
LA −36,900
FL −72,600
NH −24,200
VT −8,100
ME −20,800
MA −109,600
RI −19,800
CT −52,000
NJ −104,800
DE −10,300
MD −37,400
DC −1,600
AK −3,100
HI −300

Percent of manufacturing jobs lost
Job growth
◼ 0%–5%
◼ 5%–10%
◼ 10%–15%
◼ 15%–20%
◼ Greater than 20%

Source: U.S. Bureau of Labor Statistics
*Data not seasonally adjusted;
February 2005 data preliminary

Figure 13.2 Map of Decline in U.S. Manufacturing Jobs, 1998–2005

Source: U.S. Department of Labor (2005).

some way off when Bell's *The Coming of Post-Industrial Society* was published and French sociologist Alain Touraine was writing *The Post-Industrial Society* (1971). Nevertheless, Bell can be given credit for forecasting some of the developments, especially in ICT, that led later sociologists to refer to the emergence of an information society. We also need to recognize that Bell did not claim that society had already undergone a revolutionary change; rather, he said it was in transition. Indeed, elements of preindustrial and industrial society were coexisting with emerging postindustrial elements. It could even be argued that some of these elements or stages remain in contradiction or conflict with one another.

The theme of contradiction became more prominent in Bell's later publication, *The Cultural Contradictions of Capitalism* (1976), when he turned his focus from social structural changes to cultural changes. The book is premised on the idea that the three focal realms are governed by contrary axial principles: for the economy, it is efficiency; for the polity, equality; and for culture, self-realization (or self-gratification) (Bell 1976: xi–xii). Bell's main concern here is with the conflict between the techno-economic and cultural realms: As he put it, the *techno-economic realm* still seemed to be ruled by the old character traits of self-discipline, restraint, and delayed gratification, which were in conflict with the hedonism that seemed to characterize the *cultural realm*. Bell discerned the emergence of a postmodern culture based on consumerism, "concerned with play, fun, display and pleasure" (Bell 1976: 70). He was ahead of his contemporaries in identifying some of the characteristics of the emerging postmodern culture. Among the issues that he mentioned in this connection were the dominance of visual culture, the presence of nonrationality and irrationality, the breakdown of the distinction between high and low culture, and loss of the sense of a unified self.

Among the many scenarios or visions of the future that exist today, some paint a bleak picture while others are enthusiastically optimistic. Most of the people who have encountered the postmodern debate have done so through the cultural dimension, which encompasses the arts, architecture, and film. Consider, for instance, *Blade Runner* (1982), deemed the acme of postmodern movies. A summary is provided in the box titled "Postmodern Futures."

What makes *Blade Runner* postmodern? According to sociologist David Lyon (1999), it contains several postmodern themes:

- "Reality" itself is in question within this movie. The replicants want to be real people, but the proof of "reality" is a photographic image, a constructed identity. One of the debates about postmodernity is whether it's possible to have verifiable knowledge about society and people (including our own identities). Or are we faced with a mélange of artificial images from television and other media? A more optimistic view is that postmodernity liberates us from definitions of "reality" imposed by authorities, leaving us free to shop around.
- Another theme is that, in the postmodern or postindustrial economy, information/knowledge has replaced industry and labor as the axial organizing principle. According to Tyrell, the corporation featured in the movie, developing knowledge has produced commerce "more human than human," with genetic engineering producing human simulacra (imitations). The replicants exist in a world that has overcome the limitations of time and space, thanks to the information and communications technology (ICT) of the "global village." The traditional and modern structures of space and time have been supplemented or supplanted by "virtual" spaces. The solidity and coherence of once-separate societies, whether nation-states or other territorially bounded communities, are undermined as global communications and relations erode the older sense of time and space. Production is internationalized: An automobile may be designed in one country and manufactured in another, with the company headquarters located in a third. Sociology itself is forced to become more global in its analyses as it seeks some sense of the new patterns formed by flows of people, data, images, and capital.
- A less prominent but still discernible postmodern theme is that of "consumer society," where everything is a spectacle and images are what matter. Some of the most memorable scenes in the movie feature decadent entertainment spectacles with bizarre characters and costumes. For

example, Zhora, a female replicant, dies crashing through storefront windows in a seemingly endless arcade. Everything is on offer to be consumed, no matter how strange, and boredom threatens to loom unless new excitements can be presented. One of the few things distinguishing replicants from humans is what they consume—echoing the postmodern theme that "we are what we eat." Otherwise, the difference between reality and simulacra is not obvious in the postmodern world of *Blade Runner*. It is as if America has become Disneyland for real, which is the conclusion of Frenchman Jean Baudrillard (1988), one of the foremost sociologists of postmodernity. According to Baudrillard, the postmodern cultural life of America is now so permeated with media images that it is impossible to distinguish a "real" America from that of Disneyland.

Social and cultural diversity is evident in the streets of the postmodern L.A. of *Blade Runner*, where all ethnic groups are represented. It a truly global city. We get an impression of social fragmentation and cultural pastiche—key themes of postmodernism. These tendencies were already evident in early-modern industrial society. As Karl Marx demonstrated, the meaning behind the constant revolutionizing of production was that "all that is solid melts into air." This process is accentuated in postindustrial, postmodern society, where everything has become a commodity for sale, including images and identities, and there is a constant pressure to change. In the words of one *Blade Runner* replicant, experience is "washed away in time like tears in rain."

Of course, *Blade Runner* was set in a future time, and sociologists who prefer the term *late modernity* over *postmodernity* (Anthony Giddens is one of them) argue that many of the characteristics of modernity still exist—even in the most advanced global cities of the information age, such as Los Angeles. Alongside the gleaming dream factories of Hollywood and Disneyland, we find Third World people scraping a living and forming what Marx might call an exploited postindustrial proletariat. The Hispanic service workers who clean supermarket floors and tend the homes and gardens of the middle class may even be a vestige of a preindustrial servant class that is now on the increase again after having declined during the industrial phase of modernity. But one could also argue that the term *postmodernity* is useful precisely because it does point to the contradictory tendencies that are appearing, including new localisms and fundamentalisms in response to globalization and rationalization. The Taliban Islamic fundamentalism that dominated Afghanistan until it was overthrown after September 11, 2001, is a recent example of resistance to globalization and rationalization. The Taliban sought to reestablish traditional cultural practices, such as the confinement of women in the home and family, denying them education and employment. It is not alone in reacting in this way. Christian fundamentalists in America, too, are highly suspicious of globalization, opposing bodies such as the United Nations, championing biblical creationist beliefs against the scientific theory of evolution, and attempting to promote traditional family values.

Information Society, Globalization, and Social Movements

Some observers of the information society go so far as to insist that it is profoundly changing the very contours of social structure and organization. They claim that, in place of the hierarchical form of social structure and organization typified by the centralized **welfare state** and the bureaucratic corporation, an older form of organization—that of the *network*—has risen to a new global prominence thanks to the computerization of information, knowledge, and communication (Castells 1996–1998, 2000, 2002).

The danger posed by this new form of organization is that, once programmed to achieve certain goals, it may impose its own logic on its members (human actors). All computer-based systems work on a binary logic: inclusion/exclusion. And "[w]hat is not in the network does not exist from the network's perspective, and thus must be either ignored (if it is not relevant to the network's task) or is eliminated (if it is competing in goals or in performance)" (Castells 2002: 127). Many sociologists would dispute Castells's pessimistic picture of the impossibility of bringing about internal change in the interpretation of organizations' goals. That is precisely how reforms occur in many organizations in society as groups and parties battle over the meanings that define the goals and the means to attain them. However, we can see that there is some truth in Castells's analysis wherever computer-based systems are in operation, as in global banking and financial systems, or in economic production systems that are programmed to switch production or sourcing of materials to the cheapest provider. In such cases, there may be a social struggle to assign goals to the network but afterward, members (actors) find themselves having to ply their strategies within the rules of the network. In order to bring about the assignment of different goals to the network, actors may have to challenge the network from the outside and, in fact, destroy it by building an alternative network around alternative values. Another option is to attempt to withdraw from the network and build a defensive, non-network structure (e.g., a "commune") that does not allow connections outside its own set of values. It is because global networks tend to exclude the possibility of changing their goals that there has been a growth of social movements opposing them (e.g., antiglobalization movements) and of "fundamentalist" communal movements seeking to separate themselves from them.

Castells discusses three types of social movements and identities that can be generated in response to the globalization of information flows and networks: *legitimizing*, *resistance*, and *project*. The first type—**legitimizing movements and identities**—is manifest in the mainstream institutions of society. They are generated by or in churches, labor unions, political parties, cooperatives, and civic associations. Such bodies constitute civil society—the part of political activity and influence that lies outside the state but has legitimate access to state power. Once again, Castells is more pessimistic than many other sociologists—in this case, about the possibility that such legitimizing movements and identities will bring about substantial transformations in the information society by way of state action. The reason for this pessimism, according to Castells, is that the state itself is weakened by globalization (e.g., global corporations, global capital flows, and global information flows elude state control). Its power is also eroded by the decline of the bureaucratic *welfare state* that grew up in industrial society but is no longer so firmly rooted in the information society. For example, Castells concludes that the nationally based *labor movement* now has little prospect of wielding influence to bring about the rebuilding of a welfare state that would provide all its citizens with standardized forms of social security. In America, the labor movement is weaker than ever before and the growth of a strong welfare state has been opposed by the ideology of individualism, which favors private provision of security benefits (e.g., private health care and pensions). Even in Europe, where the welfare state is more highly valued, the influence of the labor movement has weakened and a shift has occurred toward more private provision of benefits.

In early 2005, the U.S. Department of Labor's Bureau of Labor Statistics issued a press release reporting the most recent data on the decline in labor union membership. These data revealed a reduction in the number of wage and salary workers who were union members from 12.9 percent in 2003 to 12.5 percent in 2004. This proportion had steadily declined from a high of 20.1 percent in 1983, the first year for which comparable union membership-rate data were available.

Highlights from this 2005 press release include the following:

- About 36 percent of government workers were union members in 2004, compared with about 8 percent of workers in private-sector industries.
- Two occupational groups—education, training, and library occupations, on the one hand, and protective-service occupations, on the other—exhibited the highest unionization rates in 2004 (about 37 percent each). Protective-service occupations include firefighters and police officers. Farming, fishing, and forestry occupations (3.1 percent) and sales and related occupations (3.6 percent) had the lowest unionization rates.
- Men were more likely to be union members (13.8 percent) than women (11.1 percent).
- Black workers were more likely to be union members (15.1 percent) than white workers (12.2 percent), Asian workers (11.4 percent), and Hispanic or Latino workers (10.1 percent).
- About 1.6 million wage and salary workers were represented by a union on their main job in 2004, while not being union members themselves.
- In 2004, full-time wage and salary workers who were union members had median usual weekly earnings of $781, compared with a median of $612 for wage and salary workers who were not represented by unions. (U.S. Department of Labor 2005b)

The second type described by Castells comprises **resistance movements and identities.** Familiar among the resistance identities are those grounded in religious fundamentalism, race and ethnicity, queer culture, and other excluded groups. Castells describes resistance movements and the identities they produce as "defensive sociocultural formations"—that is, as products of alienation and resentment in relation to the dominant institutions and ideologies of society. He is pessimistic about the prospect that these movements will be able to bring about institutional changes, as he thinks they have little influence over the centers of state power. Other sociologists, however, have pointed to the successes of some of these groups in securing recognition for themselves and their demands.

The third type is **project movements and identities.** A project identity is formed "when social actors, on the basis of whichever cultural materials are available to them, build a new identity that redefines their position in society and, by so doing, seek the transformation of the overall social structure" (Castells 1997: 8). Castells cites the environmental movement and the women's movement as examples. In contrast to resistance movements, project movements move beyond issues of exclusion by seeking to transform existing institutions or by constructing new ones. For instance, the women's movement projects itself into society at large by undermining male dominance (patriarchy) and reconstructing the family on a new basis of equality, as well as by seeking to abolish gender distinctions in other major institutions such as work and politics. Castells notes that not all religious fundamentalisms can be ruled out as project identities; some religious communities, he argues, can be said to have transformative potential through their efforts aimed at "remoralizing society, reestablishing godly, eternal values, and embracing the whole world, or at least the whole neighborhood, in a community of believers, thus founding a new society" (Castells 1997: 357).

Social movements have attracted increasing attention from sociologists, especially those who believe we are entering a new stage of social development, such as the information society or network society described by Castells. But what are social movements, and why are they becoming so important?

Mario Diani has defined a social movement as "a network of informal interactions between a plurality of individuals, groups and/or organizations, engaged in a political or cultural conflict, on the basis of a shared collective identity" (1992: 13). Based on this definition, the key characteristics of a social movement can be summarized as follows:

- It is an *informal network* of interactions among activist groups, individuals, or organizations.
- It is defined by a sense of *collective identity* among participants.
- It is engaged in *political or cultural conflict* over social change.

Diani's definition is useful because it makes a clear distinction between social movements and other temporary episodes of collective behavior, on the one hand, and established political organizations, on the other. Consider, for example, an episode of collective behavior such as a panic caused by a leak of radioactive material from a nuclear reactor. As a temporary phenomenon it does not in itself bestow an identity, but it may evolve into an environmentalist social movement devoted to closing nuclear power stations or halting their spread. Bear in mind, however, that while a social movement may become organized and even bring together a number of organizations to pursue its objectives, it is broader and more loosely structured through an informal network than the more rigidly structured single organization.

Analysis of social movements was originally included in the study of the broad range of phenomena referred to as **collective behavior.** Sociologist Neil Smelser defined collective behavior as "mobilization on the basis of a belief which redefines social action" (1962: 8). Following is a list, based on his analysis, of the stages through which an episode of collective behavior typically develops:

- *Structural conduciveness.* Conditions exist that permit or encourage collective behavior to occur, as when a money market creates conditions conducive to a panic about a financial crash.
- *Structural strain.* Uncertainty, conflict, or some other anxiety-producing circumstance is present.
- *Growth and spread of a generalized belief.* A shared belief identifies the source of strain, gives it meaning, and specifies certain appropriate responses.
- *Precipitating factors.* An event triggers an episode of collective behavior, as when a rapid drop in the price of tech stocks leads to a panic selling.
- *Mobilization of participants for action.* Information from or actions by influential figures summon people to act, as when a respected stockbroker's advice is quoted.
- *The operation of social control.* Collective behavior occurs as a result of lack of action by those otherwise capable of controlling the situation and thereby heading off the behavior.

According to Smelser, collective behavior occurs as a result of the passage through these stages in a cumulative progression—what amounts to a *value-added process.*

This approach has been found useful for understanding the emergence of certain forms of collective behavior, such as panics. But because the overall category of collective behavior is very broad, ranging from single events to long-lasting social movements, the study of social movements has given rise to other theories as well. These include resource mobilization theory and new social movements (NSM) theory (Storr 2002).

Resource mobilization theory, as developed by John D. McCarthy and Mayer N. Zald, starts with the question Why do people get involved in social movements? The seemingly obvious answer is that they get involved because they want to bring about social change as a result of their own experiences of disadvantage or oppression. Accordingly, we might expect gay men and lesbians to join a movement for social change because they suffer homophobia or blacks to join an antiracist movement because they suffer racism. McCarthy and Zald (1987) suggest that this is an oversimplification. On the one hand, some people experience oppression but do not join a social movement—and this may be a rational choice on their part. For example, homosexual individuals who do not actively participate in the lesbian and gay movement may have decided that it is not worth "coming out" in public if they risk losing their jobs, and perhaps they hope that homophobia will end at some indefinite point in the future. On the other hand, some people who do join social movements may not have experienced discrimination or disadvantage themselves. Indeed, there are heterosexuals who have been involved in the gay and lesbian movement, just as there are white people who participate in antiracist movements.

Why do some people join a social movement and others do not? Or to put the question another way: How do social movements mobilize people to participate?

The key insight of resource mobilization theory is that social movements need resources—money, volunteers, know-how, and so on. The more resources they can mobilize, the more success they will achieve. In short, the main task of a social movement, according to resource mobilization theory, is to increase its pool of available resources. It can do this by persuading individuals to become involved as active members and to place some of their own resources at the disposal of the organization. In its search for resources, a social movement will not necessarily limit itself to those who stand to benefit directly from social change; for instance, a lesbian and gay movement may try to secure participation and resources from sympathetic heterosexuals as well as from gays and lesbians. And since there may be perfectly rational reasons for individual gays and lesbians not to join, it is no less rational for heterosexuals to join. In fact, resource mobilization theory assumes that social movements and individuals always operate on a rational basis and make rational choices. It is thus a form of *rational choice theory*, which signifies "that in acting rationally, an actor is engaging in some kind of optimization. This is sometimes expressed as maximizing utility, sometimes as minimizing cost, sometimes in other ways" (Coleman and Fararo 1992: xi). Resource mobilization theory also tends to treat social movements as if they were companies in search of investors. For instance, McCarthy and Zald (1987) explicitly compare social movements with industries and use terminology from economics to analyze them.

The major problem with resource mobilization theory, however, is that it tends to reduce all sociological analysis to a form of economic analysis. It is not really interested in the aims of social movements—the social changes these movements want to achieve or the protest actions they employ. Consequently, it has little to tell us about the *culture* of specific movements—the kinds of symbols or styles they use and the meanings attached to them. For example, an interesting feature of the gay liberation movement is that its public demonstrations often feature members dressed up in "drag" costumes. This approach might not seem the best way to attract resources, but as a form of political action directed against heterosexual gender norms it is symbolically very expressive.

The other theory introduced above—*new social movements theory*—is more interested in the analysis of culture and meaning in social movements. What is new about NSM theory is not the theory itself but the social movements that have come to the fore—and those social movements are new because, according to many sociologists, the form of society in which they are occurring is new. Indeed, new social movements have emerged in the information society, and they are engaged in struggles over information—they are attempting to bring about social change by influencing the public to see things their way. These are struggles over meanings and identities: The new social movements are more concerned with nonmaterial issues—identity and lifestyle and the inequalities they are subject to—than with economic inequality, as was the case with the older social movements of the industrial age, such as the labor movement (Inglehart 1990).

One of the leading thinkers behind new social movement theory is the Italian sociologist Alberto Melucci. His outline of the key characteristics of the new social movements in the information society includes the following:

- The centrality of *information*. Activists in the information society are centrally concerned with the production and circulation of information and meaning.
- The *self-reflexive form of action*. Because new social movements are struggles about meanings, activists must take account of the meanings generated by their own actions. Actions are primarily viewed as acts of communication; the protest action is a form of message and so is the activist himself or herself.
- The *global dimension*. New social movements are able to make links with global events and issues by using global networks of communication, especially the Internet.
- *Latency and visibility*. There are times when social movement activity is very visible and other times when it seems almost to disappear. Hence sociologists sometimes talk about different "waves" of a social movement—for example, "first-wave feminism" followed by second-wave and even third-wave feminism (editorial, *Feminist Review* 64 [2000]: 1–2). Alberto Melucci maintains, however, that a wave of activism should not be understood as a new arrival of energy, which subsequently disappears; rather, sociologists should focus on the networks of individuals and communities that periodically become visible as "waves" of activism. (Melucci 1995; Storr 2002)

A final point made by Melucci is that the success or failure of a social movement should be judged not solely by its "political" achievements but also in terms of its more subtle cultural results. Since new social movements are concerned with conveying and changing meanings, the very fact that a protest action takes place could be responsible for changing old meanings or creating new ones. The protest can make people aware of power structures and imbalances of power.

Many sociologists who subscribe to the idea that the contemporary societies with the most developed economies have become postindustrial societies or information societies would also accept that the new social movements are expressions of a postmodern culture and lifestyle. Many members of such movements seem to be engaged in constructing a lifestyle from a pastiche of elements, picking and choosing among a number of choices on offer—from dress codes and food consumption codes to sexual identity. This point is borne out if we look at some of the main examples that are given of new social movements: the gay and lesbian movement, the environmental or ecology movement, the women's movement, and so on. It has been said that people do not so much "join" such movements as "live" them. This "picking and mixing" has led to the criticism that involvement in a new social movement is often itself an expression of a postmodern lifestyle.

It's easy to draw too sharp a contrast between old and new social movements. Some of the new social movements are still engaged in a struggle over perceived inequalities, even if they are inequalities of recognition and respect (as in the gay and lesbian movement) or of power and status (as with many movements in behalf of ethnic groups and the women's movement). However, the new social movements are also concerned with lifestyle and identity—that is, with influencing public perceptions of lifestyle options and identities that seem to deviate from established mainstream opinion. But in order to wield this influence, they have to grapple with images in the mass media and the ways in which these "frame" or socially construct the issues. This phenomenon has led sociologists to develop a **frame analysis** of social movements, drawing on the earlier work of Erving Goffman (1974). Frame analysis reveals forms of interpretation that allow individuals or groups "to locate, perceive, identify, and label" events, thereby rendering meaning, organizing experiences, and guiding actions (Goffman 1974: 21). It is an approach that has been used in media studies to analyze the process by which news organizations define and construct a political issue or public controversy. Sociologists who have employed this method suggest that social movements are more likely to succeed in getting their message across if they frame it so as to be aligned with the frames of those receiving the message ("frame alignment") (Snow et al. 1986); if they ensure that the message resonates in a way that transforms the receivers' existing frame (Snow et al. 1986); or if their performance in the dramas surrounding public controversy attracts sympathetic attention to their values and beliefs, drawing on symbolic aspects of the movements' own subculture and that of the wider culture (Alexander 2006).

One of the newest social movements to attract wide support from young activists in many parts of the more economically developed world is the antiglobalization movement (sometimes referred to as the anticapitalism movement), which combines some of the characteristics of the old social movement struggle on behalf of the disadvantaged against the powerful, on the one hand, with new social movement issues of lifestyle, such as excessive consumerism and protecting the environment, on the other. It also uses many of the symbolically expressive tactics of new social movements in order to catch public attention and encourage people to think differently. As suggested earlier, demonstrators who dress in unusual outfits or stage eye-catching stunts may gain media attention, but they also run the risk of being met with derision or even of being reduced to objects of ironical discussion in the newspaper style section. A review in *Extra!* of the media coverage of the Washington, D.C., demonstrations against the International Monetary Fund and the World Bank in April 2000 illustrates the problem, as detailed in the box titled "For Press, Magenta Hair and Nose Rings Defined Protests."

Whatever success is attributable to the styles and symbols of the antiglobalization movement, it has drawn attention to a subject that many people in the poorer parts of the world believe is not sufficiently publicized in more economically developed societies. Within the latter, especially the United States, emphasis tends to be placed on the advantages of worldwide communication through new information technologies, increased international trade, and the free flow of cultural products. The policies of international agencies like the International Monetary Fund (IMF) and the World

Bank are intended to assist such developments; the antiglobalization movement seeks to publicize what it regards as their ill effects.

Globalization

Exactly what is *globalization*? The term has many definitions, but one of the simplest has been offered by David Held: "Globalization may be thought of initially as the widening, deepening and speeding up of worldwide interconnectedness in all aspects of contemporary social life, from the cultural to the criminal, the financial to the spiritual" (Held et al. 1999: 2). This seems a fairly straightforward and uncontroversial proposition. However, it is disputed on a number of grounds.

First, whereas the phrase *worldwide interconnectedness* implies a single world system, the interconnectedness may actually exist only among certain nations and regions. Indeed, evidence indicates that the majority of international trade and communication occurs between neighboring countries (e.g., the United States and Canada) and within regional groups of nations or "trading blocs" (e.g., the European Union, Asia Pacific, and North America) (Hirst and Thompson 1996).

Second, the common assumption that globalization involves a neutral process of increasing "interconnectedness" may disguise the possibility that the flows between connected points are mainly in one direction, or consist of one side dominating the other (i.e., the more economically developed societies dominating the less developed ones). In fact, research demonstrates that use of the Internet is overwhelmingly situated in North America and Europe, and that America exports more television programs than any other country and imports only a tiny amount from other countries (Held et al. 1999: 356–360).

Third, as opponents of globalization in the environmental and anticapitalist movements have argued, the pursuit of profits leads to overexploitation of global resources by the more economically developed societies. This observation does not invalidate the term *globalization*, but it does seem a valid criticism of the effects of certain aspects of globalization, particularly the overexploitation of natural resources such as fossil fuels (oil, coal, and natural gas) and some of the antiregulation policies of international institutions such as the World Trade Organization, the World Bank, and the IMF. On the other hand, the term *globalization* has also been used in the context of increasing environmental degradation. The Western predilections for the motor car and profligate energy use entail a very large release of greenhouse gases into the atmosphere that has significantly contributed to global warming. Some national governments have been reluctant to reach an international agreement to limit the growth in these and other pollutants if doing so jeopardizes their national commercial interests. The U.S. government, for example, withdrew from such an agreement—the Kyoto agreement—in 2002, on the grounds that it might adversely affect profits and jobs in America.

On balance, it is probably safe to say that there is evidence of increasing globalization in the sense of worldwide interconnections on various dimensions—communications, financial transactions, trade, cultural flows, environmental problems, and so on. But these connections are uneven and unequal in their effects. And, in any case, there have been reactions against globalization. On the one hand, national governments and regional blocs have taken action to protect their interests, and on the other, social movements, including not just the antiglobalization movement but also local and religious movements, have arisen to protest globalization.

Conclusion

It is time to return to the question posed at the beginning of this chapter: Are we living through a social revolution, a transformation of the social order from one type of society to another? *Wired* magazine's famous five "poster children" were led to believe that they could "make a difference" and play a part in bringing about the digital revolution. Their hopes were dashed, but they still had faith that long-term changes were under way. As one of them said: "Tech is going to be around forever. It was overhyped a couple of years ago when magazines like *Fortune* said the Internet was going to change the world, and it's overhyped now when people say the whole economy is crashing. Who's to say things aren't going to get better next year?" (quoted in Hubler 2001: 2).

We live in a media-saturated culture that is described as postmodern because it has become increasingly difficult to avoid the hype and to judge what is really happening. It is an information society in the sense that we have access to vast quantities of information. The problem, however, is that we may be suffering from information overload. Futurologists have exploited this scenario by joining with the media to provide exciting stories of revolutionary social change, heralding a new type of society or a "new wave"—for example, Toffler's *Third Wave* (1980). And sociologists have the task of carefully weighing the evidence and explaining where and to what extent long-term social changes are occurring. Sometimes the use of terms like *information society* can be helpful, by directing attention to significant changes; but they need to be qualified, in the sense of taking account of evidence of inequalities and reversals in these changes. Indeed, social sources of resistance to change as well as social movements influencing the course of change in a different direction can also be subjected to sociological analysis.

Key Terms

American dream   The ideology that an individual of low social status and opportunity in the United States can, through hard work and perseverance, climb to the top of the social hierarchy.

Social revolution   A revolution that involves a fundamental change in social practices (as distinct from a political revolution, which involves the overthrow of one type of political regime by another).

Evolutionary view of social change   A perspective on social change that implies a gradual transformation through a series of stages of increasing complexity (as distinct from the revolutionary view of social change, which assumes that a revolution is necessary for social change to occur).

Standardization   A characteristic of the industrial age whereby everything was produced en masse, following the same guidelines and design protocol and resulting in identical products.

Social change   The alteration of social structures with respect not only to institutions and actions but also to changes in cultural elements, such as norms, beliefs, and values.

Cultural lag   The phenomenon whereby cultural elements, such as religious beliefs, change more slowly than structural elements, such as technological innovations. The term *cultural lag* was coined by William Ogburn.

Differentiation   In the context of development of the modern social system, this process involves the separation of major social functions so that each is the specialized responsibility of an appropriate social institution.

Metanarratives   All-encompassing, macrosocial theories of development.

Social relations of production   The relationships between the main groups engaged in the production of goods for sale—workers and those who supervise them on behalf of capitalist owners. According to Marx, it is neither the factory nor technology that defines capitalism but rather the emergence of new, problematic social relations of production.

Rationalization   The process by which traditional institutions and values are replaced by those based on rational calculation regarding the most efficient means to achieve empirical ends. The market economy and modern bureaucracy are examples of this process. According to Max Weber, rationalization is the defining characteristic of modernity.

Networks   The components of an interconnected system through which social actors are organized toward the attainment of goals. Networks arguably represent the new social structure and organization replacing the hierarchical form exemplified by the welfare state.

Welfare state   A state in which the government takes responsibility for its citizens' well-being. A welfare state typically devotes a significant portion of its expenditures to programs that provide access to resources such as housing, health care, education, and/or employment for its citizens.

Legitimizing movements and identities   As described by Manuel Castells, social movements that are generated through institutions of civil society that are outside of the state, yet have legitimate access to state power.

Resistance movements and identities   As described by Manuel Castells, social movements that are based on the identity of excluded groups (i.e., racial and ethnic minorities) and are the product of resentment toward dominant institutions and alienation from mainstream ideologies.

Project movements and identities   As described by Manuel Castells, social movements that use available cultural resources to create new identities that redefine one's position in society and try to change the overall social structure. The women's movement and environmental movement are examples of project movements and identities.

Social movements Movements whose key characteristics are (1) an informal network of interactions among activist groups, individuals, and organizations; (2) a sense of collective identity; and (3) engagement in political or cultural conflict over social change.

Collective behavior As defined by Neil Smelser, mobilization on the basis of a belief that redefines social action.

Frame analysis A method of determining the ways in which social movements are socially constructed, interpreted, and represented both by actors in the movement itself and by outside influences, such as the mass media.

Exercises

Exercise 1

As noted in this chapter, a central question in research on social movements has to do with why people get involved in social movements. Have you ever participated in a social movement? Why did you decide to join? How did you convince others to get involved? Describe the goals or desired outcome of this social movement. Which of the theories discussed in this chapter best explains its success or failure?

Exercise 2

Another important concept discussed in this chapter is *cultural lag*. This term refers to the gap that often exists between cultural practices and technological innovations. The failure of culture to keep up with science is often used to explain social conflict. Do you think that American society suffered cultural lag with the introduction of the Internet? Did the introduction of this technology raise new moral and legal questions?

Study Questions

1. What is the difference between evolutionary and revolutionary social change? Are they mutually exclusive? How is social revolution different from political revolution?

2. What are Alvin Toffler's three "waves" of social development? Briefly describe each of these stages by identifying its dominant form of economic production, its basis of wealth, and its social significance. Which stage are we in now?

3. What is Wilbert Moore's definition of *social change*? What are the advantages and disadvantages of this definition? Why is *social change* so difficult to define?

4. What two types of theories of social change emerged during the nineteenth century? Who are the major theorists associated with each theory? Which one describes development in terms of evolution, and which one in terms of revolution?

5. What events prompted the first attempts to explain social change in the nineteenth century? How were the first theories of social change criticized by sociologists of the twentieth century?

6. How did Karl Marx understand the role of the factory in modern capitalism? How did Max Weber understand the role of the manufacturing firm? Does the information society constitute a radical break from the modern society that these two theorists describe?

7. Name the three social spheres described by Daniel Bell. What is the axial principle of each sphere? According to Bell, what conflict characterized the transition to postmodernism?

8. Briefly describe Manuel Castells's three types of social movements and the corresponding identities generated in response to the globalization of information flows. Which one is he most optimistic about in terms of its ability to bring about substantial changes in the information society?

9. What are the key characteristics of a social movement? What is the difference between social movements and collective behavior?

10. What is the central insight of resource mobilization theory? Why is it considered a form of rational choice theory? What is the major problem with resource mobilization theory?

11. What is David Held's definition of *globalization*? What are the main criticisms of this definition and of globalization in general?

Further Reading

Eyerman, Ron, and Andrew Jamison. 1998. *Music and Social Movements: Mobilizing Traditions in the Twentieth Century*. New York: Cambridge University Press.

Langman, Lauren. 2005. "From Virtual Public Spheres to Global Justice: A Critical Theory of Internetworked Social Movements." *Sociological Theory* 23, no. 1: 42–74.

McAdam, Doug. 1996. *Comparative Perspectives on Social Movements: Political Opportunities, Mobilizing Structures, and Cultural Framings*. New York: Cambridge University Press.

Project for Excellence in Journalism Report. 2004. "State of the News Media 2004: An Annual Report on American Journalism." Available online at http://www.stateofthenewsmedia.org/chartland.asp?id=323&ct= col&dir=&sort=&col1_box=1 (accessed July 31, 2005).

———. 2005. "State of the News Media 2005: An Annual Report on American Journalism." Table based on unpublished data from BIAfn MediaAccess Pro, available online at http://www.biafn.com. Available online at http://www.stateofthenewsmedia.org/2005/chartland.asp?id=360&ct=col&dir=&sort=&col1_box- =1&col2_box=1# (accessed January 16, 2006).

Ritzer, George. 2003. *The Globalization of Nothing*. Thousand Oaks, CA: Pine Forge Press.

Snow, David A., and Robert D. Benford. 1988. "Ideology, Frame Resonance, and Participant Mobilization." *International Social Movement Research* 1: 197–217.

Tilly, Charles. 1978. *From Mobilization to Revolution*. New York: McGraw-Hill.

U.S. Department of Labor. 2005. "Union Members Summary." USDL 05-112. Washington, DC: U.S. Bureau of Labor Statistics, Division of Labor Force Statistics. Available online at http://www.bls.gov/news.release/union2.nr0.htm (accessed July 31, 2005).

Webster, Frank. 2002. *Theories of the Information Society*. 2nd ed. Routledge.

Bibliography

Alexander, Jeffrey C. 2006. *The Civil Sphere*. New York: Oxford University Press.

Baudrillard, Jean. 1988. *America*. London: Verso.

Bell, Daniel. 1973. *The Coming of Post-Industrial Society: A Venture in Social Forecasting*. New York: Basic Books.

———. 1976. *The Cultural Contradictions of Capitalism*. New York: Basic.

Bottomore, Tom B. 1985. *Theories of Modern Capitalism*. London: Allen and Unwin.

Calhoun, Craig, Paul Price, and Ashley Timmer, eds. 1992. *Habermas and the Public Sphere*. Cambridge: Massachusetts Institute of Technology Press.

Castells, Manuel. 1996. *The Information Age, Vol. 1: The Rise of the Network Society*. Malden, MA: Blackwell.

———. 1997. *The Information Age, Vol. 2*. Malden, MA: Blackwell.

———. 1998. *The Information Age, Vol. 3: End of Millennium*. Malden, MA: Blackwell.

———. 2000. "Materials for an Exploratory Theory of the Network Society." *British Journal of Sociology* 51, no. 3: 5–24.

———. 2002. "Materials for an Exploratory Theory of the Network Society." In Tim Jordan and Steve Pile, eds., *Social Change*, pp. 123–128. Oxford, UK: Blackwell.

Coleman, James S., and Thomas J. Fararo. 1992. *Rational Choice Theory: Advocacy and Critique*. Newbury Park, CA: Sage.

Diani, Mario. 1992. "The Concept of Social Movement." *Sociological Review* 40: 1–25.

Goffman, Erving. 1974. *Frame Analysis*. Cambridge, MA: Harvard University Press.

Hamilton, Peter. 2002. "From Industrial to Information Society." In *Social Change*, edited by Tim Jordan and Steve Pile, 96–120. Oxford: Blackwell.

Held, David, Anthony G. McGrew, David Goldblatt, and Jonathan Perraton, eds. 1999. *Global Transformations: Politics, Economics, and Culture*. Palo Alto, CA: Stanford University Press.

Hirst, Paul Q., and Grahame Thompson. 1996. *Globalization in Question: The International Economy and the Possibilities of Governance*. Cambridge, UK: Blackwell.

Hubler, Shawn. 2001. "How Green Was the Valley: Five 'Poster Children' for Silicon Valley's Heady Glory Days Reflect on Money, Reality, and Changing the World." *Los Angeles Times*, March 25, 1.

Inglehart, Ronald. 1990. *Culture Shift in Advanced Industrial Society*. Princeton, NJ: Princeton University Press.

International Telecommunication Union. 2003. Digital Access Index: World's First Global ICT Ranking. New York: ITU (a UN agency). Available online at http://www.itu.int/newsarchive/press_releases/2003/30.html (accessed April 10, 2006).

Lyon, David. 1999. *Postmodernity*. Minneapolis: University of Minnesota Press.

McCarthy, John D., and Mayer N. Zald, eds. *Social Movements in an Organizational Society: Collected Essays*. New Brunswick, NJ: Transaction.

Melucci, Alberto. 1995. "The New Social Movement Revisited: Reflections on a Sociological Mis-Understanding." In *Social Movements and Social Classes: The Future of Collective Action*, edited by Lewis Maheu, 107–119. London: Sage.

Merton, Robert K. 1949. *Social Theory and Social Structure: Toward the Codification of Theory and Research*. Glencoe, IL: Free Press.

Moore, Wilbert Ellis. 1967. *Order and Change: Essays in Comparative Sociology*. New York: Wiley.

Ogburn, William Fielding. 1964. *On Culture and Social Change*. Chicago: University of Chicago Press.

Parsons, Talcott. 1951b. *The Social System*. Glencoe, IL: Free Press.

PEJ (Project for Excellence in Journalism). 2004. "State of the News Media 2004: An Annual Report on American Journalism."

———. 2005. "State of the News Media 2005: An Annual Report on American Journalism."

Serrano, Richard A. 1998. "Internet Promotes a Surge in Hate Groups, Study Finds; Racism: Organizations Showed 20% Increase Nationwide from 1996 to 1997, Report Says. Computer Network, Doomsday Rhetoric Are Blamed." *Los Angeles Times*, March 28, 10.

Smelser, Neil. 1962. *Theory of Collective Behavior*. New York: Free Press.

Snow, D. A., et al. 1986. "Frame Alignment Processes, Micromobilisation, and Movement Participation." *American Sociological Review* 51: 464–481.

Stern, Christopher. 1999a. "D.C. Spin." *Variety* (June 28–July 11): 8.

———. 1999b. "Radio Receives Rivals by Satellite." *Variety* (June 28–July 11).

Storr, Merl. 2002. "Sociology and Social Movements: Theories, Analysis, and Ethical Dilemmas." In *The Uses of Sociology*, edited by Kenneth Thompson and Peter Hamilton, 175–220. Cambridge, UK: Blackwell.

Tobar, Hector. 2000. "Column One; Heartland Tuning in to Spanish; Even in Remote Parts of the Plains and Rockies, Oldies and Talk Radio Stations Are Giving Way to Mexican Ballads and the Norteña." *Los Angeles Times*, June 23, 1.

Toffler, Alvin. 1970. *Future Shock*. New York: Random House.

———. 1980. *The Third Wave*. New York: Morrow.

Touraine, Alain. 1971. *The Post-Industrial Society: Tomorrow's Social History—Classes, Conflicts, and Culture in the Programmed Society*. New York: Random House.

Tucker, Robert C., ed. 1978. *The Marx-Engels Reader*. New York: Norton.

U.S. Census Bureau. 2001b. "Current Population Survey: Computer and Internet Use in the United States—September 2001 Detailed Tables," 1–175. Washington, DC: U.S. Department of Commerce.

U.S. Department of Education, National Center for Education Statistics. 2003a. "The Condition of Education 2003 (NCES 2003–067)," Table 15-2. Washington, DC: NCES.

———. 2003b. "Young Children's Access to Computers in the Home and at School in 1999 and 2000." Washington, DC: NCES.

U.S. Department of Labor. 2005b. *Current Employment Statistics*. Washington, DC: U.S. Bureau of Labor Statistics, Division of Current Employment Statistics.

———. 2005c. "The State Crises: Manufacturing Jobs Lost." U.S. Department of Labor, Bureau of Labor Statistics.

———. 2005d. Press Release, Union Members Summary. USDL 05-112. U.S. Department of Labor, Bureau of Labor Statistics. Available online at http://www.bls.gov/news.release/union2.nr0.htm (accessed July 31, 2005).

Weber, Max. 1904. *The Protestant Ethic and the Spirit of Capitalism*. New York: Scribner. Reprinted in 1930.

Printed in the USA
CPSIA information can be obtained
at www.ICGtesting.com
LVHW061522280723
753682LV00012B/52